Advertising and Violence

Advertising and Violence

Concepts and Perspectives

Nora J. Rifon
Michigan State University

Marla B. Royne
University of Memphis

and Les Carlson
University of Nebraska-Lincoln
EDITORS

With a Foreword by
Wally Snyder
Executive Director, Institute of Advertising Ethics

LONDON AND NEW YORK

First published 2014 by M.E. Sharpe

Published 2015 by Routledge
2 Park Square, Milton Park, Abingdon, Oxon OX14 4RN
711 Third Avenue, New York, NY 10017, USA

Routledge is an imprint of the Taylor & Francis Group, an informa business

Copyright © 2014 Taylor & Francis. All rights reserved.

No part of this book may be reprinted or reproduced or utilised in any form or by any electronic, mechanical, or other means, now known or hereafter invented, including photocopying and recording, or in any information storage or retrieval system, without permission in writing from the publishers.

Notices
No responsibility is assumed by the publisher for any injury and/or damage to persons or property as a matter of products liability, negligence or otherwise, or from any use of operation of any methods, products, instructions or ideas contained in the material herein.

Practitioners and researchers must always rely on their own experience and knowledge in evaluating and using any information, methods, compounds, or experiments described herein. In using such information or methods they should be mindful of their own safety and the safety of others, including parties for whom they have a professional responsibility.

Product or corporate names may be trademarks or registered trademarks, and are used only for identification and explanation without intent to infringe.

Library of Congress Cataloging-in-Publication Data

Advertising and violence : concepts and perspectives / edited by Nora J. Rifon, Marla B. Royne, and Les Carlson. pages cm
 Includes bibliographical references and index.
 ISBN 978-0-7656-4268-4 (hardcover : alk. paper) — ISBN 978-0-7656-4269-1 (pbk. : alk. paper)
1. Advertising—Social aspects. 2. Violence. 3. Violence in mass media. I. Rifon, Nora J., 1956– II. Royne, Marla B., 1960– III. Carlson, Les.

HF5821.A294 2014
659.1′045552—dc23
2014010000

ISBN 13: 9780765642691 (pbk)
ISBN 13: 9780765642684 (hbk)

Contents

Foreword
   Wally Snyder vii

1. Introduction
   Les Carlson, Nora J. Rifon, and Marla B. Royne 3

PART I. VIOLENCE IN MEDIA DEFINED

2. Understanding Media Violence and Its Effects
   Carlos Cruz and Brad J. Bushman 11

3. Exploring the Underlying Dimensions of Violence in Print Advertisements
   Hillary A. Leonard and Christy Ashley 23

PART II. HUMOR AND VIOLENCE IN ADVERTISING

4. It's Just a Joke: Violence Against Males in Humorous Advertising
   Charles S. Gulas, Kim K. McKeage, and Marc G. Weinberger 45

5. The Prevalence and Influence of the Combination of Humor and Violence in Super Bowl Commercials
   Benjamin J. Blackford, James Gentry, Robert L. Harrison, and Les Carlson 60

PART III. SEX AND VIOLENCE IN ADVERTISING

6. Fifty Shades of Sex and Violence: Scenes of Advertising to Come?
   Tom Reichert and Marc G. Weinberger 77

7. The Impact of Violence Against Women in Advertisements
   Michael L. Capella, Ronald Paul Hill, Justine M. Rapp, and Jeremy Kees 94

PART IV. EFFECTS OF VIOLENCE IN ADVERTISING

8. The Role of Dominance in the Appeal of Violent Media Depictions
   Laurence Ashworth, Martin Pyle, and Ethan Pancer 115

9. Celebrity Violence Outside the Ad Context: Synergies and Concerns
   Nora J. Rifon, Karen Smreker, and Sookyong Kim 134

PART V. SPECIAL CONCERNS FOR CHILDREN

10. Violence Is in the Ads, Too: Should Television Advertisements Be Rated?
    Marla B. Royne and Alexa K. Fox — 151

11. Television Commercial Violence: Potential Effects on Children
    E. Deanne Brocato, Douglas A. Gentile, Russell N. Laczniak, Julia A. Maier, and Mindy Ji-Song — 161

12. Caution, Animated Violence: Assessing the Efficacy of Violent Video Game Ratings
    Karen L. Becker-Olsen and Patricia A. Norberg — 179

PART VI. PUBLIC SERVICE CAMPAIGNS

13. Using Mass Media Domestic Violence Campaigns to Encourage Bystander Intervention
    Magdalena Cismaru, Gitte Jensen, and Anne M. Lavack — 197

14. Unintended Effects of a Domestic Violence Campaign
    Sarah N. Keller, Timothy Wilkinson, and A.J. Otjen — 215

PART VII. REGULATORY ISSUES

15. Violence, Advertising, and Commercial Speech
    Leleah Fernandez and Jef I. Richards — 237

16. Violence in Advertising: A Multilayered Content Analysis
    Tim Jones, Peggy H. Cunningham, and Katherine Gallagher — 255

About the Editors and Contributors — 291
Index — 299

Foreword

Advertising and Violence: Concepts and Perspectives, edited by Nora J. Rifon, Marla B. Royne, and Les Carlson, is an important resource for academic, government, and industry leaders. It provides the essential compendium and collection of academic research, conclusions, and recommendations on "violence in advertising."

The ethical dilemmas presented by any amount of violent advertising and the possible impact it may have on children, women, and vulnerable audiences need to be addressed for the benefit of the public. This work is balanced in its treatment of advertising violence and its potential effects, and calls for a thorough vetting by academics *with* industry leaders. Indeed, in their introduction the editors see the book as "a solid starting point for the discussion, contemplation, and elaboration that is necessary to reach appropriate and needed conclusions and recommendations that could form the basis for policy formulation as needed and/or required."

The issue for further discussion is not about the political correctness of the depiction of violence in advertising. The research findings and conclusions in the book provide a strong foundation for discussing two issues with industry leaders: (1) the communication intent and usefulness in using violent depictions and (2) the ethical dilemmas presented with violent depictions in both adult and children's advertising. These two questions are linked, because, as the authors of Chapter 16 contend, not all "violent" depictions are bad. They make the assertion that under some circumstances such depictions are justified. Whether the particular ad is ethical and responsible depends on already determined factors, including the nature of the audience, as well as the purpose of the use of violence, such as to prevent actual harm in the real world.

There is an excellent and detailed accounting in Chapter 15 of the government's role in the regulation of violence in advertising, mostly the limitations imposed by the First Amendment to the U.S. Constitution. Basically, truthful advertising, even though violent, is protected under the First Amendment unless a "real" threat of the violence is proved. A California law prohibiting the sale and rental of violent video games to youth under the age of 18 was struck down by the Supreme Court. In a 7–2 vote, the justices ruled that the law was unconstitutional and that it violated the First Amendment rights of children. The Federal Trade Commission remains interested in violence in advertising aimed at children and holds hearings and publishes reports to Congress and the public on the self-regulatory actions of the music, film, and video-game industries.

It appears that any substantial change in the current depiction of violence in advertising will come about only through action taken voluntarily by the advertising industry on ethical considerations. Importantly, the authors of Chapter 16 recommend an extensive ethical construct to determine the appropriateness of violence in different advertising settings. For me, an ethical approach based upon "the right thing to do for the consumer" is the basis of real discussions between academic, industry, and government leaders. The book's research and recommendations can be helpful to the industry's ongoing self-regulatory mission, including to the Children's Advertising Review Unit (CARU).

While president of the American Advertising Federation, I had the opportunity to serve on the board overseeing CARU. It has published guidelines relating to "Inappropriate Advertising" that "only age appropriate videos, films and interactive software are advertised to children" and that "Advertising should not portray or encourage behavior inappropriate for children (e.g., violence or sexuality) or include material that could unduly frighten or provoke anxiety in children; nor should advertisers targeting children display or knowingly link pages of a website that portray such behaviors or materials."

As one who represented the ad industry and served as its counselor for over twenty years, I know how important advertising is to consumers in providing commercial information on products and services in a very competitive marketplace. Also, to be effective, advertising must attract attention, build brand awareness, and influence purchase behavior. The question, which the book addresses, is what impact violence has on the effectiveness of advertising. Or, put another way, why are violent acts and threats depicted in advertising, including, as pointed out in Chapter 5, in some of the most popular Super Bowl commercials? The authors in the book address this question and provide their analyses of whether violence and aggression build consumer awareness and motivate sales. The authors of Chapter 15 suggest that the current use of violence in advertising "may come as a result of the industry's 'conventional wisdom' rather than consumer preference," citing recent research that "most viewers report preferences for less violent media content compared to more violent content." Also, the authors of Chapter 7, studying the impact of violence in advertising against women, conclude that "sexualized appeals in advertising have little value to essential marketing outcomes."

The book compiles the forms of violence contained in advertising, including advertising to children and advertising showing violence against women, including sexual violence. While the total number of violent ads may be relatively small in comparison to the vast amount of other advertising, violent ads often stand out and receive much consumer attention—favorable and unfavorable—in online discussions. Some might believe that the controversy such advertising generates builds brand awareness. But is this worth the negativity often engendered by the violent depictions? This is one question that should be included in discussions between academic and advertising professionals.

The reported research also makes clear that reactions to violence in advertising vary by gender, generational, and cultural attributes. Assuming your target is young men, some might argue a violent depiction is an effective way to build awareness and favorable brand purchase intentions. Yet, because of consumer information power generated by the internet, many others will learn of the violent depiction in social media and may be critical of the advertiser. These people may well include targeted consumers for other products sold by the advertiser.

Also, those offended by the violence depicted often are part of the audience targeted by the advertiser. Consider this public service campaign with the noble purpose of getting young, first-time voters to vote in the presidential election. Titled "Do Not Silence Yourself," the campaign relied on graphic depictions of silent young people. The ad showed a young woman, bound and gagged with black duct tape, with a look conveying great fear. When I asked the opinions of ad students, including those in creative classes, women almost universally condemned the ad as depicting violence against women. As one stated, "I will never respond favorably to an ad that shows violence against women." The ad also received considerable online negative attention. It appears that the PSA offended much of its target audience.

The book is a valuable resource for both the academic community and the advertising industry. It is a resource for educators preparing our next generation of ad professionals for the critical and complex role of connecting with consumers effectively and ethically. The ad industry certainly will benefit from the assessment, based upon existing and new research, as to the impact of violence in advertising. Both groups also can benefit from interacting on this important issue and moving forward together to resolve ethical dilemmas to the benefit of consumers.

Wally Snyder
Executive Director,
Institute for Advertising Ethics

Professor and Senior Advisor for Advertising Ethics,
Michigan State University

Distinguished Visiting Professor,
Missouri School of Journalism

Advertising and Violence

1

Introduction

Les Carlson, Nora J. Rifon, and Marla B. Royne

This book is derived from and represents an extension of a special issue of the *Journal of Advertising* (JA) published in winter 2010 and edited by Nora J. Rifon, Marla B. Royne, and Les Carlson. This special issue was devoted to the topic of violence and advertising and contained eight articles. We believed then that development of the violence and advertising topic was a relevant and worthwhile endeavor that could have theoretical as well as practical implications and importance; the special issue initiative was a manifestation of those beliefs. We were pleased with the content and themes that arose from that issue.

However, we also endorse and agree with views expressed in both the academic and popular press that scientific research and discussion cannot be expected to proceed along a logical and ordered sequence that has as its result a "goal of truth" (Young 1990, p. 39). Indeed, Arbesman (2013) notes that "[s]cience is far from a continuous path toward the truth. Instead, we move forward in fits and starts, with long detours and dead ends, always revising what we know, always viewing it as provisional and potentially wrong" (p. C8).

We adopt these convergent perspectives as a basis for the development and genesis of this book—an extension to our special issue—because these views suggest that the process of scientific discovery is evolving, not definitive. Specifically, we continue to believe that building and considering an array of perspectives about violence and advertising is as necessary now as it was in 2010, and it is again appropriate and useful to extend thinking on this topic because of the ever evolving nature of this area.

Consequently, we attempt to bring together here, as we did in the JA special issue, a compilation of assessments from authors who have a vested interest in violence in advertising. This book is another effort to synthesize and coalesce current thinking and perspectives on this topic.

We believe, though, that our book significantly extends and adds to what was presented in the 2010 JA special issue. Specifically, readers will find in this book articles that were an integral part of the special issue along with other JA articles that were not in the special issue but share a focus on violence and advertising. In addition, and to expand on the special issue, we have invited papers from authors who were not in the special issue but who we believe offer unique, in-depth analyses of violence in form and content because of their distinctive backgrounds and interest in this topic. We think these invited papers in conjunction with other, new manuscripts plus articles from the original JA special issue and several subsequent issues of JA will provide a compendium of assessments of this important topic that heretofore has not been compiled in a single source. Thus, while this volume will not result in conclusive "truths" about violence and advertising, it will serve to stimulate further discussion and additional research in this area.

But why is a new book or a special JA issue devoted to violence and advertising even necessary? The authors in this book provide an array of extremely thoughtful and legitimate justifications for the perspectives on this topic. Yet one piece of evidence is particularly noteworthy, relevant, and perhaps even compelling.

Bushman and Anderson (2001) indicate, despite opinions to the contrary, that there is no longer any need for further debate on the relation between exposure to violence in the media (which, of course, includes advertising) and a detrimental outcome—that is, aggression. Rather, literature reviews and meta-analyses of the conjunction of aggression and media violence all point to the same conclusion. Specifically, Bushman and Anderson (2001) note that based on numerous studies since the mid-1970s, there is a positive link between depictions of media violence and aggression. Moreover, the magnitude of this relation has increased over time, not decreased. Perhaps even more important, the significance of the correlation between violence and aggression across studies is second only to the relation between smoking and lung cancer, and even supersedes the magnitude of correlations between more "obvious" relationships such as calcium consumption and increases in bone mass (Bushman and Anderson 2001).

We believe that the data compiled by Bushman and Anderson (2001) serves as an appropriate backdrop and motivation for this book. Evidence presented by these authors may indeed suggest that a "truth" has been uncovered based on extensive prior research in a variety of disciplines—that there is a palpable relation between depictions of violence and aggression. Yet such a conclusion, while intriguing and certainly important, should not stifle additional inquiry into the nuances of what this relation might suggest. That is, a "truth" could serve as a basal starting point for expanding what we know about that truth by motivating scholars who are knowledgeable in the area to comment on the topic represented, provide their own insights pertinent to the topic, and consider other aspects of the relation that might expand (or not) on its generalizability. This book offers a platform for extending such thinking by showcasing the additional thought and perspectives that arise from consideration of an important aspect of the central media/violence relation; that is, advertising and the violent depictions that occur in this format.

As indicated, we have attempted to facilitate the genesis of this further commentary by compiling articles from our previous JA special issue and articles from other JA issues that were pertinent to the topic. We also invited other scholars to lend their unique perspectives who have considerable background in areas pertinent to violence and advertising.

The result of these efforts is a book that is organized around seven parts: Violence in Media Defined, Humor and Violence in Advertising, Sex and Violence in Advertising, Effects of Violence in Advertising, Special Concerns for Children, Public Service Campaigns, and Regulatory Issues. This introductory chapter continues with a synopsis of the articles that comprise each of the major sections.

The two chapters in the first section, Violence in Media Defined, provide background perspective for discussion of media violence. Chapter 2 is an invited chapter by Carlos Cruz and Brad J. Bushman titled "Understanding Media Violence and Its Effects." In this chapter, Cruz and Bushman set the contextual stage for understanding violence in the media in general. These authors provide definitions for aggression and violence and note that humans have exposed themselves to depictions of violence throughout virtually all of our history. They also discuss the General Aggression Model, which provides a theoretical framework for appreciating and comprehending the scope of negative effects that arise from violent depictions in the media.

In the third chapter, "Exploring the Underlying Dimensions of Violence in Print Advertisements," Hillary A. Leonard and Christy Ashley provide transition from the generalized context of violence and the media to the central focus of this book: violence in advertising. Leonard and Ashley find that viewers utilize a two-dimensional framework when reacting to violent advertisements, rather than perceiving advertising violence unidimensionally. Specifically, viewer reactions are differentiated by whether the ad that is viewed is from the victim's or the perpetrator's point of view and the degree to which victims are perceived as deserving of the violence enacted on them.

The next four chapters extend the introductory conceptual work in Part I regarding violence and the media into specific areas and contexts where such juxtapositions may be identified and found. For example, the topic in Part II, Humor and Violence in Advertising, is explored via two chapters: "It's Just a Joke: Violence Against Males in Humorous Advertising," by Charles Gulas,

Kim McKeage and Marc Weinberger (Chapter 4), and "The Prevalence and Influence of the Combination of Humor and Violence in Super Bowl Commercials," by Benjamin J. Blackford, James Gentry, Robert L. Harrison, and Les Carlson (Chapter 5). Both of these chapters focus on how humor has been combined in ads with depictions of violence. In Chapter 4, for example, Gulas, McKeage, and Weinberger find that depictions of males in advertising are often demeaning to men. In addition, these depictions may combine humor with violent portrayals such that men are revealed as inept and lethargic and deserving of scorn. Such disparaging representations of men are a relatively recent phenomenon compared to the more positive portrayals that were characteristic of advertising and programs from the television era typified by the *Andy Griffith Show*. Blackford, Gentry, Harrison, and Carlson in Chapter 5 also investigate combining humor and violence, this time within Super Bowl commercials over three consecutive time periods. These authors find that violent "acts" occur frequently in Super Bowl commercials and, moreover, that these depictions of violence are also sometimes veiled by a humorous context. Perhaps even more disquieting is that these humorous representations of violence also appear in some of the popularly rated, or most liked, Super Bowl commercials.

Part III, Sex and Violence in Advertising, also comprises two chapters and, similar to Part II, centers on pairing violence in advertising with another phenomenon, in this instance, sex. We have again invited a chapter on this topic by two scholars who have investigated the subject extensively. Tom Reichert and Marc G. Weinberger in Chapter 6, "Fifty Shades of Sex and Violence: Scenes of Advertising to Come?" provide background on two important media trends that have emerged since the 1970s: increases in sexually oriented themes as well as violent portrayals in the media. Both trends are defined in the chapter, and an assessment is provided of the prevalence and effects of utilizing sex and violence in advertising. The chapter also offers an overview of the juxtaposition of sex and violence in advertising, and while the authors believe that there is negligible occurrence of this combination in "mainstream" advertising today, they also suggest that combinations of sex and violence in ads are likely to increase in the future.

In Chapter 7, "The Impact of Violence Against Women in Advertisements," Michael L. Capella, Ronald Paul Hill, Justine M. Rapp, and Jeremy Kees investigate how sexualized violence toward women in advertising may affect viewer perceptions. Findings indicated some gender difference; specifically, women are typically unaffected by sexualized violence while men appear to be more positively oriented to such depictions. There appeared to be age-related effects as well, with younger viewers more positively oriented toward sexualized violence compared to older respondents. Consequently, the authors conclude that advertisers might approach use of such appeals with caution because of the possibility (yet untested) that younger men may be socialized into a "culture of aggression" from viewing ads that incorporate sexualized and violent images.

Part IV, Effects of Violence in Advertising, is devoted to exploration of the outcomes that may be attributable to violent portrayals in ads. In Chapter 8, "The Role of Dominance in the Appeal of Violent Media Depictions," Laurence Ashworth, Martin Pyle, and Ethan Pancer suggest that most previous work on violence has focused on the consequences of viewer exposure to violence and not on why viewers are attracted to such depictions. The authors propose it is the portrayal of dominance that makes violence appealing in video game ads because being able to dominate others has resulted in beneficial outcomes for us throughout human history. In other words, we are wired to be attracted to images that incorporate dominance, though men were found to like violent depictions that incorporated dominance while women were less attracted to such images.

In Chapter 9, "Celebrity Endorser Violence Outside the Ad Context: Synergies and Concerns," Nora J. Rifon, Karen Smreker, and Sookyong Kim introduce us to a side of violence that may be relatively "new," at least in terms of what is usually considered under the umbrella of depictions of violence. In this chapter, the authors note tendencies to engage in violence by at least some celebrities but also suggest how the media again plays a role in how violence may be processed inappropriately by viewers. That is, when the media portrays celebrities engaged in violent acts, and moreover when consequences for their violent acts are not also part of the media's portrayal of the celebrity, then viewers may form the distorted view that violence may be "okay" for some individuals but not others.

Part V, Special Concerns for Children, is composed of three chapters and is devoted to an examination of violent depictions in the media and their relevance for children. In Chapter 10, "Violence Is in the Ads, Too: Should Television Advertisements Be Rated?" Marla B. Royne and Alexa K. Fox address the question of whether television commercials should be rated based on their violent content. Television networks already have the flexibility and capability to voluntarily rate most televised programs (though some programs are exempt, as are the commercials that appear during the programs). There have been attempts by the private sector toward development of a rating system for commercials, but these efforts have been largely voluntary in nature and have not resulted in compulsory guidelines for the television industry to follow regarding rating commercials on their violent content. An exploratory study is described in which children were asked to record their television viewing together with commercials they disliked. Interestingly, children cite commercials that make them feel uncomfortable even during programs that were deemed suitable for children according to program ratings.

In Chapter 11, "Television Commercial Violence: Potential Effects on Children," authors E. Deanne Brocato, Douglas A. Gentile, Russell N. Laczniak, Julia A. Maier, and Mindy Ji-Song investigate further the effects of depictions of violence in commercials on children. Separate focus groups composed of parents and their children were used to explore how each group viewed violence. Neither parents nor their children were overly concerned about violence, though a follow-up experimental study indicated that exposure to violent commercials may elicit aggressive thoughts from children.

Karen L. Becker-Olsen and Patricia A. Norberg, in "Caution, Animated Violence: Assessing the Efficacy of Violent Video Game Ratings" (Chapter 12), also explore the efficacy of ratings systems, this time within the context of violent video games. Findings from two studies indicated that self-reported knowledge of an existing video game rating system, and where information about the video game's rating could be found, varied across parent and child respondents. Middle school students cited the highest levels of knowledge about the rating system, and all groups of children (middle school, high school, and college students) knew where a video game's rating might be located. Parents were lower on game rating knowledge and knowledge of where rating information could be found. A second study indicated that parental perceptions of a game's violence intensity supersede the frequency of violent depictions in the game regarding decisions on whether (or not) a game is appropriate for children.

The focus of Part VI, Public Service Campaigns, is how the detrimental effects of violence might be countered. In Chapter 13, by Magdalena Cismaru, Gitte Jensen, and Anne M. Lavack, "Using Mass Media Domestic Violence Campaigns to Encourage Bystander Intervention," the authors assess the efficacy of a number of advertising/public service campaigns whose purpose was to encourage bystander intervention when witnessing violence being committed on intimate partners. Twelve prior campaigns were analyzed in terms of the degree to which bystander intervention might be instigated according to a five-step model. Results suggested that at least one of these five steps is often not addressed in these campaigns—that is, identifying that a situation is a true emergency. Recommendations for enhancing bystander intervention are offered.

Chapter 14, "Unintended Effects of a Domestic Violence Campaign," by Sarah N. Keller, Timothy Wilkinson, and A.J. Otjen, examines another campaign that targeted domestic violence. Similar to results from studies described in other chapters in this book, gender differences—this time in reactions to the campaign—were once again found. That is, women exhibited more positive effects as a result of viewing the campaign. The unintended consequence of the campaign (but which was predicted by the authors) was that men manifested no change in reactions such as perceptions of severity after exposure to the campaign or, in some cases, even exhibited decreases in severity perceptions. Explanations for these disparate results included the possibility that the campaign elicited a backlash among men because the campaign's target was women.

Part VII, Regulatory Issues, then provides an examination of the regulatory environment as it pertains to violence and the media. Leleah Fernandez and Jef I. Richards in Chapter 15, "Violence, Advertising, and Commercial Speech," offer the first of two chapters in this section. We invited coauthor Richards to contribute this chapter because of his dual background and experience in both the advertising and legal environments. In it, the authors provide readers with background on what constitutes advertising violence in a variety of forms and formats as well as examples of actual ads that contain a violent overlay. The chapter then shifts to its second theme—advertising regulation and the protection afforded advertising as free speech under the First Amendment. The chapter concludes with perspectives on potential and actual regulatory forms that could play a role in controlling how violence is depicted in the media.

The second chapter in this section, "Violence in Advertising: A Multilayered Content Analysis" (Chapter 16), is contributed by Tim Jones, Peggy H. Cunningham, and Katherine Gallagher. These authors utilize a multilevel content analysis approach to investigate violent content in advertising. Specifically, previous content analyses of violence were reviewed to derive ad features that were then confirmed in another content analysis of violent ads. In the next level of the study, violent themes inherent in the violent depictions were identified. The final content analysis then centered on relating those themes with ethical principles as a means of signifying the ethicality of violent depictions in advertising. Six latent themes were found, and five ethicality principles are offered to advertisers and policymakers as potential guidelines regarding the use of violence in advertising and the media.

As noted, the intention of this book is not to determine the "truth" with respect to violence and advertising. Rather, we believe that while the evidence may indicate strongly that there is a relation between violence and negative outcomes such as aggression, there is still ample opportunity for further discussion of the myriad nuances that flow from this relation. To that end, we have structured this volume in what we believe is an ordered portrayal (in terms of part themes) of how that framework of nuances might actually be considered. That is, our discussion of violence in the media and advertising flows from conceptual foundations, to links among violence and general and/or more specific outcomes, to effects on vulnerable populations such as women and children, to how these effects might be countered, and, finally, to regulatory issues affiliated with the overall theme of this book. Consequently, we believe this book offers a solid starting point for the discussion, contemplation, and elaboration required to reach appropriate and needed conclusions and recommendations that could form the basis for policy.

We began this project with the objective of learning more about violence and advertising. We believe this book is evidence that additional insight and knowledge about the topic have been gained as a result. We invite readers to utilize this book for the generation of their own new understanding as well as additional questions that motivate further study.

REFERENCES

Arbesman, Samuel (2013), "Stumbling Toward Greatness," *Wall Street Journal,* June 8–9, C8.
Bushman, Brad J., and Craig A. Anderson (2001), "Media Violence and the American Public: Scientific Facts Versus Media Misinformation," *American Psychologist,* 56 (6/7), 477–489.
Young, Brian M. (1990), *Television Advertising and Children,* Oxford: Clarendon Press.

PART I

VIOLENCE IN MEDIA DEFINED

2

Understanding Media Violence and Its Effects

Carlos Cruz and Brad J. Bushman

Violent entertainment is not new, and it is not harmless either. The goal of this chapter is to provide an overview of violent media effects research. We begin by defining the concepts of aggression and violence. Next, we provide a historical review of violent entertainment. Many human beings seem to enjoy watching violent acts, and this has not changed over time. Next, we discuss the level of violence in various forms of media, including comic books, television, movies, and video games. We also discuss new forms of violent media being produced for our consumption. The remainder of the chapter is dedicated to an exploration of mass media effects research. We begin by outlining the General Aggression Model (GAM), the primary theoretical perspective used in understanding how violent media can have both short-term and long-term effects. Finally, we turn to effects stemming from violent media consumption, including aggressive affect, behavior, and cognition; desensitization; and fear.

CONCEPTUALIZING AGGRESSION AND VIOLENCE

It is useful to begin with definitions of aggression and violence. Lay people and researchers often use the term "aggression" differently. Lay people may describe a salesperson who tries really hard to sell merchandise as "aggressive." The salesperson does not, however, want to harm potential customers. Most researchers define human aggression as any behavior intended to harm another person who does not want to be harmed (Baron and Richardson 1994). Scientists and lay people also use the term "violent" differently. A meteorologist might call a storm "violent" if it has intense winds, rain, thunder, and lightning. Most researchers define violence as aggression that has as its goal extreme physical harm, such as injury or death (Anderson and Bushman 2001). For example, one child pushing another off a tricycle is an act of aggression but not an act of violence. One person intentionally hitting, kicking, shooting, or stabbing another person is an act of violence. Thus, all violent acts are aggressive acts, but not all aggressive acts are violent (only the ones designed to cause extreme physical harm). This is similar to the definition of violence used by most media scholars (e.g., National Television Violence Study 1996, 1997, 1998; Yokota and Thompson 2000).

VIOLENT ENTERTAINMENT IS NOT NEW

I think violence in a cinematic context can be, if handled in a certain way, very seductive.
—Kathryn Bigelow

The fascination with and appreciation of violent content is certainly not a novel phenomenon. One need only take a quick survey of history books to find they are filled with examples of violence produced for the enjoyment of the masses. One of the more infamous examples of violence as spectacle can be found in Rome during the height of the Roman Empire. As a way of entertaining the citizens of the ever-expanding Roman Empire, the emperor Vespasian oversaw the construction of the Coliseum, designed to hold 50,000 spectators. Although the Coliseum was not completed under the stewardship of Vespasian, it is one of the most famous buildings in world history. It served as a theater, at times showcasing the latest and greatest literary offerings, but the building is synonymous with gladiatorial combat. Gladiatorial fights sometimes attempted to replicate historic events, whereas other times simply pitted individuals in combat to the death. Readers may believe that this morbid fascination with violence is simply a product of an antiquated time and that contemporary sensibilities differ drastically from those of individuals living two thousand years ago, but is that really the case?

The epigraph found above is not from a Roman Emperor or anyone living in antiquity. Rather, the quote is from one of the more universally praised film directors in recent memory. In 2008, Kathryn Bigelow directed *The Hurt Locker*, one of the first films to have the Iraq War as its focal topic. *The Hurt Locker* was a huge success with moviegoers, critics, and the academy as it secured a best picture win at the 2009 Oscars. For her next film, Bigelow moved away from exploring the lives of soldiers fighting in Iraq and instead opted to examine the events leading up to the assassination of Osama bin Laden, in a film titled *Zero Dark Thirty*. Similar to *The Hurt Locker*, *Zero Dark Thirty* received near universal praise from both moviegoers and critics. However, some viewers had difficulty stomaching the host of torture scenes included in the movie, which depicted a litany of torture methods employed by U.S. officials at the time, such as physical abuse and waterboarding. Although the depiction of these behaviors is certainly accurate in a historical sense, one has to wonder about the strong focus on torture to begin the movie, given Bigelow's view that violence can be considered seductive. Were the scenes included in the movie in order to accurately reflect the tactics used by U.S. governmental officials, or were they included in order to satisfy the director's fascination with violence? The truth is difficult to discern, but it does highlight questions raised frequently by media scholars. Why does the vast majority of media produced include some form of violence, and what are the effects of such violence on viewers?

EXPOSURE TO VIOLENT MEDIA

According to estimates from media scholars, the average American child will witness 200,000 acts of violence on television alone before the age of 18 (Senate Committee on the Judiciary 1999). This number is especially staggering because it includes only one form of media exposure—television. Hollywood blockbusters would obviously serve to increase the 200,000 figure by a large margin. Adding totals derived from violent video games such as the ever-popular Grand Theft Auto and Call of Duty series would increase the figure even more. Unfortunately, it is difficult to calculate the number of violent acts witnessed by age 18 given the complete saturation of violent content across all types of media.

About 97% of teenagers play video games on the Web, on video game consoles, or on their phones (Lenhart et al. 2008). Over half of these teenagers indicated that the last time they played video games was "yesterday," so it can at least be assumed that these individuals are exposed to video games on a frequent basis. Perhaps the most notable finding is that 32% of the sample listed among their three favorite games at least one game rated by the Entertainment Software Review Board (ESRB) as being for mature or adult-only audiences. The ESRB Web site provides the following description for Mature Games, "MATURE Content is generally suitable for ages 17 and up. May contain intense violence, blood and gore, sexual content and/or strong language" (ESRB n.d.). Moreover, games intended for audiences that are ADULTS ONLY have the following advisory warning, "Content suitable only for adults ages 18 and up. May include prolonged scenes of intense violence, graphic sexual content and/or gambling with real currency" (ESRB n.d.). Clearly, these are games that should not be in the possession of minors, yet according to the research conducted by the Pew Research Center, these games are incredibly popular among minors. However, studies have shown that video game players and parents often disagree with the ratings provided to video games (Funk et al. 1999; Walsh and Gentile 2001). Research has consistently found surprising levels of violence in titles that are rated E for everyone (Thompson and Haninger 2001). Violence is not only here to stay as a component of our media diets, but now we are consuming mediated violence at rates unimaginable 20 years ago.

VIOLENT CONTENT IN DIFFERENT TYPES OF MEDIA

Violence in Comic Books

Comic books have a long and infamous history in American culture. They rose to prominence in the late 1930s with the development of Superman by Joe Siegel and Joe Shuster. The creation of the Superman character spawned the development of an entire genre: the superhero comic. Comics could not be kept on the shelf in the 1940s as hundreds if not thousands of writers took their shot at developing the next big hero to follow in the steps of Superman and Batman. This comic book boom was coupled with widespread concern from parents and legislators as they pondered the effects of comic books on young and impressionable minds. Ultimately, these concerns led to the development of the Comics Code Authority (CAA) and the Comics Magazine Association of America (CMAA). The CAA listed a host of restrictions, such as limiting the amount of extreme violence that could be included in the comic book, discouraging the inclusion of scenes that featured kidnapping and concealed weapons, and requiring good to always triumph over evil (American Social History Project n.d.). The majority of comic book companies complied with the mandates of the CAA in the immediate aftermath of the ruling, but over time the code lost its power and now none of the major comic book companies comply with the CAA tenets (Rogers 2011).

Although comic book censorship existed on levels unimaginable for contemporary video games, critical studies exploring the effects of comic book violence have been few and far between. Research has found that males showed more interest in extremely violent comics than females (Kirsh and Olczak 2001). Outside of the relationship between sex and a preference for comic book violence, researchers have explored how exposure to comic book violence affects interpretations of ambiguous situations. Researchers believed that exposure to comic book violence, much like other forms of media violence, can lead to the development of a hostile attribution bias. Individuals who have a hostile attribution bias are more likely to interpret an ambiguous act, such as an accidental tripping, as an intentionally hostile act, and are consequently more likely to react in a hostile manner (Dodge 1980). The hypothesis that exposure to violent comic books leads to the development of a hostile attribution bias has largely been supported by existing research (Kirsh and Olczak 2000, 2002). No experimental research, however, has examined the effects of violent comic books on aggressive behavior.

Violence in Music and Music Videos

The presence of violent content in music and music videos is surprisingly overlooked in public discussions of exposure to violence, especially since young people listen to about seven hours of music each week (Foehr 2006). The potential effects from exposure to music are troublesome when one considers that over 50% of the top *Billboard* songs in the rap and heavy metal genres feature violent content (Knobloch-Westerwick, Musto, and Shaw 2008). Moreover, about 15% of music videos played on music-oriented channels such as MTV, CMT, BET, and VH1 feature violent content (Rich et al. 1998). At first glance, this percentage of violent content seems low.

However, the violent content in music videos fits the criteria for observational learning. That is, violent music videos do not depict consequences to the perpetrator (Smith and Boyson 2002), and research has shown that children are more likely to imitate role models when their aggressive behaviors go unpunished (Bandura 1965). Given the prevalence of violent content both in music lyrics and music videos, this area of research remains largely understudied.

Violence in TV Programs and Films

Every year, media producers spend millions of dollars marketing and producing what they hope will be the next hit violent prime-time television show. Media producers believe that violent programming is the key to capturing the critical 18–34 demographic. This belief stands in stark contrast to the reality that historically violent programming has attracted smaller audiences than nonviolent programming (Hamilton 1998). Yet media producers continue to churn out violent products. If violent programming is not bringing eyeballs to the screen, what explains the consistent production of violent television content? Perhaps the preoccupation with violence stems from the transportability of violent media across cultural barriers. Most genres of programming require different levels of cultural understanding to comprehend a show, but a punch to the face is the same in any language (Hamilton 1998). In addition, violent programs attract younger adult viewers, 18–34 years old, who tend to have more disposable income than other adults do (Hamilton 1998).

Violence on television is inescapable in today's media environment, with estimates stating that over 60% of the television programs contain violence (National Television Violence Study 1998). Numerous studies have shown that exposure to televised violence increases aggressive thoughts and behaviors (e.g., Bushman and Huesmann 2006). Aggressive behaviors are especially likely to be mimicked if the viewer believes he or she can perform the behavior, and if the behavior went unpunished on the program (Bandura 1965).

Movies, like television programs, portray violence at rates that do not remotely resemble those in the real world (Thompson and Yokota 2004). An analysis of all movies, 1,218 in total, released between December 1992 and December 2003 with a rating PG or higher revealed 57% of these movies received their rating based on the presence of violent content (Thompson and Yokota 2004). G-rated films also contain a significant amount of violent content; one analysis found that 74 G-rated films released between 1937 and 1999 contained at least one act of violence (Yokota and Thompson 2000). Like TV producers, movie producers might assume that audiences enjoy violent content. Paradoxically, research has found that the presence of violent content increases the likelihood that someone will watch the program, but decreases enjoyment of the program (see Weaver 2011 for a review). However, warning labels and restrictive ratings are like magnets that draw minors to movies containing violence (Bushman and Cantor 2003).

Violence in Violent Video Games

To say that video games have improved graphically in the last 30 years would be an understatement, and these huge graphical leaps have upped the realism of contemporary video games. Shooting someone in a Nintendo Entertainment System (NES) game like Elevator Action (a 1983 arcade game) is comparable only to shooting someone in the newest Call of Duty game because the behavior is the same. Although video games have always had a violent component, the level of realism and blood and gore is increasing over time. Research has found that 94% of video games rated Teen contained content descriptors indicating that the game featured violence (Haninger and Thompson 2004). More unsettling is a finding that 64% of E-rated games—games assumed to be safe for consumption by everyone—featured violence (Thompson and Haninger 2001). The level of violence in games that are deemed appropriate for youth and teenage audiences is distressing, but not certainly surprising given the perspectives of media producers that violence sells. Limiting children to content-appropriate games is made tougher in light of research that found 90% of parents never examine the rating of a game prior to purchase (Walsh 2000). Thus, video games feature violence regardless of their ESRB rating. In addition, games are becoming one of the most popular ways for youth and adolescents to spend their time. Adolescent males play an average of 16.4 hours per week and adolescent females are playing an average of 9.2 hours per week (Gentile 2009).

Violence on the Internet

It is difficult to quantify the amount of violence people are exposed to on the Internet. This difficulty stems from the fact that Internet use encompasses a range of behaviors such as watching videos, participating in chat rooms, and playing in online video games. Researchers should aim to classify what features of the Internet are unique in order to better distinguish research on Internet violence from previously explored media such as video games and television.

The Rise of New Violent Media

Video games continue to surge in popularity. In addition, other forms of media violence are being developed. Technological advances have allowed all individuals to become media creators if they so choose through the popular video hosting site YouTube. YouTube affords anyone with Internet access and basic technical know-how the ability to transmit messages to millions of people around the globe. Unfortunately, one genre of video that is becoming increasingly popular is the recorded street fight. With the advent of smartphones, a significant portion of the population has the ability to record violence and distribute it to the masses. These recorded street fights often feature a screaming crowd of individuals surrounding the combatants urging them on, as opposed to breaking the fight up. Upon clicking on one of these videos, viewers may experience a brief moment of confusion as the screaming masses and bloodthirsty fighters echo the gladiatorial combat discussed at the beginning of the chapter. While YouTube places a modicum of restrictions on content that can be uploaded to the site, searching the Internet leads to the discovery of videos with extreme violence and even murder.

Another noteworthy source of new violent content is mixed martial arts (MMA). Martial arts are certainly not new. Indeed, they have been around for thousands of years. But mixed martial arts is a full contact, combat sport that allows the use of both striking and grappling techniques, both standing and on the ground. The level of exposure to MMA both on cable television and pay-per-view is at all-time high levels. MMA differs from boxing in several ways, including the use of smaller gloves that offer less padding, and the ability to hit the opponent on the ground. MMA bouts can end in a variety of ways, including knockouts (KOs), submissions, and technical knockouts (TKOs). In the case of a TKO, it is the duty of the referee to step in and make sure one fighter does not take unnecessary damage especially when it comes to blows to the head. In a fight broadcast on Fuel Television in 2012, Mark Munoz was floored with an elbow and proceeded to get punched in the head over ten times by his opponent, Chris Weidman. It was very clear that Munoz was no longer defending himself intelligently, the standard for ensuring that a fight should continue, and was instead being subjected to punishment that could almost be viewed as cruel given the circumstances. Ultimately, the referee called a stop to the fight after approximately 15 unanswered blows left Munoz in a pool of his own blood. A description of the violence cannot accurately convey the brutal punishment sustained by Munoz. Yet MMA appears to be on the fast track to becoming one of the most popular sports in America, which is surprising given its relative infancy as a broadcast sport.

Figure 2.1 **The General Aggression Model**

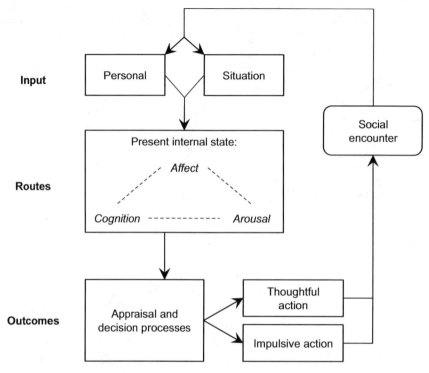

Source: Anderson and Bushman, 2001.

THEORETICAL GROUNDING: GENERAL AGGRESSION MODEL (GAM)

Researchers are not content to show that violent media have effects on people. They want to know why the effects occur. The *General Aggression Model (GAM)* is the theory that most researchers use to explain violent media effects (e.g., Anderson and Bushman 2002). This model proposes that two types of input variables can influence aggression: personal and situational (Figure 2.1). Personal variables include anything the individual brings to the situation (e.g., gender, genetic predispositions, personality traits, attitudes, beliefs, values). Situational variables include all external factors that can influence aggression (e.g., alcohol, aggressive cues, frustration, provocation, violent media, hot temperatures).

In the model, personal and situational factors influence one's internal state, for example, aggressive thoughts, angry feelings, physiological arousal levels, and brain activity such as the ability to regulate one's emotions and behavior. These internal states are all interconnected.

If people have the cognitive resources available, they may use higher-order cognitive processes to further analyze their situation. For example, they might think about how they feel, make causal attributions about what led them to feel this way, and consider the consequences of acting on their feelings. Decisions and appraisals influence whether people behave in a thoughtful, nonaggressive manner or in an impulsive, aggressive manner in a single instance.

The GAM can address long-term changes in aggressive behavior through the learning of scripts and frequent activation of violent constructs in the brain. Scripts are organized systems of knowledge that guide an individual's behavior in a situation (Anderson, Benjamin, and Bartholow 1998).

For example, a restaurant script may dictate that one should wait to be seated by the hostess rather than just sitting down at any available table. Once learned, scripts can color the interpretation of future events. Thus, frequent exposure to violent media may result in the learning of scripts that dictate violence as a solution to conflict. Similarly, heavy exposure to violent media may make aggression-related constructs more readily accessible. Exposure to violent media involves rehearsal of aggression-related constructs as one consumes the media, which increases the likelihood that these concepts will become active in memory. These long-term changes as a result of exposure to violent media ultimately become an input at the personal level, thus increasing the likelihood of aggressive behavior in the short term.

MEDIA EFFECTS

We now examine the effects of violent media exposure on aggressive behavior, desensitization, and fear.

Aggression

Over five decades of scientific data lead to the irrefutable conclusion that exposure to violent media increases aggression. Hundreds of studies involving tens of thousands of participants have been conducted. Experimental studies have shown that exposure to media violence *causes* people to behave more aggressively immediately afterward.

One experiment (Lennings and Warburton 2011) sought to understand the influence of violent music lyrics on aggressive behavior. The aggressive behavior in this particular study was the adding of chili sauce to an ostensible participant's food who hated spicy food. The study was framed as a taste test in order to avoid arousing suspicion. Participants who listened to music with violent lyrics allocated significantly more hot sauce than did participants who listened to music with nonviolent lyrics.

Experimental studies have been criticized for their somewhat artificial nature (for reviews and rebuttals of these criticisms, see Anderson, Lindsay, and Bushman 1999), but field experiments have produced similar results in more realistic settings. For example, one field experiment examined personal (trait aggressiveness) and situational (violent media exposure plus the presence of an aggressive cue) influences on aggressive behavior (Josephson 1987). The participants were 396 students ages seven to nine, who watched clips from either a nonviolent or violent television program. In addition, half the students were frustrated before watching the program while the other half of the sample were frustrated after watching the program. The frustration manipulation involved informing the children that they were going to watch some cartoons, but due to technical difficulties with the tape they were unable to watch the cartoons. Following television consumption, children were led to an arena for what they believed was a second study. This second study was actually a behavioral measure of aggression under the guise of examining what children liked to do in their spare time. Randomly assigned to half of the games were referees who were wearing walkie-talkies. The violence in the movie involved an individual that was wearing a walkie-talkie, so the research team wanted to explore the role of the walkie-talkie as a potential cue to commit violence. The idea that certain objects can trigger related thoughts or behaviors is referred to as priming. Trained observers were instructed to code a variety of aggressive behavior during the activity, a hockey game, including using a hockey stick to hit other players and elbowing other players. The data supported the hypotheses that the violent programming led to increased aggressive behavior, especially for those children with a high characteristic aggressiveness. Moreover, the presence of the walkie-talkie as a cue increased their aggressive behavior when compared to individuals who solely watched the violent program.

Cross-sectional research features the administration of a survey at a single point in time. Media scholars have employed cross-sectional study designs to study more extreme behaviors that cannot ethically be studied in experimental studies. For example, one cross-sectional study found violent media exposure was linked to delinquent behavior and conduct problems, serious physical aggression, and general aggressiveness (Boxer et al. 2009).

However, it is not so much the immediate effects of media violence that are of concern, but rather the aggregated long-term effects. Longitudinal studies typically involve the administration of surveys at numerous points over an extended period of time in order to examine how levels of one variable predict a second variable at a later point. They allow researchers to examine the cumulative, long-term effects of violent media exposure. For example, one longitudinal study examined the relationship between habitual video game exposure and measures of physical aggression in youth (Anderson et al. 2008). This study featured three different samples—two Japanese samples and one United States sample—making it one of the first studies to feature cross-cultural samples in violent video game research. Across the three samples used in the study, the weighted correlation between habitual video game exposure at time one and self-reported physical aggression at time two was .28. This study was one of the first to provide evidence for increases of aggression in both a high-violence culture (U.S. sample) and low-violence culture (Japanese samples). Other longitudinal studies have found similar effects between exposure to media violence and aggressive outcomes (Slater et al. 2003; Hopf, Huber, and Weis 2008).

Researchers refer to the study of a topic across methodologies as *triangulation*. Each research methodology is capable of addressing the limitations of the other, so triangulation represents a consensus across research methods. However, triangulation is a nice idea in theory, but is there any logical way to combine results across studies to reach a nice and neat statistical conclusion? Thankfully statisticians have developed a methodology called meta-analysis that allows one to aggregate effects across studies (see Borenstein et al. 2009). The three most common effect-sizes are the correlation coefficient, the standardized mean difference, and the odds ratio. Scholars interested in conducting a meta-analysis scour databases across the social sciences to find articles that may have examined the relationship of interest. In addition to searching databases high and low, researchers often contact renowned scholars in that subject area as they may have articles that were not published yet fit the necessary criteria for inclusion in the meta-analysis.

Numerous meta-analyses have explored different facets of the relationship between violent media consumption and aggressive outcomes. One meta-analysis (Anderson and Bushman 2001) found that violent video game play is associated with increased aggressive affect, aggressive behavior, aggressive cognitions, and desensitization to violence. Other more recent meta-analyses have come to similar statistical conclusions (Anderson et al. 2010; Anderson 2004; Bushman and Huesmann 2006). These meta-analyses summarize decades of research on violent media and have largely come to the same seemingly inescapable conclusion: exposure to violent media leads to aggressive outcomes.

Desensitization

Individuals who are consistently exposed to violence, regardless of medium, develop higher levels of tolerance for violence. Increased tolerance levels for violence means an increase in the level of violence present in the media needed to arouse typical physiological or emotional reactions. The experience of diminished reactions, physiological or emotional, to the suffering of others is called *desensitization*. These blunted reactions can be decreased physiological reactions, such as galvanic skin response (GSR), during exposure to recorded real-world violence following exposure to media-depicted violence (Carnagey, Anderson, and Bushman 2007). Desensitization is also used in reference to decreased emotional reactions and decreased helping behavior toward individuals in need. For example, one study found that after exposure to violent media, individuals were less likely to diagnose a staged fight outside of the research laboratory as an emergency, and the individuals who did diagnose it as an emergency were slower in responding to the conflict when compared to individuals who watched a nonviolent program (Bushman and Anderson 2009).

Studies exploring the willingness to help others fit in nicely with the theory of bystander intervention (Darley and Latane 1968). Physiological and emotional desensitization can occur both in the short term after brief exposure to violent content (Thomas et al. 1977; Bushman and Anderson 2009), or can be the product of exposure to violent content over time (Funk et al. 2004; Funk et al. 2003). Meta-analyses have provided evidence that desensitization should be a real concern for media scholars (Anderson et al. 2010).

Fear

On the surface, it may seem odd to discuss fear as a by-product of media consumption unless we are talking about individuals watching horror movies. However, in this context fear is not explicitly referring to horror movie consumption but rather to fear for one's safety or the safety of one's loved ones. Perhaps the most famous line of research on fear effects can be found in work examining Cultivation Theory (Gerbner 1998). According to cultivation theory, heavy exposure to television, especially violent television, increases the belief that the world portrayed on television mirrors the real world. Heavy viewers of television may be more likely to develop the belief that the world is a scary place based on the horrifying images they see on a daily basis. This belief is referred to as the *mean world syndrome* (Gerbner 1998). People who feel afraid often take steps to protect themselves, such as by buying guns, locks for their house, and watchdogs. They may also be afraid to leave their houses because they fear becoming a victim of violent crime. The basic principle underlying cultivation effects, that heavy exposure to violent media can result in the development of negative beliefs about the world, has been expanded to examine for cumulative effects of violent video game exposure (Van Mierlo and Van den Bulck 2004).

In addition to the studies on cultivation, other research has shown that children exposed to violent images on television become more fearful (see Cantor 1998 for a review—*"Mommy, I'm Scared"*). For example, studies have found that violent news coverage frightens children (e.g., Cantor, Mares, and Oliver 1993; Smith and Moyer-Gusé 2006; Smith and Wilson 2002; van der Molen and Bushman 2008).

VIOLENCE AND ADVERTISING

The influence of mediated violence on the effectiveness of advertising has been the subject of frequent scholarly research over the last few years. Scholars conducting this line of research are interested in outcomes stemming from exposure to media violence, including brand memory (Bushman 2007), brand attitudes (Shen 2001), and behavioral intention (Bushman 2005). Work in this area has consistently found that the presence of violence, whether it is during a television program (Bushman 2007; Bushman and Bonacci 2002) or in a violent video game (Yoo and Peña 2011) impedes explicit memory for the advertisements. Furthermore, implicit tests such as a brand coupon task, in which participants select a coupon from one of four generic brands, show that the presence of violence decreases the likelihood that the participant will select a coupon for the brands advertised during the program (Bushman 2005).

These findings concerning the effectiveness of violent content and advertising stand in direct contrast to media practices. Businesses are often willing to spend exorbitant amounts of money to advertise during prime-time television slots even though 60% of prime-time television programs feature violence (Signorielli 2003). Advertisement placements in video games are few and far between for the moment, although one of the more famous instances of such placement occurred during the 2008 presidential election, in which the campaign of Barack Obama placed advertisements in the popular sports franchise Madden (Barrett 2008). Scholars have reason to believe that the extra level of interactivity associated with the playing of violent video games as opposed to simply watching a television program will only serve to decrease the effectiveness of these advertisements. This area of research will continue to grow as more video games incorporate real-world advertisements.

SUMMARY

As mentioned at the beginning of the chapter, the manufacture of violent content for consumption does not appear to be on the decline. Instead, it appears that we are frequently exposed to violent content through the development of new genres and Web sites. This creep of violence into every facet of our life is especially noteworthy given the host of negative outcomes that are the result of consuming violent media. We have explored the impact of violent media on aggressive behavior, desensitization, and fear. The link between violent content and advertising served as a future directions section as that line of inquiry combines two elements that have come to define American culture: materialism and violent content. Research has shown that violent media content decreases enjoyment for the audience (Weaver 2011), but this research stands in stark contrast to the explosion of violent content across all mediums. History has shown us that violent media will not simply fade into the background, and simply denying the existence of the problem does not render all media effects nonexistent. Instead, individuals from all walks of life, including parents, legislators, and scholars, must work together to raise awareness of the potentially harmful effects of violent media.

REFERENCES

American Social History Project/Center for Media and Learning (n.d.), "Good Shall Triumph over Evil": The Comic Book Code of 1954, http://historymatters.gmu.edu/d/6543/.

Anderson, C.A., A.J. Benjamin, and B.D. Bartholow (1998). "Does the Gun Pull the Trigger? Automatic Priming Effects of Weapon Pictures and Weapon Names," *Psychological Bulletin*, 9 (4), 308–314.

Anderson, Craig A., and Brad J. Bushman (2002), "Human Aggression," *Annual Review of Psychology*, 53, 27–51.

——— (2001), "Effects of Violent Video Games on Aggressive Behavior, Aggressive Cognition, Aggressive Affect, Physiological Arousal, and Prosocial Behavior: A Meta-Analytic Review of the Scientific Literature," *Psychological Science*, 12, 353–359.

Anderson, C.A. (2004), "An Update on the Effects of Violent Video Games," *Journal of Adolescence*, 27, 113–122.

Anderson, C.A., J.J. Lindsay, and B.J. Bushman (1999), "Research in the Psychological Laboratory: Truth or Triviality?" *Current Directions in Psychological Science*, 8, 3–9.

Anderson, C.A., A. Sakamoto, D.A. Gentile, N. Ihori, A. Shibuya, S. Yukawa, M. Naito, and K. Kobayashi (2008), "Longitudinal Effects of Violent Video Games on Aggression in Japan and the United States," *Pediatrics*, 122 (5), 1067–1072.

Anderson, C.A., A. Shibuya, N. Ihori, E.L. Swing, B.J. Bushman, A. Sakamoto, H.R. Rothstein, M. Saleem, and C.P. Barlett (2010), "Violent Video Game Effects on Aggression, Empathy, and Prosocial Behavior in Eastern and Western Countries: A Meta-Analytic Review," *Psychological Bulletin*, 136 (2), 151–173.

Bandura, A. (1965), "Influence of Models' Reinforcement Contingencies on the Acquisition of Imitative Responses," *Journal of Personality and Social Psychology*, 1, 589–595.

Baron, R.A., and D.R. Richardson (1994), *Human Aggression*, 2nd ed., New York: Plenum Press.

Barrett, D. (2008), "Ads for Obama Campaign: 'It's in the Game,'" NBC News, October 14, www.nbcnews.com/id/27184857/ns/technology_and_science-games/t/ads-obama-campaign-its-game/#.UUNmNByk3Eo.

Borenstein, M., L.V. Hedges, J.P.T. Higgins, and H.R. Rothstein (2009), *Introduction to Meta-Analysis*, New York: Wiley.

Boxer, P.L., L.R. Huesmann, B.J. Bushman, M. O'Brien, and D. Moceri (2009), "The Role of Violent Media Preference in Cumulative Developmental Risk for Violence and General Aggression," *Journal of Youth and Adolescence,* 38 (3), 417–428.

Bushman, B.J. (2005), "Violence and Sex in Television Programs Do Not Sell Products in Advertisements," *Psychological Science,* 16 (9), 702–708.

——— (2007), "That Was a Great Commercial, But What Were They Selling? Effects of Televised Violence and Sex on Memory for Violent and Sexual Ads," *Journal of Applied Social Psychology,* 37 (8), 1784–1796.

Bushman, B.J., and C.A. Anderson (2009), "Comfortably Numb: Desensitizing Effects of Violent Media on Helping Others," *Psychological Science,* 20 (3), 273–277.

Bushman, B.J., and A.M. Bonacci (2002), "Violence and Sex Impair Memory for Television Ads," *Journal of Applied Psychology,* 87, 557–564.

Bushman, B.J., and J. Cantor (2003), "Media Ratings for Violence and Sex: Implications for Policymakers and Parents," *American Psychologist,* 58, 130–141.

Bushman, B.J., and L.R. Huesmann (2006), "Short-term and Long-term Effects of Violent Media on Aggression in Children and Adults," *Archives of Pediatrics and Adolescent Medicine,* 160, 348–352.

Cantor, J. (1998), *"Mommy, I'm Scared": How TV and Movies Frighten Children and What We Can Do to Protect Them,* San Diego: Harcourt Brace.

Cantor, J., M.L. Mares, and M.B. Oliver (1993), "Parents' and Children's Emotional Reactions to TV Coverage of the Gulf War," in *Desert Storm and the Mass Media,* B.S. Greenberg and W. Gantz, eds., Cresskill, NJ: Hampton Press, 325–340.

Carnagey, N.L., C.A. Anderson, and B.J. Bushman (2007), "The Effect of Video Game Violence on Physiological Desensitization to Real Life Violence," *Journal of Experimental Social Psychology,* 43, 489–496.

Darley, J.M., and B. Latane (1968), "Bystander Intervention in Emergencies: Diffusion of Responsibility," *Journal of Personality and Social Psychology,* 28, 377–383.

Dodge, K.A. (1980), "Social Cognition and Children's Aggressive Behavior," *Child Development,* 51, 162–170.

Entertainment Software Review Board (n.d.), *ESRB Ratings Guide,* www.esrb.org/ratings/ratings_guide.jsp.

Foehr, U. (2006), *The Teen Media Juggling Act: The Implications of Media Multitasking Among American Youth,* Menlo Park, CA: Kaiser Family Foundation.

Funk, J.B., H. Bechtoldt Baldacci, T. Pasold, and J. Baumgardner (2004), "Violence Exposure in Real-Life, Video Games, Television, Movies, and the Internet: Is There Desensitization?" *Journal of Adolescence,* 27, 23–39.

Funk, J.B., D.D. Buchman, J. Jenks, and H. Bechtoldt (2003), "Playing Violent Video Games, Desensitization, and Moral Evaluation in Children," *Journal of Applied Developmental Psychology,* 24, 413–436.

Funk, J.B., G. Flores, D.D. Buchman, and J.N. Germann (1999), "Rating Electronic Games: Violence Is in the Eye of the Beholder," *Youth and Society,* 30, 283–312.

Gentile, D.A. (2009), "Pathological Video Game Use Among Youth 8 to 18: A National Study," *Psychological Science,* 20, 594–602.

Gerbner, G. (1998), "Cultivation Analysis: An Overview," *Mass Communication and Society,* 1, 175–194.

Hamilton, J.T. (1998), *Channeling Violence: The Economic Market for Violent Television Programming,* Princeton, NJ: Princeton University Press.

Haninger, K., and K.M. Thompson (2004), "Content and Ratings of Teen-rated Video Games," *Journal of the American Medical Association,* 291, 856–965.

Hopf, W., G.L. Huber, and R.H. Weis (2008), "Media Violence and Youth Violence: A 2-Year Longitudinal Study," *Journal of Media Psychology,* 20, 79–96.

Josephson, W.L. (1987), "Television Violence and Children's Aggression: Testing the Priming, Social Script, and Disinhibition Predictions," *Journal of Personality and Social Psychology,* 53, 882–890.

Kirsh, S.J., and P.V. Olczak (2000), "Violent Comic Books and Perceptions of Ambiguous Provocation Situations," *Media Psychology,* 2, 47–62.

——— (2001), "Rating Comic Book Violence: Contributions of Gender and Trait Hostility," *Social Behavior and Personality,* 29 (8), 833–836.

——— (2002), "The Effects of Extremely Violent Comic Books on Social Information Processing," *Journal of Interpersonal Violence,* 17, 1830–1848.

Knobloch-Westerwick, S., P. Musto, and K. Shaw (2008), "Rebellion in the Top Music Charts: Defiant Messages in Rap/Hip-hop and Rock Music 1993 and 2003," *Journal of Media Psychology: Theories, Methods, and Applications,* 20 (1), 15–23.

Lenhart, A., J. Kahne, E. Middaugh, A.R. Macgill, C. Evans, and J. Vitak (2008), *Teens, Video Games, and Civics,* Pew Internet and American Life Project, www.pewinternet.org/Reports/2008/Teens-Video-Games-andCivics.aspx.

Lennings, H.B. and W.A. Warburton (2011), "The Effect of Auditory Versus Visual Violent Media Exposure on Aggressive Behavior: The Role of Song Lyrics, Video Clips and Musical Tone," *Journal of Experimental Social Psychology,* 47 (4), 794–799.

National Television Violence Study (1996), *National Television Violence Study* (Vol. 1), Thousand Oaks, CA: Sage.

——— (1997), *National Television Violence Study* (Vol. 2), Studio City, CA: Mediascope.

——— (1998), *National Television Violence Study* (Vol. 3), Santa Barbara, CA: The Center for Communication and Social Policy, University of California, Santa Barbara.

Rich, M., E.R. Woods, E. Goodman, S.J. Emans, and R.H. DuRant (1998), "Aggressors or Victims: Gender and Race in Music Video Violence," *Pediatrics,* 101 (4), 669–674.

Rogers, V. (2011), "The Comics Code Authority—Defunct Since 2009?" www.newsarama.com/comics/comics-code-authority-defunct-since-2009-110124.html.

Senate Committee on the Judiciary (1999), "Children, Violence, and the Media: A Report for Parents and Policy Makers," www.indiana.edu/~cspc/ressenate.htm.

Shen, F. (2001), "Effect of Violence and Brand Familiarity on Responses to Television Commercials," *International Journal of Advertising,* 20 (3), 381–397.

Signorielli, N. (2003), "Prime-Time Violence 1993–2001: Has the Picture Really Changed?" *Journal of Broadcasting and Electronic Media,* 27, 36–57.

Slater, M.D., K.L. Henry, R. Swaim, and L. Anderson (2003), "Violent Media Content and Aggression in Adolescents: A Downward-Spiral Model," *Communication Research,* 30, 713–736.

Smith, S.L., and A.R. Boyson (2002), "Violence in Music Videos: Examining the Prevalence and Context of Physical Aggression," *Journal of Communication,* 52, 61–83.

Smith, S.L., and E. Moyer-Gusé (2006), "Children and the War on Iraq: Developmental Differences in Fear Responses to TV News Coverage," *Media Psychology,* 8 (3), 213–237.

Smith, S.L., and B.J. Wilson (2002), "Children's Comprehension of and Fear Reactions to Television News," *Media Psychology,* 4, 1–26.

Thomas, M.H., R.W. Horton, E.C. Lippincott, and R.W. Drabman (1977), "Desensitization to Portrayals of Real-Life Aggression as a Function of Television Violence," *Journal of Personality and Social Psychology,* 35, 450–458.

Thompson, K.M., and K. Haninger (2001), "Violence in E-Rated Video Games," *Journal of the American Medical Association,* 286, 591–598.

Thompson, K.M., and F. Yokota (2004), "Violence, Sex, and Profanity in Films: Correlation of Movie Ratings with Content," *Medscape General Medicine,* 6 (3), www.ncbi.nlm.nih.gov/pmc/articles/PMC1435631/.

van der Molen, J.H., and B.J. Bushman (2008), "Children's Direct Fright and Worry Reactions to Violence in Fiction and News Television Programs," *Journal of Pediatrics,* 153 (3), 420–424.

Van Mierlo, J.V., and J. Van den Bulck (2004), "Benchmarking the Cultivation Approach to Video Game Effects: A Comparison of the Correlates of TV Viewing and Game Play," *Journal of Adolescence,* 27 (1), 97–111.

Walsh, D.A. (2000), *Interactive Violence and Children: Testimony Submitted to the Committee on Commerce, Science, and Technology, United States Senate,* Minneapolis, MN: National Institute on Media and the Family, March 21, www.gpo.gov/fdsys/pkg/CHRG-106shrg78656/pdf/CHRG-106shrg78656.pdf (accessed March 20, 2013).

Walsh, D.A., and D.A. Gentile (2001), "A Validity Test of Movie, Television, and Video Game Ratings," *Pediatrics,* 107, 1302–1308.

Weaver, A. (2011), "A Meta-Analytical Review of Selective Exposure to and the Enjoyment of Media Violence," *Journal of Broadcasting and Electronic Media,* 44 (2), 232–250.

Yokota, F., and K. Thompson (2000), "Violence in G-Rated Animated Films," *Journal of the American Medical Association,* 283, 2716–2720.

Yoo, S.-C., and J. Peña (2011), "Does Violence in Video Games Impair In-Game Advertisement Effectiveness? The Impact of Game Context on Brand Recall, Brand Attitude, and Purchase Intention," *Cyber Psychology, Behavior, and Social Networking,* 14 (7–8), 439–446.

3

Exploring the Underlying Dimensions of Violence in Print Advertisements

Hillary A. Leonard and Christy Ashley

Advertisers aspire to create ads that stand out, break through the clutter, and attract consumer attention—a scarce resource (Unnava and Sirdeshmukh 1994). One strategy for attracting attention in advertising is the use of violent images. Marketers attract attention by using violent ads to shock consumers into paying attention (De Pelsmacker and Van Den Bergh 1996) and as part of a humor appeal (e.g., Creamer and Parekh 2008; Potter and Warren 1998).

The ability of violence in advertising to capture consumer attention can overshadow marketers' considerations of the effect of the use of violence. Even when violent advertising campaigns have provoked a strong negative reaction from consumers, marketers have perceived the campaign to be successful. For example, Mars Inc. stopped broadcasting a Snickers ad that showed Mr. T machine-gunning Snickers bars at an effeminate man because it received complaints that the ad condoned violence against gays. However, the creative force behind the ad was optimistic that the ad's censure would help generate buzz for the brand (Creamer and Parekh 2008). This approach may be shortsighted.

Offending audiences with violence may attract attention in some cases, but this attention may come at high cost. Controversial advertising frequently ends up the subject of derision on personal blogs and YouTube, which can damage a firm's reputation and harm a brand's equity (Roehm and Brady 2007). Considering the potential for costly negative consequences associated with its misuse, it is important for marketers to understand how consumers respond to violence depicted in advertising.

The wide range of violence depicted in advertising and differing consumer responses to it suggests that consumers do not perceive advertising violence as a single, unidimensional concept. Research on advertising violence tends to use simple dichotomies that characterize ads as violent or nonviolent (e.g., Gunter, Furnham, and Pappa 2005), shocking or not shocking (e.g., Dahl, Frankenberger, and Manchanda 2003), including or not including death (e.g., Manceau and Tissier-Desbordes 2006). A more complex, multifaceted view of consumer perceptions of violence in advertising is lacking. Identification of the dimensions underlying other advertising-related attributes, such as beauty and humor, led to insights on how to use those attributes more effectively in marketing (Alden, Mukherjee, and Hoyer 2000; Ang, Lee, and Leong 2007; Solomon, Ashmore, and Longo 1992). Similarly, marketers would be able to use advertising that depicts violence more effectively to gain a desired consumer response if they understood the dimensions of consumer perceptions of advertising violence.

To begin to address this gap in the literature, we conduct an exploratory study of the underlying dimensions of consumers' perceptions of advertising violence. By revealing the underlying cognitive structures that shape consumers' perceptions and inform consumer reactions to violent-themed advertising, this study offers marketers a more comprehensive view of violent advertising. Cognitive structures, or schemas, contain information about the traits of a concept and the relationships between the traits (Fiske and Taylor 1984). Because cognitive structures impact whether information is understood, how information is stored, and whether information is retrieved, marketers are keenly interested in understanding them (e.g., Fiske and Taylor 1984; Meyers-Levy and Tybout 1989).

BACKGROUND

Violence Depicted in Advertising

While use of violence in advertisements is widespread (Scharrer et al. 2006), research on and understanding of the effects of violence in advertisements are limited. Most research examines the consequences of violent advertising on the consumer of the ad or advertised product such as the effectiveness of violent-themed advertising in fashion (e.g., Andersson et al. 2004) or the effect of violent content on memory (e.g., Gunter, Furnham, and Pappa 2005). When the style of advertising is considered, such as its humor, research has found that violence in advertising can result in positive feelings because it is humorous (Scharrer et al. 2006). To date, much of the research on violence-themed advertising has been equivocal. Studies have found that violent advertisements viewed in the context of violent programming leads to decreased memory of the ad (Bushman and Bonacci 2002) or improved memory of the ad (Gunter, Furnham, and Pappa 2005). With equivocal findings and research focused on outcomes, advertisers have a limited understanding of how consumers make sense of the violence used in advertising.

The Study of Violence in the Social Sciences

This study aims to enhance understanding of how consumers make sense of violent advertising by identifying the dimensions that shape consumers' interpretation of violent ads. Different disciplines have recognized different dimensions and typologies of violence. Their dimensions and typologies reflect the specialized focus of the research and the relevant questions of the disciplines. For example, sociologists interested in the institutional causes of violence have created typologies based on the structure of groups and the morality of the ties within and between the groups (Collins 1974), while psychologists interested in predicting violent behavior have recognized two dimensions of causes of violence: person-related and situational (Anderson and Huesmann 2003).

It is an empirical question whether consumers interpret violent-themed advertising using an existing typology or whether they recognize unique dimensions of violence. Unlike the violence more commonly studied in the social sciences, the violence in advertising is used as a communication tool to help persuade the receiver. However, the wide range of dimensions and variables relevant to violence studied in other fields and contexts serve as a starting point for identification of possible dimensions of consumer perceptions of violent advertising.

Type and Level of Harm

Violence has previously been described using the types and degree of violence. When collecting data on injuries, the World Health Organization considers both physical and psychological violence (World Health Organization 2002). Others have distinguished dimensions based on the degree to which the violence is commonplace, such as muggings, beatings, and threats, versus extraordinary acts of violence, such as bombings or sniper attacks (Rosenthal and Wilson 2003). In studying trends in occurrences of violence in the media and responses to violent content, media scholars have recognized differences based on the severity of the violence as a function of degree of blood and gore, outcomes perceived as harmful, or the realism of the pain portrayed, as well as the portrayal of the violence as glamorized, trivialized, punished, or praised (Wilson et al. 2002), or the realism of the violence (Kirsh 2006). More abstract, conceptual characteristics of types of violence have been recognized, including affective versus instrumental, impulsive versus premeditated, or proactive versus reactive violence (see Anderson and Huesmann 2003).

To examine social structures of violence, scholars have classified types of violence on macrolevel, abstract dimensions such the structure of groups and the morality of the ties within and between groups (Collins 1974) or direct, organized, and potential violence (Derriennic 1972). These categorizations may be useful in understanding how consumers respond to different acts of violence. In print advertising, however, the limited narrative frame and short exposure time to advertising may limit the consumers' ability to make judgments about the conceptual characteristics of violence.

Actors

In addition to studying types of harm, researchers of violence examine a range of dimensions associated with the actors involved in violent episodes: the perpetrators, victims, and bystanders or audience of violent acts. The motivations of perpetrators of violence have been widely considered in typologies of violence (e.g., Cooney and Phillips 2002). Dimensions of motivations for violence have differentiated between moralistic and predatory violence. With moralistic violence, perpetrators commit violence when seeking justice or vengeance in response to what is perceived as deviant behavior. In contrast, predatory violence is exploitative. It is violence for gain or benefit (Cooney and Phillips 2002). This distinction has also been posited as violence with a goal of harm versus a goal of benefit (Anderson and Huesmann 2003). Baumeister and Campbell (1999) have proposed three motivations for performing violent acts: deriving pleasure from the suffering of others (sadism); thrill seeking or escape from boredom; and violent responses in defense of or retaliation for attacks against one's image (threatened egotism).

The relationship between the perpetrators and victims of violence has formed the basis for distinguishing between stranger versus acquaintance versus family violence and animal violence (e.g., Messner and Tardiff 1985; Van Zomeren and Lodewijkx 2005). Other researchers have distinguished victims of violence from witnesses to violence (Rosenthal and Wilson 2003). Furthermore, although the actors are distinguished between victims, perpetrators, and witnesses in some literature, consumers of violent advertising may be more likely to focus on distinctions based on the gender or the portrayal of the perpetrator or victim as a human, animal, cartoon, or object, which were previously identified in media studies (e.g., Wilson et al. 2002).

It is possible that consumers' perceptions of advertising violence will be structured by judgments of perpetrators' motivations for violent behavior. As with conceptual characteristics of violence in advertising, however, it is possible that the limited narrative frame and short exposure time to advertising may limit consumers' ability to recognize motivations for violence. Consumers of violent advertising may be more likely to differentiate between ads based on perceptions of the *advertiser*'s motivation for using violence.

Context

Many scholars have recognized contextual factors when categorizing different forms of violence. Most commonly, they have considered the presence of weapons, whether violence occurred at home versus outside of the home (Rosenthal and Wilson 2003), the punishment or rewards for violence, and the consideration or portrayal of the consequences of violence. Within media studies, distinctions are recognized based on the type of program in which the violence is portrayed, including whether the shows were prosocial or whether the shows were humorous (Wilson et al. 2002). These factors may also shape consumers' responses to advertising violence.

Scholars have delineated a wide range of typologies and characterizations of violence, including ones focused on the nature of violence, predictors of violence, the effects of violence, and the social role of violence. Advertising as a form of unsought persuasive communication (Dyer 1988) offers a domain of violence different from those from which existing dimensions and typologies of violence have been derived. While it is likely that some, and possibly all, of these previous typologies and dimensions of violence could inform our understanding of consumers' interpretation of violent ads, it is not clear which dimensions are most relevant or whether additional dimensions might be missing. Therefore, this study aims to determine what dimensions of violence inform consumers' cognitive structure of advertising violence.

OVERVIEW OF STUDY DESIGN

To uncover the underlying cognitive structures that shape consumers' perceptions and inform consumers' reactions to violent advertising, we used an unconstrained pile sort (Boster and Johnson 1989; Solomon, Ashmore, and Longo 1992). The pile sort is sometimes called a "structural knowledge elicitation technique." This technique uncovers how individuals organize knowledge in their minds through a process in which they categorize items in a given topic (Harper et al. 2003). Through this process, pile sorts facilitate exploration of relationships among items and generate data that indicate these relationships in terms of cognitive distances, or how dissimilar the items are perceived (Ryan and Bernard 2003).

For our study, the pile sort determined people's associations between different ads that use violent images and themes. By using an unconstrained pile sort, we allowed the respondents to categorize stimuli without the bias of predetermined categories. This is best when understanding of a concept is limited, as is the case with consumers' perceptions of violence.

METHOD

Stimuli

In pile sort procedures, the sorted stimuli should represent an inclusive sample of the issue under study as it occurs in the world (Giguere 2006). The diverse stimuli set helps to ensure that results represent a complete as possible description of the structures underlying individual perceptions regarding the topic. This study used a set of 40 violent print advertisements chosen to represent a broad range of print advertisements available to consumers. The set of ads represented different factors enumerated in previous categorizations, including contextual factors (e.g., weapons present/not present, alcohol present/not present, relationships between perpetrators and victims), the actors (e.g., perpetrators and victims of different genders, ages, species, and realism), and different types and levels of violence (e.g., death, injury, unobserved, and violence that results from carelessness versus execution). It also included examples of ads for a mix of products and causes (or nonprofits), and those that used humorous overtones and sexual overtones. (See Table 3.1 for a short profile of each ad in the final set.)

While the ads were chosen to completely represent all categories of violence in print advertising, the goal was to achieve this with the smallest number of ads so as to limit participant fatigue (Van Exel and de Graaf 2005). The ads were chosen from advertisements found online on Web sites devoted to the profession of marketing and or advertising (e.g., adsoftheworld.com and adweek.com) and selected based on information that identified the ads as controversial due to the presence of violence or violent images. All ads were in color and approximately 8 × 10 inches in size.

Table 3.1

Two-Dimensional Solution (with Description of Ads)

Descriptions of ads	1 Viewpoint	2 Type of victim
Cluster 1: "From the Victim's Perspective"		
Protect Wildlife: Seal (shows an adult seal with a club in its mouth standing over a bloody human baby and includes copy that says, "Don't Treat Others the Way You Don't Want to Be Treated")	1.629	.6169
Hooked (direct response ad with photo of woman with a fishhook in corner of her mouth promoting service for smoking cessation, called get unhooked)	1.7098	.4294
Don't Speed (blond female child's bloody head and face smashed into a cracked windshield with copy that says, "Don't Speed Near Schools. It's for your own good")	1.6932	.3017
Child Labor (boy with Nike symbol branded onto his chained foot suggesting consumers avoid shoes produced using child labor [from UNICEF])	1.6051	.2298
iPod (PSA: young man lying in the street with white headphone cords replacing a police chalk outline with copy that says, "Watch for cars when wearing headphones")	1.5797	-.1662
Verbal Abuse (Juvenile Protection Agency ad features a crying boy being choked by words in the shape of a hand around his throat)	1.5286	.1417
Domestic Abuse (shows the x-ray image of an arm with a pin repairing a break and a diamond bracelet copy indicates, "he gave me this [bracelet] on our anniversary," but "he gave me this [broken arm] for nothing at all")	1.6506	-.3143
RSCPA (beaten boy shown with ad copy stating that animal welfare inspectors help prevent not just animal abuse but child abuse as well)	1.3673	.16
Organ Donor (overhead shot of a person lying in front of a car with blood under their head)	.972	-.7967
Breast Cancer (shows torso of a woman in a white tank top that is printed with a message of plans to physically assault and kill breast cancer and then tie a pink ribbon on it)	.9366	-.9269
Lego (man with pixelated image of a gun pointed to his head while sitting next to a liquor bottle with ad copy that says, "Kids shouldn't watch too much TV")	.3644	-1.0399
PETA (actress Persia White holds a skinned fox with the head and paw fur intact with copy that says, "Here's the rest of your fur coat" [promoting the Web site FurIsDead.com])	1.1202	-.4324
Game Over (image of child holding another child at gunpoint in a modification of the famous Pulitzer prize photo of an execution during the Vietnam War with copy advocating against training children to kill through shooter video games)	1.4632	-.0716
Secondhand Smoke (Canadian Public Health Organization parody of Marlboro man ad with image of a cowboy standing over a dead horse in desert scene)	.6668	1.5397
NOAH (photo of woman's legs in boots fashioned from a crocodile that is biting the woman's leg and copy that urges people to support the struggle against illegal animal trade)	1.1657	1.3571

Descriptions of ads	1 Viewpoint	2 Type of victim
Cluster 2: "Undeserving Victims from the Perpetrator's Perspective"		
Little Boys Smoked Venison Sausages (cartoon features two boys in a tree lighting a grenade while looking down on a deer drinking from a pond with copy that says, "Doing what comes naturally")	−.6643	1.6302
Don't Leave Pets (cartoon features outline of Snoopy buried with Woodstock on his stomach crying as Charlie Brown walks away smiling with the shovel; copy indicates 50,000 house pets are abandoned or killed because people fail to make arrangements when they go away on vacation)	−.2975	1.4269
Magnum Bullets (shows an imprint outline of a deer in leaves with copy that indicates triple seven magnum bullets have serious knockdown power so you can eliminate blood trails and avoid letting another deer get away)	.0938	1.568
SPCA—It's Time to Neuter Your Dog (photograph shows flying winged "cupid" dog with a bow shooting heart-tipped arrows into a man's calf as he washes the car; copy states, "It's time to neuter your dog" and "To stop animal aggression and stop unplanned pregnancies, call SPCA")	−.5821	1.1944
Pepsi Max (shows one "lonely" calorie committing suicide—drinking poison, shooting itself in the head, with a noose/beaver gnawing at the stump he stands on)	−.6955	.7741
Condom (shows armed military group on patrol, one is nude except for an automatic weapon with the message "Don't Be Stupid. Protect Yourself.")	−.947	.444
Bud (photo of aquarium filled with Budweiser beer and ice while the fish are placed in a plastic bag next to the aquarium, with a party of people)	−1.054	1.2069
Dr. Scholl's (photograph of a dead parrot in a cage above someone's sneakers with copy that says, "Foot Odor!" with Dr. Scholl's logo)	−1.1663	1.233
Alka Seltzer (photo shows disheveled man washing dishes with kitten, with copy that says, "Hangover is dangerous")	−1.1272	1.1457
Killer Heels (shows drawn image of a man completely impaled through the chest and lying lifeless on the heel of an enormous stiletto shoe, with blood stains around the wound)	−1.3811	.4221
Cluster 3: "Deserving Victims from the Perpetrator's Perspective"		
Crime Stoppers (shows a person whose image is pixilated being beaten by three people, suggesting that those who report crimes remain anonymous)	−.2276	−1.5626
Plax (photo of four blindfolded men in a firing squad lineup formation with a fifth man who has his mouth bound instead of his eyes and copy that suggests Plax kills the germs that cause bad breath)	−.4314	−1.2124
Trident (shows a woman raising a chair over her head to be at a human-sized donut to show Trident Splash helps you "fight back" against hunger)	−.5108	−1.023
Axe (shows a young man swinging a wooden sword at another man, whose head is tucked in his shirt so he looks headless; behind him on a chalkboard is a graphic, colored chalk drawing of a flying, bloody, head. In the corner is a small graphic showing a can of Axe, a man surrounded by women, and "Get a Girlfriend")	−.5267	−.8733

Descriptions of ads	1 Viewpoint	2 Type of victim
Prius (man in distance dragging a person in a body bag from a Toyota Prius toward a lake with copy that says, "Well at least he drives a Prius")	−.618	−1.0037
Hitman (cellist in a tuxedo with slit throat, with copy "Classically Executed" advertising the Hitman video game release in Spring 2006)	−.6288	−1.1082
D & G (Elizabethan-style image of two women, one holding a silver, two-pronged carving fork at the throat of another; the other is holding a Dolce & Gabbana handbag)	−.7283	−1.0147
Parade (shows two women scantily clad in caveman attire with clubs running after shoes to promote a three-day sale at Parade of Shoes)	−.7552	−.9884
Old Khaki (shows a woman in panties on a bed being paddled by a shirtless man in khaki pants in a room with animal skulls and drying animal skins)	−.8582	−.7851
Raid (shows blank sheet music with *Flight of the Bumblebee* printed at the top and music notes collapsed at the bottom under the empty staffs, with the message "Raid. Kill them Dead." next to a can of insecticide)	−.9037	−.9567
FTD (shows elderly woman collapsed in front of an unwrapped jack-in-the-box; copy states, "Flowers would have been better," with FTD logo)	−.9247	−.9192
Electric Bikes (a matador faces off with a bull while hiding a pistol behind his back; copy states, "Why Make the Effort?" to promote Electric Bikes for WattWorld)	−.9333	−.3158
Super Soaker (shows a cartoon battlefield of many children engaged in war with their Super Soaker water guns)	−.9616	−.0344
Crunch—Paparazzi Step Class (shows women's sneakers and the bottom of their calves as they step on the faces of wincing men lying on the ground with cameras on their necks)	−1.2532	−.0832
Nutcracker (shows a stick figure of a man in a top hat kicking a large cartoon mouse and childish script indicating the nutcracker kicks the mouse's butt)	−1.3694	−.1925

Notes: PSA = public service announcement;
RSCPA = Royal Society for the Prevention of Cruelty to Animals;
PETA = People for the Ethical Treatment of Animals;
NOAH = Northwest Organization for Animal Help;
SPCA = Society for the Prevention of Cruelty to Animals.

Participant Sampling

A purposive sample of 20 participants was recruited through fliers on a college campus and through snowball sampling. As an incentive for recruitment, researchers offered participants entry into a lottery to win a cash prize or a comparable donation to a nonprofit. With purposive sampling (also called judgment samples) the researcher selects a sample to best answer the research question (Marshall 1996). For this study, we specifically used a maximum variation sample (Marshall 1996) for which the researchers sought to create a sample of participants that would ensure representation of a diverse set of perspectives on violence in advertisements (Van Exel and de Graaf 2005).

By using a purposive sample, the researchers were able to seek participants to fill out a variety of perspectives rather than randomly sampling which, with such a small sample, would be likely to introduce too much bias (Marshall 1996). The sample included people with conservative, liberal, and no political affiliations; the respondents included a PETA (People for the Ethical Treatment of Animals) member, a terrorism expert, two cancer survivors, five parents, and nine pet owners. The focal sample was 60% female ($n = 12$) and 40% male ($n = 8$), with an age range of 20 years to 71 years (median = 36). All participants in the sample had a college degree except for one undergraduate student and 25% ($n = 5$) had at least some graduate education. Initial screening indicated that each member of the sample was exposed to print advertisements through their use of media.

Procedure

A researcher met individually with each participant to complete the sorting task. After introducing herself, the researcher explained to the participant that the goal of the research was to learn more about how they think about advertisements. The researcher gave the participant a deck of the 40 advertisements selected as the stimuli. The advertisements were printed in color on 8×10-inch paper. Each ad was numbered on the back for data recording purposes.

Participants were asked to sort the ads into piles of similar ads. To limit researcher-introduced bias and to uncover the categories of meaning relevant to the participants, no further sorting criteria was offered. Participants could sort the ads into as many piles as they chose, with as many ads as they desired in each pile. The respondents were told there were no right or wrong answers, and were told to take as much time as necessary. By leaving the sorting activity unstructured, the participants sorted the ads on the dimensions they deemed relevant rather than using an a priori structure imposed by the researcher (Weller and Romney 1988; Whaley and Longoria 2009). The researcher then recorded by paper and pencil the numbers of each ad sorted into each pile. Piles were not ordered and were not recorded in any specific order.

Participants were instructed to "think out loud" while they performed the sorts so that the researchers would better understand their rationales for sorting advertisements. The conversations that took place while each participant was sorting served to offer additional insights into the participants' thought processes and perspectives on the advertisements (Bettman and Zins 1977; Rosenberg and Kim 1975). In most cases, the participants volunteered explanations of the piles. In the cases in which participants were less forthcoming, however, the researcher asked for elaboration on what each pile represented. The discussion between the researcher and the participant during the sorting procedure was audio recorded and handwritten discussion notes were transcribed to enable review and analysis to assist in the interpretation of the results. This information was used to assist the authors in interpreting the clusters and dimensions uncovered in this study (Rosenberg and Kim 1975). Completion time for the unconstrained sorting task and discussion ranged from 45 minutes to two and a half hours.

RESULTS

The results of the pile sort were analyzed using multidimensional scaling (MDS) and a hierarchical cluster analysis of the MDS estimates. Both cluster analysis and multidimensional scaling (MDS) are frequently used to uncover the underlying knowledge structures from pile sort data and are particularly suited for analyzing data from complex stimuli such as advertisements (Kruskal 1964; Weller and Romney 1988). Both methods are used to provide a visual presentation of similarities and patterns among items sometimes called a cognitive or perceptual map. Like a real map, this output represents distance between items that can be interpreted to reveal the collective organization and structure of knowledge (Ryan and Bernard 2003).

MDS analysis uses accumulated subjective comparisons to uncover the shared bases, or dimensions for the comparisons. It is particularly useful when the basis for how the items are compared is unknown (Garson 2009). In the sorting task, participants sorted similar ads together; however, the basis on which they made their judgments of similarity was unknown. MDS transforms these similarity/dissimilarity judgments into a scatter plot in which the axes are the underlying dimensions revealing collective knowledge structure.

Cluster analysis is a classificatory tool used to identify subgroups within a larger sample that show maximum similarity within the group and maximum dissimilarity between groups. Using cluster analysis with MDS can help identify subregions within the dimensional space estimated by MDS. This enables the researchers to move beyond the continuums identified as dimensions and see patterns along the continuums. As a result, MDS and hierarchical cluster analyses are frequently used together by researchers studying meaning systems such as anthropology (e.g., Burton and Romney 1975), management (e.g., Jackson and Trochim 2002), and psychology (e.g., McLaughlin, Carnevale, and Lim 1991).

Both MDS and cluster analysis are descriptive, atheoretical tools that require interpretation of results by the researchers. To aid in interpretation, pile sort methods frequently rely on qualitative data derived from discussions during the sorting procedure. To this end, we examined the discussion surrounding the sorting procedures for themes and insight into consumers' meaning systems, or cognitive structures regarding violent advertising. Audio recordings of the sorting discussions as well as handwritten notes taken during the procedure were reviewed and discussed in light of the MDS and cluster solutions. In an iterative process, new notes were created to find themes and commonalties across comments as they related to the dimensions and clusters.

It is important to note that while the discussions during the sorting procedures included participants' reactions to the ad stimuli, the discussions concentrated on the participants' judgments of similarities and dissimilarities between ads. Because we focus on our participants' commentaries to interpret the meaning of the resulting multidimensional scaling solution and cluster solution, our resulting framework illuminates a shared, emic perspective of our participants.

Multidimensional Scaling Analysis of Sorting Data

Multidimensional scaling analysis (MDS) was used to transform the pile sort data into a map of the differences between the ads. In MDS, this visual representation of the relational structures between the advertisements is created through transformation of a dissimilarity matrix into Euclidean distances. Ads that were grouped in the same pile because they were similar to each other were located close together, while dissimilar ads were located far apart. The spatial representation indicates the perceptual structure used to differentiate among ads depicting violence.

To do the MDS analysis, an $N \times N$ (where N is the total number of ads) binary symmetric dissimilarity matrix was developed for each respondent. If the ads were grouped in the same pile, a 0 was put in the matrix at the intersection of the two ads. If the ads were grouped in different piles, a 1 was put in the cell. Dissimilarity judgments were calculated by adding the 20 matrices together. The numbers on the off diagonals represented the number of times the ads were not sorted in the same piles. The numbers on the diagonal were zeroes. The matrix was symmetrical.

From the aggregated dissimilarity matrix, MDS created coordinate estimates for solutions that ranged from one to six dimensional solutions using ALSCAL (SPSS 16.0). Solutions that indicate the distance between the dimensions were created, resulting in the following goodness-of-fit measures for one through six dimensional solutions, respectively: stress (and R^2) values .32 (.73), .19 (.82), .13 (.87), .10 (.91), .07 (.93), .06 (.95). The two-dimensional configuration was selected for ease of interpretability and because of the smaller decrease in stress between the two- and three-dimensional solutions (relative to the one- and two-dimensional solution) (Burton and Romney 1975). Consistent with this choice of solution, methodologists have suggested, "when an MDS configuration is desired primarily as the foundation on which to display clustering results, then a two-dimensional configuration is far more useful than one involving three or more dimensions" (Kruskal and Wish 1978, p. 58). The coordinate estimates and a two-dimensional map of the distances between the ads based on the sorts of 20 respondents are shown in Figure 3.1.

Dimensions

As we saw above, Table 3.1 includes the list of ads and their ratings on each of the two dimensions. While the MDS fits the ads into dimensions to help identify the bases of the cognitive structures, the graphical output needs to be interpreted for meaning. The results combine the output from the mathematical algorithms and the subjective interpretations based on the think-aloud discussion of the pile sort process. The analysis of the discussions regarding why the piles were created was particularly useful for labeling dimensions. The two dimensions suggest participants distinguished between the ads based on whom they identify with (victim or perpetrator) and the type of victim portrayed in the ad.

The first dimension of the multidimensional scaling solution represents the perspective from which the ad depicts violence. The sorting suggests respondents separated ads by the actor they identified with in the ad. At the high end of this dimension, the ad takes the victim's perspective of the violence. For example, at the extreme end of this dimension, an ad shows a young woman with a large fishhook pulling her lip. The ad copy refers to addicted smokers, and states, "Get unhooked." This ad elicited a visceral response in many of the participants that indicates a strong level of identification with the victim. At the other end of the first dimension, the ads take the point of view of the perpetrators of the violence. The low end is typified by an advertisement for a production of the *Nutcracker*, which shows a cartoon stick figure kicking a mouse, with the copy encouraging attendance to see the nutcracker "kicking the butt of a mouse."

The vast majority of ads that focus on the victim's perspective advertise cause-related issues and the ads from the perpetrator's perspective promote commercial messages. While this arrangement could indicate that the participants were simply recognizing cause-related ads as different from commercial messages, the data point to alternate explanations. For example, an ad for Crime Stoppers, which encourages witnesses to report crimes and guarantees them anonymity, falls toward the middle of this dimension. The image shows a gang of men beating someone up. The victim's identity is pixilated, making it unclear whom to identify with—victims or the perpetrators of the victim. While the cause-related ads were not located at both ends of this dimension, there were three cause-related ads interspersed with ads with commercial messages in the middle of Dimension 1.

The second dimension of the multidimensional scaling represents the degree to which the victims portrayed in the ads are deserving of violence. Deservingness for one's fate is a psycho-

UNDERLYING DIMENSIONS OF VIOLENCE IN PRINT ADVERTISEMENTS   33

Figure 3.1   **Two-Dimensional MDS Coordinate Map of Violent Ads**

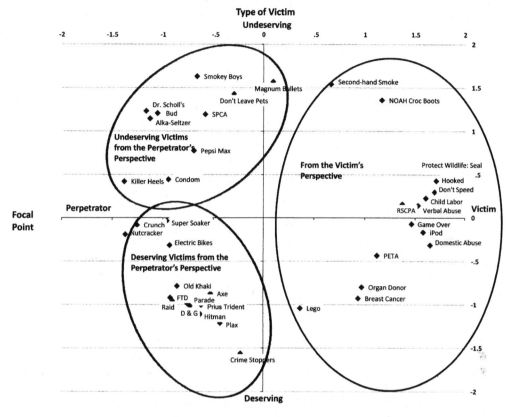

Notes: MDS = multidimensional scaling; SPCA = Society for the Prevention of Cruelty to Animals; RSCPA = Royal Society for the Prevention of Cruelty to Animals.

logical concept. This corresponds with sorting discussions during which participants explained perceptions of ad similarities based on the victims portrayed and their innocence or culpability regarding violence depicted. At the high end of the second dimension, the victims of the violence are not deserving of their fate. For example, at the extreme end of this dimension, two ads portray deer as victims of violence. Multiple participants referred to these as the "Bambi ads." Bambi is a children's cartoon character that is further associated with symbols of childhood and innocence (Lerner and Kalof 1999; Martinez, Prieto, and Farfan 2006). Ads at the opposite end of this dimension are characterized by their portrayal of victims that may be perceived as more deserving of violence: male gang members, criminals in an execution lineup, and the victim of a mafia hit.

Research has found that judgments of deservingness for one's fate encompass elements of perceived responsibility, likability, and in-group/out-group relations (Feather 1999). Cognitive ability increases inferences of responsibility (Weiner 1995) so that animals and children, such as the victims at the high end of the second dimension would be less likely to be perceived as responsible for or deserving of their outcome than adults. This corresponds to the pattern revealed by examining the victims in the ads sorted on this dimension: It begins with animals at the high end and moves to children, women, and ultimately, adult men at the low end.

The two dimensions uncovered through MDS suggest that the viewpoint of the ads (victim or perpetrator perspective) and the degree of the victim's deservingness are used to organize consumers' knowledge and activate different schemas that affect the processing of the violence-themed advertisements. To increase our understanding of the subregions that can be used to segment ads that fall across these two dimensions, the MDS results were analyzed using hierarchical cluster analysis.

Cluster Analysis

After the appropriate multidimensional solution was identified, the resulting MDS coordinates from the solution were analyzed using hierarchical cluster analysis in SPSS (Ryan and Bernard 2003). Hierarchical cluster analysis was appropriate because the structure of the categories of ads was unknown. The goal of the hierarchical cluster analysis was to look for homogeneous subsets of ads within the two-dimensional space to help with the interpretation of the two-dimensional solution. Ward's algorithm was used to develop a hierarchical agglomerative cluster analysis for a range of potential grouping structures for classifying the MDS estimates from the sorting task results.

A hierarchical cluster analysis was done on 2–10 clusters to decide on the appropriate cluster solution. The output was examined to evaluate whether the way the ads merged in each cluster solution was appropriate. We selected the appropriate cluster solution by interpreting the structure of the agglomeration schedule to create a conceptualization that represented the respondents' ideas about violence depicted in advertisements. The Euclidean distances from each ad's cluster center for each of the nine solutions were also calculated. There was less improvement in the average distance from the centroid between the three- and four-cluster solutions than there was for the lower solution (Punj and Stewart 1983). This average distance from the centroid is used as the intragroup error for each solution. Comparing the intragroup error across different cluster solutions indicates that the improvement from the two cluster solution intragroup error (.89) to the three cluster solution intragroup error (.53) yielded a higher improvement (.35) than the change in intragroup error between the three cluster solution and the four cluster solution (.48; difference = .05). Therefore, based on interpretability and the lack of improvement between the higher-level cluster solutions, the ads were grouped into three clusters for additional interpretation.

To label and interpret the three derived clusters, we focused on the ads that were closest to the centroid of each cluster, and the characteristics and data related to the remaining ads in each cluster (Griffin and Hauser 1993). The clusters allow us to detect patterns in the data in addition to the dimensions previously described.

Figure 3.1 displays the results of the cluster analysis with labels for clusters. The three clusters were named: (1) From the Victim's Perspective, (2) Undeserving Victims from the Perpetrator's Perspective, and (3) Deserving Victims from the Perpetrator's Perspective. Figure 3.1 summarizes the results of the multidimensional scaling and cluster analysis in a perceptual map. The cluster each ad falls into matches the categories listed in Table 3.1.

To examine the nature of the differences between the three clusters along the two dimensions of the MDS analysis, we conducted a multivariate analysis of variance (MANOVA) (see Table 3.2). A 3 × 1 MANOVA, using the score on each dimension as the dependent variables and the cluster number as the independent variable, showed the three clusters were different, Wilks's λ (4, 72) = .043, $p < .001$. On the first dimension (viewpoint of ad), the cluster "From the Victim's Perspective" ($M = 1.30$) was significantly different from "Undeserving Victims from the Perpetrator's Perspective" ($M = -.78$) or "Deserving Victims from the Perpetrator's Perspective," $M = -.78$; $F(2, 37) = 137.00$; $p < .001$. The latter two clusters do not differ from each other on this dimension, as both consist of ads presented from the perpetrator's viewpoint. On the second dimension (deservingness of the victim), the analysis also showed the "Undeserving Victims from the Perpetrator's Perspective" group ($M = 1.11$) was significantly different from the "From the Victim's Perspective"

Table 3.2

MANOVA of Clusters and Dimensions

	Dimensions	
	Viewpoint: Means (Standard Error)	Type of victim: Means (Standard Error)
"From the Victim's Perspective"	1.297 (.099)	.069 (.148)
"Undeserving Victims from the Perpetrator's Perspective"	−.782 (.121)	1.105 (.182)
"Deserving Victims from the Perpetrator's Perspective"	−.775 (.099)	−.805 (.148)

Note: MANOVA = multivariate analysis of variance.

($M = .07$) and the "Deserving Victims from the Perpetrator's Perspective," $M = -.81$; $F(2, 37) = 33.34$; $p < .001$. Each of the clusters differed significantly on the second dimension, where the "Undeserving Victims from the Perpetrator's Perspective" group had the most undeserving victims, the "From the Victim's Perspective" group had a mix of deserving and undeserving victims, and the "Deserving Victims from the Perpetrator's Perspective" group had the victims most deserving of the violence. Below, we summarize the characteristics of each cluster.

Cluster 1: "From the Victim's Perspective"

The first cluster includes 15 ads (14 cause-related ads and one commercial message). In this cluster, all the ads are located on one side of Dimension 1, which aligns with the interpretation that these ads are distinct in portraying the victim's viewpoint. Ads closest to the centroid in this cluster include ads portraying a child victim of verbal abuse crying and wincing from the figurative chokehold of violent words and a bruised and battered child victim of physical abuse.

Even though the ads in this cluster are characterized by taking the perspective of the victim, they vary in the deservingness of the victim portrayed. In this cluster, the victims range from horses, to babies, to adult men. The ads provoked comments indicating widely disparate views concerning the level of violence in the ads, the appropriateness of the use of the violence, the effectiveness of the execution of the ads, and the likability of the ads. However, comments relating to the ads in this cluster suggest a general consensus that they were grouped together because they focused on the victim regardless of whether the victim deserved the violence, which reflects the knowledge structure of advertisements depicting violence.

Cluster 2: "Undeserving Victims from the Perpetrator's Perspective"

This cluster comprises 10 ads, 2 of which are cause-related and 8 of which are commercial messages. These ads are characterized by taking the perpetrator's perspective, but portray victims that are less deserving of violence. Four of the 10 ads show cartoon victims, while other ads show victims less deserving of violence, such as a kitten, a parrot, and a young child. One of the ads closest to the centroid of this cluster shows a fish tank in which the goldfish have been replaced with beer for a party. In this ad, the consumer identifies with enjoying the party and cold beer (the perpetrator's viewpoint), yet the pet goldfish do not seem to deserve their violent fate of being relegated to a crowded plastic bag.

Cluster 3: "Deserving Victims from the Perpetrator's Perspective"

Fifteen ads comprise the third cluster, 14 of which are commercial messages. This cluster is distinguished by ads that take the perspective of the perpetrator of violence against powerful victims or victims associated with criminality or lower moral standards and thus more likely to be perceived as deserving of their fate. Research suggests powerful victims are considered more deserving of their fate because they are perceived to have done something to provoke the violence (Bradac, Hemphill, and Tardy 1981). The victims in this cluster include paparazzi, gang members, criminals in a firing line, the victim of a mob hit, and women fighting over fashion items. One of the ads closest to the centroid of this cluster depicts a woman in underwear apparently enjoying a spanking. The participants' comments while sorting indicated that the sexual nature of the violence in this ad and two others as well as the victims' apparent pleasure relates to their perceptions of the victims as complicit in the violence. This is consistent with research that shows that sexual women are perceived to have lower moral character (Cowan and O'Brien 1990). Victims of lower moral character, like the victims in this cluster, are perceived to be more deserving of their fate (Oliver 1993). The discussions with the participants suggest that while these ads are portrayed from the perpetrator's perspective, the victims' deservingness figured into their sorting judgments.

DISCUSSION

Our results indicate that consumers organize their thoughts about violent advertising in consideration of the deservingness of the victim and whether the ad presents the victim's or perpetrator's perspective. Arranged as a visual display of the perceived similarities between the ads, our results demonstrate a shared common cognitive structure of advertising depicting violence. Understanding this cognitive structure suggests that marketers using violent advertisements should consider whether their ads portray the viewpoint of the perpetrators or victims, and how this will impact their message. If their ad is promoted from the perpetrator's viewpoint, they also need to consider the deservingness of the victim. These results suggest specific areas for additional research to find a more complex and nuanced understanding of how consumers perceive and react to violent advertising.

Patterns resulting from the multidimensional scaling, cluster analysis, and means analysis suggest conceptualizing dimensions of violence in advertising based on deservingness of the victim and the point of view of the actors may be preferred to the application of conceptualizations that were designed for other purposes in other disciplines. Previously identified factors, including the level of violence, the consequences of violence, the presence of a weapon, and whether the violence is humorous do not appear to entirely shape the *shared* way in which consumers organize knowledge about advertising violence. These elements were discussed by many of the participants as a basis for some of their judgments of similarity between ads. However, the fact that resulting visual representation of the ads did not reflect these judgments indicates that individual judgments of these issues vary and do not represent *shared* knowledge.

Future research might examine whether different segments of consumers share perceptions regarding humor, level of violence, portrayal of consequences, and the relevance of the presence of weapons. A segmentation study might identify common individual differences in how segments of consumers react to violent advertising on the basis of types of victims portrayed and the viewpoint of the ad. This nuanced understanding might help marketers appropriately target violent ads to avoid confusing or offending consumers.

Dimensions

The first dimension we identified suggests that respondents distinguish between the ads based on the viewpoint of the ad: victim or perpetrator. This dimension also links to distinctions between cause-related ads and commercial messages. Ads with a commercial message generally show the perspective of the perpetrator, who is usually a consumer of the product being promoted. More frequently, the playful ads in our sample were commercial messages. This potential relationship may be linked to the finding that comedic elements in ads signal that seriousness should be downplayed (Kirsh 2006). While cause-related advertising may use a playful context (our sample contains examples), the converse, a serious, victim-focused commercial message, may be less common. It is possible that serious commercial messages portraying the victim's perspective may run counter to consumers' shared understandings of violent advertising and thus have the potential to confuse viewers. One exception may be advertisements for products that protect the victim (e.g., tires, burglar alarms). Considering this, additional research might examine the intersection of comedic versus serious ad executions portrayed from the perpetrator's perspective.

Ads portraying the victim's perspective in our study were primarily cause-related ads. Because empathy when viewing cause-related ads is linked to helping behavior (Bagozzi and Moore 1994), it is likely that marketers use a victim focus with hopes of engendering empathy in consumers. The ads on this dimension with a victim focus sometimes show the consequences of violence. This has been found to increase identification with victims (Dill and Dill 1998). Thus, marketers seeking to encourage helping behavior might create ads that portray the victim's perspective and the consequences of the violence. Fruitful directions for future research include exploration of the effect of the viewpoint (victim or perpetrator) in cause-related ads and the impact of whether the consequences of violence or the acts of violence are portrayed.

In addition to differentiating between ads based on the viewpoint they take, our analyses indicate a second dimension by which consumers distinguish between deserving and undeserving victims. Perceptions of deservingness figure prominently in violence research. Media studies research on violence found evidence that people enjoy viewing violence more if the victim deserved it (Oliver 1993). On the other hand, Tamborini, Stiff, and Zillmann (1987) suggest that the enjoyment of violence is linked to a desire to see social norms violated, such as attacks on vulnerable victims. Based on our findings, it appears that consumers differentiate between violent ads depicting animal victims versus human victims, and within human victims, by age and gender. It would be useful to further understand whether this distinction relates to an interference with (or enhancement of) the message.

Cluster Analysis

Our cluster analysis identifies three clusters. The first cluster is associated with ads from a victim viewpoint, whereas the other two clusters are located in the area representing ads that portray the perpetrator's viewpoint. Here the cluster analysis offers subregions of the MDS analysis of consumers' perceptions, indicating that consumers make additional distinctions between ads with a perpetrator's viewpoint. Specifically, while all ads portrayed from the victim's perspective regardless of the apparent deservingness of that victim are categorized similarly, in ads with a perpetrator viewpoint, they differentiate between ads with deserving victims and ads with undeserving victims.

The ads in the "Undeserving Victims from the Perpetrator's Perspective" cluster take the perspective of a perpetrator, but the victims do not appear deserving of their fate. Despite this, for many ads in this cluster, the tone is light and in some cases the violence is portrayed with cartoons and whimsy. Ads with lower realism (including animated or farcical) are less likely to be considered violent (Kirsh 2006). Depicting violence in a fanciful manner may help consumers to identify with perpetrators of violence against less deserving victims. Further research regarding this tactic may offer insight into how to minimize chances for offense.

In the cluster "Deserving Victims from the Perpetrator's Perspective," the ads portray victims that are less desirable and more powerful, and thus more likely to be perceived as deserving of their fate. Research supports that people react to powerful, disliked, or deserving victims differently. Media studies report that viewers experience positive moods when disliked characters suffer negative outcomes (Zillmann 1988). In the courtroom, powerful victims are believed to be more deserving of their fate because they are perceived to have done something to provoke the violence (Bradac, Hemphill, and Tardy 1981). Furthermore, research has found that if one can blame the victim, one is less likely to try to help (Van Zomeren and Lodewijkx 2005). This suggests that additional research into portrayals of victims in ads from the perpetrator's perspective should consider the effects on helping behavior and enjoyment of the ad.

In the third cluster, "From the Victim's Perspective," the ads are only distinguished by portraying the viewpoint of the victim. Consumers do not distinguish the ads by the deservingness of the victim. Taking the perspective of the victims seems to wipe out considerations of the deservingness of that victim. It is possible that deservingness of the victims in ads from the perpetrator's viewpoint is linked to perceptions of appropriateness of the violence.

This study indicates a prominent role of characters in how consumers make judgments about violent ads. Past research reveals an important role of identifying with characters in communication (Cohen 2001; Huesmann, Lagerspertz, and Eron 1984). DeRosia (2008) notes that when ad characters suggest brand claim, consumers use the whole context of the ad to decode, or derive meaning from, the ad elements using common, culturally bound rules. However, character theorization as it relates to violence and communication in general is undertheorized (Cohen 2001; Johnston 1995). In our study, the narrative viewpoint of victim versus perpetrator, as well as the type of victim portrayed, form the underlying dimensions of how consumers make distinctions between violent ads. This suggests that developing a deeper understanding of the role and effects of characters in violent advertisements warrants further research.

Limitations and Directions for Future Research

Two common critiques of MDS and cluster analysis are that they are atheoretical and the results may be sample-specific. The first criticism stems from concern that theory is required to interpret and make sense of the dimensions and clusters identified in the analysis. While this is of particular concern when testing hypotheses, to interpret the clusters and dimensions, this study uses the voice of the consumer through "think out loud" discussions of participants. This ensures that the results represent the consumers' shared structures of understanding rather than relying on proposed theories to explain cognitive structures. The second issue concerns the generalizability of the results. Like qualitative studies, the pile sort research design is representative rather than generalizable. Samples of both participants and stimuli were purposively (rather than randomly) selected so that the study would represent the widest possible range of consumers and violent ads. However, the participants in our sample were of higher educational levels than the broader population. Research suggests that education is positively related to less tolerant views regarding violence (Harris 1996). Also, ads were selected to represent a heterogeneous pool of different forms of violence and with different perpetrators and victims. To create this diversity in our set of stimuli, we relied on both domestic and international advertisements. Therefore, some of the brands and advertising strategies were less familiar to the respondents from the United States. Considering these limitations, it would be beneficial to replicate the study with different ads and participants.

A replication of the study could address how consumers' cognitive structure of advertising varies across cultures and advertising media. Because the meaning of violence is socially constructed and draws on shared cultural meanings (Muehlenhard and Kimes 1999), different participants may draw on different cultural resources to understand how the images related to the product or cause. Future research should examine how consumers' belief structures and perceptions vary across cultures and other demographics to build on this contribution. Also, this study only examined print advertisements. However, studies indicate that sound in violent media exerts a powerful effect (e.g., Furnham and Gunter 1987). Therefore, future research studies should examine consumers' perceptions of violent television or video advertising (e.g., YouTube), which includes sound and motion dimensions that may change consumer evaluations of violent images.

Finally, the focus of the current study is to identify the underlying cognitive structures of consumers' perceptions of violence. It did not examine the role of violence on likability of ads, message recall, or attitude toward the brand. Future studies should examine how victims portrayed in ads and the viewpoint of the ad impacts these relationships.

CONCLUSION

In conclusion, due to the widespread consumption of violence in consumer culture, we would be remiss to oversimplify how consumers respond to violent advertising. In contrast to previous research, which uses a unidimensional perspective of violence in advertising, our exploratory study identified dimensions in consumer perceptions of violent advertisements. We found that consumers distinguished ads based on the perspective from which the violence is presented (the victim or the perpetrator) and the deservingness of the victim.

These dimensions and clusters offer a picture of the elements that structure how consumers think about advertising violence. This suggests that greater attention be paid to the point of view of violence in advertising and the type of victim in violent advertisements. Our research suggests that these underresearched dimensions of violent advertising are important to consumers' perceptions. Expanding research to consider these dimensions may help to clarify unresolved questions regarding the effects and effectiveness of violent advertising and lead to a more nuanced and complex understanding of violent advertising.

REFERENCES

Alden, Dana L., Ashesh Mukherjee, and Wayne D. Hoyer (2000), "The Effects of Incongruity, Surprise and Positive Moderators on Perceived Humor in Television Advertising," *Journal of Advertising,* 29 (2), 1–15.

Anderson, Craig A., and L. Rowell Huesmann (2003), "Human Aggression: A Social-Cognitive View," in *The Sage Handbook of Social Psychology,* Michael A. Hogg and Joel Cooper, eds., Thousand Oaks, CA: Sage, 296–323.

Andersson, Svante, Anna Hedelin, Anna Nilsson, and Charlotte Welander (2004), "Violent Advertising in Fashion Marketing," *Journal of Fashion Marketing and Management,* 8 (1), 96–112.

Ang, Swee Hoon, Yih Hwai Lee, and Siew Meng Leong (2007), "The Ad Creativity Cube: Conceptualization and Initial Validation," *Journal of the Academy of Marketing Science,* 35 (2), 220–232.

Bagozzi, Richard P., and David J. Moore (1994), "Public Service Advertisements: Emotions and Empathy Guide Prosocial Behavior," *Journal of Marketing,* 58 (January), 56–70.

Baumeister, Roy F., and W. Keith Campbell (1999), "The Intrinsic Appeal of Evil: Sadism, Sensational Thrills, and Threatened Egotism," *Personality and Social Psychology Review,* 3 (3), 210–221.

Bettman, James R., and Michel A. Zins (1977), "Constructive Processing in Consumer Choice," *Journal of Consumer Research,* 4 (2), 75–85.

Boster, James S., and Jeffrey C. Johnson (1989), "Form or Function: A Comparison of Expert and Novice Judgments of Similarity Among Fish," *American Anthropologist,* 91 (4), 866–889.

Bradac, James J., Michael R. Hemphill, and Charles H. Tardy (1981), "Language Style on Trial: Effects of

'Powerful' and 'Powerless' Speech Upon Judgments of Victims and Villains," *Western Journal of Communication*, 45 (4), 327–341.

Burton, Michael, and Kimball Romney (1975), "A Multidimensional Representation of Role Terms," *American Ethnologist*, 2 (3), 397–407.

Bushman, Brad J., and Angelica M. Bonacci (2002), "Violence and Sex Impair Memory for Television Ads," *Journal of Applied Psychology*, 87 (3), 557–564.

Cohen, Jonathan (2001), "Defining Identification: A Theoretical Look at Identification of Audiences with Media Characters," *Mass Communication and Society*, 4 (3), 245–264.

Collins, Randall (1974), "Three Faces of Cruelty: Towards a Comparative Sociology of Violence," *Theory and Society*, 1 (4), 415–440.

Cooney, Mark, and Scott Phillips (2002), "Typologizing Violence: A Blackian Perspective," *International Journal of Sociology and Social Policy*, 22 (7/8), 75–108.

Cowan, Gloria, and Margaret O'Brien (1990), "Gender and Survival Vs. Death in Slasher Films: A Content Analysis," *Sex Roles*, 23 (3/4), 187–196.

Creamer, Matthew, and Rupal Parekh (2008), "How to Cut Through But Not Offend? Verizon, Snickers Latest to Fail Test," *Advertising Age*, 79 (29), 3, 30.

Dahl, Darren W., Kristina D. Frankenberger, and Rajesh V. Manchanda (2003), "Does It Pay to Shock? Reactions to Shocking and Non-Shocking Advertising Content Among University Students," *Journal of Advertising Research*, 43 (3), 268–281.

De Pelsmacker, Patrick, and Joeri Van Den Bergh (1996), "The Communication Effects of Provocation in Print Advertising," *International Journal of Advertising*, 15 (3), 203–222.

DeRosia, Eric D. (2008), "The Effectiveness of Nonverbal Symbolic Signs and Metaphors in Advertisements: An Experimental Inquiry," *Psychology and Marketing*, 25 (3), 298–316.

Derriennic, Jean-Pierre (1972), "Theory and Ideologies of Violence," *Journal of Peace Research*, 9 (4), 361–374.

Dill, Karen E., and Jody C. Dill (1998), "Video Game Violence: A Review of the Empirical Literature," *Aggression and Violent Behavior*, 3 (4), 407–428.

Dyer, Gillian (1988), *Advertising as Communication*, New York: Routledge.

Feather, Norman T. (1999), "Judgments of Deservingness: Studies in the Psychology of Justice and Achievement," *Personality and Social Psychology Review*, 3 (2), 86–107.

Fiske, Susan T., and Shelley E. Taylor (1984), *Social Cognition*, Reading, MA: Addison-Wesley.

Furnham, Adrian, and Barrie Gunter (1987), "Effects of Time of Day and Medium of Presentation on Immediate Recall of Violent and Non-Violent News," *Applied Cognitive Psychology*, 1 (4), 255–262.

Garson, G. David (2009), "Multi-Dimensional Scaling: StatNotes," North Carolina State University, available at http://faculty.chass.ncsu.edu/garson/PA765/mds.htm, February 8, 2009 (accessed May 2010).

Giguere, Gyslain (2006), "Collecting and Analyzing Data in Multidimensional Scaling Experiments: A Guide for Psychologists Using SPSS," *Tutorial in Quantitative Methods for Psychology*, 2 (1), 27–38.

Griffin, Abbie, and John R. Hauser (1993), "The Voice of the Customer," *Marketing Science*, 12 (1), 1–27.

Gunter, Barrie, Adrian Furnham, and Eleni Pappa (2005), "Effects of Television Violence on Memory for Violent and Nonviolent Advertising," *Journal of Applied Social Psychology*, 35 (8), 1680–1697.

Harper, Michelle E., Florian G. Jentsch, Devon Berry, H. Cathy Lau, Clint Bowers, and Eduardo Salas (2003), "TPL-KATS-Card Sort: A Tool for Assessing Structural Knowledge," *Behavioral Research Methods, Instruments and Computers*, 35 (4), 577–584.

Harris, Mary B. (1996), "Aggression, Gender, and Ethnicity," *Aggression and Violent Behavior*, 1 (2), 123–146.

Huesmann, L. Rowell, Kristi Lagerspertz, and Leonard D. Eron (1984), "Intervening Variables in the TV Violence-Aggression Relation: Evidence from Two Countries," *Developmental Psychology*, 20 (5), 746–775.

Jackson, Kristin M., and William M. K. Trochim (2002), "Concept Mapping as an Alternative Approach for the Analysis of Open-Ended Survey Responses," *Organizational Research Methods*, 5 (4), 307–336.

Johnston, Deirdre D. (1995), "Adolescents' Motivation for Viewing Graphic Horror," *Human Communication Research*, 21 (4), 522–552.

Kirsh, Steven J. (2006), "Cartoon Violence and Aggression in Youth," *Aggression and Violent Behavior*, 11 (6), 547–557.

Kruskal, Joseph (1964), "Non-Metric Multidimensional Scaling: A Numerical Approach," *Psychometrika*, 29 (March), 115–129.

———, and Myron Wish (1978), *Multidimensional Scaling*, Beverly Hills: Sage.

Lerner, Jennifer E., and Linda Kalof (1999), "The Animal Text: Message and Meaning in Television Advertisements," *Sociology Quarterly*, 40 (4), 565–586.

Manceau, Delphine, and Elisabeth Tissier-Desbordes (2006), "Are Sex and Death Taboos in Advertising? An Analysis of Taboos in Advertising and a Survey of French Consumer Perceptions," *International Journal of Advertising*, 25 (1), 9–33.

Marshall, Martin N. (1996), "Sampling for Qualitative Research," *Family Practice*, 13 (6), 522–525.

Martinez, Inmaculada Jose, Maria Dolores Prieto, and Juana Farfan (2006), "Childhood and Violence in Advertising: A Current Perspective," *International Communication Gazette*, 68 (3), 269–287.

McLaughlin, Mary E., Peter Carnevale, and Rodney G. Lim (1991), "Professional Mediators' Judgments of Mediation Tactics: Multidimensional Scaling and Cluster Analyses," *Journal of Applied Psychology*, 76 (3), 465–472.

Messner, Steven F., and Kenneth Tardiff (1985), "Social Ecology of Urban Homicide: An Application of the Routine Activities Approach," *Criminology*, 23 (2), 241–267.

Meyers-Levy, Joan, and Alice Tybout (1989), "Schema Congruity as a Basis for Product Evaluation," *Journal of Consumer Research*, 16 (June), 39–54.

Muehlenhard, Charlene L., and Leigh Ann Kimes (1999), "The Social Construction of Violence: The Case of Sexual and Domestic Violence," *Personality and Social Psychology Review*, 3 (3), 234–245.

Oliver, Mary Beth (1993), "Adolescents' Enjoyment of Graphic Horror: Effects of Viewers' Attitudes and Portrayals of Victim," *Communication Research*, 20 (1), 30–50.

Potter, W. James, and Ron Warren (1998), "Humor as Camouflage of Televised Violence," *Journal of Communication*, 48 (2), 40–57.

Punj, Girish N., and David W. Stewart (1983), "Cluster Analysis in Marketing Research: Review and Suggestions for Application," *Journal of Marketing Research*, 20 (May), 134–148.

Roehm, Michelle L., and Michael K. Brady (2007), "Consumer Responses to Performance Failures by High-Equity Brands," *Journal of Consumer Research*, 34 (December), 537–545.

Rosenberg, Seymour, and Moonja Park Kim (1975), "The Method of Sorting as a Data-Gathering Procedure in Multivariate Research," *Multivariate Behavioral Research*, 10 (4), 489–502.

Rosenthal, Beth Spenciner, and W. Cody Wilson (2003), "The Association of Ecological Variables and Psychological Distress with the Exposure to Community Violence Among Adolescents," *Adolescence*, 38 (151), 459–479.

Ryan, Gery W., and H. Russell Bernard (2003), "Techniques to Identify Themes," *Field Methods*, 15 (1), 85–109.

Scharrer, Erica, Andrea Bergstrom, Angela Paradise, and Qianqing Ren (2006), "Laughing to Keep from Crying: Humor and Aggression in Television Commercial Content," *Journal of Broadcasting and Electronic Media*, 50 (4), 615–634.

Solomon, Michael, Richard D. Ashmore, and Laura C. Longo (1992), "The Beauty Match-Up Hypothesis: Congruence Between Types of Beauty and Product Images in Advertising," *Journal of Advertising*, 21 (4), 23–34.

Tamborini, Ron, James Stiff, and Dolf Zillmann (1987), "Preference of Graphic Horror Featuring Male Versus Female Victimization," *Human Communication Research*, 13 (4), 529–552.

Unnava, H. Rao, and Deepak Sirdeshmukh (1994), "Reducing Competitive Advertising Interference," *Journal of Marketing Research*, 31 (August), 403–411.

Van Exel, Job, and Gjalt de Graaf (2005), "Q Methodology: A Sneak Preview," available at www.fsw.vu.nl/en/Images/Q%20methodology_tcm31–41687.pdf, Version 5.03 (accessed August 2008).

Van Zomeren, Martijn, and Hein F. M. Lodewijkx (2005), "Motivated Responses to 'Senseless' Violence: Explaining Emotional and Behavioural Responses Through Person and Position Identification," *European Journal of Social Psychology*, 35 (6), 755–766.

Weiner, Bernard (1995), "Inferences of Responsibility and Social Motivation," in *Advances in Experimental Social Psychology*, Mark P. Zanna, ed., San Diego: Academic Press.

Weller, Susan C., and A. Kimball Romney (1988), *Systematic Data Collection*, Irvine, CA: Sage.

Whaley, Arthur L., and Richard A. Longoria (2009), "Preparing Card Sort Data for Multidimensional Scaling Analysis in Social Psychological Research: A Methodological Approach," *Journal of Social Psychology*, 149 (1), 105–115.

Wilson, Barbara J., Stacy L. Smith, W. James Potter, Dale Kunkel, Daniel Linz, Carolyn M. Colvin, and Edward Donnerstein (2002), "Violence in Children's Television Programming: Assessing the Risks," *Journal of Communication*, 52 (March), 5–35.

World Health Organization (2002), *World Report on Violence and Health*, Elienne G. Krug, Linda L. Dahlberg, James A. Mercy, Anthony B. Zwiand, and Rafael Lozano, eds., Geneva: World Health Organization.

Zillmann, Dolf (1988), "Mood Management Through Communication Choices," *American Behavioral Scientist*, 31 (3), 327–340.

PART II

HUMOR AND VIOLENCE IN ADVERTISING

4

It's Just a Joke

Violence Against Males in Humorous Advertising

Charles S. Gulas, Kim K. McKeage, and Marc G. Weinberger

All of us who professionally use the mass media are the shapers of society. We can vulgarize that society. We can brutalize it. Or we can help lift it onto a higher level.
—William Bernbach

Advertising reflects the culture in which it appears. As noted by Pollay (1986), the reflection occurs, however, in a distorted mirror. One of the emergent reflections of our culture is that of violence. There is extensive literature in the past two decades documenting both the presence and the impact of violence in the media (Wilson et al. 2002; Wood, Wong, and Chachere 1991). These studies have examined violence on television programs, on sporting events, in music and video games (Bushman and Anderson 2001; Funk et al. 2004; Tamburro et al. 2004). Murray (2008) identified over 500 studies focused just on violence and television. Sharrer et al. (2006) examined the issue of violence in television advertising. More recently, an experimental study (Brown, Bhadury, and Pope 2010) examined and documented a significant effect of comedic violence in viral video advertising.

The people portrayed in ads are not a random sample of consumers, nor are they even a reasonably representative one. The actions and values of characters in ads reflect real-world actions but in a highly fictionalized manner. Yet this incomplete and distorted reflection helps to shape the culture (Pollay 1986). Kilbourne states: "Advertising often sells a great deal more than products. It sells values, images, and concepts of love and sexuality, romance, success, and perhaps more important, normalcy. To a great extent, it tells us who we are and who we should be" (1999, p. 74). The focus of the current study is the confluence of violence, gender, and humor in advertising.

Beginning with content analysis studies of women and minorities, researchers in the 1970s examined how various groups are portrayed in advertising (Bush, Solomon, and Hair 1977; Courtney and Lockeretz 1971). The depth of analysis evolved and matured in the work of Kilbourne (1999) and others. This social criticism began to influence advertising portrayals of women and minorities. Excluded from this literature has been the white male.

This paper investigates the male narrative as it intersects with portrayals of violent aggression and humor. Using Kilbourne's approach to gender analysis, the following question is posed: How is the male role constructed through violence and aggression in current humorous advertising?

LITERATURE REVIEW

Humor is a complex construct that has been studied by linguists, philosophers, psychologists, and scholars from many disciplines, including, of course, advertising (for a review, see Gulas and Weinberger 2006). There are many theories of humor, most of which fall broadly into three general categories: cognitive-perceptual (including the incongruity theories), superiority (including disparagement and affective-evaluative theories), and relief (including psychodynamic theories).

Humor often includes elements of either physical or psychological violence. Speck (1987) outlined five types of humor that result from the combination of these three categories. Two of the humor types, satire (composed of incongruity and disparagement) and full comedy (composed of incongruity, disparagement, and arousal-safety), include disparagement and accounted for about 30% of the 125 prime-time CBS television ads in his sample. Full comedy, which uses all three humor mechanisms, accounted for 16% of the television ads. It is the addition of disparagement to incongruity and arousal-safety that transforms Speck's "sentimental wit" category into "full comedy" with its higher perceived humor level.

Morreall (1983) posits that disparagement is probably the oldest and most widespread theory of laughter. There are many proponents of disparagement theory (see La Fave, Haddad, and Maesen 1976; Morreall 1983; Zillmann 1983; Zillmann and Cantor 1976). Proponents of disparagement theory also include Aristotle and Hobbes. Aristotle viewed laughter as a form of derision and even wit as a form of educated insolence. Moreover, Freud's (1960) "tendentious wit" includes disparagement. Rapp (1951) traced the evolution of laughter from primitive physical battles of triumph. In the modern era, the physical derision is often substituted by ridicule. In genial humor, this ridicule is tempered by love or affection.

Perhaps because it relies on an explicit verbal or physical put-down, disparagement (superiority) has been traditionally used with some caution by advertisers to avoid alienating an audience who may either miss the play signals that help convert raw aggression into mirth, or who associate themselves with the target of the disparaging humor. Empirical evidence suggests, however, that one form of disparagement, aggressive humor, now appears in a significant number of television ads (Sharrer et al. 2006). In an analysis of over 4,000 broadcast television ads, Scharrer et al. (2006) found some form of aggression in 12.3% of the ads. Scharrer et al. further found that 53.5% of the ads featuring aggression also contained elements of humor. If movie trailers and television promos are removed from the analysis, the link between humor and aggression is more pronounced, with 87.7% of aggressive ads containing a humorous element. Scharrer and her colleagues also found that 77.9% of the victims of fortuitous (unintentional) aggression were male. Only 5.5% of the victims were female; the remainder represent missing data. In the cases of intentional aggression, 80.8% of the perpetrators and 89.3% of the victims were male. As shown by Scharrer et al. (2006), the target of violence in humorous advertising is often a male character.

Targets in Humorous Disparagement

In disparagement, the humor process includes an agent, an object, and an audience (Gulas and Weinberger 2006). The agent is the source of the humor, the joke teller. In the case of advertising, the agent is the advertiser. The audience is the recipient of the humor, and the object is the butt of the joke. These components can sometimes be collapsed. For example, in self-deprecating humor, the agent is also the object of the humor. In other situations, the audience may be the object of the humor. Generally, however, the object or butt of the joke is a third party.

The third-party humor object may be a specific, known individual. For example, it is common for politicians and celebrities to be the object of humor in comedy acts. However, in the case of advertising, the humor is typically directed at a more general target, such as an anonymous, hapless blunderer. Even an anonymous individual can be associated with some group, though, such as blondes, men, children, or older adults, either by design or by default.

The nature of the object in disparaging humorous advertising has changed over time. In early U.S. advertising, racist humor was common (Gulas and Weinberger 2006). Although racial and ethnic humor have faded from mainstream advertising, sexist humor remains. For example, a recent Mercedes-Benz ad features an attractive blonde woman who tries to order French fries, a burger, and a milk shake. When the woman behind the counter informs her that she is in a library, she pauses, looks around the room full of bookshelves and people reading, and then repeats the order in a whisper. The tag line for the ad is "beauty is nothing without brains." This ad makes use of a standard humor archetype, the attractive, but intellectually challenged, woman. These women are generally portrayed as blondes. Indeed, "blonde jokes" defines an entire genre of humor but is used infrequently in current advertising.

Much has been written about the portrayal of women in advertising (e.g., Cortese 2008; Kilbourne 1999). Most of the research exploring images of women in advertising has focused on the objectification of women in advertising (e.g., Zimmerman and Dahlberg 2008). A separate stream of research explores the effect that idealized advertising imagery has on women who are exposed to this advertising (e.g., Martin and Gentry 1997). Both of these streams of inquiry converge on the question of how gender is constructed in society and how advertising both uses and supports social expectations of gender (Goffman 1979). In spite of the gains of feminism over the past few decades, the objectification of women in advertising continues (Plakoyiannaki et al. 2008). As long as gender is an important social category, advertisers will continue to construct gender representations in ads. The objectification of women in advertising has now, apparently, been joined by physical violence against men and the denigration of men in humorous advertising.

Gender Portrayals in Television and Advertising

Given that the duration of a modern video ad is as short as 15 seconds, clearly the construction of a subtle, inaccessible narrative is impossible. Consumers must grasp the point and grasp it quickly. Therefore, ads must use themes that are familiar and easily recognized by their audience. Traditionally, ads include recognizable themes such as "men are rational/women are emotional" (Solomon 1988) and "men are aggressive/women are passive" (Goffman 1979). Goffman noted that in the power dynamics in gender portrayals, men were generally portrayed as active, in control, and in superior positions. Women were generally portrayed as subordinate to men and childlike.

These traditional themes are not, however, entirely supported in current advertising. The trend in advertising discourse now admits adults into the fantasy world of children where they are allowed to be "bad" and enjoy freedom from adult constraints and worries (Cross 2002). Today it is the man's behavior that leads to problems and censure, and the traditional family metaphor is turned upside down.

These traditional advertising images were echoed by the popular television shows of the day. Popular television dads included Andy Taylor on the *Andy Griffith Show*, Ward Cleaver on *Leave It to Beaver*, Mike Brady on *The Brady Bunch*, and Cliff Huxtable on *The Cosby Show*. Each of these characters was stable, financially secure, and confident. While there were notable exceptions, such as Fred Flintstone and Archie Bunker, television dads generally served as a voice of reason when, in a typical episode, the children got into some sort of problem. The exemplar of this role was the character Jim Anderson on the aptly named *Father Knows Best*.

The modern era of television is defined by a very different type of dad. This dad is often bumbling, or lazy, or self-centered, or some combination of these. The voice of reason on these shows is nearly always the wife, the children, or a secondary character. These dads include Homer Simpson on *The Simpsons*, Ray Barone and his father, Frank Barone, on *Everybody Loves Raymond*, Tim Taylor on *Home Improvement,* and Peter Griffin on *Family Guy*. From the 1950s through the 1990s, the portrayal of the father figure in television programming changed significantly (Scharrer 2001). An analysis of sitcom characters from the 1950s through the 1990s revealed that female characters tell significantly more jokes at the expense of father characters in later decades than in earlier decades (Scharrer 2001). In addition, the overall foolishness of portrayal of the father figure increased significantly in later decades compared to earlier decades (Scharrer 2001). Scharrer notes that this trend is due primarily to changes between programs rather than changes within a program, since fathers tend to be portrayed as wise or foolish consistently within a program across episodes. In other words, recent television series are more likely than television series of the past to have a foolish father character.

As the typical portrayal of fathers on popular television shows switched from Andy Taylor to Tim Taylor, a new type of humorous ad began to emerge. Cross proposed that "maturity and responsibility" in advertising portrayals of adults might have declined, to be replaced by images of "self-gratification and youthful coolness" (2002, p. 445)—or youthful foolishness, in the case of some ads. He calls for researchers to examine the three-way relationship between children and advertising *and* parents, for evidence of shifting understandings of childhood and the role of childhood innocence in regulating consumption. While Cross (2002) does not explicitly say so, the examination of the adult role must further be broken down by gender, as it appears that in many cases, the license for childishness is largely issued to the male parent in these ads.

The shift in gender portrayals through humorous executions is a key to understanding our current social discourse. Gender is a particularly important social category, and Jhally (1990) notes that advertising, given its prominence in our daily lives, has a particularly important role in the discourse on gender. Furthermore, he notes that advertisements tend to exaggerate key aspects of their narrative—making them more recognizable, but not untrue. Eagleton (1983) notes that discourses from films, television, fiction, and other sources are closely related to the maintenance or transformation of our existing systems of power. Shifts in our discourse thus signify potential shifts in power. If there has been some upheaval of the status quo in the 30 years since Goffman's (1979) *Gender Advertisements*, it should be explored.

METHOD

Following the methodology employed by Stern (1996), our first analysis is a "close reading" of the portrayal of men in recent humorous advertising. The initial sample for the ads in this study was drawn similarly to previous advertising deconstructions (Goffman 1979; Kilbourne 1999). Goffman selected ads that he described as "easy to hand—at least to my hand" (1979, p. 24). Kilbourne (1999) noticed a pattern in the portrayal of women in ads and began compiling a clippings file. Likewise, through work on other research projects, preparation of class materials, and general exposure to advertising, we perceived an emerging pattern in the portrayal of men in humorous advertising and began compiling examples over the past few years. For the current study, we supplemented this sample with a sample drawn more systematically. We analyzed all the ads broadcast during the Super Bowl in 1989, 1999, and 2009. We also analyzed the television advertising of the five most advertised brands in 2008.

Our analysis reveals two broad themes of violence in the context of humorous advertising. The first is explicit physical violence toward men. The second is denigration, which is a form of psychological violence (Candib 2000; Montminy 2005).

FINDINGS

In many of the ads discussed in this paper, physical violence against men is intended to be humorous. There are two subcategories of this type of advertisement. In one type, the violence is of a general nature. In the other, the violence is presented as a reasonable response to something that the man has done.

General violence against men occurs in an ad for the Dodge Ram pickup truck that depicts a wedding scene. As the minister approaches the part of the ceremony when a kiss is customary, the bride chooses instead to head-butt the groom and knocks him unconscious. She then carries him out to her pickup truck. This type of violence can also be seen in several recent examples in Bud Light advertising. Thirty-four television ads aired for Bud Light in the United States between January 1, 2009, and December 2, 2009. All these ads used humor. Of these ads, eight included some form of physical violence. In seven ads, the violence is directed against men. For example, in one ad, a woman breaks up with her boyfriend by pushing him out the door of a moving car. In another, a woman attaches a boutonniere to a man's tuxedo with seven nails shot from a nail gun. The man grimaces in agony from what would be in reality a life-threatening assault (see Figure 4.1). Similar violence occurs in a Pepsi Max ad that appeared during the 2010 Super Bowl. Five different men are portrayed as the victims of physical violence. In at least two of these violent acts, the victim would likely have been hospitalized or killed if the events portrayed actually happened.

Violence against men in ads is often portrayed as justified within the context of the ad. For example, in a Visa credit card ad, a woman walks into a room where a man is watching TV and eating popcorn. A children's cartoon is playing on the TV, and the man is laughing uproariously and dropping popcorn all over the floor. The woman says that she has bought a new vacuum cleaner, but the man is too engrossed in the childish cartoon to react to her statement. He continues to ignore her as she starts vacuuming. When she gets near his feet, he says, "You missed a spot." Her reaction is to point the vacuum at him. As the computer-animated version of the man gets sucked into the vacuum cleaner, the woman looks satisfied. She says in a pleased tone, "It works." This scene is followed by a flashback to buying the machine—with her Visa card—and the salesman saying the machine will be good for her biggest problem areas.

Burger King promoted its "Steakhouse Burger" with an ad featuring two male teachers in a faculty lunchroom eating Steakhouse Burgers. A female teacher walks in and says to one of the men, "A Steakhouse Burger—what did you do to deserve that?" The man replies, "I gave half of my salary to charity." Satisfied with the answer, she then asks the second man the same question. He replies, "I was just hungry." The woman slaps him violently across the face, then hits him on top of the head. In one version of the ad she says, "I hope you don't teach your students to be as arrogant as you." In another version she says, "What kind of a reason is that, you self-important narcissistic bas . . ." The audio cuts off before she completes the word "bastard."

Mike's Hard Lemonade aired an ad in which a woman and a man are sitting at a bar talking. A second man approaches and uses a bad pickup line. The woman responds with a slightly annoyed look and turns back toward the man she had been talking to. The ad fades to black. In the next scene, we see that the pickup artist has returned for another try. He gets the same response. The man returns for yet a third attempt. At this point, the woman's male companion stands up and starts to tell the pickup artist to move on. Before he can complete his statement, however, the woman stands up and head-butts the interloper, knocking him to the ground.

In a smartphone ad, a woman is frantically looking for her lost Sprint Blackberry when two male colleagues ask if everything is all right. She then hears the phone ring in one of the colleague's pockets. She gives him an angry look, and he replies in a frightened tone that he was just making a joke. The next scene is set in a hospital, where the woman is texting the message that Frank might be late. The shot widens to show one of the men being treated by the medical staff and the other man sitting next to the woman, holding an ice pack on his head.

Progressive Insurance ran an ad in which a woman is using a Web site to make a virtual voodoo doll. The doll is labeled "Cheatin' Boyfriend." The woman inflicts pain with pins and flames in various spots on the man's body as he is shown in a bar with another woman. One version of the ad culminates with the woman shrinking the man's head. In another version, the final infliction shows the woman dragging virtual pliers toward the man's genitals. We see the man recoil in pain just as he was about to kiss the other woman. There is a look of glee on the face of the ex-girlfriend as she sits at the computer. And a man does not have to be unfaithful to deserve attack. An animated banner ad on the *Detroit News* Web site warned that men who buy the wrong Valentine's Day gift might be subject to a beating (see Figure 4.1).

50 HUMOR AND VIOLENCE IN ADVERTISING

Figure 4.1 **Violence Against Men Is Humorous**

Bud Light Boutonniere Ad

Web Banner *Detroit News* Web Site

Two recent Bud Light ads also "justify" violence. In one of these ads, a female restaurant patron is attempting to get the attention of a waiter who is ignoring her. She eventually gets his attention by tripping him. He falls across a table, where another man is dining, and through a plate-glass window, almost landing on a third man seated in the patio area of the restaurant. All three men are hit by falling glass. In the Bud Light "meeting" ad, a man gets thrown out of a third-story window for suggesting that the company could save money by cutting back on its beer purchases.

In all the ads discussed in this section, the attempted humor derives from physical violence targeted at men. In the context of the ad, the violence often appears to be "justified" in some way. This suggests approval of the "blame the victim" mentality that has been condemned in domestic violence literature for decades.

In addition to subjecting men to physical violence, ads attempt to generate humor by subjecting men to several types of psychological violence through denigration. The subcategories of denigration found in the ads include portraying men as animals, as childish, lazy, incompetent, and ignorant. These ads also suggest that men have an inflated view of themselves and, consequently, deserve scorn (see Table 4.1).

Table 4.1

Psychological Violence Through Denigration

Theme	Examples
Men are animals	*Sony Cybershot* The dad is portrayed literally as a horse's ass. The children refer to the hindquarters as "Dad," and the wife refers to the hindquarters as "sweetie." The payoff of the joke is, "your dad is not a horse's behind. A *Sony Cybershot* camera knows this." The implication is that the family may not know this but the camera does. *Buy.com* A Super Bowl ad that shows a man crawling on his hands and knees toward a large dog. The man then proceeds to sniff the dogs behind.
Men are childish	*Fidelity* A man dressed in business attire plays with a toddler ring-stacking toy in a doctor's waiting room and proclaims his success to a preadolescent girl (who is clearly too old to be interested in such a simple toy) and then to the other people waiting. "Did you see how fast I did that? I am like the king of that thing." *Subway* A man throws a tantrum. He stomps his feet and holds his breath when his wife refuses to comply with his request to get a Big Philly Cheese Steak sandwich. She responds, "that's real mature." His young child joins in the condemnation angrily stating, "yeah, Dad, grow up."
Patronizing behavior toward men is acceptable	*Fidelity* A couple speaking to the camera about their retirement planning. The wife says, "We don't know much about handling money." The man counters, "When I switched jobs, who handled the turnover?" "Rollover," the wife corrects him. She continues that *Fidelity* did it all. "They would have signed your name if they could have." She adds, "You can't get the dog to roll over." The man sheepishly replies, "It's your dog." *Sonic* A man and woman are ordering food. The woman says, "I will have the hickory grilled chicken junior wrap and so will you." The man replies, "I really thought I wanted the light ranch grilled chicken." The characters then begin talking over each other. He says awkwardly, "I guess I was wrong." The woman says, "You don't know what you like." The man continues, at this point speaking more to himself than to the woman, "I don't know what to eat, ever."
Men are lazy	*SAM Store and Move* A woman is loading household items into a large storage container in the yard of a suburban house. The voice-over explains that *SAM Store and Move* is perfect for moving and renovating. As the woman struggles dragging a sofa, the voice-over continues, "Or if you just need to get some things out of the way for awhile." The shot then widens to show that the reason that the sofa is so heavy is that a man is sleeping on it with a TV remote in his hand. The woman loads the couch with the man on it into the storage container, taking the remote control with her when she returns to the house. *Klondike* A man brings a drinking glass into the kitchen and puts it on the counter, then picks it up and puts it in the dishwasher as his wife looks on in amazement. The tag line is, "Give that man a *Klondike* bar."

52　HUMOR AND VIOLENCE IN ADVERTISING

Table 4.1 *(continued)*

Theme	Examples
Men are incompetent and ignorant	*FluMist* Ad shows a father incapable of preparing his children for school. On the radio in the background the weather forecast calls for heavy snow, yet the children are dressed in lightweight summer clothes. The kitchen is a mess and the man is clearly overwhelmed. All of this is due to the mom's illness, which presumably could have been prevented with *FluMist*. *Sonic* A man and a woman are in a car; each is holding a milk shake. The woman is drinking hers. She asks why he is not drinking his. He replies that he is waiting for it to cool. She explains to him that a hot-fudge sundae is not literally hot. He tries it hesitantly and realizes that she is correct, but he still fails to grasp the basic concept of a milk shake. *National Bank and Trust* In a radio commercial, a man and a woman are talking about online banking services that the company offers. The man seems overwhelmed by the technology. The woman concludes, "plenty of features for people like me—easy to use for people like you." *Verizon* A man is demonstrating a computer to his son. The father gets all of the terminology wrong. He is repeatedly corrected by the son. The father also says that the computer is "screaming fast" when, in fact, it is very slow when he attempts a download.
Men have an inflated view of their worth and therefore deserve scorn	*Kingsford Match Light* A group of people is gathered for a backyard cookout. A woman approaches a charcoal grill. A man urgently calls out, "Honey, wait!" He explains that lighting charcoal requires a technique. He proceeds to light a match and place it on the pile of charcoal, which ignites. The woman mockingly says, "wow." She then turns to the crowd and proclaims in a mocking manner, "it's okay, everyone." *Fidelity* The ad opens with a man and a woman in a car. The frame shows the man driving. He says, "First the one, and then the deuce," as he turns the steering wheel one way and then another. It appears as though he is maneuvering the car into a difficult parking space. He proclaims, "Perfect!" and lifts his hand toward the woman next to him and says, "High five." She looks at him with utter contempt and refuses to respond to the high-five request. As the shot widens, we see that what the man has succeeded in doing was to park his car in a huge, nearly empty parking lot and he has parked far away from the buildings when there are hundreds of closer parking spots. *Verizon* In an ad for DSL service, a hapless dad is attempting to help his approximately 8-year-old daughter with her homework. It is apparent that she knows more than the dad. The mom arrives on the scene and the dad states that he is helping her with her homework. The mom tells the dad to wash the dog. When he hesitates, she tells him to "leave her alone." Upon further hesitation, she sharply demands his exit from the room and he jumps to comply.

Table 4.2

The Use of Aggressive Humor in Super Bowl Advertising

	1989	1999	2009
Percent using any humor	61.9%	70.5%	76.9%
Percent of humorous ads with males as target of aggression	13.6%[a]	29.6%[b]	73.4%[c]
Percent of humorous ads with females as target of aggression	0%	13.3%[d]	10.8%[e]
	n = 71	n = 139	n = 60

Notes: Ads using physical aggression out of pool of aggressive ads: [a]2 of 6 ads used physical aggression; [b]5 of 29 ads employed physical aggression; [c]13 of 34 ads employed physical aggression; [d]4 of 13 ads employed physical aggression; [e]1 of 5 ads employed physical aggression.

To examine the prevalence of portrayals like those described and to ascertain whether there has been a change in the portrayal of men in advertising, we examined Super Bowl advertising from 1989, 1999, and 2009 (see Table 4.2). The ads were obtained from the online archive available at http://adland.tv/SuperBowlCommercials/.

The 2010 Super Bowl delivered the largest U.S. television audience in history, with over 106 million viewers, and each of the four previous Super Bowls drew over 90 million viewers (Flint 2010). Between 1972 and 2002, the Super Bowl delivered a television audience that comprised more than 40% of U.S. households in every year except 1990, when the broadcast was viewed by 39% of U.S. households (Kelley and Turley 2004). With these large audiences, the Super Bowl is the remaining remnant of television as a true mass medium (McAllister 1999). As such, it has attracted the attention of many advertising scholars. In fact, Super Bowl advertising has been the sample used in numerous academic studies exploring a wide range of advertising-related topics (see, e.g., Alessandri 2009; Chung and Zhao 2003; Jin, Zhao, and An 2006; Nail 2007; Youn et al. 2001). In addition, McAllister (1999) posits that Super Bowl advertising is unique due to its "cultural spillage." There is pre-event discourse regarding the advertising, discourse about the advertising during the event, and postevent discourse about the advertising. According to McAllister (1999), this discourse elevates Super Bowl advertising to the level of culture and influences the broader culture as a whole. The large audience and the cultural relevance of Super Bowl advertising makes it attractive as a sample for the current study.

The ads were coded by two independent coders. Ads for movies and television programs were discarded. The interrater reliability measures were Holsti's reliability .929 = humor, male target of aggression = .966, female target of aggression = .981; Scott's π .841 = humor, male target of aggression = .895, female target of aggression = .755. The reliability for female target of aggression was lower due to the small number of examples found. With a small number of ads in the category, a discrepancy in coding with only a few ads has a major impact on the reliability scores calculated using Scott's π.

In 1989, just 13.6% of ads using humor involved aggressive or disparaging humor, none of which used physical violence. In 1999, aggression was used in almost a third of the ads using humor, and physical humor mainly aimed at men became more common. In 2009, over 70% of the humorous ads used some form of aggression. More notable is that 13 out of 34 of these ads use males as the victims of physical violence, in contrast to only one ad in which women were the victims. The advertisers using physical violence with male victims in the 2009 sample include Coke Zero, Bud Light, Audi, Frito-Lay, Doritos, Castrol, SoBe, and Pepsi Max. The pattern illustrates a clear increase in the use of disparagement, particularly physical aggression, targeting males over the 20-year cross section of ads.

In 2008, the brands with the largest advertising budgets were Verizon, AT&T, Macy's, Sprint, and Wal-Mart, respectively (http://adage.com/datacenter/). To further examine the prevalence of aggressive humor in advertising, text descriptions of all the television ads placed by these advertisers in 2008 were obtained from TNS Media Intelligence.[1] An analysis of these text descriptions reveals that three of the top five brands—Verizon, AT&T, and Sprint—each used humor that denigrates men; some of this humor was also violent.

For example, Sprint aired an ad in which a man gets hit in the head with pipes from a truck and loses his memory. He has to rely on his phone to look up his name and to find out where he lives. One AT&T ad featured brother and sister taekwondo experts. When the brother asks the sister how fast her AT&T broadband service is, she demonstrates by kicking him and knocking him to the ground.

The analysis of Super Bowl ads from 1989, 1999, and 2009, and the analysis of the ads from the five largest brand advertisers in 2008, suggest that the ads examined in this paper are not isolated examples. The use of aggressive humor with primarily male victims is now a part of the cultural landscape.

DISCUSSION

The literature shows that advertising reaches far beyond the primary effect of company and brand-related information and attitude formation. The secondary effects of advertising are social and, as can be seen in the studies of the effect of idealized images of girls and women in advertising, are often negative (Martin and Gentry 1997; Richins 1991). Men are also affected by the social effects of ads. They compare themselves to advertising images, a comparison that can have a negative effect on their self-perceptions (Gulas and McKeage 2000).

From a social perspective, these secondary effects of advertising actually may be the primary effect. Twitchell argues that within commercial speech "resides the essence of what draws us together, what we share, what our culture is" (1996, p. 10). This sentiment is echoed by Johnson (2008), who posits that advertising can change perceptions of the social world. For example, it is largely through advertising that the wrinkle-free face has become normative for middle-aged women (Johnson 2008). Cross (2002) concurs, noting that while desire to preserve an innocence of childhood was originally justified within the sacred prerogatives of parenthood, it is the marketplace and advertising that now dictates to parents the appropriate relationship between consumption and restraint for children.

Unique Power of Humor to Demean and Degrade

The humorous portrayals in the ads noted in our findings are powerful. Humor allows a husband and father to be equated with a horse's ass because, after all, the portrayal is just a joke. Although no one seriously suggests that all husbands and fathers are horses' asses, or even that some anonymous man is, the derogatory suggestion is there. Because advertising must use symbols and meanings that are easily recognized by the audience, then this comparison of men to horses' asses must be recognizable to both those who construct the ad and those who view it. Denigration, which is found in many humorous ads, is a form of psychological violence (Candib 2000; Montminy 2005), and is correlated with physical aggression (Gormley and Lopez 2010). It is unlikely that a large advertiser would present denigration in a serious manner. However, humor gives the ability to denigrate in a "softer" manner.

Humor gives broad license to the humorist, allowing statements that, if delivered in a serious manner, would not be tolerated (Lewis et al. 2008). The options for response to derogatory humor are limited. By laughing at or ignoring a humorous attack, the target tacitly supports or accepts it. A protest is likely to result in the accusation that the target does not have a sense of humor. By eliminating an appropriate response, ridicule becomes more humiliating than verbal abuse or physical violence (Lewis et al. 2008) and is equally dangerous. Research suggests, for example, that racist or sexist joking promotes discriminatory behavior in a work environment. Serious presentations of derogatory sexist or racist statements, which are likely to bring condemnation, do not have as strong an effect on attitudes and behavior as humor (Lewis et al. 2008).

Humor also allows the suggestion that physical violence (sometimes extreme) is a reasonable response to minor offenses, as shown in the Blackberry and Bud Lite ads previously discussed. A serious recommendation of assault or tossing a colleague out a window would be universally denounced. Yet these behaviors and many more are presented as acceptable in some sense because they are presented humorously. The violence is, after all, just a joke.

Mitigating Factors

Many of the ads discussed above have been criticized on various Web sites, but the criticism has resulted in a significant backlash. Apparently, many people are less offended by these ads than they are offended by the critics. Some of the backlash, especially as posted by men, is a result of the attitude that the violence is just a joke and the critics should lighten up. The backlash from women seems to originate in shared victimization. Men are now experiencing the violence that has been historically directed at women, so now the men "know how we feel."

Another factor that may help explain the backlash against those who complain about the ads is the authorship of the ads. All ten people listed in the credits for the Bud Light "meeting" ad in which a man gets thrown out of the window are male (www.coloribus.com/adsarchive/tv-commercials/bud-light-meeting-536602/). A recent report found that 92% of the creative directors for ads that appeared in the 2010 Super Bowl were white males (Patel 2010). Members of a group are typically "licensed" to make fun of that group in ways that outsiders are not (Gilbert 2004). By this standard, it is acceptable for male copywriters to mock men; in fact, it is the only group that they are given license to mock.

Violence Against Men

We may not see women victimized in ads in the same way that men are because of a widespread cultural understanding that violence against women is real and thus is not funny. Breaking up with your girlfriend by throwing her out the door of a moving car is not funny, but breaking up with your boyfriend in that manner is. However, violence against men is also real. Men are more likely to be the perpetrators of violent crime than women, but men are also more likely to be the victims of violent crime (U.S. Department of Justice 2010). Men are also victims of intimate partner violence (IPV).

Women sustain 62% of the injuries from IPV (Archer 2000) and are more likely to be under "terroristic control" of a partner than men (Cunradi, Bersamin, and Ames 2009). Studies have shown, however, that women's use of IPV against male partners is widespread (e.g., Straus 2008, 2009). In fact, women are slightly more likely to use physical aggression against intimate partners than men (Archer 2000; Straus 2008), and women use physical aggression more frequently than men (Archer 2000).

The extensive evidence of female-initiated IPV is not generally known to the public (Straus 2009). This may be one reason that violence against men may seem laughable. Furthermore,

Nathanson and Young (2001) report that, unlike misogyny, misandry tends to be excused, trivialized, or even justified.

In most of these ads, if we substitute a woman in the ad as the butt of the joke, the ad loses humor, and, in some cases, becomes downright tragic. This is especially true, as previously noted, for the ads depicting violence. Similarly, given all the jokes about women drivers, the ad with a driver parking in a nearly empty lot would just seem insulting if the driver were a woman—and not fresh or new, given the aforementioned history.

Questions Raised by the Findings

The heart of the paper is a deconstruction of advertising imagery and a content analysis. We have conducted the deconstruction in the spirit of Goffman (1979), Jhally (1990), Kilbourne (1999), and Stern (1996). No research is totally immune from author influence. At the very least, the author decides the areas upon which to conduct research. However, we believe that the analysis provided in our paper is as free from bias as is possible. Each of the authors of this paper brings a different perspective and research history to the work that we hope helps to mitigate any potential bias. Yet we acknowledge that the interpretative nature of this sort of analysis constitutes a limitation of the research. We see this research as exploratory and believe that it raises more questions than it answers. We hope that this paper can begin a discourse.

Kilbourne (1999) states that popular culture, including advertising, mocks men who have real intimacy with women, especially men who appear to be married. This insight is borne out by the ads described above. Often it is the middle-class married men and fathers who are victimized by physical violence in ads intended as humorous. Men are often portrayed as ignorant, lazy, or childish. Father characters who are attempting to help children with homework, play games with children, attempt household repairs, and engage in other appropriate parental activities are portrayed as buffoons. Men are mocked by wives, girlfriends, and children. Adult men act in childish ways. Has the meaning of what it means to be a mature man changed as Cross (2002) suggests?

What effect does exposure to the ads discussed above have on the men who view them? Cross (2002) notes the trend toward advertising portrayals of adults as irresponsible and childish and deems these as evidence of adults' playing out fantasies of freedom from constraint for a few brief moments on screen. However, as we have seen, these are largely portrayals of men's freedom and childishness. The ads use a construction that at least some viewers would say echoes women's frustrations with male partners' ineptitude. But are they really portrayals of true denigration of men and their roles? Or, alternatively, are these instead male fantasies of freedom once again couched in a style that will be tolerated by women, perhaps even perceived as amusing and nonthreatening?

What message does the advertising imagery discussed here send to young boys regarding how they are expected to behave? Parents can choose, to a large extent, the television programs to which their children are exposed, and programs are rated to aid in these choices. Parents have far less control over the ads that children see, yet children are affected by the content of ads. What message do the ads discussed here send to children regarding the role of the father in the family? How are the themes found in these ads getting replicated in other aspects of the commercial consumer landscape? Recently a shirt was marketed toward adolescent girls with the slogan "Boys are stupid. Throw stones at them." Like the violence used in the advertising discussed in this paper, this was intended as humorous.

The imagery of advertising has been demonstrated to affect body image in young girls (McLellan 2002). Imagery of thin models in ads has been linked to eating disorders among those who are exposed to the ads. Given that children emulate the sexual imagery that they see in advertising (Kilbourne 2005), one can assume some effect from exposure to the imagery discussed in this paper.

All six finalists in the Doritos "Crash the Super Bowl" competition in 2010, in which consumers submit ads to potentially run during the Super Bowl, portrayed men in a derogatory manner. In five of the ads, men are victims of physical violence. Are these ads typical of the more than 4,000 submissions? If so, what motivated so many people to use this creative strategy? If the ads are atypical, on what criteria were they judged to emerge as the best?

Researchers have found that the race of a character in an ad affected how the character was portrayed (e.g., Bush, Solomon, and Hair 1977; Dominick and Greenberg 1970). Researchers have also found that women in ads were typically shown as submissive or subservient to men (e.g., Goffman 1979; Kilbourne 1999). Both of these findings were used to draw implications about U.S. culture.

We have deconstructed the portrayal of men in advertising and identified physical violence and denigration in advertising intended as humorous. The data from TNS Media Intelligence indicates that aggressive humor with primarily male victims is used by some of the largest advertisers in the United States. The data from a cross section of 20 years of Super Bowl ads shows that this type of advertising is now widely used in the biggest advertising venue in the United States. A key question is raised by these findings: What do these ads suggest about current U.S. culture?

DIRECTIONS FOR FUTURE RESEARCH

To address some of the questions posed above, additional in-depth analysis is warranted. We have just scratched the surface of these ads and their meaning. There are many more ads like those addressed here, each of which could be examined in more detail, including taking a look at the social discourse around the ads (and their companies) that exists. Misattribution Theory (Zillmann and Bryant 1980) may prove to be a helpful tool in understanding how these ads are perceived by audiences. This theory could provide insights as to how (or if) the humor changes if the victim changes.

An examination of the institutional dynamics behind these ads is also warranted. An examination of who creates the ads might suggest that a lack of diversity in the advertising industry is a contributing factor to the targeting of men in humorous ads. Perhaps men are the last acceptable targets for humor, since men are the authors, but if so, why use this sort of aggressive humor?

If the significant effects of violent humor in online viral advertising found by Brown, Bhadury, and Pope (2010) can be replicated in more mainstream traditional media and with broader audiences, it is likely that we will see more violence in television advertising because they may be effective for advertisers. Based on the trend we have uncovered, the violence and denigration are likely to be directed at men because, after all, it is just a joke.

NOTE

1. Data acquired from TNS Media Intelligence, www.kantarmediana.com/intelligence/.

REFERENCES

AdLand (2009), "39 Years of Super Bowl Commercials," available at http://adland.tv/SuperBowlCommercials/ (accessed December 22, 2009).

Alessandri, Sue Westcott (2009), "Promoting the Network Brand: An Exploration of Network and Local Affiliate On-Air Promotion During the Super Bowl, 2001–2006," *Journal of Promotion Management,* 15 (1/2), 150–164.

Archer, John (2000), "Sex Differences in Aggression Between Heterosexual Partners: A Meta-Analytic Review," *Psychological Bulletin,* 126 (5), 651–680.

Brown, Mark R., Roop K. Bhadury, and Nigel K. Ll. Pope (2010), "The Impact of Comedic Violence on Viral Advertising Effectiveness," *Journal of Advertising*, 39 (1), 49–65.

Bush, Ronald F., Paul J. Solomon, and Joseph F. Hair (1977), "More Blacks in TV Ads," *Journal of Advertising Research*, 17 (1), 21–25.

Bushman, Brad J., and Craig A. Anderson (2001), "Media Violence and the American Public: Scientific Facts Versus Media Misinformation," *American Psychologist*, 56 (6), 477–489.

Candib, Lucy M. (2000), "Primary Violence Prevention," *Journal of Family Practice*, 49 (10), 904–906.

Chung, Hwiman, and Xinshu Zhao (2003), "Humour Effect on Memory and Attitude: Moderating Role of Product Involvement," *International Journal of Advertising*, 22 (1), 117–144.

Cortese, Anthony J. (2008), *Provocateur: Images of Women and Minorities in Advertising*, Lanham, MD: Rowman & Littlefield.

Courtney, Alice E., and Sarah Wernick Lockeretz (1971), "A Woman's Place: An Analysis of the Roles Portrayed by Women in Magazine Advertisements," *Journal of Marketing Research*, 8 (1), 92–95.

Cross, Gary (2002), "Valves of Desire: A Historian's Perspective on Parents, Children, and Marketing," *Journal of Consumer Research*, 29 (3), 441–447.

Cunradi, Carol B., Melinda Bersamin, and Genevieve Ames (2009), "Agreement on Intimate Partner Violence Among a Sample of Blue-Collar Couples," *Journal of Interpersonal Violence*, 24 (4), 551–568.

Dominick, Joseph R., and Bradley S. Greenberg (1970), "Three Seasons of Blacks on Television," *Journal of Advertising Research*, 10 (2), 21–27.

Eagleton, Terry (1983), *Literary Theory: An Introduction*, Oxford: Blackwell.

Flint, Joe (2010), "Saints' Super Bowl Win Nips 'MASH' Finale for Most-Watched Show Ever," *Los Angeles Times*, available at http://latimesblogs.latimes.com/entertainmentnewsbuzz/2010/02/saints-super-bowl-win-is-.html (accessed June 19, 2010).

Freud, Sigmund (1960), *Jokes and Their Relation to the Unconscious*, New York: Norton.

Funk, Jeanne B., Heidi Bechtoldt Baldacci, Tracie Pasold, and Jennifer Baumgardner (2004), "Violence Exposure in Real-Life, Video Games, Television, Movies, and the Internet: Is There Desensitization?" *Journal of Adolescence*, 27 (1), 23–39.

Gilbert, Joanne R. (2004), *Performing Marginality: Humor, Gender, and Cultural Critique*, Detroit: Wayne State University Press.

Goffman, Erving (1979), *Gender Advertisements*, New York: Harper & Row.

Gormley, Barbara, and Frederick G. Lopez (2010), "Psychological Abuse Perpetration in College Dating Relationships: Contributions of Gender, Stress, and Adult Attachment Orientations," *Journal of Interpersonal Violence*, 25 (2), 204–218.

Gulas, Charles S., and Kim K. McKeage (2000), "Extending Social Comparison: An Examination of the Unintended Consequences of Idealized Advertising Imagery," *Journal of Advertising*, 29 (2), 17–28.

———, and Marc G. Weinberger (2006), *Humor in Advertising: A Comprehensive Analysis*, Armonk, NY: M.E. Sharpe.

Jhally, Sut (1990), *The Codes of Advertising*, New York: Routledge, Chapman & Hall.

Jin, Hyun Seung, Xinshu Zhao, and Soontae An (2006), "Examining Effects of Advertising Campaign Publicity in a Field Study," *Journal of Advertising Research*, 46 (2), 171–182.

Johnson, Fern L. (2008), *Imaging in Advertising: Verbal and Visual Codes of Commerce*, New York: Routledge.

Kelley, Scott W., and L. W. Turley (2004), "The Effect of Content on Perceived Affect of Super Bowl Commercials," *Journal of Sport Management*, 18 (4), 398–420.

Kilbourne, Jean (1999), *Deadly Persuasion: Why Women and Girls Must Fight the Addictive Power of Advertising*, New York: Free Press.

——— (2005), "What Else Does Sex Sell?" *International Journal of Advertising*, 24 (1), 119–122.

La Fave, Lawrence, Jay Haddad, and William Maesen (1976), "Superiority, Enhanced Self-Esteem, and Perceived Incongruity Humour Theory," in *Humour and Laughter Theory, Research and Application*, Antony J. Chapman and Hugh C. Foot, eds., London: John Wiley & Sons, 63–92.

Lewis, Paul, Christie Davies, Giselinde Kuipers, Rod A. Martin, Elliott Oring, and Victor Raskin (2008), "The Muhammad Cartoons and Humor Research: A Collection of Essays," *Humor*, 21 (1), 1–46.

Martin, Mary C., and James W. Gentry (1997), "Stuck in the Model Trap: The Effects of Beautiful Models in Ads on Female Pre-Adolescents and Adolescents," *Journal of Advertising*, 26 (2), 19–33.

McAllister, Matthew P. (1999), "Super Bowl Advertising as Commercial Celebration," *Communication Review*, 3 (4), 403–428.

McLellan, Faith (2002), "Marketing and Advertising: Harmful to Children's Health," *Lancet*, 360 (9338), 1001.

Montminy, Lyse (2005), "Older Women's Experiences of Psychological Violence in Their Marital Relationships," *Journal of Gerontological Social Work*, 46 (2), 3–22.

Morreall, John (1983), *Taking Laughter Seriously*, Albany: State University of New York Press.

Murray, John P. (2008), "Media Violence: The Effects Are Both Real and Strong," *American Behavioral Scientist*, 51 (8), 1212–1230.

Nail, Jim (2007), "Visibility Versus Surprise: Which Drives the Greatest Discussion of Super Bowl Advertisements?" *Journal of Advertising Research*, 47 (4), 412–419.

Nathanson, Paul, and Katherine K. Young (2001), *Spreading Misandry: The Teaching of Contempt for Men in Popular Culture*, Montreal: McGill-Queen's University Press.

Patel, Kunur (2010), "Study Finds Super Bowl Ad Creators Overwhelmingly White," *Advertising Age* (May 5), available http://adage.com/article?article_id=143711/ (accessed May 7, 2010).

Plakoyiannaki, Emmanuella, Kalliopi Mathiodaki, Pavlos Dimitratos, and Yorgos Zotos (2008), "Images of Women in Online Advertisements of Global Products: Does Sexism Exist?" *Journal of Business Ethics*, 83 (1), 101–112.

Pollay, Richard W. (1986), "The Distorted Mirror: Reflections on the Unintended Consequences of Advertising," *Journal of Marketing*, 50 (2), 18–36.

Rapp, Albert (1951), *The Origins of Wit and Humor*, New York: E.P. Dutton.

Richins, Marsha L. (1991), "Social Comparison and the Idealized Images of Advertising," *Journal of Consumer Research*, 18 (1), 71–83.

Scharrer, Erica (2001), "From Wise to Foolish: The Portrayal of the Sitcom Father, 1950s–1990s," *Journal of Broadcasting and Electronic Media*, 45 (1), 23–40.

———, Andrea Bergstrom, Angela Paradise, and Qianqing Ren (2006), "Laughing to Keep from Crying: Humor and Aggression in Television Commercial Content," *Journal of Broadcasting and Electronic Media*, 50 (4), 615–634.

Solomon, Jack (1988), *The Signs of Our Time*, New York: Harper & Row.

Speck, Paul Surgi (1987), "On Humor and Humor in Advertising," Ph.D. dissertation, Texas Tech University, Lubbock.

Stern, Barbara B. (1996), "Deconstructive Strategy and Consumer Research: Concepts and Illustrative Exemplar," *Journal of Consumer Research*, 23 (2), 136–147.

Straus, Murray A. (2008), "Dominance and Symmetry in Partner Violence by Male and Female University Students in 32 Nations," *Children and Youth Services Review*, 30 (3), 252–275.

——— (2009), "Why the Overwhelming Evidence on Partner Physical Violence by Women Has Not Been Perceived and Is Often Denied," *Journal of Aggression, Maltreatment and Trauma*, 18 (6), 552–571.

Tamburro, Robert F., Patricia L. Gordon, James P. D'Apolito, and Scott C. Howard (2004), "Unsafe and Violent Behavior in Commercials Aired During Televised Major Sporting Events," *Pediatrics*, 114 (6), 694–698.

Twitchell, James B. (1996), *Adcult USA: The Triumph of Advertising in American Culture*, New York: Columbia University Press.

U.S. Department of Justice (2010), "Criminal Victimization in the United States, 2007 Statistical Tables: National Crime Victimization Survey," available at http://bjs.ojp.usdoj.gov/index.cfm?ty=pbdetail&iid=1743/ (accessed May 7, 2010).

Wilson, Barbara J., Stacy L. Smith, W. James Potter, Dale Kunkel, Daniel Linz, Carolyn M. Colvin, and Edward Donnerstein (2002), "Violence in Children's Television Programming: Assessing the Risks," *Journal of Communication*, 52 (1), 5–35.

Wood, Wendy, Frank Y. Wong, and J. Gregory Chachere (1991), "Effects of Media Violence on Viewers' Aggression in Unconstrained Social Interaction," *Psychological Bulletin*, 109 (3), 371–383.

Youn, Seounmi, Tao Sun, William D. Wells, and Xinshu Zhao (2001), "Commercial Liking and Memory: Moderating Effects of Product Categories," *Journal of Advertising Research*, 41 (3), 7–13.

Zillmann, Dolf (1983), "Disparagement Humor," in *Handbook of Humor Research*, vol. 1, Paul McGhee and Jeffrey Goldstein, eds., New York: Springer-Verlag, 85–107.

———, and Jennings Bryant (1980), "Misattribution Theory of Tendentious Humor," *Journal of Experimental Social Psychology*, 16 (2), 146–160.

———, and Joanne R. Cantor (1976), "A Disposition Theory of Humor and Mirth," in Humour and Laughter: Theory, Research and Application, Antony J. Chapman and Hugh C. Foots, eds., London: John Wiley & Sons, 93–116.

Zimmerman, Amanda, and John Dahlberg (2008), "The Sexual Objectification of Women in Advertising: A Contemporary Cultural Perspective," *Journal of Advertising Research*, 48 (1), 71–79.

5

The Prevalence and Influence of the Combination of Humor and Violence in Super Bowl Commercials

Benjamin J. Blackford, James Gentry,
Robert L. Harrison, and Les Carlson

A bowling ball falls on a man's head to advertise a soft drink. Employees hurl a coworker out a window because of the mere suggestion that a specific beer should no longer be provided at meetings in order to reduce expenses. In another office setting, coworkers use a snow globe to break into a snack machine in pursuit of a certain snack food and to injure a supervisor. This is but a snapshot of the television commercials being aired that use humor in combination with violent acts to promote various products. How common is media content such as this in commercials? What effect does it have on the audience's reaction to the ad?

The effects of viewing violent media are the subject of a large body of research across a number of disciplines including psychology, sociology, public policy, law, and marketing. Initial research in this area began to appear in the mid-1950s with a variety of studies (Anderson et al. 2003). For example, Bandura, Ross, and Ross (1963) found that children who viewed live violent acts or televised violent acts tended to imitate these actions and engage in more violent actions themselves. A recent review article by Murray (2008) identified 1,945 research articles in the last 50 years examining the effects of television. Of these articles, approximately 600 focused on the issue of violence (Murray 2008).

A related topic that has received limited attention in the literature is the use of humor in combination with the portrayal of violence. Such studies have generally found that the use of humor in conjunction with violence lessens the perception of violence. King (2000) suggests one reason for using humor in combination with violence is to relieve or reduce audience stress from dramatic scenes. Humor may also serve to suggest to the audience that the events are not to be taken seriously. If the audience is affected by this cue, humor may trivialize the violence that is occurring, as suggested by Potter and Warren (1998). Potter and Warren raise a concern, based on work by Bandura (1994), that the trivialization of violence leads to a greater likelihood of such acts being imitated. In fact, Potter and Warren (1998) use the term "camouflage" to refer to the consumer's reaction to violence in the presence of humor, whereas Scharrer et al. (2006) use the term "desensitize." If this is the case, it becomes important to identify how often humor is combined with violence in various forms of media, as this combination may have an influence as large as or larger than the display of violent acts in isolation.

Given the potential adverse consequences attributable to combining these factors, this research seeks to provide further insight into the prevalence of the use of humor in combination with violence and their joint influence on ad popularity. Prior content analyses have approached this issue in a variety of ways, including analysis of violence in commercials during sporting events (Tamburro et al. 2004), as well as examinations of combinations of violence and humor occurring during nightly television programming (Potter and Warren 1998) and prime-time television commercials (Scharrer et al. 2006). Our study combines the approach of several of those just mentioned, as we examine violence and humor as depicted in television commercials occurring during a sporting event for three nonconsecutive years over a period of five years.

Our research also investigates the likability of these commercials by integrating results from two ratings systems of commercial popularity. As such, three primary research questions were identified for this study: (1) How often are violence and humor combined in commercials aired during the Super Bowl? (2) How has this changed since 2005? and (3) Is there an association between the combination of humor and violence and the likability of ads?

BACKGROUND

Prevalence of Violence in Media

The most extensive study of violence in U.S. television was the National Television Violence Study (NTVS), conducted from 1994 to 1998 (Wilson et al. 1997, overviewed by Wilson et al. 2002). The NTVS collected 2,700 hours of television programming per year for three years, sampling from 23 television channels randomly over a 20-week period. In the report, five elements were identified that, in concert, would result in a high-risk portrayal: the violence is realistic to the viewer, the victim faces at least minimal consequences, the violence is unpunished, the violence seems justified, and the individual undertaking the violent act is attractive. Wilson et al. (2002) found that a higher percentage of children's programming contained violence (69% versus 57% for adult programs), as well as almost three times as many violent acts when compared with programming not targeted to children. They also found that a greater percentage of children's programming showed rewards for violence when compared with programming not aimed at children (32% versus 21%) and that 81% of violent acts went unpunished in children's programming. Moreover, 76% of the violent acts in children's programming took place in a humorous context, whereas only 24% of the violent acts in other programming involved a humorous context.

More recent research has continued to find high levels of violence in television programming. Smith, Nathanson, and Wilson (2002) found that 61% of all programs contained violence, with 32% including nine or more violent acts, and an average of 6.63 violent acts per hour in prime-time programs. Glascock (2008) found an average of 9.5 aggressive acts per hour. More extensive reviews of this literature can be found in Gunter (2008), Kirsh (2006), and in the *Journal of Advertising* special issue on violence in advertising (2011).

While the presence of violence in television programming is well documented, there is less evidence concerning the presence of violent content in television advertising (Scharrer et al. 2006). As noted by Scharrer et al., the issue of violence and humor in commercials is a special case because it is more difficult for viewers to identify commercial content beforehand when compared with program content, which may lead to unintended viewer exposure. Anderson (2000) found that during the 1998 Major League Baseball Playoffs, 8.8% of the commercials contained violence. Of these 137 commercials, 76.6% were promotions for television programs and 16.8% were advertisements for movies. Tamburro et al. (2004), whose study also involved sports programming, found that 6% of the 1,185 commercials sampled contained violence. Contrary to Anderson (2000), Tamburro et al. found that movie advertisements accounted for 65% of violent ads, whereas television program ads accounted for 15%. Gentry and Harrison (2010) found that nearly 10% of the commercials during sports programming showed men in violent roles. Thus, while violence appears to be less prominent in advertising than it is in programming, it is still quite evident.

Processes of Media Effects

Several explanations for the possible linkage between viewers seeing violence on television and then engaging in violent acts have been offered. Huesmann (1986) suggested that violent behavior is learned through modeling behaviors (observational learning) and through positive reinforcement (only the aggressive seem to receive reinforcement). Anderson et al. (2003) noted two other underlying processes: (1) arousal-transfer, and (2) desensitization. Arousal-transfer is based on the excitement that may result from viewing violence. Such arousal can make it more likely that an individual will pursue the dominant activity at that time. Desensitization occurs when violent acts are viewed repeatedly, thus reducing the emotional reaction to being exposed to violent acts (Gunter 2008). We explore these notions by investigating the prevalence of acts of violence that are associated with humor in television advertising. The study of this phenomenon within the context of television advertising is particularly important because commercials may reappear frequently, thereby strengthening their effects, whereas television programs may, at best, be repeated only once during the broadcast off-season.

Humor in Advertising

In the current advertising landscape, humor is frequently used in television commercials, with approximately one out of five television ads containing humorous appeals (Beard 2005). Moreover, for over one hundred years, scholars have searched for a theoretical understanding of humor (Buijzen and Valkenburg 2004) and pondered its place in advertising (Beard 2005). Of the multiple theories and perspectives, three major approaches have emerged: relief theory, whereby people laugh because they need to reduce physiological tension from time to time (Berlyne 1972); superiority theory, whereby people laugh because they feel triumph over others (Meyer 2000); and incongruity theory, whereby people laugh at things that are unexpected or surprising (Berger 1998a, 1998b). Modern humor theorists believe that these three theories are complementary and that many instances of humor can be explained by more than one theory (Buijzen and Valkenburg 2004).

Research on humor has also resulted in typologies such as that by Speck (1990), which was specific to advertising and related closely to these three humor theories, and Martin et al. (2003), which outlined the four dimensions utilized in this study related to the differences in functional uses or types of humor. Their approach distinguishes between humor that can enhance or be detrimental to relationships, the individual, or others. Most applicable to this study is their inclusion of aggressive humor that enhances the individual while being detrimental to others. The remaining dimensions from Martin et al. include self-enhancing, affiliative, and self-defeating humor, and are determined by intent and target. A 2 × 2 matrix adapted from Martin et al. (2003) including these dimensions is presented in Figure 5.1.

The Humor and Violence Interface

As noted earlier, there is only limited literature investigating the role of the desensitization of violence through the use of humorous contexts. Potter and Warren (1998) investigated the humor/violence interface in the context of television programming and found that comedy programs contained more violent acts per hour than other programming. More specifically, they observed 5,970 violent acts during 168 hours of programming, with 31% of these acts involving humorous content. Based on their results, Potter and Warren state that humor is not being used to reduce aggression in viewers by providing a break from violent content, but rather to trivialize the violence. This is of special concern because trivialized violence is the most likely to be imitated. Research has also found humor to have a significant negative correlation with the perceived violence in a program

Figure 5.1 **Human Styles**

	Enhances Self	Enhances Relationships
Benevolent (Intent)	Self-enhancing	Affiliative
Detrimental (Intent)	Aggressive	Self-defeating

Source: Adapted from Martin et al. (2003).

(Sander 1997). Similarly, Bandura (1990) found that perpetrators of violent acts in television programs use humor to dehumanize victims to undermine the emotional responses from viewers.

Scharrer et al. (2006) specifically considered combinations of humor and violence in advertising. Their sample included 536 commercials containing aggressive behavior during a week of prime-time programming on six major broadcast networks. These commercials represented 12.3% of the total commercials during that time. Once again, advertisements for movie and television programs were the most likely to contain violent actions. Over half (53.5%) of the commercials included humorous elements. If the movie and television program ads were not considered, 87.7% of the violent commercials included humor.

We expand on this prior work in a number of ways. First, we analyze longitudinally the occurrence of humor and violence in advertising in a different media context (during a highly watched sporting event, i.e., the Super Bowl) and through the inclusion of a richer set of humor and violence variables. In addition, in our study, we do not analyze duplicate commercials, as was the case in Scharrer et al., which we believe provides a more conservative assessment of the incidence of commercials that combined humor and violence. Also, we incorporated consumer judges to identify the humorous/violent acts in the commercials, rather than the researchers themselves or graduate assistants as in prior research. This provides insight into how the "average" consumer views violence and humor in advertisements. Finally, we also include currently available assessments of commercial popularity to gauge consumer opinion of commercials that combine acts of humor and violence. While prior research has addressed some of these areas (e.g., Tamburro et al. considered violence in commercials during sporting events, but not humor), there has been no study to our knowledge that has taken all the above approaches into account. Further, we investigate the relationship between humor, violence, and their combination in terms of ad popularity, which has not been done heretofore.

Goals of the Study

One of our goals was to ascertain the level of violence in commercials by identifying the percentage of commercials that included violent acts and the number of violent acts within each commercial. Another goal was to identify the number of humorous acts in each commercial and the number of commercials with at least one humorous act. The third goal was to determine the prevalence of the humor/violence interface by identifying the percentage of commercials in which humor and violence were combined and to determine the number of such acts in each commercial. The final goal was to investigate the relationships between the combination of humor and violence and ad popularity.

METHOD

To provide a longitudinal analysis, Super Bowl commercials were examined from three different years over a five-year time span. These commercials were provided to three consumer raters who identified the number of violent and humorous acts within the commercial. The first rater was a 30-year-old male customer service representative. The second rater was a 29-year-old female social worker. A 63-year-old female former academic administrator at a small Southern college was the final rater. The data collected from the raters was then compared with audience likability ratings from two different sources. The methodology is discussed in detail in the following section.

Sample

The television broadcasts selected for our content analysis were the Super Bowl telecasts for 2005, 2007, and 2009, allowing the examination of violence and humor occurring in commercials on a longitudinal basis. Because of ratings and share of audience data, the Super Bowl is considered to be a major event and advertisers dedicate massive resources to take full advantage of this unique opportunity. Consequently, telecasts of the Super Bowl provide an interesting opportunity for longitudinal analyses examining how the content of Super Bowl advertising may have changed across years. Technological advances, such as the zapping and zipping of commercials and the drop in network ratings due to cable television and advertising clutter, combine to make network television advertising exposure much less than in previous decades (McAllister 1999). The Super Bowl may be an exception, however, because its audience may prefer to watch commercials occurring during the broadcast rather than zap them (McAllister 1999).

The 2009 Super Bowl was the second most-watched television event of all time, with an average viewership of 98.7 million. Nielsen reports 151.6 million different people watched at least six minutes of the broadcast, the largest number ever for a television event (Lewis 2009). Furthermore, the 2008 Super Bowl was viewed by approximately 14 million children (Lewis 2009), and parents may be less able to prevent children from being exposed to this programming and its accompanying commercials (Anderson 2000). In addition, the Super Bowl is the only venue where a vast majority of consumers will view new ads for the first time. These ads are often used in the long run by advertisers, being shown over and over, long after the Super Bowl has ended. Another factor contributing to the importance of Super Bowl commercials as a sample is the newsworthiness of the ads. For example, Kim and Morris (2003) investigated the influence of advertising during the Super Bowl on stock price; commercials shown in other types of programming typically do not receive similar attention.

All paid commercials, except promos for networks or nonprofits during the three Super Bowls (2005, 2007, and 2009), were obtained via listings and video files from nielsenmedia.com, which resulted in a sample of 180 commercials. Three consumer judges were asked to assess all Super Bowl commercials for the three years considered in the sample, coding all commercials for the number of violent acts, the number of humorous acts, and the number of simultaneous occurrences. Average pairwise percentage agreement between the raters was 82%. The ratings of the three judges were averaged to obtain the final rating for each commercial in all categories. Ratings for commercial popularity came from *USA Today,* which are available to the public, and AdBowl ratings, which were obtained from the company sponsors.

Conceptual Definitions

Potter (1999) discussed the complexity of defining violence in research, noting that the number of violent acts that will be identified depends on how violence is defined. Given the nature of our research, development of our definitions must include special consideration for violent acts within a humorous context. When Potter and Warren (1998) considered violence and humor in their study of television programs, they noted that this necessitated expanding the definition of violence to include the less serious forms that may be associated with humor. We drew on the definitions of violence from a number of previous studies, noting common themes to develop the definition of violence used for this study. Some of these common themes included the use of, or the credible threat of, force (Anderson 2000); actions that can harm physically or psychologically (Mustonen and Pulkkinen 1997); and targets that include animals and inanimate objects (Mustonen and Pulkkinen 1997). Based on this work, violence is defined here as "an overt depiction or credible threat of force or other actions, including implicit threats or nonverbal behaviors, intended (or conveying the intention) to physically or psychologically harm oneself, another person, other living things, or inanimate objects."

Scharrer et al. (2006) considered any aspect that was designed to be funny to the viewer as a presentation of humor. Our research expands on this by integrating the four dimensions of humor developed by Martin et al. (2003) discussed in the literature review. The dimensions are outlined in Figure 5.1. The matrix is also based on what is enhanced or detrimentally impacted by the humor.

The three raters were provided descriptions of Martin's four dimensions of humor, as well as the above definition of violence, for reference while coding. Actual examples of these dimensions from our commercial sample included an individual making light of forgetting their sword while preparing for battle (self-defeating) and a koala being punched repeatedly in a dream by a person who doesn't like his or her job (aggressive).

This approach was different from that often taken in the literature, in that we examined the intent of the humor rather than the type of humor or the underlying mechanism. In line with work by Potter and Warren (1998), the commercials were also coded for a number of characteristics with regard to the violent act. These included whether the perpetrator of the violence showed remorse, whether the act was presented as harming the victim, whether the perpetrator was punished, and whether the violent act was rewarded. Commercials were also coded for whether the target viewer was likely to identify with the perpetrator.

RESULTS

As was mentioned previously, the combination of humor and violence has the potential to desensitize viewers to violent acts and add to the likability of advertisements. Thus, this research was guided by three primary research questions that guide our understanding of the frequency and likability of the phenomenon and how it has changed over time. The discussion of the results addresses each research question in the order in which they were presented in the study.

How Often Are Violence and Humor Combined in Commercials Aired During the Super Bowl?

Several interesting findings, summarized in Table 5.1, emerge from the results addressing the first research question. The content analysis identified 234 total acts of violence (humorous and non-humorous) in the approximately one hour and 50 minutes of commercials, a rate of 2.13 violent

Table 5.1

Summary for Occurrence of Acts of Interest

Type of act	Total actions	Acts per minute	Unaccompanied acts (not in association with other acts)	Percentage of acts tied to other variable of interest
Violence	234	2.13	89	61.3
Humor	520	4.73	377	27.5

acts per minute. Out of all the commercials, 86, or 47.8%, were identified by at least one rater as containing a violent act. Of the 234 violent acts, 89 occurred outside of a humorous context. Only seven of the commercials containing violence were completely lacking in humor. There were 377 humorous incidents that did not include violence. Out of 180 commercials, 86 contained humor with no reference to violence by any rater. A total of 9 commercials (5%) contained no acts of violence, humor, or the combination coded by any of the raters.

Humor and violence were combined in 143 acts, representing 61.3% of all violent acts. In addition, 27.5% of all humorous acts were tied to a violent act. Just under 40% of all commercials aired were identified by at least one rater as containing an act combining violence and humor. Eight additional commercials contained acts of both violence and humor, but no acts that combined both. It comes as no surprise that 71 of these acts combining humor and violence were in conjunction with the "aggressive" dimension of humor (Martin et al. 2003), more than twice the number of acts for the next category, self-defeating (34).

How Has This Changed Since 2005?

The second research question concerned how humor and violence in Super Bowl commercials has changed since 2005. An overview of the findings for each of the years analyzed is presented in Table 5.2. It is interesting to note that instances of humor, violence, and the combination thereof all increased year to year, with the greatest increase occurring between 2007 and 2009. The 2009 Super Bowl commercials contained on average almost three times as many violent acts and acts combining humor and violence when compared to 2005, which represents a substantial increase given that it occurred over a time span of only five years. There was also an increase of almost 50% between 2005 and 2009 in the number of humorous acts identified.

Table 5.2

Summary Comparing Sampled Years (2005, 2007, and 2009)

	No. of commercials	Time	Acts including violence	Acts including humor	Acts including both
2005	60	0:35:25	51	154	29
2007	58	0:37:43	64	156	46
2009	62	0:37:50	119	210	68
Totals	180	1:50:58	234	520	143

Note: Total elapsed time is approximate.

Is There an Association Between the Combination of Humor and Violence and the Likability of the Ads?

The final research question asked how humor and violence influence the audience. To answer this question, two different independent rankings (the USA Today AdMeter and the AdBowl.com ballot) of consumers' reactions to Super Bowl commercials in terms of popularity were obtained for the three years sampled. Table 5.3 provides the top 10 and bottom 10 ads from each ranking. For each ad, the number of acts identified by the raters as humorous only, violent only, and humorous and violent at the same time are provided. In addition, scores for popularity with consumers were calculated for the linear combination of the USA Today AdMeter and AdBowl ratings.

Table 5.3

Comparison with Composite Factor from Two Rating Systems (*USA Today* and AdBowl)

Advertiser	Ad description	Only violence	Only humor	Combined	Ad rating*
2009	**Top 10**				
Doritos	Crystal ball sees free Doritos	0	.33	3	2.04499
Bridgestone	Mr. and Mrs. Potato Head take a drive	.33	2.33	1	2.03949
Bridgestone	Space travelers visit Saturn	0	2.33	1	1.56632
Anheuser-Busch	A Clydesdale can fetch	0	1.67	0	1.55211
Anheuser-Busch	Clydesdale's romance with circus horse	0	1.67	.67	1.34719
Coca-Cola	Bugs make off with a guy's Coke	0	3.67	0	1.28564
Doritos	Superpowers of Doritos' crunch	0	1.33	4	1.27200
Pedigree	Dog is better pet than an ostrich or rhino	0	2.67	2	1.24265
Anheuser-Busch	Corporate bean counter proposes no Bud Light at meetings to cut budget	0	.67	2.67	1.11505
Pepsi Max	"I'm good", say battered guys	0	0	6.33	.97959
	Bottom 10				
Coca-Cola	Coke transforms monster avatar into a pretty girl	0	5.67000	0	−.60778
Pepsi	Saturday Night Live's MacGruber changes name to PepSuber	1.33	3.00000	3.33	−.64912
Cash4Gold	Ed McMahon and MC Hammer trade gold mementoes for needed cash	0	9.00000	0	−.69605
Hyundai	Rivals unhappy Genesis sedan named Car of the Year	1	2.00000	0	−.75096
Gatorade	Tiger Woods and others talk about G	0	.33000	.67	−.94221
GoDaddy.com	Shower scene	0	1	0	−.95616
GoDaddy.com	Danica Patrick says she "enhanced"	0	3.67	1	−1.20038
Hyundai	Hyundai Assurance Program	0	0	0	−1.45012
Toyota	Diversity of new Venza's appeal	0	0	0	−1.45842
Vizio	Flat-panel televisions	0	1.33	0	−2.05080
2007	**Top 10**				
Anheuser-Busch	Rock, Paper, Scissors game for beer	0	.67	1.33	2.13746
Anheuser-Busch	Stray dog and the Clydesdales	0	2	0	1.72230
Blockbuster	Using mouse to rent movies	0	.33	3.67	1.60346
Anheuser-Busch	Immigrants learn to ask for Bud Light	0	5	0	1.53148
Doritos	Guy in car, girl show Dorito's qualities	0	1	1.67	1.52682
Anheuser-Busch	Wedding shortened by auctioneer	0	2.67	0	1.45944
Anheuser-Busch	Scary hitcher gets ride for Bud Light	.33	1.33	1	1.43785
Anheuser-Busch	Crabs worship Bud Light	0	3.33	0	1.37604
Anheuser-Busch	Ape loses out on beer while posing	0	2	0	1.00607
Snickers	Mechanics enjoy candy bar	0	2	.67	.97337

(*continued*)

Table 5.3 *(continued)*

Advertiser	Ad description	Only violence	Only humor	Combined	Ad rating*
2007					
	Bottom 10				
GoDaddy.com	GoDaddy marketing department parties	0	1.67000	0	-.86314
Toyota	Tundra tows load on see-saw ramp	0	.67000	0	-.91827
Pride Movie	Movie trailer for Pride	0	1.00000	0	-1.00291
Honda	Fuel efficiency of Hondas	0	.33000	0	-1.09879
Honda	Elvis' Burning Love for new CR-V	0	.33000	0	-1.12563
Van Heusen	Man dressed for any occasion	0	1.67	0	-1.21907
Garmin	GPS navigator versus paper map monster	1	1	3	-1.48872
Revlon Colorist	Sheryl Crow sings new song	0	2.33	0	-1.92510
Flomax	Prostate drug lets men bike, kayak	0	.33	0	-1.99490
Salesgenie.com	Salesgenie.com helps sales success	0	1	0	-2.16159
2005					
	Top 10				
Anheuser-Busch	Pilot jumps out of plane for six-pack of Bud Light after skydiver refuses	0	2	1	2.12446
Anheuser-Busch	American troops get standing ovation thank you at airport	0	.33	0	1.96964
Ameriquest	Store customer's cell phone chat misunderstood to be robbery	1	0	5.5	1.48412
Ameriquest	Romantic dinner goes awry after cat knocks over spaghetti sauce	0	1	1.5	1.47290
Careerbuilder.com	Guy sits on whoopee cushion as prankster monkey colleagues laugh	0	4.33	0	1.04161
Diet Pepsi	Cindy Crawford, other women eye handsome Diet Pepsi drinker	0	4.67	0	1.01365
Anheuser-Busch	Ostrich, giraffe, kangaroo, and cute pig audition to join the Clydesdales	0	2.67	0	.97542
Careerbuilder.com	Guy in boardroom won't kiss-up to monkey boss—but one monkey does	0	2.33	0	.88465
Anheuser-Busch	Cedric is designated driver who gets clubgoers doing his driving dance	0	4.67	0	.58857
Emerald Nuts	Nut-loving dad takes grief from unicorn, Santa Claus, and the Easter Bunny	0	2.67	.67	.54491
	Bottom 10				
Sahara movie	Studio promotes upcoming film *Sahara*	3	.00000	0	-1.15151
Batman Begins movie	Studio promotes upcoming film *Batman Begins*	4.33	.67	0	-1.17278
Honda	New Honda pickup drives on mountain ridge	0	0	0	-1.24488
McDonald's	Couple hold Web auction for french fry that looks like Abraham Lincoln	0	3	0	-1.29967
Anheuser-Busch	Introduction of Budweiser Select low-carb beer with no aftertaste	0	.33	0	-1.36304
MBNA	Gladys Knight tears up the field as rugby star in Affinity credit card ad	1.67	1	1.67	-1.56193
Volvo	Rocket launches with "My Other Vehicle is a Volvo XC90" bumper sticker	0	.33	.33	-1.60862
Cialis	Couples in romantic settings ogle to classic song "Be My Baby"	0	2	0	-1.77939
Napster	Feline at game holds up sign comparing price of new Napster service	0	1.33	0	-1.83544
Novartis	People float in bubbles for O2OPTIX silicone hydrogen contact lenses	0	1.67	0	-2.20482

*Ad rating is a linear combination computed from ratings by *USA Today* and *Ad Bowl*.

Table 5.4

Correlations of Observed Acts

	Violence	Humor	Both	Popularity	Rankings	Year
Violence	—					
Humor	−.171	—				
Both	.096	−.271*	—			
Popularity	−.192	.155	.344**	—		
Rankings	−.243	.15	.328*	.952**	—	
Year	−.204	.094	.218	.098	0	—

*Significant at the .05 level.
**Significant at the .01 level.

Table 5.4 provides the correlations among the variables in the study. It is interesting to note that the number of acts combining humor and violence is correlated to our ad popularity measure ($r = .344$, $p < .01$). A between-groups analysis of variance (ANOVA) examined the number of the various acts observed by the raters compared across our two groups of ads (Top 10 versus Bottom 10). There was a significant difference between the Top 10 (mean = 1.26 acts) and Bottom 10 (mean = .33 acts) in terms of the number of observed acts that combined humor and violence, with the Top 10 having more combined acts, $F(1, 58) = 7.00$, $p < .01$. There was no difference for acts of only humor, $F(1, 58) = 1.34$, $p > .05$, or only violence, $F(1, 58) = 3.62$, $p > .05$.

To further examine the relationships, a multiple regression analysis was performed, the results of which are presented in Table 5.5. To do so, the popularity values obtained from a linear combination of the *USA Today* and AdBowl ratings were entered as the dependent variable. Humorous acts, violent acts, acts combining both, and the year of the ad were entered as the independent variables. Results indicated a positive relationship between the combination of violence/humor acts and commercial popularity ($p < .001$). The influence of humorous or violent acts in isolation on commercial popularity was not significant ($ps > .05$). A correlation analysis was performed to determine whether violence in combination with certain specific types of humor contributed to the popularity score. In this analysis examining the four types of humor and the popularity score, aggressive humor/violence was the only form correlated with popularity ($r = .34$, $p < .01$). The other three humor/violence combinations from Martin et al. (2003) were not correlated with popularity. A χ^2 analysis was also undertaken to identify whether a significantly different number of ads in the Top 10 most popular commercials contained acts of violence, humor, or both when compared to the Bottom 10. This analysis was not significant for humor and violence separately; however, there was a significant difference ($p < .003$) in the relationship for ads that combined humor and violent acts, that is, commercials with acts combining both humor and violence were more likely to be in the Top 10 ads than the Bottom 10 ads. Twenty-four of the 30 Bottom 10 ads contained no combined acts, whereas only 13 of the 30 ads identified in the Top 10 contained no such acts.

Regarding additional characteristics of the violent acts and perpetrators, only 11 commercials were identified by any rater as containing a violent act for which the perpetrator showed any remorse. It is interesting to note that out of 180 commercials, only 15 total displays of remorse were identified by the raters. At the same time, 52 of the 86 commercials (60%) containing violence were coded as having perpetrators with whom the target audience was likely to identify. Moreover, many of the commercials did not provide a realistic depiction of the harm suffered by the victim. Of the 86 commercials with violent acts, half of them were not identified by even one

Table 5.5

Results of the Regression Analysis

	B	Standard error	β	t	Significance
Constant	111.059	220.252	.504	.616	
Acts of violence only	−.397	.239	−.205	−1.661	.102
Humorous acts only	.21	.108	.246	1.955	.056
Acts of humor and violence combined	.448	.13	.444	3.461	.001
Year	−.056	.11	−.064	−.507	.614

rater as displaying harm to the victim. When considering the possible outcomes of the violence, neither punishments nor rewards were identified by raters in 44.2% of the commercials. Only 15 of the commercials showed any form of punishment for committing a violent act. Thirty-three of the commercials actually showed the violent acts being rewarded according to at least one of the raters. One example of this was a Doritos commercial from 2009 in which an act of violence is rewarded with free snacks. Moreover, this commercial was also ranked first overall in the annual *USA Today* Ad Meter ratings of best-liked Super Bowl commercials. This is an issue of concern because of the possibility that the most-liked ads may be more likely to be rerun and imitated by other advertisers.

DISCUSSION

Overall, our findings suggest that the most popular commercials during a Super Bowl will be those that include acts combining humor and violence. Correlations, a regression analysis, and a χ^2 analysis all support this assertion. We also note an upward trend in these acts over the years included in this study. Acts of violence and acts combining humor and violence have both increased greatly, in both cases more than doubling when 2005 and 2009 are compared.

Implications

That the number of acts including violence and violence and humor in Super Bowl commercials has increased by approximately 133% and 135%, respectively, over the five-year time span should be of concern to members of the academic community. Furthermore, we find that the portrayal of violence is unrealistic for several reasons. Some violent acts (10%) are shown to reward the perpetrator for their actions. The vast majority also depict no harm to the victim (90%) and no punishment for the perpetrator (98%). Perhaps even more troubling is that at least some of these violent but humorous commercials were well liked by viewers. Our analyses indicated that positively rated ads had significantly more acts that combined violence and humor than did those rated in the bottom 10 by consumers. Clearly, the combination of humor and violence seems to appeal to consumers. Research is needed to investigate the effects of viewers (especially children) seeing such acts in a positive context.

We agree with previous researchers who assert that this combination of humor and violence desensitizes viewers in terms of reacting negatively to the violence, thus subtly resulting in the conclusion that violence is acceptable if presented in a humorous context (Potter and Warren 1998). The desensitization to violent portrayals that may arise when violence is combined with humor appears to be an appealing mix to some viewers, at least based on our popularity analyses. Perhaps the result (i.e., liking/popularity) of this juxtaposition can be explained by the approaches to understanding humor and its effects that were previously noted. For example, viewers may "like" violence depicted in a humorous context because the presentation is unexpected (incongruity theory), enables viewers to feel better than a hapless victim (superiority theory), or provides viewers with the means to reduce the psychological tension that could arise when actors in a commercial are engaged in violent acts unaccompanied by humor (relief theory). In sum, it seems that combining violence and humor provides a number of potential recourses for viewers to find more acceptable what on the surface seems to be an odd mix of execution strategies, that is, combining violence with humor in commercials.

Perhaps most significant is that our Ad Meter and AdBowl information indicates viewers find these commercials more than merely acceptable; they also like at least some of them. Thus, combining humor with violence appears to not only lessen the impact of violent portrayals but, more important, may also result in increased liking of violent depictions when they are shown in a humorous context. This would indeed be an unfortunate outcome of these commercial formats if viewers actually find violence more acceptable and likable when portrayed with humorous overtones. The next logical step in this transition would be to investigate whether these combinations affect actual behavior. These concerns represent viable issues and questions for additional academic research, but they also pose considerations for public policy. For example, should commercial portrayals that lead consumers to not only discount the impact of violence but also to increase their liking of the violent acts being shown continue to qualify as protected free speech as is the case now with most commercial content?

In addition, we believe that the viability of parental gatekeeping may be somewhat compromised in contexts such as those that could occur during the viewing of a Super Bowl. As noted previously by Scharrer et al. (2006), exposure to commercials is more difficult for viewers to control because viewers are less likely to know the content of a commercial prior to actually seeing it, and unintended viewer exposure may be the result. Consequently, parents' ability to act as television gatekeepers during the viewing of commercials embedded within programs may be less than what they might exert regarding decisions concerning which programs to watch. The high level of violence found in Super Bowl ads, coupled with watching relaxed adults laugh at violent acts, may suggest to children who are also present during the telecast that violence inflicted on others isn't as bad when cast as being "funny." We, of course, do not know whether this possibility actually exists and, consequently, the above discussions present an important avenue for future research, that is, the behavioral influence on viewers from being exposed to violence and humor in commercials.

Limitations

The Super Bowl was chosen due to its acknowledged high viewership and reach. However, the factors that make it a unique broadcast may mean the results do not generalize completely to normal prime-time viewing. The distinctive nature of the Super Bowl may draw viewers more inclined to watch commercials during the Super Bowl than during regular prime-time programming. Another limitation is that NFL football may be viewed as a violent sport and the violence witnessed in the game may make the inordinate display of violence in the commercials more acceptable to viewers. We must be careful not to draw conclusions that are not justified by the methodology used or the results that were found (Carlson 2008), though our results do allow us to state that the record number of viewers for Super Bowl XLIII and the viewers of other Super Bowl broadcasts could be exposed to many acts of violence, humor, and combinations thereof. There were 2.13 violent acts per minute of commercials and 143 acts combining humor and violence. Thus, while the results of our content analysis do not allow for any conclusions regarding the effects of viewing this content on subsequent behavior, we can state that viewers are regularly being exposed to such acts during Super Bowl commercials.

CONCLUSION

Overall, if future research does identify negative outcomes resulting from viewing violence in a humorous context within commercials, we can say that there is no shortage of exposure to these formats based on the commercials aired during recent Super Bowl broadcasts. In addition, commercials that combine humor and violence are better liked by viewers, which could mean that these commercials will become more prevalent as advertisers identify and perhaps attempt to capitalize on this relationship. Both of these findings add to prior work in the literature and provide important reasons for research in the area to continue. From a public policy standpoint, additional consideration should be provided to the prevalence of violence combined with humor in commercials. While such content is identified and limited to certain time frames in television programming, parents attempting to limit their children's exposure in commercials are not provided the tools needed to effectively address these concerns. It appears that public policy has overlooked an important avenue through which viewers are being exposed to violence, especially that which is trivialized by its association with humor.

REFERENCES

Anderson, Charles R. (2000), "Television Commercial Violence During Nonviolent Programming: The 1998 Major League Baseball Playoffs," *Pediatrics,* 106 (e46), 1–4.

Anderson, Craig A., Leonard Berkowitz, Edward Donnerstein, L. Rowell Huesmann, James D. Johnson, Daniel Linz, Neil M. Malamuth, and Ellen Wartella (2003), "The Influence of Media Violence on Youth," *Psychological Science in the Public Interest,* 4 (3), 81–110.

Bandura, Albert (1990), "Selective Activation and Disengagement of Moral Control," *Journal of Social Issues,* 46 (1), 27–46.

——— (1994), "Social Cognitive Theory of Mass Communication," in *Media Effects: Advances in Theory and Research,* Jennings Bryant and Dolf Zillman, eds., Hillsdale, NJ: Lawrence Erlbaum.

———, Dorothea Ross, and Sheila A. Ross (1963), "Imitation of Film-Mediated Aggressive Models," *Journal of Abnormal and Social Psychology,* 66 (1), 3–11.

Beard, Fred K. (2005), "One Hundred Years of Humor in American Advertising," *Journal of Macromarketing,* 25 (1), 54.

Berger, Arthur A. (1998a), *An Anatomy of Humor,* New Brunswick, NJ: Transaction.

——— (1998b), "Laughing Matter: A Symposium: Anatomy of a Joke," *Journal of Communication,* 26 (3), 113–115.

Berlyne, Daniel E. (1972), "Humor and Its Kin," in *The Psychology of Humor,* Jeffrey Goldstein and Paul McGhee, eds., Oxford: Academic Press, 43–60.

Buijzen, Moniek, and Patti M. Valkenburg (2004), "Developing a Typology of Humor in Audiovisual Media," *Media Psychology,* 6 (2), 147–167.

Carlson, Les (2008), "Use, Misuse, and Abuse of Content Analysis for Research on the Consumer Interest," *Journal of Consumer Affairs,* 42 (1), 100–105.

Gentry, James W., and Robert L. Harrison (2010), "Is Advertising a Barrier to Male Movement Toward Gender Change?" *Marketing Theory,* 10 (1), 74–96.

Glascock, Jack (2008), "Direct and Indirect Aggression on Prime-Time Network Television," *Journal of Broadcasting and Electronic Media,* 52 (2), 268–281.

Gunter, Barrie (2008), "Media Violence: Is There a Case for Causality?" *American Behavioral Scientist,* 51 (8), 1061–1122.

Huesmann, L. Rowell (1986), "Psychological Processes Promoting the Relation Between Exposure to Media Violence and Aggressive Behavior by the Viewer," *Journal of Social Issues,* 42 (3), 125–139.

Kim, Jooyoung, and Jon D. Morris (2003), "The Effect of Advertising on the Market Value of Firms: Empirical Evidence from the Super Bowl Ads," *Journal of Targeting, Measurement and Analysis for Marketing,* 12 (1), 53–65.

King, Cynthia M. (2000), "Effects of Humorous Heroes and Villains in Violent Action Films," *Journal of Communication,* 50 (1), 5–24.

Kirsh, Steven J. (2006), "Cartoon Violence and Aggression in Youth," *Aggression and Violent Behavior,* 11 (6), 547–557.

Lewis, Aaron (2009), "Nielsen Says Bud Light Lime and Godaddy.com are Most-Viewed Ads During Super Bowl XLIII," Nielsen Company, press release (February 5).

Madden, Thomas J., and Marc G. Weinberger (1984), "Humor in Advertising: A Practitioner View," *Journal of Advertising Research,* 24 (4), 23–29.

Martin, Rod A., Patricia Puhlik-Doris, Gwen Larsen, Jeanette Gray, and Kelly Weir (2003), "Individual Differences in Use of Humor and Their Relation to Psychological Well-Being: Development of the Humor Styles Questionnaire," *Journal of Research in Personality,* 37 (1), 48–75.

McAllister, Matthew P. (1999), "Super Bowl Advertising as Commercial Celebration," *Communication Review,* 3 (4), 403–428.

Meyer, John C. (2000), "Humor as a Double-edged Sword: Four Functions of Humor in Communication," *Communication Theory,* 10 (3), 310–31.

Murray, John P. (2008), "Media Violence: The Effects Are Both Real and Strong," *American Behavioral Scientist,* 51 (8), 1212–1230.

Mustonen, Anu, and Lea Pulkkinen (1997), "Television Violence: A Development of a Coding Scheme," *Journal of Broadcasting and Electronic Media,* 41 (2), 168–189.

Potter, W. James (1999), *On Media Violence,* Thousand Oaks, CA: Sage.

———, and Ron Warren (1998), "Humor as Camouflage of Televised Violence," *Journal of Communication,* 48 (2), 40–57.

———, Kartik Pashupati, Robert Pekurny, Eric Hoffman, and Kim Davis (2002), "Perceptions of Television: A Schema Explanation," *Media Psychology,* 4 (1), 27–50.

Sander, Ingo (1997), "How Violent Is TV Violence? An Empirical Investigation of Factors Influencing Viewers' Perceptions of TV Violence," *European Journal of Communication,* 12 (1), 43–98.

Scharrer, Erica, Andrea Bergstrom, Angela Paradise, and Qianqing Ren (2006), "Laughing to Keep From Crying: Humor and Aggression in Television Commercial Content," *Journal of Broadcasting and Electronic Media,* 50 (4), 615–634.

Smith, Stacy L., Amy I. Nathanson, and Barbara J. Wilson (2002), "Prime-Time Television: Assessing Violence During the Most Popular Viewing Hours," *Journal of Communication,* 52 (1), 84–111.

Speck, Paul S. (1990), "The Humorous Message Taxonomy: A Framework for the Study of Humorous Ads," *Current Issues and Research in Advertising,* 13 (1), 1–44.

Tamburro, Robert F., Patricia L. Gordon, James P. D'Apolito, and Scott C. Howard (2004), "Unsafe and Violent Behavior in Commercials Aired During Televised Major Sporting Events," *Pediatrics,* 114 (6), 694–698.

Wilson, Barbara J., Stacy L. Smith, W. James Potter, Dale Kunkel, Daniel Linz, Carolyn M. Colvin, and Edward Donnerstein (2002), "Violence in Children's Television Programming: Assessing the Risks," *Journal of Communication,* 52 (1), 5–35.

———, Dale Kunkel, Daniel Linz, W. James Potter, Edward Donnerstein, Stacey L. Smith, Eva Blumenthal, and Tim Gray (1997), "Television Violence and Its Context: University of California, Santa Barbara Study," in *National Television Violence Study,* vol. 1, Margaret Seawell, ed., Thousand Oaks, CA: Sage.

PART III

SEX AND VIOLENCE IN ADVERTISING

6

Fifty Shades of Sex and Violence
Scenes of Advertising to Come?
Tom Reichert and Marc G. Weinberger

During the summer of 2011, *Fifty Shades of Grey* became the fastest selling paperback novel of all time. The book is an erotic novel that topped best-seller lists around the world, including in the United Kingdom and the United States. The second and third volumes are titled *Fifty Shades Darker* and *Fifty Shades Freed*, respectively, and were equally well received by readers if not by literary critics. Within its first two years the series sold over 70 million copies, with book rights in at least 37 countries. The not-so-subtle themes involving sexual practices such as bondage/discipline, dominance/submission, and sadism/masochism are a landmark for the mass market in our cultural landscape.

The *Fifty Shades* trilogy is the latest manifestation of an increase in two separate media social trends since the 1970s—the increase in sexual themes (Kunkel et al. 2007; Reichert, Carpenter-Childers, and Reid 2012) and the increase in violence (Bushman and Anderson 2001; McIintosh et al. 2003). What is different in the *Fifty Shades* series is the confluence of both of these trends—sex and violence—in the same mass-market vehicle. These books and the trend toward sexual material and violence are even more notable by their contrast to several decades in which we have been challenged by authors such as Jean Kilbourne (1999), organizations such as the Media Education Foundation, and the feminist movement as a whole to condemn how women have been sexualized in the media and advertising, and in which there has been more awareness and condemnation of rape and violence directed at women. There are chapters elsewhere in this volume that critically examine violence directed at women in ads (Capella et al.) and domestic violence mainly toward women (Keller, Wilkinson, and Otjen). Another chapter in this book examines the disparagement of men as a target of physical and verbal ridicule in ads (Gulas, McKeage, and Weinberger).

The irony of the coupling of sex and violence in *Fifty Shades* has not gone unnoticed by critics on the left and right, the former condemning sexual violence toward women and the latter condemning increased sexual content and moral decay in media. The disparate portrayals of women as submitting to and even craving subservient and violent sex versus condemnation of sexualization and violence directed at women in particular create an interesting conundrum for advertisers wanting to gain attention but wishing to avoid extreme controversy.

In the remainder of this chapter we look at the developments and impact of these emergent themes: sex and violence in advertising. Are we on the verge of a new explosion of advertising that pushes over the edge to romanticize the combination of sex and violence? Is it desirable? That is, does sex and violence in advertising work? We address these questions by examining what we know about the prevalence and impact of using either sex or violence in advertising, and finally speculate what the combination of sex and violence might look like and what its effects might be.

BACKGROUND

In the 1980s, a pioneering female advertising executive asked whether we have to make women mad to buy our products. Rena Bartos (1980, 1981) was challenging advertisers to examine the way they were portraying females in ads that were stereotypical, outdated, and offensive. She questioned the prevailing view that "a little irritation is necessary to break through the competitive clutter." Lever Bros. admitted the company kept the Wisk "ring around the collar" theme for 22 years even though management knew people hated it (Freeman 1989). Pokrywczynski and Crowley (1993) point out that that advertising can and often does irritate people, as is well documented in research they cite. Wells, Leavitt, and McConville (1971) identified "irritation" as one of six stable (though negative) response dimensions to TV commercials. Schlinger's (1979) seven dimensions of response include one she called "alienation." Aaker and Bruzzone (1985) offered four dimensions, among them, "dislike."

Another attention-getting aspect that has the potential to irritate and offend is the shock value of advertising. Deliberate attempts to shock an audience by violating social norms may break through the clutter to gain greater attention. Dahl, Frankenberger, and Manchanda (2003) suggest, "Offense is elicited through the process of norm violation, encompassing transgressions of law or custom (e.g., indecent sexual references, obscenity), breaches of a moral or social code (e.g., profanity, vulgarity), or things that outrage the moral or physical senses (e.g., gratuitous violence, disgusting images)" (p. 268). These same authors point to advertisers such as Benetton and Calvin Klein, who have been deliberately shocking. A 2013 outdoor advertising campaign in the UK pushes the edge of sex and vulgarity by promoting an energy drink called Pussy with the taglines, "the drink's pure, it's your mind that isn't" and "Cunningly Delicious." Media use of sex and violence, and more specifically their use in advertising, have the potential to irritate, shock, and offend by violating commonly held social norms. According to Dahl, Frankenberger, and Manchanda's (2003) model, shocking ads violate social norms, create surprise, and have an impact on a range of measures of advertising success, suggesting that shock like irritation may break through the clutter. Unanswered in this model is whether some audiences may be irritated, offended, and take their feelings and attitudes out on the advertiser and brand.

The fact that the *Fifty Shades* media blitz has largely flown below society's norm violation radar is fascinating and speaks to how moral standards have changed. As sex and violence have become more common in the media and part of our culture, advertisers wanting to be edgy but not on the bleeding edge of creativity have incorporated these themes into traditional and digital media campaigns.

It is the cultural context that determines what is an acceptable and benign norm violation versus a violation that is malign and rejected by the public, sponsors, and formal or informal social regulators. Abstractly, culture is the knowledge base that forms values, tastes, and ideologies (Bourdieu 1983; Swidler 1986, 2001). It provides the lens through which people and regulators view, categorize, and understand the world; but, like one's heartbeat, it is constantly at work in the background. We learn culture through socialization, experiences, and education. As a result, one's social context or social fields fundamentally influence their values, norms, and meanings that are used to interpret everything in the environment. "There are social norms established in every group within society. These norms carry sanctions, which are used to encourage conformity and obedience. Sanctions also work to discourage violation of social norms carried out through informal and formal types of social control" (Brown 2010).

Clearly, culture evolves and norms change. However, the media can drive rather than just reflect such changes. But when and how does a malign violation of social norms in the media become innocuous and benign? In the 1960s, Jack Paar, the famous *Tonight Show* host, was censored from using the word *toilet* on his show (in its place he used the euphemism *water closet*). Moving forward 30 years, the HBO series *Sex and the City* was on the moral edge of TV and was available only to subscribers after 10:00 p.m. on HBO. The themes were considered adult and were restricted. In less than five years, reruns of the series began appearing on regular cable channels in the United States and before that in European countries in the early 2000s. For younger children or teenagers, the episodes they were seeing for the first time were no less sexual than they were for cable audiences, who had been partially shielded from this programming a few years earlier on subscription cable-only channels. Younger audiences who were protected by congressional pressure to restrict violence on TV Westerns in the 1960s were replaced with kids being exposed to levels of violence in video games, movies, and TV programming that made violence in 1960s episodes of TV shows like *Gunsmoke* look quaint.

Has a moral switch opened? The 1990s was an interesting cultural period in the United States with the introduction of Viagra, open discussion of sexually transmitted infections, and the widespread news coverage and comedic lampooning of President Bill Clinton's sexual affair with White House intern Monica Lewinsky. Politics became more polarized, comedians took aim, and advertisers jumped on the liberalized trend to adopt more aggressive and lewd language and images in ads. Programming such as *Family Guy,* Adult Swim, sitcoms, and movies with more frequent sexual references and/or gratuitous violence and humor became accessible to a broad population newly groomed by mention of oral sex and the president on the nightly news and violent video games like Grand Theft Auto.

One recent commentary suggests that *Fifty Shades* also reveals just how pornographic our culture has become over the last decade or so. "While the old Harlequin romance novels had narcissistic heroes who toyed, sexually and psychologically, with their much younger prey, however remote and emotionally challenged he was, the hero did not have a torture chamber tucked away in his basement. *Fifty Shades of Grey* is Harlequin on steroids, a kind of romance novel for the porn age in which overt sexual sadism masquerades as adoration and love. New as this is, the ending remains depressingly the same for real women who end up falling for the Mr. Greys of the world" (Dines 2012). Perhaps this newly popular genre represents another cultural shift that lowers the bar defining the difference between images that are shocking or not and whether they are benign or malign violations of social norms in our current culture.

To consider the types and effects of sexual violence in advertising, we must first review each type of appeal to gain a better understanding of what they are and how consumers respond to them. We provide brief overviews of academic research for each appeal, beginning with sex in advertising followed by violence in advertising.

SEX IN ADVERTISING

Definition

We intuitively know it when we see it, but Courtney and Whipple (1983) provide a clear definition of sex in advertising: "sexuality in the form of nudity, sexual imagery, innuendo, and double entendre . . . employed as an advertising tool for a wide variety of products" (p. 103). In other words, sex in advertising is an ad that contains sexual content. Types of content people commonly ascribe as sexual within ads includes physically attractive models in clothing that accentuates or reveals their bodies. Obviously, instances of sexual behavior—come-hither stares, flirty behavior and provocative poses, or a steamy embrace—also qualify.

Words and phrases can have sexual meaning as well. For example, French Connection UK grabbed attention in the early 2000s by prominently featuring its acronym—FCUK—in ads. More common is the double entendre or suggestive headline that has sexual meaning when paired with a sexual image. An ad for Kenneth Cole fragrance for men features the headline "Wear me out." The message has additional meaning when paired with a visual of woman grabbing a man's shirt as they are about to kiss. Headlines themselves can have sexual meaning but, overall, images of people constitute the vast majority of sexual content in advertising.

Sexual content can be integrated within an advertisement or promotional message at several levels. In the Kenneth Cole example, sex is the central brand message. On the other end of the spectrum, sexual content has no obvious connection to the brand and is merely present to attract attention to the brand. Such uses are generally referred to as "decorative." Sexual content used for this purpose is famously, and rather derisively, referred to by David Ogilvy (1985) as borrowed interest, meaning that advertisers were taking the easy road by using attention generated by the sexual image to direct attention to the brand, instead of highlighting the brand based on its merits.

Despite Ogilvy's criticism, advertisers appear to be more likely to use sex as a reason for buying or using a brand than previously assumed. Studies show that up to 70% of sexual ads for products (Reichert and Lambiase 2003), and up to 90% of ads for cosmetic surgery (Hennink-Kaminski and Reichert 2011), centrally feature a sex-related brand message. These ads imply or directly state that buying and using the product or service can make one more sexually attractive, have more or better sex, or simply have more sexual self-confidence. "Enhance your attractiveness factor," states the headline in one ad. Unfortunately, most of what we know about sex in advertising is based on its decorative function instead of its persuasive function. Future research should attempt to assess the believability and credibility of sexual appeals in addition to their recall and recognition scores.

Prevalence

The prevalence of sex in advertising is not uniform within or across media. For example, viewers of cable programming on MTV and Spike networks are more likely to see sexually themed commercials than are viewers of prime-time, broadcast network newscasts. Similarly, magazine readers are more likely to see sexual ads in *Cosmopolitan* and *Maxim* than in *Field and Stream* or *Time*. Overall, however, magazine readers are more likely to see sexual ads than are television or online viewers (Paek and Nelson 2007; Ramirez 2006). In one of the earliest studies, Soley and Reid (1988) examined ads in high-circulation magazines. They found that sexual content was more likely to appear in women's magazines and that women constituted most of the content in sexual ads. Their study also indicated that sexual appeals became more prevalent over time. Updates of that study revealed similar trends (Reichert, Carpenter-Childers, and Reid 2012). For example, there was an increase from 15% to 27% in ads with sexual content from 1983 to 2003.

Sexual content in television advertising commercials is less common. Lin (1998) reported that about 8% of television ads contained sexual content but that about 18% of models were judged to be "very sexy." Other studies have reported similar results (Fullerton and Kendrick 2001; Hetsroni 2007). An online study found that sexual content was present in up to 20% of online banner ads posted on high-traffic news sites (Ramirez 2006).

A recent content analysis shows that sexual content is more likely to be used in ads for low-involvement products as well as high-risk, transformational products such as fashion (Reichert, Carpenter-Childers, and Reid 2012). That same study shows that sex is most likely to be used in the following product categories: health and hygiene, beauty, clothing and accessories, entertainment, and travel. Research has shown that viewers rate sexual ads more favorably if there is a connection between the use of sex and the product category (Baker and Churchill 1977; Peterson and Kerin 1977; Simpson, Horton, and Brown 1996). Although ingenious copywriters can make a connection between sex and brand for almost any product, consumers are more accepting of it if there is a link to enhanced physical attractiveness, such as for fashion and cosmetic products.

Effects of Sex in Advertising

Early published work sought to determine the effectiveness of sexual content in advertising. Researchers were primarily interested in decorative appeals containing sexual images of women with no meaningful link to the product. In the 1950s and 1960s, these decorative appeals were common in ads for a range of products such as soft drinks, cigarettes, and automobiles (Reichert 2003). These ads were so commonplace that in 1968, Thomas Shepard, publisher of *Look* magazine, remarked that nudity is a fad and "the next step will be to put clothing on the models to attract attention."

Researchers applied an information-processing lens, which assumes that persuasion occurs in a linear manner—from attending to a message to yielding (i.e., buying the brand). These studies measured recall and recognition for the visual and message factors with the assumption that you must attend to and encode information before it is entered into memory. Results consistently showed that viewers direct their attention toward the scantily clad female, not to important information such as the brand name, copy points, and the logo (Alexander and Judd 1978; Baker and Churchill 1977; Reid and Soley 1983; Severn, Belch, and Belch 1990). The overall conclusion was that sex in advertising should not be used because it distracts viewers from processing and storing brand information: money is wasted if one can remember the ad but not the advertised brand.

It is important to note that recall and recognition were statistically lower in the presence of sexual content but they were not zero. Studies show that even though people are less likely to process the message, they are more likely to report being persuaded or indicate higher purchase intention for sexual ads compared to nonsexual ads (Dudley 1999; Grazer and Keesling 1995; Reichert, Heckler, and Jackson 2001; Severn, Belch, and Belch 1990). So whereas sexual ad content tends to inhibit processing of brand information, it may positively influence consumers' in-store behavior, especially for low-involvement products, if used in point-of-purchase or in-store promotional material.

Researchers also examined the emotional responses people have to sexual images and subsequent effects on advertising and brand indicators. Sex in advertising does not evoke intense levels of sexual arousal but does influence pupil dilation, heart rate variation, and self-reported excitement. The nature of the affect a person assigns to the arousal depends on a variety of factors such as intensity of the material, context, taste, gender, and relevant personality factors of the viewer. In a typical study, participants are shown versions of ads that are the same except for sexual content (nonsexual, low-, moderate-, and high-sexual content; e.g., LaTour 1990). Findings were that affective responses correspond with sexual content but are moderated by respondent gender (Belch et al. 1981; LaTour and Henthorne 1994, 2003). For example, females experienced more affect and arousal toward ads as sexual content increased but dropped dramatically in the high-sex condition. Males, on the other hand, exhibited a fairly direct relationship between female nudity and arousal and affect. Overall, images of opposite-sex models elicit most favorable reactions, and female and male viewers respond similarly to sexual images of heterosexual couples (Reichert, LaTour, and Kim 2007).

A recent study indicates that exposure to sexual images of women in ads or even handling garments such as women's intimate wear can influence men's judgment (Van den Bergh, DeWitte, and Warlop 2008). The finding indicates that men are likely to make snap decisions and seek immediate gratification without critically considering implications or outcomes. According to the authors, "induced sexual appetite instigates a greater urgency to consume anything rewarding" (p. 94). This finding supports previous research showing that sexual ads, while distracting, can result in a behavioral advantage for low-involvement products.

More recent work in this area examines the influence of personality on responses to sexual content. Studies have shown some indication that a concept known as sexual self-schema—a person's sexual self-view based on past experiences—predicts responses (Reichert, LaTour, and Ford 2011). Generally, men and women with higher, or more positive, schemas respond more positively to sexual ads than people with low or negative schemas. Other studies have shown that sensation seeking, ethical judgments, and need for cognition also influence responses to sexual ads (Davies, Zhu, and Brantley 2007; Putrevu 2008; Reichert, LaTour, and Kim 2007).

VIOLENCE IN ADVERTISING

The issue of violence in society—in schools, video games, road rage, workplace violence, bullying, and in sports—has been of interest to policymakers and researchers for decades. There are spikes in social concern after high-profile events such as the Columbine and Newtown shootings, but such events merely underscore the broader issues. Efforts to curb exposure to violence are often thwarted by powerful industry lobbies and conflicting conclusions from the evidence. There is quite compelling but not universal agreement about the effects of such exposure to violence. While Bushman and Anderson (2001) review over 1,000 studies and conclude that there is strong evidence of a link between violent media content and aggression, Freedman (2002) suggests that the basis for such a conclusion is questionable.

Research about violence in the media has a history in communication and has been studied since the 1950s by numerous communication researchers (Anderson et al. 2003). In the 1960s, congressional concern about violence in TV Westerns resulted in guidelines restricting the number and type of violent scenes per episode. Research studying the connection between exposure to violent incidents in the media and increased audience aggression (Bushman and Anderson 2001; Paik and Comstock 1994) concluded that viewing television violence can lead to increased antisocial and violent behavior. Researchers have also documented that the level of TV and video game violence is related to the levels of societal violence and individual aggression (Bushman and Anderson 2001).

Definition and Prevalence

There are many definitions of violence, but the one we use is quite broad and is the one that Scharrer et al. (2006) employed when conducting a landmark content analysis of violence in television advertising. Violence is "physical aggression enacted by a perpetrator with the intent to harm, physical aggression with no such intent, verbal aggression, and fortuitous aggression" (p. 617). This definition includes attempts to demean or humiliate through word or action. The type of sexual violence in *Fifty Shades,* whether implied or explicit, fits within this broad definition of violence.

Scharrer and her colleagues (2006) found that 12% of the commercials appearing in a week of prime-time advertising in 2004 contained some type of aggression, a percentage considerably higher than 3% seen in daytime ads in the mid-1990s (Maguire, Sandage, and Weatherby 2000) and 9% by Anderson in the late 1990s (Anderson 2000). Scharrer et al. found that 80% of the violent commercials for products used humor to cloak their aggression. The use of images of waiters being tripped and falling through plate glass windows, men being hit in the groin by flying objects, and flowers being attached with a nail gun to a man in a tuxedo represent a significant departure from historical trends where advertisers rarely employed violence or, even more rarely, violence with humor. This trend toward employing advertising humor with TV violence is discussed by Gulas, McKeage and Weinberger in this book. They found that the percentage of Super Bowl ads using humor and violence rose from 18.9% in 1989 to about 33% in 1999 and over 40% in 2009. The brands using physical violence with male victims in the 2009 sample included Coke Zero, Bud Light, Audi, Frito-Lay, Doritos, Castrol, SoBe, and Pepsi Max, brands owned by large mainstream advertisers. Scharrer notes: "it appears to be common practice to present the harm and injury that befalls a character in a commercial as humorous, a depiction that past research has suggested may lead to a diminished, even desensitized, perception of the severity of aggression, a trivialization of violence (as well as to the possibility of an aggressive behavioral response" (Scharrer et al. 2006, p. 630).

Effects of Violent Advertising

The increased prominence of aggressive humor in advertising leads to questions about how such possibly more shocking ads are processed and whether they are effective or even perhaps irritating. A number of scholars have offered reasons why irritating advertising may, indeed, benefit the advertiser (Buller 1986; Nelson, Duncan, and Frontczak 1985; Silk and Vavra 1974). Among the possible benefits of irritating commercials are their ability to get attention and possibly reduce counter-arguments, as well as to enhance their memorability. On the other hand, Pasadeos (1990) found irritating ratings of ads to be inversely related to informativeness ratings for the same ads.

As with irritation, the evidence is mixed on whether shock and violence are good for advertisers. When examining ads for HIV/AIDS prevention, Dahl, Frankenberger, and Manchanda (2003), mentioned earlier, looked at the value of shocking content and concluded that it enhanced attention, short-term recall, and recognition. The key, they argued, was the violation of social norms, an aspect that may also play a role in advertising irritation. Brown and his colleagues (2010) examined the impact of violence in online advertising and found that the more extreme the violence the greater the ad likability, recall, and the increased likelihood that the ad would be passed along to others. The implication is, therefore, that this form of disparaging humor may benefit advertisers.

The evidence is more negative when attitudinal measures are considered. When studying violent video games, Jeong, Bohil, and Biocca (2011) found that while recall of brand logos was enhanced, attitudes toward brand logos were harmed in this context. In a test of humor paired with violence, Swani, Weinberger, and Gulas (2013) found that women liked the ads and brands that used humor with extreme violence less than men, and that men and women both preferred ads with extreme violence less than humorous ads with no violence or less extreme violence. They found that extreme violence, even cloaked in humor, violated female social norms more than male social norms, a view supported by Wilson and O'Gorman (2003), who argue that there is clear evidence that sex differences exist in response to norm-breaking events, with males more prone to violence than females.

The model of shocking advertising of Dahl and coauthors (2003) is silent on whether the violations of social norms impact attitudes as studied by Swani, Weinberger, and Gulas (2013) and by Jeong, Bohil, and Biocca (2011), but it is an important issue of whether ads that irritate and put consumers off have a negative halo effect of brand attitudes and purchase behavior. The question raised by Bartos (1980, 1981) about irritating advertising might be raised here: "Do we have to make them hate us to buy our products?"

SEX AND VIOLENCE IN ADVERTISING

With the success of *Fifty Shades of Grey*, it is likely that ads with the elements discussed in this chapter—sex and violence—will increase in prevalence. Advertisers often reflect popular culture in their campaigns in order to resonate with consumer experiences. In the 1980s, for example, after the success of the film *9½ Weeks*, a film that featured sex play with bondage, food, and ice cubes, Revlon ran a campaign for its Fire and Ice fragrance with remarkably similar images and themes from the movie. We suspect that the images and themes in *Fifty Shades of Grey* will begin appearing in advertising as well.

Overall, however, there appears to be very little sexual violence in mainstream advertising. Soley and Reid (1985) reported that 12.9% of ads in *TV Guide* for network program promotion contained both sexual and violent elements, though there was no indication if the two elements were related. A more recent and comprehensive analysis of 3,252 television commercials reported zero instances of sexualized violence (Hetsroni 2011). One explanation for its absence is that sexual violence is fairly rare in television advertising because it can offend viewers. An alternate hypothesis, however, is that sexual violence is typically operationalized as very overt instances, thus excluding subtle references to violence. In the Soley and Reid (1985) study, for instance, examples of violent content included references to "crazed killers" and "murderers," and visuals of "a man choking another," two men "fighting over a knife," and "a woman pointing a gun." Similarly, Hetsroni's (2011) study considered violence as bare-handed assault, assault with weapons, rape, and acts of war. These acts are clearly violent, but either reflect the advertised product (network programming) or fail to consider subtle allusions to violence characteristic of that found in *Fifty Shades of Grey*. It is also possible that use in advertising of such images as seen in online digital media and more targeted print publications has not been accounted for by studies focusing just on TV. In sum, most studies have either content analyzed sex or violence in advertising but not both; further, those that included both did so in a manner that used a coding scheme unable to detect subtle forms of violence. Finally, up until now it is possible that images of sex and violence have occurred in media other than television. A comprehensive study that examines both elements, and considers more nuanced forms of both types of content in more varied media, offers a ripe opportunity for future research.

There have been some occasional examples of maverick brands that have utilized sexual violence to violate social norms and get noticed. Most of these instances have been largely restricted to fashion brands developing a sexual brand positioning with ads in very specialized publications with narrow target audiences. For example, an ad for clothier Duncan Quinn features him pulling on a necktie worn by a seemingly dead woman draped across the hood of a sports car. She is clad only in her underwear. Another well-known ad is for fashion importer Loula, based in Australia. The company has run a series of ads showing staged crime scenes featuring women wearing Loula footwear. In the best-known print ad, a woman's leg and hand are dangling from the trunk of a Mercedes. It is clear that she is dead, but at the end of her bare leg is imported fashion footwear from Loula. Although not fashion related, in 2013, personnel at JWT India entered a series of print ads in a regional ad contest. It was discovered that the ads were fake, but, more important, the ads created a firestorm because one featured a Ford with its hatchback raised to reveal three scantily clad young women bound and gagged with a smiling Silvio Berlusconi, former Italian prime minister, in the front seat. The ads elicited much negative press for JWT and Ford and provide a clear example of what may happen when sexually violent ads violate the bounds of acceptability.

In the following section, we speculate what happens when you cross sex and violence in advertising. We will look at that answer from two perspectives: implications for brands and social implications.

Ad and Brand Effects

What can we ascertain about the effects of sex and violence in advertising for brands? First, we must consider that not all instances of sex and violence are the same. As we know, effects can vary as a result of content intensity, explicitness, and intent, as well as additional message factors such as humor, context, and prevailing tone.

One way to consider the likely effects of sex and violence is through a simple framework with two levels (low, high) of both variables (sex, violence; see Table 6.1). Overall, sexual content will vary by explicitness and graphic nature. Low-sex content is characterized by physically attractive models, toned physiques, and subtle references of sexual double entendre. Images of high-sex content would consist of implied nudity and sexual behavior between models. Instances of low-

Table 6.1

A Framework for Considering Sexual and Violent Content and Effects in Advertising

Violence	Sexual Explicitness Low	Sexual Explicitness High	
Low	Example: Keystone Light "Beer Cooler"	Example: Miller Light "Pillow Fight"	Description (low-violence): Inadvertent violence such as push or shove.
	Effects: Favorable memory and attitude effects; least chance of consumer criticism.	Effects: Unfavorable memory and attitude effects; potential consumer criticism.	Minor violation of social norms if any.
High	Example: Pepsi MAX "Love Hurts"	Example: Dolce & Gabbana "Dream"	Description (low-violence): Aggressive violence or implied rape.
	Unfavorable memory and attitude effects; potential consumer criticism.	Effects: Least favorable memory and attitude effects; highest risk of consumer backlash.	Major violation of social norms.
	Description (low-sexual explicitness): Attractive models, revealing clothing, and/or flirtation/poses.	Description (high-sexual explicitness): Models in intimate wear or implied nudity, and/or sexual behavior.	
	Minor violation of social norm if any.	Major violation of social norms.	

violence content would consist of an inadvertent push or shove, or implied violence. High-violence content would be characterized by serious violence that is likely to result in physical or emotional harm, and sexualized violence.

An example of content in the low-sex, low-violence quadrant is a commercial for Keystone Light beer. In the spot, a man inadvertently knocks over an attractive woman who came over to help him open the door to a beer cooler in a convenience store. The campaign focused on men's mishaps and the slogan, "You can't always be smooth but your beer should be." Another example could be two men competing for the attention of an attractive woman. Both could be playfully jockeying for the woman's attention. If the competition became extreme, the commercial would be an example of low-sex, high-violence content. To turn the tables, a 2011 commercial for Pepsi MAX titled "Love Hurts" features a woman kicking, pushing, and putting soap in her husband's mouth when she catches him eating unhealthy food. When he shares a moment with an attractive female jogger, the wife knocks out the jogger with a Pepsi can she throws at her ducking husband.

Content in the high-sex quadrants would be more sexually explicit with regard to nudity and behavior. An example of a high-sex, low violence commercial aired several years ago as Miller Lite refreshed its "Tastes great/Less filling" slogan with a series of commercials. One spot featured Pamela Anderson and two other women—all in their underwear—engaged in a pillow fight. Another commercial from that campaign, titled "Catfight," garnered a good deal of attention for its gratuitous nature. The spot featured two women in a physical fight over whether Miller Lite "Tastes great" or is "Less filling." Their fight was especially violent but also involved their losing articles of clothing during the altercation—and kissing in the extended online version. Where

"Pillow Fight" is an example of high-sex, low-violence, the "Catfight" commercial is clearly an example of a high-sex, high-violence advertisement. Table 6.1 provides examples and descriptions of ads containing both sexual and violent content. Additionally, the table summarizes memory and attitudinal effects described in the following sections that can be expected for exemplar advertisements within each quadrant, and when a social norm is likely to be violated.

Memory Effects

If recall and recognition are important goals, ads containing sex and violence should be a winning combination. As discussed, from an attention standpoint both types of content attract attention. Combining them in one message should generate ultimate awareness for an advertisement. On the other hand, both elements have been shown to be distracting such that retention of brand information would be at a disadvantage in sexually violent ads.

There is relevant research that tested both sex and violence—though not in the same ad—which may provide an indication of memory effects. Bushman (2007) examined the influence of programming context on ad effectiveness. He crossed three types of programming (violent, sexual, and neutral) with three types of commercials (violent, sexual, and neutral). He reported that products in commercials aired during neutral programming were much better recalled than commercials aired in either violent or sexual programming. Overall, violent and sexual ads had lower product recall scores, with violent ads recalled the least. This work builds on his previous studies showing that memory of commercials is inhibited if they are aired during violent or sexual programming (Bushman and Bonacci 2002).

Bushman's studies suggest that when it comes to memory effects, violent and sexual ads are at an overall disadvantage compared to neutral ads. Whereas he does not directly test messages that contain sexually violent content, his findings are such that violent or sexual ads embedded within violent or sexual content are also at a distinct disadvantage. His findings suggest that sex and violence in the same commercial may attract attention and memory for the ad—as borne out in previous research—but brand information will not be well remembered. It remains to be seen, however, if the distraction effect is additive if both sexual and violent content are used in an ad, or if the memory disadvantage is no worse than if either sex or violence were used. Additionally, it is unclear whether Bushman tested what could be considered high- or low-sex/violence commercials. In either case, the evidence from Bushman's study suggests that sexually violent commercials will not benefit brand recall and recognition.

We must remember, however, that opportunities for advertising exposure today are far greater than what is aired during a television program. Many commercials are posted online and are available for mass viewing. If a viewer wants to see them again, he easily can. Advertisers also post extended cuts and out-takes, which can enhance the experience of a 30-second commercial. We do know that sex is a top search term, so there is opportunity for consumers to find a sexually violent ad and experience multiple viewings, which can mitigate negative memory effects found in an experimental one-exposure setting.

Emotional Response Effects

Beyond brand recall, emotional effects are potentially more relevant to consider for sexually violent advertising. As described, sexual content in ads evokes more negative reactions as the images move beyond the moderately explicit. LaTour (1990) has shown that viewers experience more negatively valenced arousal when the graphic nature of the appeal violates what viewers consider acceptable. Those reactions translate to less favorable attitudes toward the ad and less brand interest. Women especially are more negative as the graphic nature of the appeals increases and are more likely to report boycotting or complaining about the advertised brand. The same is true for violence. In this sense, ads that are high-sex and high-violence are likely to evoke negative responses. This is important because research has shown for both types of appeals that negative emotional responses are directly linked to attitudes toward the ad.

For this reason, a clear recommendation would be to avoid any high-sex or high-violence categories. If a marketer were to include both elements in their ads, the research would suggest that low-sex and low-violence would result in the most positive (or least negative) responses compared to the other options.

Beyond lower evaluations of the ad, sexually violent ads can result in public outcry and can cause public image concerns for a brand. Research by Ford, LaTour, and Middleton (1999) found that women were likely to boycott brands that offended them with graphic forms of sexual content. Brands today must be aware of social media and the ability of citizens to complain publically about an ad they find controversial. Today, viewers can post or write about ads they find particularly offensive and perceive to violate the social norms described by Dahl, Frankenberger, and Manchanda (2003). One recent example of a backlash was reaction to an ad by fashion designer Dolce and Gabbana (Schrobsdorff 2007). The ad, labeled "Dream" in Table 6.1, featured what some described as a rape scene—a man holding down a woman as four other men appeared to wait their turn. The ad was quickly pulled after online protests and criticism from the president of the National Organization for Women (NOW). The creators claimed the intent of the scene was misperceived, and that it was intended to portray a dream. Regardless of intent, the ad and negative criticism continue to live online, coming up prominently in any related search about women in advertising. Similarly, an ad for Calvin Klein jeans was banned by the Australian Standards Bureau in 2010 because it depicted a rape scene (Doherty 2010). The bureau claimed that the ad "was demeaning to women by suggesting that she is a plaything of these men. It also demeans men by implying sexualized violence against women." Both of these examples can be considered high-sex, high-violence, and both met with public sanctioning. Even though viewers may not be in the target audience, it will not stop them from negatively commenting on and critiquing ads.

There are relevant moderators that influence how people interpret sex and violent content. For example, violence in advertising is often accompanied by humor. Similarly, humor can seem to defuse tension in a sexual commercial. The Miller Lite "Catfight" example previously discussed is arguably more sexual and violent than the ads by Dolce and Gabbana and Calvin Klein, but it did not receive the same level of criticism as those ads. The lack of criticism is partly because the commercial did not allude to or could not be perceived as depicting sexual assault and the action was couched in humor. Similarly, context and prevailing tone influence interpretations as well. What might be acceptable in a women's fashion magazine, surrounded by similar, avant-garde ads for other high-fashion brands, is likely to seen as a norm violation when viewed in isolation online or through social media, or when viewed by a general audience on television.

Last, gender can play a role as well. As noted, it is clear that males are more favorable toward sex in advertising than are females—primarily because females represent most sexual content in advertising. But the same is true for violence. In the context of humor, we have seen that extreme violence is more effective with males than females, but in general, it may underperform when compared with ads that use no violence or lower levels of violence. Again, these variables and their interplay with sexually violent advertising present an understudied area ready for further inquiry.

Social Effects

Aside from brand effects, the social effects of sexual violence in advertising should be considered as well. The attitudinal and behavioral effects of sexual violence have been studied by some researchers within the context of pornography. In fact, there is a great deal of literature that has verified the impact of aggressive pornography. This form of pornography has been defined by Cline (1994) as consisting of sexual coercion in which physical force is either used or implied to engage in sexual acts or sexually arousing situations that involve violence.

In a meta-analysis of the aggressive pornography literature, Lyons, Anderson, and Larson (1994) reported that "with fairly impressive consistency . . . exposure to [aggressive pornography] has a negative effect on attitudes toward women and perceived likelihood to rape" (p. 305). Specifically, they report that exposure to this form of pornography is linked to negative attitudes toward women. Attitudes are more callous toward women as measured by greater acceptance of rape myths, hostility and acceptance of violence toward women, and higher perceptions of normative aggressive sexual behavior compared to viewers of nonviolent pornography. Behaviorally, men have been shown to emulate the aggression they view and to report an increased likelihood of rape if there were no consequences (Lyons, Anderson, and Larson 1994). Cline (1994, p. 239) argues that these effects are undeniable when one considers that viewers are "associating sexual arousal with inflicting injury, rape, humiliation, or torture on females."

The leap from pornography to advertising may not be as large as it was in the past. For one, pornographic themes are showing up with more frequency in mainstream advertising. Consider, for example, an advertisement for Pornstar clothing in a skateboarding magazine that featured two scantily clad women standing in front of an elementary-school classroom, one spanking the other. Similarly, a recent ad for Revelstoke whiskey featured a close-up shot of a man enjoying a lap dance in a gentleman's club. As these examples attest, explicit themes are present in advertising as well as in everyday media.

In addition, and more important, there is evidence that even standard forms of sex in advertising can contribute to violent attitudes toward women. MacKay and Covell (1997) showed study participants 10 ads featuring either sexual or non-sexual images of women. They reported that participants viewing the sexual images—regardless of gender—were more accepting of aggression toward women on a number of indicators and reported less support toward feminism overall. More than 10 sexual ads featuring women are commonplace in most high-circulation fashion magazines. A related study found that males who viewed sex in advertising featuring women were more likely to be accepting of rape toward women and had more callous attitudes toward women (Lanis and Covell 1995). We speculate that these effects would be heightened if the ads also contained violent images.

On a related note, research shows that exposure to sex in advertising, or similar types of images of women, makes women feel negative about themselves and their bodies (Lavine, Sweeney, and Wagner 1999). Images that fail to inspire self-confidence and self-satisfaction may lead one to be more accepting of violence and degradation toward herself. At any level, violence against women is unacceptable in any form. Advertisers would be well advised to avoid creating such ads and to seriously consider findings from research that show the indirect contribution to violent attitudes.

CONCLUSION

With the success of the *Fifty Shades of Grey* series and movies to follow, we should expect edgy advertisers to work themes of forbidden sex and violence into advertising and promotion as they attempt to appeal to the millions of readers of this series. Even if not directly because of *Fifty Shades*' success, we should expect sexually violent content to increase in prevalence as both sex and violence have—and will continue to do—in most major media platforms. With sexual and pornographic themes increasingly part of broadcast and cable television, why shouldn't we expect "lighter" types of sexual violence, such as those exemplified in *Fifty Shades of Grey*—especially if both protagonists are fully on board? The social norms that provide a boundary for such images have shifted dramatically in established and new media but there is still an edge beyond which broadcasters and advertisers risk scorn and condemnation.

After reading this chapter, you should have a good sense of definitions of both sex and violence in advertising as well as research into their effects. The two appeals share several commonalities: both attract attention to the advertisement, both tend to inhibit memory of brand information, both elicit negative reactions if they violate the normative bandwidth, and both are liked more by males than females—all things being equal. Overall, emotional responses appear to be the key to understanding both brand effects as well as negative public reactions to their use. Despite the similarities, we hesitate to predict with much certainty the effects if the two types of content are combined. Are the effects cumulative or no greater than what could be expected if only one element were present in an advertisement? If advertisers do attempt to integrate themes of sex and violence into their messages, it is likely to be transformational products such as sexy underwear, perfumes, fashion clothing, jewelry, sports cars, motor cycles, upscale liquors, and tobacco products where such themes might be more compatible with product positioning and audience purchase motivations.

Overall, we see that much opportunity exists for aspiring researchers who are willing to test and analyze the content and effects of sexually violent advertising content. As evident in the second half of this chapter, very little research exists that documents either the prevalence of sexual violence or its effects. To facilitate these efforts, we presented two ways of conceptualizing further work in this area. For one, we suggest Dahl, Frankenberger, and Manchanda's (2003) normative bandwidth model as a way of considering the outcomes of extreme instances of sexual violence on brand communication. To move beyond extreme instances, we also proposed a framework for both categorizing and anticipating effects of sexually violent content. It is obvious that memory and attitudinal responses will vary as a function of the explicitness, extremity, and gratuity of sexually violent depictions.

Beyond further research, are there any guideposts for advertisers? In another chapter in this book, Jones, Cunningham, and Gallagher provide some guidelines about the appropriate use of violence in advertising that may be useful for advertisers considering the use of violence and sex. Can depiction of scenes from *Fifty Shades* adapted for an ad be used ethically? Beyond the ethics, what is the likely audience response? Is it shocking, repugnant, offensive, or irritating? Is it okay if it increases attention, gets passed along virally? Is it okay if it is just aimed at, and exposed to, a restricted audience that enjoys the combination of sex and violence? For example, is the ad for the Pussy energy drink referred to earlier better if it is in a magazine for men than on a billboard for all to see? McGraw and Warren (2010) suggest that if it is perceived as wrong but benign, people will be amused. Most advertisers looking to gain attention but wanting to avoid irritating their audiences walk a fine line attempting to predict the point where the use of sex and violence might be seen as a malign violation, offensive and irritating to the point that it creates harmful attention and exposure that may damage the brand.

Further, there are social implications for using sexually violent advertising. As mentioned, aggressive pornography—and even objectifying examples of sex in advertising—can lead to antisocial sexual attitudes and behaviors. Considering *Fifty Shades of Grey*, what effects should be expected if in an advertising context sexual violence against a woman is depicted but the woman welcomes it and affection is involved. Is the taboo against violence toward women lifted because it is wrapped in some affection? Does it matter if she likes the sex and violence? In the context of shocking advertising in Table 6.1, the violence toward a woman and the sex create the shock, a norm violation, surprise, and follow-on impact on recall and downstream variables. However, if the norm violation is malign and taboo, advertisers adapting such scenes for their brands could become the targets of moral outrage. Is the trade-off between greater awareness and exposure worth it, and when it could be offset by individual offense, dislike and irritation and possible public condemnation and boycotts? We believe the answer is clear. Any use of violence against women, in any form, is wrong and should not be tolerated at any level.

Regardless of our stance, advertisers, as with media storytellers, can create and use characters that violate social norms but are loved for it. The following commentary on *Fifty Shades* from one website suggests that there are clear norm violations:

> In his book on batterers, Lundy Bancroft provides a list of potentially dangerous signs to watch out for from boyfriends. Needless to say, Mr. Grey is the poster boy of the list ... with his jealous, controlling, stalking, [and] sexually sadistic behavior.... And yet women of all ages are swooning over this guy and misreading his obsessive, cruel behavior as evidence of love and romance. (www.antipornography.org)

As the success of this series suggests, consumers will buy what they desire, even if the messages may result in antisocial outcomes. When it comes to advertising, however, consumers are less forgiving. Determining how much and in what contexts is the responsibility of enterprising researchers.

REFERENCES

Aaker, David S., and Donald E. Bruzzone (1985), "Causes of Irritation in Advertising," *Journal of Marketing,* 49 (2), 47–57.

Alexander, Michael W., and Ben B. Judd (1978), "Do Nudes in Ads Enhance Brand Recall?" *Journal of Advertising Research,* 18 (February), 47–50.

———, (1986), "Differences in Attitudes Toward Nudity in Advertising," *Psychology: A Quarterly Journal of Human Behavior,* 23 (1), 26–29.

Anderson, Charles R. (2000), "Television Commercial Violence During Nonviolent Programming: The 1998 Major League Baseball Playoffs," *Pediatrics,* 106 (4), e46.

Anderson, Craig A., Leonard Berkowitz, Edward Donnerstein, L. Rowell Huesmann, James D. Johnson, David Linz, Neil Malamuth, and Ellen Wartella (2003), "The Influence of Media Violence on Youth," *Psychological Sciences in the Public Interest,* 4 (3), 81–110.

Baker, Michael J., and Gilbert A. Churchill (1977), "The Impact of Physically Attractive Models on Advertising Evaluations," *Journal of Marketing Research,* 24 (November), 538–555.

Bartos, Rena (1980), "Do We Really Have to Make Them Mad to Sell Them?" Presentation to Advertising Research Foundation 26th Annual Conference, Advertising Research Foundation, New York, March 17–19.

——— (1981), "Ads That Irritate May Erode Trust in Advertised Brands," *Harvard Business Review,* 59 (4), 138–140.

Belch, Michael A., B.E. Holgerson, George E. Belch, and J. Koppman (1981), "Psychophysical and Cognitive Responses to Sex in Advertising," in *Advances in Consumer Research,* vol. 9, Andrew A. Mitchell, ed., Ann Arbor, MI: Association for Consumer Research, 424–427.

Bourdieu, Pierre (1983), "Forms of Capital," in *Handbook of Theory and Research for the Sociology of Education,* J.C. Richards, ed., New York: Greenwood Press.

Brown, Kimona (2010), "Social Norms and Sanctions," *Suite 101,* December 16, http://suite101.com/a/social-norms-sanctions-a321549 (accessed February 13, 2013).

Brown, Mark R., Roop K. Bhadury, and Nigel K. Ll. Pope (2010), "The Impact of Comedic Violence on Viral Advertising Effectiveness," *Journal of Advertising,* 39 (1), 49–65.

Buller, David, B. (1986), "Distraction During Persuasive Communication: A Meta-Analytic Review," *Communication Monographs,* 53, 91–114.

Bushman, Brad J. (2007), "That Was a Great Commercial, But What Were They Selling? Effects of Violence and Sex on Memory for Products in Television Commercials," *Journal of Applied Social Psychology,* 37 (8), 1784–1796.

———, and Craig A. Anderson (2001), "Media Violence and the American Public: Scientific Facts Versus Media Misinformation," *American Psychologist,* 56 (6), 477–489.

———, and A.M. Bonacci (2002), "Violence and Sex Impair Memory for Television Ads," *Journal of Applied Psychology,* 87, 557–564.
Cline, Victor B. (1994), "Pornography Effects: Empirical and Clinical Evidence," in *Media, Children, and the Family: Social Scientific, Psychodynamic, and Clinical Perspectives,* Dolf Zillmann, Jennings Bryant, and Aletha Bryant, eds., Hillsdale, NJ: Erlbaum, 229–247.
Courtney, Alice E., and Thomas W. Whipple (1983), *Sex Stereotyping in Advertising,* Lexington, MA: Heath.
Dahl, Darren W., Kristina D. Frankenberger, and Rajesh V. Manchanda (2003), "Does It Pay to Shock? Reactions to Shocking and Nonshocking Advertising Content Among University Students," *Journal of Advertising Research,* 43 (3), 268–280.
Davies, John, He Zhu, and Brian Brantley (2007), "Sex Appeals That Appeal: Negative Sexual Self-Schema on Affective Responses to Sexual Content in Advertising," *Journal of Current Issues and Research in Advertising,* 29 (Fall), 79–89.
Dines, G. (2012). "Why are Women Devouring Fifty Shades of Grey?" *Counterpunch,* July 27–29, www.counterpunch.org/2012/07/27/why-are-women-devouring-fifty-shades-of-grey/.
Doherty, Elissa (2010), "Advertising Watchdog Orders Violent Calvin Klein Ads to Be Taken Down," *Herald Sun News* (Australia), October 19, www.heraldsun.com.au/archive/news/violent-ads-spark-sex-fury/story-e6frf7l6-1225940899235 (accessed May 29, 2013).
Dudley, Sid C. (1999), "Consumer Attitudes Toward Nudity in Advertising," *Journal of Marketing Theory and Practice,* 7 (Winter), 89–96.
Ford, John B., Michael S. LaTour, and Courtney Middleton (1999), "Women's Studies and Advertising Role Portrayal Sensitivity: How Easy Is It to Raise 'Feminist Consciousness'?" *Journal of Current Issues and Research in Advertising,* 21 (Fall), 77–87.
Freedman, Jonathan L. (2002), *Media Violence and Its Effect on Aggression: Assessing the Scientific Evidence,* Toronto: University of Toronto Press.
Freeman, L. (1989), "Wisk Rings in New Generation," *Advertising Age,* September 18, 5.
Fullerton, Jami, and Alice Kendrick (2001), "Comparing Content of Commercials from General Market and Spanish-Language Television," *Southwestern Mass Communication Journal,* 17 (1), 53–62.
Grazer, William F., and Garland Keesling (1995), "The Effect of Print Advertising's Use of Sexual Themes on Brand Recall and Purchase Intention: A Product Specific Investigation of Male Responses," *Journal of Applied Business Research,* 11 (Summer), 47–58.
Hennink-Kaminski, Heidi J., and Tom Reichert (2011), "Using Sexual Appeals in Advertising to Sell Cosmetic Surgery: A Content Analysis from 1986 to 2007," *Sexuality and Culture,* 15 (November), 41–55.
Hetsroni, Amir (2007), "Sexual Content on Mainstream TV Advertising: A Cross-Cultural Comparison," *Sex Roles,* 57, 201–210.
——— (2011), "Violence in Television Advertising: Content Analysis and Audience Attitudes," *Atlantic Journal of Communication,* 19, 97–112.
Jeong, Eui Jun, Corey J. Bohil, and Frank A. Biocca (2011), "Brand Logo in Violent Games: Memory and Attitude Change," *Journal of Advertising,* 40 (3), 59–72.
Kilbourne, Jean (1999), *Deadly Persuasion: Why Women and Girls Must Fight the Addictive Power of Advertising,* New York: The Free Press.
Kunkel, Dale, Keren Eyal, Edward Donnerstein, Kristie M. Farrar, Erica Biely, and Victoria Rideout (2007), "Sexual Socialization Messages on Entertainment Television: Comparing Content Trends 1997–2002," *Media Psychology,* 9 (May), 595–622.
Lanis, Kyra, and Katherine Covell (1995), "Images of Women in Advertisements: Effects of Attitudes Related to Sexual Aggression," *Sex Roles,* 32 (9/10), 639–649.
LaTour, Michael S. (1990), "Female Nudity in Print Advertising: An Analysis of Gender Differences in Arousal and Ad Response," *Psychology and Marketing,* 7 (Spring), 65–81.
———, and Tony L. Henthorne (1994), "Ethical Judgments of Sexual Appeals in Print Advertising," *Journal of Advertising,* 13 (September), 81–90.
——— (2003), "Nudity and Sexual Appeals: Understanding the Arousal Process and Advertising Response," in *Sex in Advertising: Perspectives on the Erotic Appeal,* Tom Reichert and Jacqueline Lambiase, eds., Mahwah, NJ: Erlbaum, 91–106.
Lavine, Howard, Donna Sweeney, and Stephen H. Wagner (1999), "Depicting Women as Sex Objects in Television Advertising: Effects on Body Dissatisfaction," *Personality and Social Psychology Bulletin,* 25 (August), 1049–1058.
Lin, Carolyn A. (1998), "Uses of Sex Appeals in Prime-Time Television Commercials," *Sex Roles,* 38 (March), 461–475.

Lyons, John S., Rachel L. Anderson, and David B. Larson (1994), "A Systematic Review of the Effects of Aggressive and Nonagressive Pornography," in *Media, Children, and the Family: Social Scientific, Psychodynamic, and Clinical Perspectives*, Dolf Zillmann, Jennings Bryant, and Aletha Bryant, eds., Hillsdale, NJ: Erlbaum, 271–310.

MacKay, Natalie J., and Katherine Covell (1997), "The Impact of Women in Advertisements on Attitudes Toward Women," *Sex Roles,* 36 (9/10), 573–583.

Maguire, Brendan, Diane Sandage, and Georgie Ann Weatherby (2000), "Violence, Morality, and Television Commercials," *Sociological Spectrum,* 20, 121–144.

McGraw, A. Peter, and Caleb Warren (2010), "Benign Violations: Making Immoral Behavior Funny," *Psychological Science,* 21 (8), 1141–1149.

McIntosh, William D., John D. Murray, Rebecca M. Murray, and Sunita Manian (2003), "What's So Funny About a Poke in the Eye? The Prevalence of Violence in Comedy Films and Its Relation to Social and Economic Threat in the United States, 1951–2000," *Mass Communication and Society,* 6 (4), 345–360.

Nelson, James, Calvin Duncan, and Nancy T. Frontczak (1985), "The Distraction Hypothesis and Radio Advertising," *Journal of Marketing,* 49, 60–70.

Ogilvy, David (1985), *Ogilvy on Advertising,* Vintage: New York.

Paek, Hye-Jin, and Michelle R. Nelson (2007), "A Cross-Cultural and Cross-Media Comparison of Female Nudity in Advertising," *Journal of Promotion Management,* 13 (Spring/Summer), 145–167.

Paik, Haejung, and George Comstock (1994), "The Effects of Television Violence on Antisocial Behavior: A Meta-Analysis," *Communication Research,* 21 (4), 516–546.

Pasadeos, Yorgo (1990), "Perceived Informativeness of and Irritation with Local Advertising," *Journalism Quarterly,* 67 (1), 35–39.

Peterson, Robert A., and Roger A. Kerin (1977), "The Female Role in Advertisements: Some Experimental Evidence," *Journal of Marketing,* 41 (October), 59–63.

Pokrywczynski, James, and John H. Crowley (1993), "The Influence of Irritating Commercials on Radio Listening Habits," *Journal of Radio Studies,* 2, 51–67.

Putrevu, Sanjay (2008), "Consumer Responses Toward Sexual and Nonsexual Appeals: The Influence of Involvement, Need for Cognition (NFC), and Gender," *Journal of Advertising,* 37 (Summer), 57–69.

Ramirez, Artemio (2006), "Sexually Oriented Appeals on the Internet: An Exploratory Analysis of Popular Mainstream Websites," in *Sex in Consumer Culture: The Erotic Content of Media and Marketing,* Tom Reichert and Jacqueline Lambiase, eds., Mahwah, NJ: LEA, 141–157.

Reichert, Tom (2003), *The Erotic History of Advertising,* Amherst, NY: Prometheus.

———, Courtney Carpenter-Childers, and Leonard Reid, (2012), "How Sex in Advertising Varies by Product Category: An Analysis of Three Decades of Visual Sexual Imagery in Magazine Advertising," *Journal of Current Issues and Research in Advertising,* 33 (May), 1–19.

———, Susan E. Heckler, and Sally Jackson (2001), "The Effects of Sexual Social Marketing Appeals on Cognitive Processing and Persuasion," *Journal of Advertising,* 30 (Spring), 13–27.

———, and Jacqueline Lambiase (2003), "How to Get 'Kissably Close': Examining How Advertisers Appeal to Consumers' Sexual Needs and Desires," *Sexuality and Culture,* 7 (Summer), 120–136.

———, Michael S. LaTour, and John B. Ford (2011), "The Naked Truth: Revealing the Affinity for Graphic Sexual Appeals in Advertising," *Journal of Advertising Research,* 51 (June), 436–448.

———, Michael S. LaToo, and JooYoung Kim (2007), "Assessing the Influence of Gender and Sexual Self-Schema on Affective Responses to Sexual Content in Advertising," *Journal of Current Issues and Research in Advertising,* 29 (Fall), 57–71.

Reid, Leonard N., and Lawrence C. Soley (1983), "Decorative Models and the Readership of Magazine Ads," *Journal of Advertising Research,* 23 (April/May), 27–32.

Scharrer, Erica, Andrea Bergstrom, Angela Paradise, and Qianging Ren (2006), "Laughing to Keep from Crying: Humor and Aggression in Television Commercial Content," *Journal of Broadcasting and Electronic Media,* 50 (4), 615–634.

Schlinger, Mary J. (1979), "A Profile of Responses to Commercials," *Journal of Advertising Research,* 19 (2), 37–46.

Schrobsdorff, Susanna (2007), "Menacing or Marketing: D and G's Controversial Ad," *If It's Hip, It's Here,* March 24, http://ifitshipitshere.blogspot.com/2007/03/menacing-or-marketing-d-controversial.html (accessed May 29, 2013).

Severn, Jessica, George E. Belch, and Michael A. Belch (1990), "The Effects of Sexual and Non-sexual Advertising Appeals and Information Level on Cognitive Processing and Communication Effectiveness," *Journal of Advertising,* 19 (Spring), 14–22.

Silk, Alvin, and Terry G. Vavra (1974), "The Influence of Advertising's Affective Qualities on Consumer Response," in *Buyer/Consumer Information Processing,* G. David Hughes and Michael Ray, eds., Chapel Hill: University of North Carolina Press.

Simpson, Penny, Steve Horton, and Gene Brown (1996), "Male Nudity in Advertisements: A Modified Replication and Extension of Gender and Product Effects," *Journal of the Academy of Marketing Sciences,* 24 (Summer), 257–262.

Soley, Lawrence, and Leonard Reid (1985), "Baiting Viewers: Violence and Sex in Television Program Advertisements," *Journalism Quarterly,* 62 (Spring), 105–131.

——— (1988), "Taking It Off: Are Models in Magazine Ads Wearing Less?" *Journalism and Mass Communication Quarterly,* 65 (Winter), 960–966.

Swani, Kunal, Marc G. Weinberger, and Charles S. Gulas (2013), "The Impact of Violent Humor on Advertising Success: A Gender Perspective," *Journal of Advertising,* 42 (4), 308–319.

Swidler, Ann (1986), "Culture in Action: Symbols and Strategies," *American Sociological Review,* 51 (April), 273–286.

——— (2001), *Talk of Love: How Culture Matters,* Chicago: University of Chicago Press.

Van den Bergh, Bram, Siegfried DeWitte, and Luk Warlop (2008), "Bikinis Instigate Generalized Impatience in Intertemporal Choice," *Journal of Consumer Research,* 35 (June), 85–97.

Wells, William D., Clark Leavitt, and Maureen McConville (1971), "A Reaction Profile for TV Commercials," *Journal of Advertising Research,* 11 (December), 11–17.

Wilson, David, and Rick O'Gorman (2003), "Emotions and Actions Associated with Norm-Breaking Events," *Human Nature,* 14 (3), 277–304.

7

The Impact of Violence Against Women in Advertisements

Michael L. Capella, Ronald Paul Hill, Justine M. Rapp, and Jeremy Kees

From high above the storied Sunset Strip on a glorious June day, a bound and bruised woman on a billboard gazed down at the citizens of Los Angeles. She was the centerpiece of a new advertising campaign for the Rolling Stones' 1976 album Black and Blue, *part of a national promotion by Atlantic Records that featured print ads, radio spots, and in-store displays. At 14 by 48 feet, she dominated the busy skyline, and traffic snarled up and down the boulevard as drivers slowed to get a better look. The woman wore a lacy white bodice, strategically ripped to display her breasts. Her hands were tied with ropes, immobilized above her head, and her bruised legs were spread apart. She straddled an image of the Stones, with her pubic bone positioned just above Mick Jagger's head. Her eyes were half closed and her mouth hung open in an expression of pure sexual arousal, as if the rough physical treatment had wakened her desires and now she wanted more. Her enjoyment was captured in the ad copy: "I'm Black and Blue from the Rolling Stones and I love it!"*

(Bronstein 2008, p. 418)

This passage comes from a recent chronicling of an advocacy group's work to stop a large media conglomerate from continuing an advertising campaign in the 1970s that glorified violence against women. Their fear was that such portrayals reinforce the inappropriate belief that women experience sexual pleasure from physical abuse. This mythic connection denies most standard definitions that violence occurs against the will of the victim rather than with their tacit agreement (see Andersson et al. 2004). Social science literature captures this mentality as "rape myths"; false stereotypes that females enjoy being sexually abused despite their protests to the contrary (Boddewyn and Kunz 1991). Statistics regarding sexual violence against women are alarming; every hour, 16 women confront rapists and every six minutes a woman is raped in the United States, clearly demonstrating that this is a major social problem (Woodruff 1996).

The term *rape myth* was coined by Burt (1980) and refers to beliefs that individuals hold about the act of sexual assault by men on women, with a central focus on the conviction that the victim bears partial or even primary responsibility. According to the rape myth, rapists assume little or no personal responsibility for their aggressive actions. Thus, the rape myth constitutes a set of beliefs that represents fundamental misconceptions about sexualized violence because the "myths" run counter to well-known evidence about sexual assault and its victims. The issue is whether exposure to images of sexualized violence in the media increases the degree of personal acceptance of these attitudes by men. If exposure leads to the adoption of such beliefs, then media violence may inadvertently promote antisocial behavior.

Unfortunately, the depiction of women in stereotypical contexts continues to exist in advertisements for several product categories, leading to the inaccurate conclusion that females may appropriately be viewed as sexual objects for the pleasure of male consumption. Research shows, "By viewing women as exclusively sexual beings whose purpose is to sexually arouse and gratify men, a power differential is created in which women generally are subordinate. This power hierarchy may support development of perceptions of women as appropriate targets for sexually aggressive behaviors" (Lanis and Covell 1995, p. 647). Continuation and propagation of this mentality throughout the media, from music videos to video games, imply to advertisers and marketers that these displays are appealing to broad audiences and innocuous. Indeed, one of the more egregious examples is the "RapeLay" video game from Japan that allows players to choose various methods to assault a teenage girl on the subway, including graphic, interactive scenes of rape (Lah 2010). As a result, distinguished scholars and other social observers have monitored the rise of serious objections, starting with the modern women's liberation movement to the present time (Boddewyn and Kunz 1991; Bronstein 2008). Needless to say, arguments against these representations are based on convictions that they exacerbate traditional attitudes about and behaviors toward women on the acceptability of certain acts of violence (Donnerstein and Linz 1986). Thus, the purpose of our investigation is to examine the influence of sexualized violence as an advertising appeal on consumers' beliefs, attitudes, and intentions.

Much of the research on this topic has examined the broader media, with an emphasis on the longer-term impact of such portrayals, with relatively consistent results. For example, using a triangulation strategy, researchers found a positive link between media violence and aggressive behavior regardless of the research method used by investigators (Anderson and Bushman 2002). In addition, Bushman (2005) looked at research across several hundred investigations spanning decades and states unequivocally that violent television programs beget generalized violence in society. More specific to our purposes, Bronstein (2008) summarizes a large body of research, with a focus on sexualized media violence, and confirms a significant relationship between use of these images and several factors associated with sexual aggression toward females by males.

Consistent with previous research, *sexualized violence* is an overarching term used to describe any violence, physical or psychological, carried out through sexual means or by targeting sexuality. In a broader sense, sexualized violence is about abusing power and encompasses a range of offenses that involve nonconsenting victims (Basile and Saltzman 2009). Our focus is sexual violence perpetrated by men and directed toward women. Therefore, the goal of this study is to demonstrate that the prevalence of media violence poses a societal dilemma, with a specific emphasis on how much, if any, is attributable to the potential negative consequences of sexualized violence in advertising. Of particular interest are the effects such advertising depictions have on rape myth beliefs and consumer attitudes.

CULPABILITY OF ADVERTISING

Scholarship involving magazine advertising has found that sexually oriented appeals are widespread, visible, and increasing (Soley and Kurzbard 1986). According to LaTour and Henthorne (1994), it is commonplace for readers of all ages to pick up any general-interest consumer magazine and find an ad featuring provocatively posed and attired models for many products. Indeed, the use of overt sexual appeals in print advertising has increased considerably in contemporary advertising practice. Recent advertising research suggests, "sex in advertising is worthy of consideration because of its pervasiveness" (Reichert, LaTour, and Kim 2007, p. 63). Furthermore, these authors state, "In magazine advertising, the proportion of sexualized women rose from less than one-third in 1964 to one-half in 2003" (Reichert, LaTour, and Kim 2007, p. 63).

Research clearly shows that the sexual content in mainstream advertising has become more pervasive throughout the 1980s and beyond based on the premise that sex sells, but only if it is more shocking and more graphic than preceding campaigns (Reichert et al. 1999). Consequently, advertisers may feel compelled to "push the envelope" and employ more shocking appeals to "break through the clutter" in the future. The prevalence of violence against women in advertising is significant, with many examples of such sexualized violence as advertising themes in mainstream media outlets (Lukas 2009). Various scholars have found that it is increasingly common for advertising to connect sexuality with aggression or violence against women (e.g., Benokraitis and Feagin 1995). However, there have been few empirical studies that have examined this issue. For instance, Wolf (1991) states that "beauty sadomasochism" is one explanation for the prevalence of violence and sex in many ads, but there has been no research to date that examines the impact of sexually violent ads on consumer behavior.

Furthermore, leading scholars who examine the depiction of women in advertisements have sounded the alarm that many constituencies find the advertising industry negligent in their responsibilities because of possible "glorification of violence against women" (Ford and LaTour 1993, p. 43). Indeed, use of shock appeals by advertisers (designed to deliberately offend their audiences) depicting sexual references and violence is not uncommon (e.g., Andersson et al. 2004; Dahl, Frankenberger, and Manchanda 2003). Yet this indictment has not fostered studies to determine the underlying causes, various expressions across media, and consequences for ads, brands, sponsors, and the larger society. Instead, concerned parties rely heavily on scholarship involving advertising that is tangential to their purposes. For instance, one television study reports that viewers give greater attention to violent programs than nonviolent programs, as well as to sexually explicit versus nonsexual offerings (Bushman 2005). The unspoken conclusion is that the combination must be very powerful, attracting a wide swath of viewers and consumers.

Nonetheless, research exists that gives an alternative understanding of the possible impact of violence against women in advertisements. General findings show that men actually enjoy violent content, especially when compared to women (Haridakis 2006). However, advertising studies involving what LaTour, Pitts, and Snook-Luther (1989) refer to as "erotic communications appeals" seem to elicit both negative and positive reactions from consumers. Other research provides mostly bad news for advertisers, demonstrating that violence and sex on television inhibit memory formation for advertised products embedded in such programming, along with lower intentions to buy (Bushman 2005). A final set of investigations finds that, compared with men, females are more offended by sexualized violence toward women, and the resulting deleterious impact on attitudes toward ads and brands and behavioral intentions are more severe for women versus men (Reichert, LaTour, and Kim 2007).

From a societal perspective, the most important issue is whether violence depicted in advertising contributes to the subjugation of women and to an increase in the acceptance of violence toward them. Once again, evidence is tangential and suggests that *any* emphasis on dominance and aggression by men based on stereotypical sex roles causes development of rape-permissive attitudes (Walker, Rowe, and Quinsey 1993). By way of example, Donnerstein and Linz (1986) assert that viewing "sexually aggressive films" positively influences acceptance of both interpersonal violence and rape myth beliefs. Of course, advertisements typically do not garner the time or attention associated with watching movies. Yet Anderson and colleagues (2003) describe how even short-term exposure to violence has the power to elicit aggressive thinking and feelings by priming preexisting violent scripts and triggering the human tendency for imitation consistent with social learning theory described next.

SOCIAL LEARNING THEORY

Our previous discussion implies that societal acceptance of violence against women is acquired over time through exposure to violent messages and contexts. One potential frame for understanding how it occurs is Social Learning Theory (SLT), which demonstrates that human behavior is obtained through modeling by observing other people and consequences of their actions (Akers 1977; Bandura 1965, 1977, 1986). In addition, much of this learning takes place without intention to learn and without awareness that learning has occurred. Bandura (1977) believes that the best explanation is in terms of continuous and reciprocal interactions between cognitive, behavioral, and environmental factors. Thus, SLT posits that the person and his or her environment do not function as independent units but instead simultaneously determine each other. Such experiences and their consequences also determine what a person perceives as possible, which affects subsequent behaviors.

SLT goes beyond operant learning by recognizing the role of vicarious processes (i.e., modeling), the effects of covert cognitive processes, and the influence of self-control processes. Bandura (1977) notes that within these parameters, learning occurs deliberately and inadvertently through the influence of examples. Most external influences affect behavior via intermediary cognitive processes that determine, in part, which external events are attended to, how they are interpreted, and whether they leave any lasting effects. SLT also recognizes the impact of self-regulatory functions on the control of behavior based on internal self-evaluative consequences as well as perceptions regarding possible external or environmental consequences. In other words, people are affected not only by external influences on behavior but also by the punishments and rewards that they give themselves.

Another influential source of social learning is the symbolic modeling provided by visual media. Research shows that both children and adults acquire attitudes, emotional responses, and new styles of conduct through mass media, which play an important role in shaping behavior and social attitudes (Bandura 1973; Liebert, Neale, and Davidson 1973). More specifically, SLT emphasizes imitative and disinhibitive effects of media violence (Bandura 1973). If depicted relationships involve aggressive or violent behavior, then these values may be adopted by audience members under certain circumstances. For example, programs that contain sexualized violence against women where male perpetrators are rewarded with arousal and gratification may create a model to imitate (Allen et al. 1995). Moreover, habitual exposure to violent media may also reduce viewers' inhibitions against aggression and violence. Building on SLT, Huesman (1986) proposed a social cognitive theory of media-related aggression. He shows that when children observe violence in the mass media, they learn aggressive scripts for social behavior. Our premise, then, is that sexualized violence in advertisements may trigger or prompt these aggressive scripts and act as positive reinforcement for previously held attitudes.

OUR INVESTIGATION

Our review of relevant social science and advertising literature within the framework of SLT allows for research propositions that guided the selection of appropriate methodology and analytic protocol. For example, while advertisers often assume violence and sex sell goods and services, our discussion suggests that the opposite may occur. Relevant work shows that violent or sexual themes may have an adverse effect on memory, with sexually explicit ads leading to a decrease in brand-related information recall from print advertising (Alexander and Judd 1978). More contemporary work by Reichert, Heckler, and Jackson (2001) support this result and indicate that ads with sexual images stimulate fewer cognitive responses toward the message than nonsexual appeals. Bushman and Bonacci (2002) and Bushman and Phillips (2001) concur and show that televised violence and sex impaired memory for commercial messages both immediately after exposure and following one day. Bushman (2005) provides an extension and found that violence and sex in television programs do not support sales of products contained within embedded ads.

These consequences of exposure to violence against women in advertisements may not be uniform. As might be expected, viewer characteristics may dampen or heighten their reactions in significant ways. For instance, research shows that certain demographic factors such as gender and age are influential in the formation of attitudes about the use of another "shock" appeal (female nudity) in advertisements (LaTour, Pitts, and Snook-Luther 1989). Other researchers found that similar characteristics mediate relationships between exposure to media violence and the series of aggressive outcomes noted previously (e.g., Harris 1996). These findings also emerge from scholarship involving violent content on television (Anderson et al. 2003). For instance, in younger demographic groups such as Generation Y, female consumers have been shown to oppose use of sexual appeals (Maciejewski 2004), with females in general more averse to such media portrayals, particularly those depicting violence (McDaniel, Lim, and Mahan 2007).

For the purposes of this investigation, the most salient results show that males are more aggressive than females and younger people are more aggressive than older people, suggesting that advertising appeals using sexualized violence may follow the same pattern.

H1a: *Consumers will hold less positive attitudes toward the advertisement, as advertisements exhibit increased levels of sexualized violence.*

H1b: *Consumers will hold less positive attitudes toward the advertiser, as advertisements exhibit increased levels of sexualized violence.*

H1c: *Consumers will have lower purchase intentions for the advertised product, as advertisements exhibit increased levels of sexualized violence.*

H2a: *Females will hold less positive attitudes toward the advertisement than their male counterparts, as advertisements exhibit increased levels of sexualized violence.*

H2b: *Females will hold less positive attitudes toward the advertiser, as advertisements exhibit increased levels of sexualized violence.*

H2c: *Females will have lower purchase intentions for the advertised product than their male counterparts, as advertisements exhibit increased levels of sexualized violence.*

H3a: *Older consumers will hold less positive attitudes toward the advertisement than their younger counterparts, as advertisements exhibit increased levels of sexualized violence.*

H3b: *Older consumers will hold less positive attitudes toward the advertiser than their younger counterparts, as advertisements exhibit increased levels of sexualized violence.*

H3c: *Older consumers will have lower purchase intentions for the advertised product than their younger counterparts, as advertisements exhibit increased levels of sexualized violence.*

SLT argues that people use stimuli around them to learn about their surroundings; specifically, mass media images "teach" about the world beyond the personal and create the possibility of contributing to an understanding of social interaction patterns. Furthermore, the review of SLT suggests a positive correlation between exposure to sexualized violence toward women in advertising and rape myth acceptance for males since such material shows successful outcomes of these actions (Allen et al. 1995). Exposure to sexualized violence in this context may activate a complex set of associations related to aggressive ideas and emotions, thereby temporarily increasing accessibility to aggressive thoughts, feelings, and scripts (Anderson et al. 2003). As a consequence, research has shown a correlation between exposure to sexually violent media and development of attitudes that support violence against women (Malamuth and Briere 1986). If this social learning perspective is correct, then one should find a positive correlation between exposure to sexually violent media and rape myth acceptance.

Considerable previous research also indicates that males are more accepting of interpersonal violence, rape myths, and adversarial sexual relations than females (e.g., Malamuth and Check 1981).

H4: *Consumers will show greater acceptance of violence against women and rape myths, as advertisements exhibit increased levels of sexualized violence.*

H5: *Males will show a greater acceptance of violence against women than their female counterparts, as advertisements exhibit increased levels of sexualized violence.*

H6: *Younger consumers will show a greater acceptance of violence against women than their older counterparts, as advertisements exhibit increased levels of sexualized violence.*

METHOD AND RESULTS

As mentioned, this study extends the diverse body of research across disciplines on mass media into the narrower field of advertising. To this end, several advertisements were amassed from current and previous campaigns using sexualized violence toward women as an advertising appeal. A subset of three ads that varied significantly from one another in perceived violence was selected as stimuli for the full investigation after pretesting. Consumers were exposed to one of these promotions and subsequently asked to respond to questions from well-known measures of attitude toward the ad, attitude toward the advertiser (firm), and behavioral intentions. They also completed scales that measure perceptions of violence toward women, emphasizing rape myth acceptance. The final set of questions involves some demographic data deemed relevant by previous research outside the advertising domain (e.g., Harris 1996).

Our first step involved an extensive and systematic review of current and past print magazine advertisements for relevant portrayals of sexualized violence against women. The search process included online resources and archived ads collected by universities, advocacy groups, and media using Internet search terms such as "sexualized violence in advertisements." Multiple sites were examined in their entirety and a subset of ads was selected for additional consideration. The review was limited to actual advertisements for branded products and excluded public service announcements because the intended responses are (obviously) drastically different from ads for consumer goods and services. In a limited number of cases, violent acts by men against men or women against women were found but ultimately not included because they were deemed lacking in sexualized violence relevant to our study.

Consideration was given to altering the facial expressions of the recipients of violent acts in order to manipulate viewers' perceived levels of ad violence. Because all of the victims portrayed showed expressions of serenity or pleasure, our belief was that adding distress or disgust might represent a third dimension. Of course, use of this caricature is common among public service announcements. Nonetheless, after much deliberation, the decision was reached to use advertisements as they existed in the marketplace in order to maintain external validity and to allow for managerial recommendations on current practice. As a consequence, stimuli used in our investigation are made up of examples of sexualized violence against women in magazine advertising that consumers may be exposed to depending on media and shopping habits.

To meet research needs, the ads containing sexualized violence against women by men were reviewed and tested for their perceived levels of violence. From the publicly available advertisements, a subset of 100 was chosen for additional review. Three of the four authors individually examined them and selected exemplars for pretesting. They then came together and discussed the merits of each ad, with several receiving consensus as potentially appropriate for study. After pretesting, a 3 (ad: low, moderate, high violence) × 2 (gender: male, female) × 3 (age: tercile split)[1] factorial design was used to explore the impact of sexualized violence in print advertising. Study participants were exposed to full-color ads of existing goods and services while completing scales associated with dependent variables. A more complete description of pretest and main study procedures follows.

Pilot Studies

The pretest was employed to select ads for our primary investigation. The principal goal was to find advertisements that varied in perceived violence without much variation on other related affective/emotional dimensions; thus, it served as a manipulation check so that the main study would be as internally valid as possible. As noted, initial evaluation involved culling through 100 ads deemed sufficiently violent to warrant additional review. Specifically, ads that demonstrated sexualized violence against women and depicted both the victim and assailant were appropriate for our research purposes. Criteria for inclusion in the pilot study were that ads must show people (e.g., no cartoons or animation), and preference was given to ads identifying male perpetrators of the violent acts. After an exhaustive search from current and past magazine campaigns that portrayed violence against women, eight ads were selected for pilot study that seemed to vary in sexualized violence based on the authors' unanimous agreement. A within-subjects experimental design was used in the analysis.

With existing literature as a guide (Gunter, Furnham, and Pappa 2005), the pilot study consisted of having consumers view each of the eight ads followed by a 12-item scale to assess the perceived level of violence of each individual ad. A total of 93 adults (female = 46) completed the paper-and-pencil survey at a national coffeehouse, and respondents were offered free drinks in exchange for doing so. Participants examined eight ads separately, and evaluated each ad on the following items ranging from 1 (not at all) to 10 (extremely): absorbing, hostile, arousing, disturbing, engaging, entertaining, enjoyable, exciting, happy, violent, involving, and interesting. As depicted in Table 7.1, ensuing analysis resulted in two factors—one associated with generalized "violence" and the other associated with "enjoyment." However, only the three-item measure of perceived violence reached the appropriate reliability level ($\alpha = .83$). Notably, confound checks suggest that the three ads did not vary on any relevant emotional responses.

Most importantly, three different levels of violence manifested, leading to selection of least violent and most violent ads for the main study. To capture the middle ground, a third advertisement with moderate levels of violence also was chosen that respondents perceived as equally enjoyable as the least violent ad but significantly different in violence from both test advertisements (see the Appendix for visual representations). The overall univariate F-test ($F = 100.4$, $p < .01$) demonstrates that differences in perceived violence across the three ads are significant. Comparisons indicate that the "high-violence" ad ($M = 8.67$) was seen as more violent than the "moderate-violence" ad ($M = 5.93$; $t = 67.34$, $p < .01$), which was viewed as more violent than the "low-violence" ad ($M = 4.90$; $t = 9.56$, $p < .01$).

Given that real ads (vs. mockups) were used in the main study, there was some concern that these advertisements might differ across other dimensions besides perceived violence. To address this issue, a separate study was conducted to examine the extent to which the three test ads differed across potentially confounding variables. Forty-six nonstudent participants were exposed to one of the three ads used in the main study and asked to respond to various measures of interest.[2] Results show that the three ads did not significantly differ across perceived ad target audience ($F = 1.04$, $p = .36$), ad execution style ($F = .98$, $p = .38$), ad type ($F = 1.57$, $p = .22$), company position ($F = .28$, $p = .76$), company history ($F = .26$, $p = .77$), or explicitness ($F = .77$, $p = .47$). These findings support our use of these ads.

Main Study

Four hundred eighty-four nonstudent U.S. adults drawn from a large marketing research firm participated in our study online. The sample was equally split between males and females and the average age of participants was 48 ($SD = 13.5$). Median household income of participants

Table 7.1

Pilot Test Factor Analysis Showing Two-Factor Solution

	Component	
	Enjoyment	Violence
Absorbing	.644	.079
Hostile	−.188	.842
Arousing	.680	.240
Disturbing	−.326	.758
Engaging	.747	.280
Entertaining	.803	.106
Enjoyable	.880	−.012
Exciting	.880	−.039
Happy	.690	−.281
Violent	−.191	.855
Involving	.764	.161
Interesting	.800	.221

was between $40,000 and $50,000 and 75% had graduated from high school. Respondents were provided information about the purpose of the investigation as well as their right to decline participation. Upon agreement, they then were randomly assigned to one of the three advertising conditions and exposed to the test ad continuously as they answered questions on violence against women, attitude toward the ad, attitude toward the firm, and purchase intentions. Respondents next completed measures of demographic variables. These copy-testing methods are supported in the literature (Andrews and Maronick 1995; Maronick 1991).

A common (Lee 2000) five-item scale measured attitude toward the ad (A_{ad}), exhibiting robust levels of reliability ($\alpha = .97$). Items were "I dislike the ad (r)," "The ad is appealing to me," "The ad is attractive to me," "The ad is interesting to me," and "I think the ad is bad (r)." Attitude toward the firm (A_{firm}) used "unpleasant/pleasant," "unfavorable/favorable," "bad/good," "negative/positive," and "not reputable/reputable," with reliability ($\alpha = .87$) consistent with previous research (e.g., Lohse and Rosen 2001; MacKenzie and Lutz 1989; Meuhling 1987). Finally, purchase intentions (PI) included "I am eager to check out the product because of this ad," "I intend to try this product," "I plan on buying this product," "It is likely that I will buy this product when it becomes available," and "I would consider purchasing this product" ($\alpha = .96$). All items used seven-point scales with anchors of "strongly disagree" and "strongly agree."

Also consistent with previous research, acceptance of interpersonal violence was used as a proxy for violence against women, with an emphasis on rape myth agreement. For example, the Acceptance of Interpersonal Violence Against Women Scale (AIV) measures the relative acceptability of using violence toward women as it pertains to satisfaction of male sexual desires (Burt 1980). These metrics are capable of examining the link between exposure to media sexualized violence and the acceptance of rape myths using the simple premise that such violence against women portrays them as objects of male pleasure. Factor analysis suggested two distinct scales: acceptance of interpersonal *sexual* violence (AIV-Sexual) and acceptance of interpersonal *general* violence (AIV-General), with only AIV-Sexual deemed appropriate for our investigation. AIV-Sexual has three items: "Being roughed up is sexually stimulating to many women," "Many times a woman will pretend she doesn't want to have intercourse because she doesn't want to seem loose, but she's really hoping the man will force her," and "Sometimes the only way a man can get a cold woman turned on is to use force." The coefficient α for this three-item measure was .77. All used seven-point scales with anchors of "strongly disagree" and "strongly agree," and they were coded

Table 7.2

Cell Means for AIV, A_{ad}, A_{firm}, and PI

Independent variables	AIV	A_{ad}	A_{firm}	PI
Low-violence ad				
Male				
Young	2.33	2.66	2.73	2.70
Middle	2.35	2.72	2.17	1.88
Older	2.33	2.42	2.42	1.68
Female				
Young	2.16	2.90	2.67	2.21
Middle	1.88	1.56	1.71	1.46
Older	1.74	2.26	1.94	1.34
Moderate-violence ad				
Male				
Young	2.78	4.30	3.88	3.15
Middle	2.32	2.90	2.50	2.05
Older	2.21	2.45	2.22	1.74
Female				
Young	2.72	3.27	2.82	2.18
Middle	2.02	2.26	2.08	1.83
Older	2.65	2.06	1.62	1.48
High-violence ad				
Male				
Young	2.24	2.50	2.63	2.25
Middle	1.91	2.15	2.47	1.80
Older	1.91	2.23	2.79	1.83
Female				
Young	2.28	2.86	2.38	2.09
Middle	1.49	1.64	1.69	1.23
Older	2.00	2.77	2.12	2.15

AIV = Acceptance of Interpersonal Violence Against Women Scale; A_{ad} = attitude toward the ad; A_{firm} = attitude toward the firm; PI = purchase intentions.

so that higher scores indicate greater acceptance of interpersonal violence. Table 7.2 shows cell means for each independent variable across the various dimensions described above.

Major Findings

To test our original research propositions, a multivariate analysis of covariance (MANCOVA) with income and education levels as covariates was run. As shown in Table 7.3, there are significant multivariate main effects for violent ad (H1: Wilks's $\lambda = .95$, $F = 2.60$, $p < .01$), gender (H2: Wilks's $\lambda = .94$, $F = 6.37$, $p < .01$), and age (H3: Wilks's $\lambda = .92$, $F = 3.97$, $p < .01$). In addition, there are significant two-way interactions for violent ad × gender (Wilks's $\lambda = .96$, $F = 1.99$, $p < .05$), violent ad × age (Wilks's $\lambda = .93$, $F = 1.64$, $p < .05$), and gender × age (Wilks's $\lambda = .95$, $F = 2.30$, $p < .05$). Findings demonstrate that the manipulation was successful and our dependent variables were affected accordingly. To examine specific propositions, several individual univariate tests were also run and reviewed as described below.

Results show a number of interesting interactions. First, findings reveal that gender moderates the effects predicted in our hypotheses for A_{ad} ($F = 2.83$, $p < .05$). As portrayed in Figure 7.1, planned comparisons indicate that men report a significantly higher A_{ad} for the moderate-violence ad condition versus the low- and high-violence ad conditions ($t = 2.35/3.33$, respectively, $p < .01$ for both). Women report lower and similar (not statistically significant) A_{ad} across the three

Table 7.3

Multivariate and Univariate Results for Study Dependent Variables

Independent variables	MANCOVA results		Univariate			
	Wilks's λ	F-value	AIV	A_{ad}	A_{firm}	PI
Main effects						
Violent ad	.95	2.60**	5.92**	6.01**	1.23	1.24
Gender	.94	6.37**	3.42*	6.31**	16.03**	9.21**
Age	.92	3.97**	4.12**	15.45**	11.52**	16.69**
Interaction effects						
VA × gender	.96	1.99*	1.27	2.83*	.44	.79
VA × age	.93	1.64*	.51	3.16*	2.89*	2.09*
Gender × age	.95	2.30*	.90	2.70*	.18	.95
VA × age × gender	.97	.76	.37	1.24	.64	.81

Notes: MANCOVA = multivariate analysis of covariance; AIV = Acceptance of Interpersonal Violence Against Women Scale; A_{ad} = attitude toward the ad; A_{firm} = attitude toward the firm; PI = purchase intentions; VA = violent ad.

[a]To account for education level and income, these variables were included as covariates in the analysis. Education had a significant effect on the AIV-Sexual variable, A_{ad}, and A_{firm}.

* $p < .05$.
** $p < .01$.

Figure 7.1 **Ad × Gender Interaction for A_{ad}**

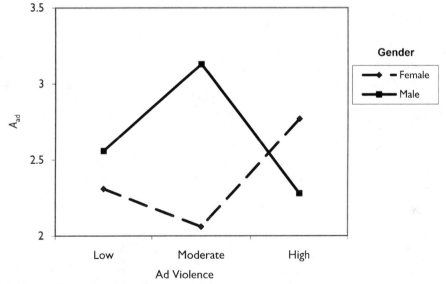

Note: A_{ad} = attitude toward the ad.

conditions. Findings thus suggest that the results supporting our predictions are driven largely by male participants in our study and that females may be less receptive to *all* ads containing sexualized violence.

Also, results demonstrate that age moderates effects for A_{ad} ($F = 3.16, p < .05$), A_{firm} ($F = 2.89, p < .05$), and PI ($F = 2.09, p < .05$). Figure 7.2 displays the pattern of results, which reveals that younger consumers report higher overall levels of A_{ad}, A_{firm}, and PI versus middle and older

104 SEX AND VIOLENCE IN ADVERTISING

Figure 7.2 **Ad × Age Interaction for A_{ad}, A_{firm}, and PI**

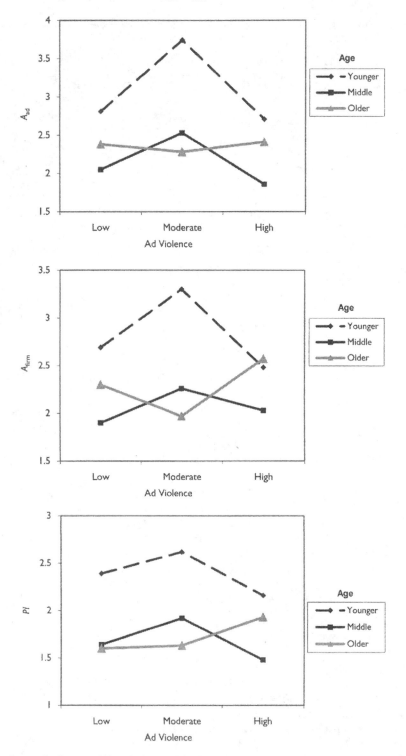

Notes: A_{ad} = attitude toward the ad; A_{firm} = attitude toward the firm; PI = purchase intentions.

age groups. Again, the moderate-violence ad appealed to younger consumers. Planned comparisons show that younger respondents reported significantly higher attitude toward the ad for the moderate-violence ad condition versus the low ($t = 3.26$, $p < .05$) and high ($t = 3.54$, $p < .05$) violence ads. A similar pattern of results was found for A_{firm} such that the moderate-violence ad condition resulted in higher values than the low ($t = 2.13$, $p < .05$) and high ($t = 2.81$, $p < .05$) violence ad conditions. These results suggest that while young adults may be positively aroused by a moderate level of sexualized violence in ads, middle-aged and older adults seem to display little appreciation for such ad themes.

Univariate tests indicate a significant main effect for violence on A_{ad} (H1a: $F = 6.01$, $p < .01$), but not on attitude toward the firm sponsoring the ad or on PI (H1b, H1c). Therefore, partial support is found for H1; specifically, only H1a is found to be significant. In addition, planned comparisons (modified Bonferroni procedure) were used to examine differences in each of the three ad conditions. Participants exposed to the moderate-violence ad reported significantly higher A_{ad} ($M = 2.83$) than those exposed to either the high-violence ad ($M = 2.56$; $p < .01$) or the low-violence ad ($M = 2.48$; $p < .01$). Univariate tests also reveal a gender main effect on dependent variables of A_{ad} (H2a: $F = 6.31$, $p < .01$), A_{firm} (H2b: $F = 16.03$, $p < .01$), and PI (H2c: $F = 9.21$, $p < .01$). Thus, H2 is fully supported. As expected, women reported significantly less positive evaluations than men across dependent variables of A_{ad} ($M_F = 2.39$ vs. $M_M = 2.66$), A_{firm} ($M_F = 2.14$ vs. $M_M = 2.62$), and intentions to buy ($M_F = 1.74$ vs. $M_M = 2.07$). Finally, univariate tests show a main effect for age on dependent variables A_{ad} (H3a: $F = 15.51$, $p < .01$), A_{firm} (H3b: $F = 11.52$, $p < .01$), and PI (H3c: $F = 16.69$, $p < .01$). As a result, H3 is also fully supported. In general, younger participants reported more positive evaluations of ads than older participants.

Univariate tests indicate a main effect for violent ads on the dependent variable of AIV-Sexual ($F = 5.92$, $p < .01$), giving support for H4. But contrary to expectations that the high-violence ad condition would generate the highest levels of violence acceptance, the moderate-violence ad resulted in significantly higher levels for AIV-Sexual ($M = 2.45$) than the other two advertisements (all $ps < .01$). As predicted and in support of H5 and H6, females reported lower levels of acceptance of sexualized violence than males (H5: AIV-Sexual, $M_F = 2.12$ vs. $M_M = 2.25$), and younger participants reported higher levels of acceptance than the two older groups of participants (H6: AIV-Sexual, $M_Y = 2.41$; $M_O = 2.07$).

DISCUSSION AND CONCLUSIONS

Summary of Findings

As previously mentioned, the purpose of this research is to examine the influence of sexualized violence as an advertising appeal on consumers' beliefs, attitudes, and intentions within the theoretical framework of social learning. The ads selected are from real promotional campaigns. Materials were pretested using adult subjects who responded to a variety of measures to ensure that the manipulation effects were caused by perceived violence. Three advertisements that differ significantly from one another and provided the greatest possible distinctions subsequently were chosen for the study. Traditional attitude and behavioral intentions measures common in advertising research were administered concurrent with this exposure. Measures of interpersonal violence acceptance were also included, along with some relevant demographic questions.

Our findings reveal that attitude toward the ad varied significantly across the three ad conditions, but exposure to ads with increased levels of sexualized violence did not directly influence consumers' attitudes toward the firm or behavioral intentions. Results suggest that this ad main effect is moderated by both gender and age. Female respondents reported relatively low levels of attitude toward the ad across conditions, whereas males generally held more positive responses for attitude toward the ad (as well as attitude toward the sponsor/purchase intentions). However, contrary to the linear effects articulated in H1, males' reactions to the ads are curvilinear. Parallel outcomes also occur when age is taken into account. The curvilinear pattern of results observed in the ad by gender interaction is evident in the ad × age interaction across dependent variables of attitude toward the ad, attitude toward the firm, and behavioral intentions. Finally, younger consumers generally evaluated ads more positively than the older cohorts; however, evaluations did not decrease in a progressive manner as expected across ads for the oldest subgroup.

From a societal perspective, the larger concern is whether sexualized violence as an advertising appeal affects acceptance of interpersonal violence. Consistent with SLT, results indicate that sexual aggression dimensions were influenced by viewership of the ads, but the impact was curvilinear and similar to the attitude toward the ad findings. Nevertheless, males and females responded in the same way, and their reactions are a matter of degree rather than direction, with the former more accepting of sexualized violence in comparison to the latter. Once again and as predicted, the younger respondents were more susceptible to the implicit manipulation of perspective by sexualized violence as an advertising appeal, and they demonstrated changes in acceptance consistent with attitude toward the ad reactions.

Implications for Theory and Practice

As Kilbourne aptly states: "Sex has long been used in advertising to sell just about everything—from champagne to shampoo, from chainsaws to chewing gum" (2005, p. 119). She goes on to remark that these sexualized images have become increasingly graphic over time, and their larger impact is "sexist, demeaning, and harmful to everyone," with "a cumulative effect that is profoundly anti-erotic" (Kilbourne 2005, p. 119). Yet such prognostications seem to fall mostly on deaf ears with advertisers. Even when academic research goes against conventional wisdom and suggests that use of these highly attractive and sexually enticing women produces mixed results at best, the myth of their effectiveness endures (see Bower 2001). Thus, diminution of usage in appeals to consumers is unlikely to happen, even if the only legitimate result is to attract attention without subsequent movement toward purchase. Indeed, previous scholarship clearly indicates that the emotional nature of sexual information in advertising attracts attention and directs processing resources toward the sexual stimulus rather than the brand (Reichert, Heckler, and Jackson 2001).

For the most part, our findings support these conclusions when females are considered the primary target audience (also see Lanis and Covell 1995). Women generally were unmoved in their attitudes and intentions after exposure to sexualized violence, regardless of its level and intensity. Men were more positive across the board, however, suggesting important differences that played out principally in elevated attitude toward the ad. Similar results occurred with the younger respondents who seemed more positive in their reactions when compared to their older counterparts, helping drive attitude toward the ad measures as well. Of course, the potential for a curvilinear relationship between sexualized violence and attitude toward the ad with these groups merits further exploration. Interestingly, this curvilinear pattern mirrors results found in research focused on arousal by ads (e.g., Henthorne, LaTour, and Nataraajan 1993; LaTour, Pitts, and Snook-Luther 1989). Specifically, this research suggests that sexual tension generates energy up to a certain point, and beyond that "threshold" additional increases arouse anxiety and deplete one's energy. When studies are conducted, scholars must recognize the complexities associated with arousal as described by LaTour (2006), and how such a multidimensional view modifies the traditional conceptualizations of threshold levels.

Of greater consequence perhaps is the impact of violence against women in ads on the potential for increased acceptance of such behavior. Researchers have reported as many as one-fourth of

American women and half of female college students are subjected to some form of male sexual aggression (Malamuth and Briere 1986). Recent data also reveal that images of female "pleasure" coupled with male sexual aggression trigger thought patterns that encourage violence against women, and long-term exposure to these counterintuitive beliefs leads to greater acceptance by men of their sexual harassment (Dill, Brown, and Collins 2008). Desensitization theory often is used to explain this phenomenon, suggesting that prosocial attitudes operating to empower women are pushed into the background when such antisocial behaviors dominate popular culture images (Linz, Donnerstein, and Penrod 1988), but our work reveals that SLT may provide a better framework.

Our results should cause some pause within the advertising community since they mirror, to some extent, what mass media scholars have been articulating for some time (see Donnerstein and Linz 1986). The predominant concern expressed by feminists and other interested observers is that men may perceive these images as reinforcement for violence against women (Bronstein 2008). Further, socialization of younger men into a culture of aggression (as posited by SLT) in their relationships with women elicits more apprehension because it helps perpetuate existing cycles of violence. Indeed, this investigation lends some credence to both perspectives, with men in general and younger consumers in particular finding advertisements with sexualized violence more appealing.

Although it is beyond the original purpose of our investigation to discuss all ethical and moral issues involved, it is nonetheless important to recognize the potential limits to employing sexualized violence in advertisements. Specifically, use of sexualized violence is fraught with a host of problems, including potential risks of increasing aggression toward women, of exposing viewers to materials that they find distressing, and of contributing to the desensitization and socialization of aggressive behavior. Obviously, use of this form of sexual appeal should be employed with care. Indeed, because female consumers dislike such gratuitous advertisements, reconsidering use of sexualized violence appeals may help advertisers insulate themselves from unethical missteps in the marketplace (Maciejewski 2004).

As is the case with any study, these findings must be tempered by their limitations. For example, our results are only for short-term attitudinal effects, and the design does not provide the environment necessary for a true experiment. Although this tactic was a deliberate decision made to maximize realism, future research is needed that uses more controlled environments and experimental designs. Also, another plausible explanation for our results is that in the high-violence ad condition, respondents focused relatively more attention on the violent nature of the ad as compared to the sexualized violence of the other two ad conditions. And while our sample of 484 nonstudent adults is large for an investigation of this nature, data were collected online and thus are not random. In addition, the inclusion of more than one ad per treatment could enhance the generalizability of our findings, especially if other associated factors from our pretests are relevant. Future research may address these limitations in myriad ways that extend our findings. For instance, since prior scholarship suggests that fear and shock appeals are often ineffective, even leading to an increase of the targeted behavior(s) (Hastings, Stead, and Webb 2004), any follow-up could examine this phenomenon as it pertains to public service announcements depicting violence against women.

Closing Remarks

Advertising scholars with an interest in ethics and social responsibility may seek to parcel out that portion of damage to women elicited by such promotions. Indeed, some policy-oriented research has examined this issue and raised concerns regarding its impact (see Gould 1992). Yet the oft-heard excuse that marketing strategies and tactics follow rather than lead cultural icons and myths is a poor defense for increasing the amount of advertising portraying violence against women perpetrated by men. At any rate, the evidence that sexualized appeals in advertisements have little value to essential marketing outcomes leads to the conclusion that public costs are not balanced by private gains, even among the most callous and calculating executives. Practitioners and researchers must ponder life lessons young boys and girls may discover when they regularly view images of unattainable beauty who are subjected to such physical and sexual abuse without recourse. Even assuming that the role of advertising on consumers is relatively minor, what code of conduct would support this blatant disregard?

Nonetheless, if attitudes and behaviors concerning interpersonal violence and rape are learned, then both men and women are able to "unlearn" them as well (Donnerstein and Linz 1986). Studies dating as far back as the early 1970s demonstrate that various forms of participant modeling have the capacity to change behaviors in significant ways, including the reduction of aggression among incarcerated and unincarcerated populations (see Bandura 1973). Efforts by feminist organizations, nonprofit firms, and governmental agencies to reduce the availability of these images and provide counter-programming examples are encouraging, at least in claims to their successes (Bronstein 2008). Still, the ad industry should do more than sit idly by and accept little blame for our current situation. Instead, our goal should be to provide socially appropriate role models that encourage healthy behaviors *and* increase positive responses to offerings.

NOTES

1. The means for the three age conditions are as follows: young = 32, middle = 49, and old = 62.
2. We thank the reviewers for suggesting this additional study and helping to identify potential confounding variables.

REFERENCES

Akers, Ronald L. (1977), *Deviant Behavior: A Social Learning Approach*, 2d ed., Belmont, CA: Wadsworth.

Alexander, M. Wayne, and Ben Judd, Jr. (1978), "Do Nudes in Ads Enhance Brand Recall?" *Journal of Advertising Research*, 18 (1), 47–50.

Allen, Mike, Tara Emmers, Lisa Gebhardt, and Mary A. Giery (1995), "Exposure to Pornography and Acceptance of Rape Myths," *Journal of Communication*, 45 (1), 5–25.

Anderson, Craig A., and Brad J. Bushman (2002), "The Effects of Media Violence on Society," *Science*, 295 (5564), 2377–2379.

———, Leonard Berkowitz, Edward Donnerstein, L. Rowell Huesmann, James D. Johnson, Daniel Linz, Neil M. Malamuth, and Ellen Wartella (2003), "The Influence of Media Violence on Youth," *Psychological Science in the Public Interest*, 4 (3), 81–110.

Andersson, Svante, Anna Hedelin, Anna Nilsson, and Charlotte Welander (2004), "Violent Advertising in Fashion Marketing," *Journal of Fashion Marketing and Management*, 8 (1), 96–112.

Andrews, J. Craig, and Thomas J. Maronick (1995), "Advertising Research Issues from FTC Versus Stouffer Foods Corporation," *Journal of Public Policy and Marketing*, 14 (2), 301–309.

Bandura, Albert (1965), "Influence of Models' Reinforcement Contingencies on the Acquisition of Imitative Responses," *Journal of Personality and Social Psychology*, 1 (6), 589–595.

——— (1973), *Aggression: A Social Learning Analysis*, Englewood Cliffs, NJ: Prentice Hall.

——— (1977), *Social Learning Theory*, Englewood Cliffs, NJ: Prentice Hall.

——— (1986), *Social Foundations of Thought and Action: A Social Cognitive Theory*, Englewood Cliffs, NJ: Prentice Hall.

Basile, Kathleen C., and Linda E. Saltzman (2009), "Sexual Violence Surveillance: Uniform Definitions and Recommended Data Elements," Centers for Disease Control and Prevention, National Center for Injury Prevention and Control, Atlanta, available at www.cdc.gov/ViolencePrevention/pub/SV_surveillance.html (accessed October 2, 2010).

Benokraitis, Nijole, and Joe Feagin (1995), *Modern Sexism: Blatant, Subtle, and Covert Discrimination*, 2d ed., Englewood Cliffs, NJ: Prentice Hall.

Boddewyn, Jean J., and Heidi Kunz (1991), "Sex and Decency Issues in Advertising: General and International Dimensions," *Business Horizons*, 34 (5), 13–20.
Bower, Amanda (2001), "Highly Attractive Models in Advertising and the Women Who Loathe Them: The Implementations of Negative Affect for Spokesperson Effectiveness," *Journal of Advertising*, 30 (3), 51–63.
Bronstein, Carolyn (2008), "No More Black and Blue: Women Against Violence Against Women and the Warner Communications Boycott," *Violence Against Women*, 14 (4), 418–436.
Burt, Martha R. (1980), "Cultural Myths and Supports for Rape," *Journal of Personality and Social Psychology*, 38 (2), 217–230.
———, and R. Albin (1981), "Rape Myths, Rape Definitions, and Probability of Conviction," *Journal of Applied Social Psychology*, 11 (3), 212–230.
Bushman, Brad J. (2005), "Violence and Sex in Television Programs: Do Not Sell Products in Advertisements," *Psychological Science*, 16 (9), 702–708.
———, and Angelica M. Bonacci (2002), "Violence and Sex Impair Memory for Television Ads," *Journal of Applied Psychology*, 87 (3), 557–563.
———, and Colleen M. Phillips (2001), "If the Television Program Bleeds, Memory for the Advertisement Recedes," *Current Directions in Psychological Science*, 10 (2), 44–47.
Dahl, Darren W., Kristina D. Frankenberger, and Rajesh V. Manchanda (2003), "Does It Pay to Shock? Reactions to Shocking and Nonshocking Advertising Content Among University Students," *Journal of Advertising Research*, 43 (3), 268–280.
Dill, Karen E., Brian P. Brown, and Michael A. Collins (2008), "Effects of Exposure to Sex-Stereotyped Video Game Characters on Tolerance of Sexual Harassment," *Journal of Experimental Social Psychology*, 44 (5), 1402–1408.
Donnerstein, Edward, and Daniel Linz (1986), "Mass Media Sexual Violence and Male Viewers: Current Theory and Research," *American Behavioral Scientist*, 29 (5), 601–618.
Ford, John B., and Michael S. LaTour (1993), "Differing Reactions to Female Role Portrayals in Advertising," *Journal of Advertising Research*, 33 (5), 43–52.
Gould, Stephen J. (1992), "The Production, Marketing, and Consumption of Sexually Explicit Material in Our Sexually Conflicted Society: A Public Policy Dilemma," *Journal of Public Policy and Marketing*, 11 (2), 135–148.
Gunter, Barrie, Adrian Furnham, and Eleni Pappa (2005), "Effects of Television Violence on Memory for Violent and Nonviolent Advertising," *Journal of Applied Social Psychology*, 35 (8), 1680–1697.
Haridakis, Paul M. (2006), "Men, Women, and Televised Violence: Predicting Viewer Aggression in Males and Female Television Viewers," *Communication Quarterly*, 54 (2), 227–255.
Harris, Mary B. (1996), "Aggressive Experiences and Aggressiveness: Relationship to Ethnicity, Gender, and Age," *Journal of Applied Social Psychology*, 26 (10), 843–870.
Hastings, Gerard, Martine Stead, and John Webb (2004), "Fear Appeals in Social Marketing: Strategic and Ethical Reasons for Concern," *Psychology and Marketing*, 21 (11), 961–986.
Henthorne, Tony L., Michael S. LaTour, and Rajan Nataraajan (1993), "Fear Appeals in Print Advertising: An Analysis of Arousal and Ad Response," *Journal of Advertising*, 22 (2), 59–69.
Huesman, L. Rowell (1986), "Psychological Processes Promoting the Relation Between Exposure to Media Violence and Aggressive Behavior by the Viewer," *Journal of Social Issues*, 42 (3), 125–139.
Kilbourne, Jean (2005), "What Else Does Sex Sell?" *International Journal of Advertising*, 24 (1), 119–122.
Lah, Kyung (2010), "RapeLay Video Game Goes Viral Amid Outrage," CNN.com, March 30, available at http://articles.cnn.com/2010-03-30/world/japan.video.game.rape_1_game-teenage-girl-japanese-government?_s=PM:WORLD/ (accessed April 8, 2010).
Lanis, Kyra, and Katherine Covell (1995), "Images of Women in Advertisements: Effects on Attitudes Related to Sexual Aggression," *Sex Roles*, 32 (9/10), 639–649.
LaTour, Michael S. (2006), "Retrospective and Prospective Views of 'Fear Arousal' in 'Fear Appeals,'" *International Journal of Advertising*, 25 (3), 409–413.
———, and Tony L. Henthorne (1994), "Ethical Judgments of Sexual Appeals in Print Advertising," *Journal of Advertising*, 23 (3), 81–90.
———, Robert E. Pitts, and David C. Snook-Luther (1989), "Female Nudity, Arousal, and Ad Response: An Experimental Investigation," *Journal of Advertising*, 19 (4), 51–62.
Lee, Yih Hwai (2000), "Manipulating Ad Message Involvement Through Information Expectancy: Effects on Attitude Evaluation and Confidence," *Journal of Advertising*, 29 (2), 29–43.
Liebert, Robert M., John M. Neale, and Emily S. Davidson (1973), *The Early Window: Effects of Television on Children and Youth*, New York: Pergamon Press.

Linz, Daniel G., Edward Donnerstein, and Steven Penrod (1988), "Effects of Long-Term Exposure to Violent and Sexually Degrading Depictions of Women," *Journal of Personality and Social Psychology*, 55 (5), 758–768.

Lohse, Gerald L., and Dennis L. Rosen (2001), "Signaling Quality and Credibility in Yellow Pages Advertising: The Influence of Color and Graphics on Choice," *Journal of Advertising*, 30 (2), 73–85.

Lukas, Scott A. (2009), "The Gender Ads Project," available at www.genderads.com (accessed December 20, 2009).

Maciejewski, Jeffrey J. (2004), "Is the Use of Sexual and Fear Appeals Ethical? A Moral Evaluation by Generation Y College Students," *Journal of Current Issues and Research in Advertising*, 26 (2), 97–105.

MacKenzie, Scott B., and Richard J. Lutz (1989), "An Empirical Examination of the Structural Antecedents of Attitude Toward the Ad in Advertising Pretesting Context," *Journal of Marketing*, 53 (2), 48–65.

Malamuth, Neil A., and John Briere (1986), "Sexual Violence in the Media: Indirect Effect of Aggression on Women," *Journal of Social Issues*, 42 (3), 75–92.

———, and James V. P. Check (1981), "The Effects of Mass Media Exposure on Acceptance of Violence Against Women: A Field Experiment," *Journal of Research in Personality*, 15 (4), 436–446.

Maronick, Thomas J. (1991), "Copy Tests in FTC Deception Cases: Guidelines for Researchers," *Journal of Advertising Research*, 31 (6), 9–17.

McDaniel, Stephen R., Choonghoon Lim, and Joseph E. Mahan, III (2007), "The Role of Gender and Personality Traits in Response to Ads Using Violent Images to Promote Consumption of Sports Entertainment," *Journal of Business Research*, 60 (6), 606–612.

Meuhling, Darrel D. (1987), "Comparative Advertising: The Influence of Attitude-Toward-the-Brand on Brand Evaluation," *Journal of Advertising*, 16 (4), 43–49.

Reichert, Tom, Susan E. Heckler, and Sally Jackson (2001), "The Effects of Sexual Social Marketing Appeals on Cognitive Processing and Persuasion," *Journal of Advertising*, 30 (1), 13–27.

———, Michael S. LaTour, and JooYoung Kim (2007), "Assessing the Influence of Gender and Sexual Self-Schema on Affective Responses to Sexual Content in Advertising," *Journal of Current Issues and Research in Advertising*, 29 (2), 63–77.

———,———, Jacqueline J. Lambaise, and Mark Adkins (2007), "A Test of Media Literacy Effects and Sexual Objectification in Advertising," *Journal of Current Issues and Research in Advertising*, 29 (1), 81–92.

———, Jacqueline Lambiase, Susan Morgan, Meta Carstarphen, and Susan Zavoina (1999), "Cheesecake and Beefcake: No Matter How You Slice It, Sexual Explicitness in Advertising Continues to Increase," *Journal of Mass Communication Quarterly*, 76 (Spring), 7–20.

Soley, Lawrence C., and Gary Kurzbard (1986), "Sex in Advertising: A Comparison of 1964 and 1984 Magazine Advertisements," *Journal of Advertising*, 15 (3), 46–54.

Walker, William D., Robert C. Rowe, and Vernon L. Quinsey (1993), "Authoritarianism and Sexual Aggression," *Journal of Personality and Social Psychology*, 65 (5), 1036–1045.

Wolf, Naomi (1991), *The Beauty Myth: How Images of Beauty Are Used Against Women*, New York: Doubleday.

Woodruff, Katie (1996), "Alcohol Advertising and Violence Against Women: A Media Advocacy Case Study," *Health Education Quarterly*, 23 (3), 330–345.

Appendix 7.1

Appendix 7.1a

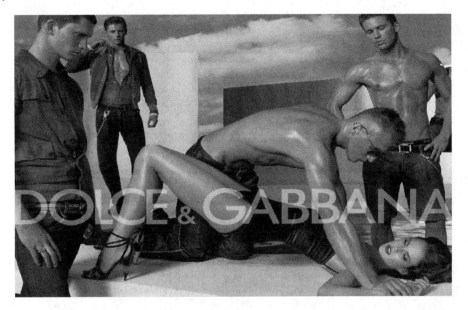

Low-Violence Ad (Based on Pilot Test Results)

Appendix 7.1b

Moderate-Violence Ad

Appendix 7.1c

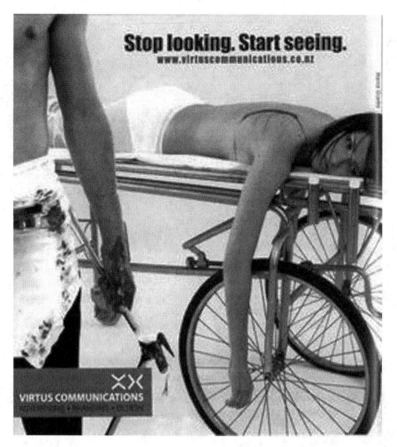

High-Violence Ad

PART IV

EFFECTS OF VIOLENCE IN ADVERTISING

8

The Role of Dominance in the Appeal of Violent Media Depictions

Laurence Ashworth, Martin Pyle, and Ethan Pancer

Existing work on violent media content has focused almost exclusively on the *consequences* of exposure. There appears to be a reasonable consensus in the literature that exposure to violent depictions increases aggressive tendencies in viewers. Much recent research has, in consequence, turned to identifying the psychological mechanisms by which exposure to violent media affects aggression. In addition to contributing to basic knowledge about the causes of aggressive behavior, this approach has clearly been motivated by concerns about societal welfare, with frequent calls to limit or otherwise regulate violent content. Nevertheless, violent media is extremely popular—Grand Theft Auto 4, for example, an intensely violent, action-adventure game, recently broke all entertainment records for first-day sales ($310 million) and first-week sales (over $500 million) (Ortutay 2008). Research has largely ignored this phenomenon, focusing on the consequences of *exposure* rather than the *appeal* of violent media. The purpose of the current work, then, is to investigate why violent media may be appealing. In addition to contributing to our understanding of this phenomenon, such an approach may help inform attempts at balancing marketing interests in the creation of violent media and societal concerns about the consequences.

The starting point for the current work is that violent media content often involves depictions of physical domination. Based on research in evolutionary psychology and work on fundamental human motivations, we argue there are likely intrinsic rewards associated with physical domination, especially in men. In the context of interactive media, such as video games, consumers experience domination directly, as they battle, and presumably at some point defeat, opponents in the game. We also argue, however, that consumers can react in a similar manner to the simple *portrayal* of domination, such as that found in the noninteractive media of television, film, and even print. It is this possibility that we explore in the current work. In short, we argue that reactions to domination, whether directly experienced or simply portrayed, provide one basis for the appeal of violence in media. We examine this basic proposition across two experiments and develop a series of additional hypotheses relating to the scope of this effect.

Our experiments are conducted in the context of advertisements for video games. Video games frequently feature violent content, and the advertisements for such games provide one context where we can study reactions to the *portrayal* of violence and domination rather than its direct experience. Furthermore, the use of advertisements for video games allowed us to manipulate domination and various hypothesized moderators while controlling the level of violence and other factors, such as perceived competence, that would be difficult to hold constant during actual gameplay.

BACKGROUND

Popularity of Violent Media and Violent Video Games

Exposure to violent media content is widespread in North America and, indeed, in much of the developed world. In the United States, the average person watches approximately four hours of television each day (Nielsen Media Research 2006), 70% of which contains violent content (Federman 1998). In addition to the violence portrayed on television, many individuals are now exposed to violence in the form of video games. Sixty-eight percent of U.S. households now play video games (Entertainment Software Association 2009), and games with *advertised* violent content account for nearly 40% of all sales—content analyses suggest the actual percentage is much higher (Haninger and Thompson 2004). In short, exposure to graphic portrayals of violence is endemic in North American society.

Consequences of Exposure to Violent Media

For more than 50 years, researchers have explored the consequences of exposure to violent acts (e.g., Bandura 1961; Eron et al. 1972). Since that time, a sizeable body of literature has amassed, documenting a variety of undesirable psychological and behavioral consequences of exposure to violent television and film. Most of this research has focused on the impact of violent media on aggression in one form or another (for reviews, see Bushman and Anderson 2001; Murray 2008; Paik and Comstock 1994). Despite some suggestions to the contrary (e.g., Savage and Yancey 2008), there appears to be substantial consensus that exposure to portrayals of violent acts increases the likelihood of aggressive thoughts and behaviors and decreases physiological arousal (i.e., desensitizes individuals to violent behavior) (e.g., Carnagey, Anderson, and Bushman 2007). As the popularity of video games has soared (unit sales have doubled in the past decade, compared to relatively static film consumption), researchers' attention has turned to the effects of violent video games. Recent reviews document similar findings—playing violent video games increases aggression, desensitizes players to violent acts, and has been shown to decrease helping behaviors (Anderson and Bushman 2001; Huesmann 2007).

Regulation of Violent Media

Despite the abundance of research demonstrating the repercussions of exposure to violent media, regulation (at least in the United States) has been fraught with difficulty, in part because of the strict scrutiny standards associated with any limitations on First Amendment rights (Collier, Liddell, and Liddell 2008). For all practical purposes, then, there is very little preventing individuals from being frequently exposed to graphic portrayals of violence—whether that be a deliberate consumption choice or incidental exposure. One of the barriers to effective regulation and, indeed, attitude change in the public domain stems from apparent misgivings regarding evidence for the causal link between violent media exposure and aggression (Bushman and Anderson 2001; Collier, Liddell, and Liddell 2008). While research has repeatedly demonstrated this link, it is not clear that exposure to violent media leads to *criminal behavior* (Savage and Yancey 2008), something that would have to be demonstrated to meet the requirements of the strict scrutiny standard (Collier, Liddell, and Liddell 2008). Nevertheless, increases in aggressive tendencies alone seem to provide sufficient cause for concern, regardless of whether such tendencies have been causally related to *criminal* violence. Consequently, much of the theory development in this area has focused on identifying the mechanisms by which violent portrayals impact viewers' psychological state and, consequently, their behavior.

Mechanisms by Which Exposure to Violent Media Causes Aggression

In the short term, violent media can function to prime existing aggression-related schemata (Huesmann 2007). Once activated, these knowledge structures can influence expectations (Bushman and Anderson 2002); attributions of others' and individuals' own behavior (Uhlmann and Swanson 2004); and, most important, in the case of aggression, chosen courses of behavior and responses to provocation (Anderson and Dill 2000). In the longer run, repeated exposure to violent portrayals can strengthen and expand those very cognitive structures—including beliefs about social norms—increasing the likelihood that they will be applied to everyday behavior (Huesmann and Guerra 1997). In young children, witnessed violent acts may also be mimicked (Bandura 1961)—a symptom of a rather general form of learning in human and primate neonates (Meltzoff and Moore 2002).

Other work has emphasized the role of excitation, or arousal, in aggressive behavior (Zillmann 1998). Consistent with this perspective, much of the research looking at the effects of exposure to violent media has examined arousal—as both a consequence and a mediator of behavior. As a consequence, the physiological arousal elicited by violent portrayals can decrease with repeated exposure (desensitization), which can lower perceptions of the severity of violent acts, increase blame on victims, and reduce helping behaviors (Carnagey, Anderson, and Bushman 2007; Linz, Donnerstein, and Adams 1989). As a mediator, arousal from violent media exposure can transfer to other contexts, increasing the likelihood of "hostile" or "affective" aggression (in contrast to "instrumental" aggression, characterized by forethought, a lack of affect or arousal, and the pursuit of some other goal) (Bushman and Anderson 2001).

Many of these ideas are integrated in the General Aggression Model (GAM) (Bushman and Anderson 2002). According to the GAM, exposure to violent media can prime existing aggressive schemata, induce an angry affective state, and increase arousal. The impact of each on social interaction (where any aggression would ultimately be enacted), however, is determined by a combination of automatic appraisals and controlled, effortful reappraisals. Furthermore, the model suggests that each violent exposure contributes to the development and accessibility of hostile knowledge structures, with sufficient exposures ultimately contributing to the development of an aggressive personality.

MOTIVATION FOR THE CURRENT WORK

Existing work on media violence has focused almost exclusively on the consequences of exposure. While the consequences are clearly important, understanding the reasons for its appeal in the first place is an important step in the development of theory that is likely to have implications for marketers and regulators alike. As Zillmann pointed out, "social psychologists and others have investigated the antisocial consequences of exposure to fictional violence . . . [b]ut they have essentially bypassed the issue of the appeal of fictional and nonfictional violence as a salient element of entertainment," and "theories that might explain the extraordinary appeal of portrayals in question and the empirical exploration of this appeal have been neglected" (1998, p. 181). Consequently, the current work represents an initial attempt to develop and test a simple model of the appeal of violent portrayals.

Why Is Violent Media Appealing?

Although there is a paucity of research in this area, there have been a number of arguments that speak to the appeal of violence. Some of these arguments relate to reasons for *engaging* in violence, whereas others are more relevant to the current context—the appeal of violent *depictions*.

Baumeister and Campbell (1999), for instance, tackled the problem of how people may come to enjoy "evil acts"—acts that engender gross harm to others. Two of their explanations seem particularly relevant to the context of witnessing violent portrayals: sadism—enjoyment of others' suffering, and sensation seeking—attempts to experience extreme physiological arousal. While true sadistic pleasure appears to be a rare phenomenon (e.g., Toch 1993), there is some support for the role of sensation seeking in the appeal of violent media (Hoffner and Levine 2005). Along these lines, Jansz (2005) argued that one of the reasons violent games are so popular with adolescent males is because such games allow them to experience a variety of emotions, including socially sanctioned emotions and those that may help sustain a dominant masculine identity. Consistent with this last point, Zillmann et al. (1986) showed that viewing violent films allowed men to portray their mastery of fear while at the same time allowing women to appear helpless, in attempts to bolster their respective attractiveness. Zillmann (1998) has also provided another explanation for why violence can be appealing, specifically, when moral circumstances dictate that a transgressor *should* be punished—that is, when the violence is justified.

What these explanations have in common is that they suggest that the appeal of violent media is not in the violence per se, but rather in its ability to satisfy some other set of needs, such as impression management, sensation seeking, or justice. In fact, Zillmann (1998) has even argued that witnessing violence is actually distressing, and is *only* satisfying when it does something else for the viewer. Research that has directly manipulated violent content appears to be consistent with this proposition. Sparks, Sherry, and Lubsen (2005), for instance, found that viewers enjoyed a popular movie no less after all violent content had been edited out, and Hansen and Hansen (1990) found that increasing levels of violence in a rock music video actually lowered the appeal of the video.

The Role of Dominance in the Appeal of Violent Media

Consistent with the notion that violence can facilitate the satisfaction of certain other needs, rather than appeal itself, we argue that one important reason for the appeal of violence is in its ability to convey the domination of one party by another. That is, the domination inherent to many violent portrayals is one element of their appeal. Violence in media has been defined as depictions of the intentional harm of one individual by another (Anderson and Bushman 2001). While violence does not necessarily imply domination, violent acts typically resolve when one party successfully suppresses the other, and the successful suppression of another—whether forcibly, as in a violent encounter, or nonviolently, as a consequence of the others' submission—is what is at the heart of domination. It is this aspect of violence that we argue is innately appealing.

For much of human evolutionary history, the ability to physically dominate other members of the species has afforded individuals certain survival and reproductive advantages (Cummins 1996). In consequence, the motivation and ability to dominate others should lead to fitness advantages that increase the prevalence of relevant physical and psychological phenotypes. The consequences of such selection on physical characteristics are obvious in the sexual dimorphism that exists between male and female humans (and, indeed, many other nonhuman species) (Cummins 1996). Males are larger and stronger, due to a combination of competition within males for access to resources and females (*intra*sexual selection), and preferential selection by females for such characteristics (*inter*sexual selection) (Buss 1988). That does not mean that the ability to dominate in some form cannot be rewarding to females, but certainly there appears to have been less selection pressure on traits related to *physical* domination. Similarly, there should be corresponding psychological characteristics that provide an accompanying motivation to dominate. Consistent with the operation of most psychological needs, this suggests that domination is likely to be intrinsically rewarding (McClelland 1985). In the context of *physical* domination, the same differential selection pressures that have resulted in discrepant physical morphology would suggest that men are also more likely than women to find physical domination intrinsically rewarding—a notion we explore in our first experiment.

Reactions to Domination in Violent Media

Video games are somewhat unique among popular media in that they allow the consumer direct experience of depicted events. Violent acts are enacted by or upon the player, and it is consumers themselves who dominate or are dominated by other characters in the game. As such, enjoyment (or frustration) is assumed to stem directly from the actions and experience of the gamer. This is consistent with Ryan, Rigby, and Przybylski's (2006) supposition that video games are appealing because they satisfy a variety of specific psychological needs: autonomy (personal freedom and control), competence (challenge and self-efficacy), and relatedness (connection with others). Especially in the context of violent video games, we would add dominance to that list.

In other media, however, the consumer is a mere witness to the violence and other experiences of the characters at hand, and therefore any reactions based on the experiences of those individuals, including domination, are necessarily vicarious. This raises the question of whether viewers are likely to experience similar reactions to the domination of one character by another, as they might to the dominance they experience during video game play. The simple answer is that we believe they can. Viewing media can induce strong emotions—we feel terror at the impending harm about to befall an otherwise expendable character, we rejoice at the victories of our heroes, we take satisfaction in violent retribution imposed on the villain, and we cry when long-lost love interests reunite. Zillmann (1998) referred to this as the "witness perspective," and the basic idea is that viewers can, under certain conditions, experience the same reactions to the fictional portrayal of characters as they would to nonfictional persons.

In short, while there are clear differences between the experience of playing a video game and the experience of viewing noninteractive media, both are capable of inspiring reactions to the depicted content. Thus, the simple portrayal of physical domination in violent media should be capable of inspiring similar reactions to the actual domination consumers might experience in violent video games or otherwise. The current work focuses exclusively on consumer reactions to *portrayals* of violence and domination. We also examine a number of conditions that we believe are likely to serve as important moderators in this context. We explore these next.

Moderation of Reactions to Depictions of Violent Domination

Any reaction to the experiences of fictional characters, especially in the context of noninteractive media, likely depends on the extent to which consumers are involved with the media and the characters within. One factor likely to impact involvement is the extent to which the consumer identifies with the chief protagonist. Identification is an important factor in other vicarious reactions, such as basking in reflected glory (Cialdini et al. 1976). Moreover, it is consistent with Zillmann's (1998) proposition that the development of a nonneutral "disposition" toward characters (i.e., positive or negative feelings) is necessary for vicarious reactions to their experiences. Zillmann further argued that the valence of this disposition moderates consumers' vicarious reactions: positive character experiences (such as successfully dominating other characters) should inspire positive reactions in consumers when they foster positive dispositions toward that character but negative reactions when consumers foster negative dispositions. Similarly, negative character experiences, such as violent injury, will inspire negative reactions when the character is liked and positive reactions when that character is disliked (e.g., retribution for past wrongdoings). Note that only two of these four combinations should be gratifying—good things happening to the characters we support or identify with and bad things happening to those we vilify. In the current context, we focus on characters we believe the viewer will generally support as the protagonist. However, we do examine the role of identification as a potential moderator to consumers' vicarious reactions to the protagonist's dominance.

A second important moderating influence on reactions to the dominative content of violent media depictions stems from factors likely to influence the appeal of the domination itself. First, there are social norms that *proscribe* certain acts of domination and, in consequence, likely limit the appeal of such acts. Second, domination that does not elevate, or at least maintain, an individual's position within the relevant status hierarchy should be relatively less rewarding. It should be noted that these factors are likely closely related—gratuitous domination (domination that does not elevate or maintain status) is also less likely to be socially tolerated. Nevertheless, domination should be most appealing when it is meaningful, in terms of an individual's position within the status hierarchy, and is not in violation of relevant social norms of acceptable behavior. Domination of others who clearly pose no threat to an individuals' position would be an example of domination that is both irrelevant to the dominator's status and likely to be normatively unacceptable. We would therefore expect depictions of such domination to be less appealing than depictions of meaningful, normatively acceptable domination. In the context of violent video games, this could occur when a powerful character in the game dominates clearly weaker opponents or nonthreatening characters in the game.

One important implication of this reasoning is that the same dominative behavior may be more or less satisfying depending on the extent to which the domination is deemed meaningful and socially acceptable. We posit that individuals who are frequently exposed to violent video games possess quite different standards about what constitutes acceptable domination relative to individuals who have not been exposed to this media to the same extent. Frequent gamers are more likely to have a well-developed sense of the nature of video gameplay. They are more likely to understand the features that are common to a particular genre, and, over time, such features are likely to become accepted. Consistent with this idea, there is evidence that norms of acceptable behavior spontaneously develop in online gaming communities (Blanchard 2007), and, more generally, behavior that is commonly engaged in tends to become accepted as an appropriate norm for the way people should behave in particular situations (Cialdini, Reno, and Kallgren 1990). As such, we expect frequent gamers to be more likely to apply a different set of norms to the gaming environment than nongamers. These norms should reflect features that are common to particular genres of game. In violent video games, it is often the case that gamers can, typically without penalty and sometimes with reward, kill or otherwise dominate *all* other in-game characters. In other words, domination of much weaker opponents is likely to be accepted, and even condoned, in a gaming environment. In contrast, in the absence of gaming-specific norms, nongamers are more likely to apply the same normative standards they would when evaluating nonfictional behavior. This suggests that depictions of domination that would be deemed socially unacceptable by nongamers may well be deemed acceptable by, and therefore be more appealing to, gamers. We test this prediction in the second study.

The Current Context

As noted, we examine our predictions in the context of advertisements for violent video games. We believe that the experience of domination is a powerful motivation for playing such games. However, the domination experienced in most violent video games is direct, and it is not clear whether reactions in this context would generalize to reactions to *depictions* of domination as might be portrayed in other, noninteractive media. By examining *advertisements* for violent games, we can examine the role of domination in a context where it is both ecologically valid and relevant to depictions of violence more generally.

SUMMARY OF PREDICTIONS

More formally, we make the following predictions:

H1: *Advertisements for violent video games that depict domination by the protagonist will lead to more favorable evaluations of the game and the advertisement than when the protagonist is dominated.*
H2: *The effect of H1 will be mediated by positive arousal.*
H3: *The effects of H1 will be stronger for men than for women due to differences in the extent to which domination is intrinsically rewarding.*
H4: *The effects of H1 will be moderated by the extent to which the consumer identifies with the protagonist. This should be most apparent within men due to the effects of H3 (i.e., a three-way interaction between domination, gender, and identification).*
H5: *Violent depictions that involve the domination of nonthreatening individuals will lead to less favorable reactions toward the game than domination of threatening individuals.*
H6: *The effect of H5 will be moderated by gaming frequency such that nongamers will react to the domination of nonthreatening individuals more negatively than gamers.*

EXPERIMENT 1

The purpose of the current experiment was to examine our basic proposition that portrayals of domination in violent media are one reason for their appeal. To do this, we created an advertisement for a soon-to-be released violent video game, Resident Evil 5, by editing sequences of high-definition teaser trailers, cut-scenes (short clips presented between gameplay), and actual gameplay footage. This is typical of the way in which games of this sort are advertised. We chose Resident Evil 5 for several reasons: first, it had not yet been released, meaning it was unlikely any of our participants would have played the game prior to the current experiment; second, the game is violent—it involves graphic portrayals of violence against humans, animals, and various "undead" creatures; third, clips of cut-scenes and gameplay that were available to us showed a large variance in the extent to which the protagonists were able to successfully dominate their opponents, which meant there was sufficient footage to create both high- and low-dominance advertisements; finally, the game has both a male and female protagonist, which meant we could manipulate the depicted protagonist's gender—our operationalization of identification—in the created advertisements.

Method

One hundred thirty-seven undergraduate students participated in return for credit toward their course. The experiment was a 2 (Protagonist Dominance: high vs. low) × 2 (Protagonist Gender) × 2 (Subject Gender) between-subjects factorial design. To test H1, domination was manipulated by creating sequences that showed situations where the protagonist was largely defeating his or her foes in one case (high dominance), and sequences where the protagonist was repeatedly suffering at the hands of those same foes (low dominance). We also manipulated the gender of the protagonist. This manipulation was designed to affect viewers' identification with the protagonist via perceived similarity, providing a test of H4. Together, these manipulations resulted in four different versions of the advertisement for the game. Each advertisement was three and a half minutes in length (longer than the typical television advertisement, but comparable in length to the full-length version of game and movie advertisements), used the same music sequence, and contained comparable levels of blood, gore, and violence.

Procedure

Participants were first briefed that they were going to watch an advertisement for an upcoming video game and would then be asked a series of questions regarding their impression of the game. Participants were told that the advertisement was for Resident Evil 5, a survival-horror, third-person shooter game. They were also told that the advertisement contained graphic portrayals of violence and that they could choose to participate in an alternative study if they wanted (no participants chose this option). Participants were then ushered into a room in groups of 8 to 36 participants, randomly shown one of the four advertisements on a large screen at the front of the room, and then directed to complete the questionnaire online using their personal computer.

Measures

All the items were measured using six-point agreement scales, where the points were labeled "strongly disagree," "disagree," "slightly disagree," "slightly agree," "agree," and "strongly agree" unless otherwise indicated. Participants first completed a six-item measure of their attitude toward the game (sample items include "I feel very positively toward this game" and "This game looks as though it would be good"). They then completed a three-item measure of their attitude toward the advertisement (sample items include "I did *not* enjoy watching this clip" (reverse scored) and "I feel very positively toward the clip"). Participants also completed a three-item measure of affective arousal (they rated the extent to which the clip made them feel excited, enthusiastic, and pumped), embedded in a 27-item affect inventory (items were rated on 6-point scales from "not at all" to "very much so"). Finally, participants completed measures of the domination and violence depicted in the clip as well as measures of the implied levels of autonomy and competence in the game to ensure that these aspects did not vary as a function of the experimental manipulations.

Results

Preliminary Analyses

An analysis of variance (ANOVA) performed on character domination showed that the dominance manipulation had the intended effect, $Ms = 5.07$ versus 4.02; $F(1, 129) = 43.62, p < .001$. There were no effects of the experimental manipulations on perceptions of violence, in-game autonomy, or competence ($ps > .10$).

Primary Analyses

ANOVAs performed on attitude toward the game revealed a significant main effect of Subject Gender and Protagonist Gender, $Fs(1, 129) = 28.27$ and 4.16, $ps < .001$ and $< .05$, respectively. These indicated that men's attitudes were, overall, more positive toward the game than those of women, ($Ms = 3.82$ vs. 2.73), and that attitudes toward the game were more positive when the protagonist was male ($Ms = 3.49$ vs. 3.07). These effects were qualified, however, by significant Protagonist Dominance × Subject Gender and Protagonist Gender × Subject Gender interactions,

Figure 8.1 **The Effect of Level of Domination Depicted in an Advertisement for a Violent Video Game on Attitude Toward the Game for Men and Women** (Study 1)

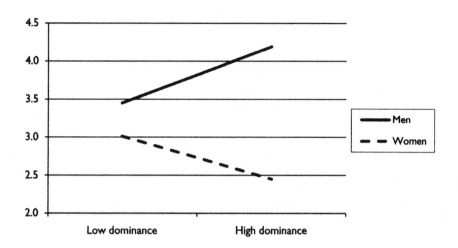

$F(1, 129) = 10.06$ and 10.98, $ps < .01$, respectively. In the first case, follow-up analyses showed that high Protagonist Dominance increased liking of the game for men, $Ms = 4.19$ versus 3.45; $F(1, 129) = 5.82$, $p < .05$, and actually decreased liking for women, $Ms = 2.45$ versus 3.01; $F(1, 129) = 4.24$, $p < .05$, consistent with H3 (Figure 8.1). Follow-up analyses to the Protagonist Gender × Subject Gender interaction showed that men preferred the game when it portrayed a male protagonist (irrespective of Protagonist Dominance), $Ms = 4.37$ versus 3.27; $F(1, 129) = 12.94$, $p < .001$, while women showed no preference ($F < 1$). One of the predictions of the current work was that men in particular should find Protagonist Dominance most appealing when they identify with that character (H4) (i.e., when Protagonist Gender was male). Although the three-way interaction was not significant ($F < 1$), we conducted a more focused contrast analysis to investigate this hypothesis specifically. This showed that the effect of Protagonist Dominance was significant for men when the protagonist was male, $Ms = 4.79$ versus 3.94, $t(59) = 2.24$, $p = .028$, but not female ($p > .15$), consistent with the idea that to be appealing, depicted domination requires identification with the protagonist (H4).

Attitudes toward the advertisement showed the same main effects of Subject Gender and Protagonist Gender, $Fs(1, 127) = 25.87$ and 6.56, $ps < .001$ and $< .05$, respectively, but only the Protagonist Dominance × Subject Gender interaction was significant, $F(1, 127) = 9.40$, $p < .01$. Follow-up analyses showed the same pattern of results as attitude toward the game—men preferred the advertisement when the protagonist dominated, $Ms = 4.21$ versus 3.61; $F(1, 127) = 4.23$, $p < .05$, while women liked the advertisement less under these conditions, $Ms = 2.63$ versus 3.22; $F(1, 127) = 5.29$, $p < .05$.

An ANOVA on the affective arousal measure showed a significant main effect of Subject Gender, $F(1, 129) = 28.72$, $p < .001$, which indicated men were more positively aroused by the advertisement than women ($Ms = 3.75$ vs. 2.59). This was qualified by significant Protagonist Dominance × Subject Gender and Protagonist Gender × Subject Gender interactions, $F(1, 129) = 12.08$ and 7.19, $ps < .01$, respectively. In the first instance, follow-up analyses showed that men were more positively aroused when Protagonist Dominance was high than when it was low, $Ms = 4.12$ versus 3.38; $F(1, 129) = 5.15$, $p < .05$, while women experienced the opposite reactions, $Ms = 2.20$ versus 2.97; $F(1, 129) = 7.15$, $p < .01$. Follow-up analyses to the Protagonist Gender Subject Gender interaction showed a marginally significant increase in positive arousal for men when the protagonist was male versus female, $Ms = 4.04$ versus 3.45, $F(1, 129) = 3.32$, $p = .071$, and the opposite effect for women, that is, a decreased positive arousal with a male protagonist; $Ms = 2.30$ versus 2.87; $F(1, 129) = 3.93$, $p < .05$.

Mediation Analyses

Separate mediation analyses were conducted for men and women to examine the role of positive arousal in the effect of Protagonist Dominance and Protagonist Gender on attitude toward the game and ad. Consistent with the ANOVA results, a regression within men showed that the independent variables (Protagonist Dominance and Protagonist Gender) predicted the dependent variables (attitude toward the game: $\beta s = .30$ and $.45$, $ps < .05$ and $< .01$; and attitude toward the ad: $\beta s = .25$ and $.37$, $ps < .05$ and $< .01$) and the hypothesized mediator variable (positive arousal: $\beta s = .31$ and $.26$, $ps < .05$). When both independent variables and the hypothesized mediator were used to predict each attitude measure, the mediator variable positively predicted each attitude measure ($\beta s = .57$ and $.54$, $ps < .001$) as did Protagonist Gender ($\beta s = .30$ and $.25$, $ps < .01$ and $< .05$), while the effect of Protagonist Dominance was no longer significant in either case ($\beta = .12$ and $.10$, $ps > .20$). Together these results suggest that, for men, positive arousal mediated the effect of Protagonist Dominance, but not Protagonist Gender, on attitudes, consistent with H2.

For women, regression analyses, consistent with the initial ANOVA, showed that Protagonist Domination, but not Protagonist Gender, predicted the dependent variables (attitude toward game: $\beta s = -.24$ and $-.11$, $ps < .05$ and $> .30$; attitude toward ad: $\beta s = -.26$ and $-.06$, $ps < .05$ and $> .60$). Protagonist Domination also predicted the hypothesized mediator variable, positive arousal, in a negative direction ($\beta = -.33$, $p < .01$). When the independent and mediator variables were used to simultaneously predict each attitude measure, the hypothesized mediator predicted each attitude ($\beta s = .55$ and $.44$, $ps < .001$), while the effect of Protagonist Domination was no longer significant ($\beta s = -.06$ and $-.12$, $ps > .25$). In short, the negative effect of Protagonist Dominance on women's attitude was also mediated by arousal, but in the opposite direction to men.

Discussion

The results of Experiment 1 showed that men preferred violence—both in terms of the advertisement and the game—when it depicted domination by the protagonist. Moreover, this effect appeared to occur primarily when men identified with the protagonist (i.e., when the protagonist was male). In short, depicted violence was most appealing to men when a protagonist they identified with dominated (H1 and H4). Finally, we found that this effect was driven by increased positive arousal in response to the domination (H2).

As expected, women liked the violent depiction less than men. However, we also found that dominative violence actually reduced any positive arousal women experienced as a consequence of viewing the clip, lowering their attitude toward the game and clip further. This could have occurred if the behavior in the high dominance conditions violated the norms women applied to this situation. Consistent with this, we found that 77% of women in our study never or rarely played video games, compared to 25% of men: $\chi^2(1) = 35.74$, $p < .001$, suggesting that they are unlikely to possess distinct norms for appropriate behavior within the context of video games, and therefore applied more general normative standards. It should be noted that this would not explain men's more positive reactions toward the high-dominance conditions, but it does provide one possible reason for women's more negative reactions. We more fully explore the idea that reactions to depicted domination can be moderated by the norms individuals possess in the second study.

Finally, it should be noted that the level of domination in the advertisement predicted both the appeal of the advertisement and the appeal of the actual game for men. It is possible that the effect of domination on the appeal of the video game stemmed, in part, from inferences regarding the ability of the (male) viewer to dominate in the game itself. Any such reactions would presumably be driven by the anticipation of *directly* dominating in the game as opposed to reactions to the depicted content. While this may have contributed to men's reactions to the game, the significant effects of dominance on the enjoyment of the advertisement itself suggest that men also reacted to the depicted domination. That is, regardless of whether actual domination (or, more precisely in this case, the anticipation of actual domination) is appealing, the current results suggest that mere *depictions* of domination are sufficient to enhance the appeal of violent media. In short, these results provide support for the notion that domination is one important component of the appeal of violent media depictions. Actual experiences of domination in interactive media, such as video games, may enhance this effect further.

EXPERIMENT 2

The purpose of the current experiment was to examine potential limits to the appeal of domination in violent depictions. Experiment 1 found that gender moderated the appeal of violent domination—men, but not women, enjoyed violent depictions more when the violence was associated with domination because they found this more positively arousing. Women, in contrast, found the domination less appealing, perhaps because they considered it excessive relative to the normative standards they applied. We more fully explore this possibility in the current study. Specifically, we manipulate the nature of the domination (domination over legitimate opponents vs. nonthreatening characters) to examine whether this can reduce the appeal of the depiction. We argue that domination of nonthreatening characters is likely to violate viewers' normative standards and consequently reduce the appeal of the depiction. Unlike the results of the previous study, this effect should be driven by the normative standards that individuals possess rather than different preferences for domination across gender. Consequently, individuals who possess different normative standards are likely to react differently to the nature of the domination portrayed in the violent depiction. We argue that regular gamers in particular are likely to possess gaming-specific norms that reflect the common occurrence of "no-holds-barred" domination in violent video games. Consequently, we expect the nongamers to react more negatively to violent depictions when they portray domination over nonthreatening characters than when the domination is over legitimate opponents, whereas regular gamers are likely to deem both types of domination acceptable (H6).

Method

We use the same context as the previous experiment—an advertisement for a violent video game. In this experiment, however, the game was a fictional expansion to Grand Theft Auto IV, an immensely popular, sandbox-style (a format where players are free to roam an extensive landscape), action-adventure game that features a third-person perspective of gameplay. We had to use a different game than in the previous study because the experimental manipulation now required a game that included both legitimate opponents and nonthreatening characters, which the game in the previous study did not. We called the game "GTA IV: The Fall of Liberty City," and it ostensibly involved the same protagonist and city as in the original game but introduced new story lines and plots. Two versions of the advertisement were created using edited sequences of high-definition teaser-trailers, cut-scenes, and gameplay footage from the original game. Each clip was designed to portray the same level of violent domination, was the same length of time (three and a half minutes), and included the same opening sequence and music throughout. Text introducing the clip made it clear that the game was an expansion of the original game (and therefore that viewers would not have played it previously). The opening sequence panned over the cityscape and a voice-over informed viewers that Liberty City was a corrupt, crime-ridden place, where the police force was a part of the problem. The protagonist (a Serbian immigrant attempting to make his way up the criminal ladder) was then shown dominating a series of violent encounters. In one of the advertisements, all of the violent encounters involved the police force—an obvious opponent in the context of the game—something we thought gamers and nongamers alike would appreciate. In the other advertisement, the protagonist was shown dominating characters that were clearly civilians—nonthreatening characters in the game. For nongamers, we predicted that the violent domination of civilians would represent a violation of the norms they were likely to apply—norms suggesting that domination is appropriate only over threatening opponents. Under these circumstances, we predicted that the domination is likely to be less arousing. Regular gamers, in contrast, should apply gaming-specific norms under which it would be appropriate to dominate any character in the game, consistent with H6.

Seventy-nine undergraduate students participated in a 2 (Domination Type: domination over Opponent vs. Nonopponent) × 2 (Gaming Status: Nongamer vs. Regular Gamer) between-subjects factorial design. The procedure and measures were identical to the first experiment, with the addition of the measure of gaming frequency—participants were asked how often they played video games (seven possible responses were labeled "never," "very rarely," "once or twice a month," "once a week," "a few times a week," "most days," and "multiple times each day"). Participants who indicated they never or very rarely played video games were categorized as "nongamers" (38 participants). All other participants were categorized as "gamers" (41 participants).

Results

Preliminary Analyses

ANOVAs conducted on perceptions of protagonist domination, violence, and in-game autonomy and competence showed no effects of the experimental manipulation ($ps > .08$ to $.90$).

Primary Analyses

An ANOVA conducted on attitude toward the game showed main effects of both Domination Type, $F(1, 75) = 4.18$, $p < .05$, and Gamer Status, $F(1, 75) = 28.67$, $p < .001$. Domination of opponents led to a more positive attitude toward the game than nonopponents ($Ms = 3.84$ vs. 3.29), consistent with H5, and gamers preferred the game to nongamers ($Ms = 4.23$ vs. 2.84). Consistent with H6, a significant interaction, $F(1, 75) = 5.15$, $p < .05$, indicated that the effect of Domination Type was moderated by Gamer Status. Follow-up analyses showed that nongamers liked the game less when the advertisement portrayed the domination of nonopponents compared to opponents, $Ms = 2.26$ versus 3.42; $F(1, 75) = 9.33$, $p < .01$, whereas gamers liked the game regardless, $Ms = 4.32$ versus 4.26; $F < 1$. ANOVAs conducted on the attitude toward the advertisement and arousal showed the same pattern of results—there were main effects of Domination Type (marginally significant in the case of arousal), $Fs(1, 75) = 7.90$ and 3.62, $ps < .01$ and $.061$, respectively, and Gamer Status, $Fs(1, 75) = 9.30$ and 12.13, $p < .05$ and $.001$. In both cases, the interaction failed to reach significance, $Fs(1, 75) = 2.27$ and 1.70, $ps = .20$. However, contrast analyses based on our specific predictions indicated that Domination Type affected attitude toward the advertisement and arousal for nongamers, $Ms = 3.49$ versus 2.35 and 2.50 versus 1.58; $ts(75) = 9.34$ and 5.15, $ps < .001$, but not gamers, $Ms = 3.89$ versus 3.55 and 3.12 versus 2.95, $ts(75) = .85$ and $.18$, $ps > .30$.

Mediation Analyses

Regression analyses were used to examine the prediction that the impact of Dominance Type would be mediated by arousal for nongamers (gamers' reactions were unaffected by Domination Type). In this group, only appropriate domination (i.e., the domination of opponents, but not nonopponents) should have been arousing, and therefore led to more positive attitudes. Consistent with the previous ANOVAs, regression analyses showed that the independent variable (Domination Type) predicted the dependent variables (attitudes toward the game and advertisement: $\beta s = .47$ and .49, respectively, $ps < .01$) and the proposed mediator (arousal: $\beta = .39, p < .01$). When the independent variable and proposed mediator were used to simultaneously predict the dependent variables, the mediator was significant in each case ($\beta s = .73$ and .63, respectively, $ps < .001$), while the independent variable was no longer significant in either case ($\beta s = .18$ and $.24; ps > .05$). Together these findings suggest that domination of nonopponents was indeed less arousing to nongamers and that this reduced the appeal of both the advertisement and the game.

Discussion

The current experiment was broadly designed to investigate the notion that not all types of violent domination should be appealing. Specifically, we predicted that domination of nonthreatening individuals should be considered inappropriate based on applicable social norms, in turn rendering the domination less arousing and less appealing. This effect, however, should have been crucially qualified by the particular norms that viewers deem relevant. In this context, we argued that gamers were likely to apply very different norms of appropriate conduct. Our findings were largely consistent with these predictions. Nongamers experienced less arousal in response to depictions of violent domination that was designed to be inappropriate, rendering both the advertisement and the game less appealing. Gamers, in contrast, were unaffected by differences in the individuals that were dominated, presumably because gaming norms suggested that any in-game character was "fair game."

The findings that gamers did not distinguish between the violent domination of legitimate opponents and nonthreatening characters could be taken as evidence of the desensitizing effects of regular video game play. Indeed, this is one of the primary findings from work on the consequences of violent video game consumption. This is, however, somewhat inconsistent with our argument that gamers were simply applying a different set of norms. Moreover, our findings do not really support a general conclusion of desensitization, although there are effects that could be described as desensitization of a different sort.

Desensitization is typically shown by demonstrating that individuals show *less* arousal to particular stimuli—in this case, exposure to violent media. Contrary to this, gamers in the current study showed *greater* arousal in response to the viewing of violent depictions. They did, however, appear not to distinguish between domination over nonthreatening characters and domination over legitimate opponents. Here, it could be argued that they have been desensitized to distinctions in the target of a domination attempt. While this could reflect a desensitization of sorts, it could also reflect the development of (more lenient) domination norms specific to the gaming context—the latter explanation being consistent with our initial theorizing. This is also almost exactly the opposite of a desensitizing explanation in that it argues viewers have become more rather than less discerning across different situations.

We conducted a brief follow-up study to examine these possibilities. Participants were asked to read a short scenario that described a violent encounter involving the inappropriate domination of nonthreatening individuals. Half of the participants were told that the description was taken from a newspaper article and the remaining participants were told that it described a scene from a video game. Had gamers become desensitized to violent domination, then we would expect them to rate the encounter as less inappropriate than nongamers, regardless of whether they believed the situation described to be real or a scene from a video game. While gamers did consider the situation to be more acceptable than nongamers when they believed it described a scene from a video game, they rated it just as inappropriate when they believed it described a real event. In short, gamers were more likely to distinguish between contexts than nongamers, suggesting that gamers' greater tolerance for "inappropriate" domination in video games is caused by the application of different norms rather than a general desensitization to violent domination. We also included a direct measure of the extent to which individuals agreed that it was wrong for video games to portray behavior that would be considered inappropriate in real life. Consistent with the assertion that regular gamers hold different in-game norms, we found that gamers were significantly less likely to agree with this than nongamers, $Ms = 2.46$ versus 3.48, $t(161) = 4.89$, $p < .001$.

GENERAL DISCUSSION

By far, the majority of research on violence in media has focused on demonstrating its negative effects. Yet this approach, although important, overlooks a fundamental question in the study of violent media: Why are such portrayals appealing? The current work sought to investigate this question. Our central premise was that depictions of physical domination present in most violent encounters contribute to its appeal. Based on research in evolutionary psychology and work on fundamental human motivations, we argued that domination, including physical domination, should be intrinsically rewarding, especially in men. Interactive media, such as video games, allow consumers to experience such domination directly. We also suggested, however, that reactions to dominance would, under certain conditions, extend to depictions of domination portrayed in noninteractive media. We studied this by examining advertisements for violent video games—a context where viewers' reactions were based on depictions of violence and domination rather than the experience per se.

Our results largely supported our predictions. Men found violence more appealing, both in terms of the appeal of the portrayal (the advertisement) and the appeal of the associated interactive experience (the video game), when it was associated with high levels of domination by the protagonist. We also found partial support for the idea that the appeal of violent domination requires some sort of identification with the protagonist. Specifically, we found that the effect of protagonist domination in violent depictions was strongest when the protagonist was also male. This is consistent with Zillmann's (1998) proposition that the development of some nonneutral disposition toward the protagonist is necessary for vicarious reactions to their experiences. We did not, however, set out to understand the specific factors that foster such dispositions, and we did not examine whether such effects would be reversed in the case of a negative disposition toward the protagonist. We think this would be a worthwhile avenue for future research.

As expected, women found the violent advertisements and the games they portrayed significantly less appealing than did men. Such findings are entirely consistent with statistics relating to the popularity of violent video games—they are overwhelmingly consumed by men, not women (Lucas and Sherry 2004). What we did not expect, however, was that women would react negatively to increased levels of domination. In retrospect, we believe this might have been caused, in part, by the fact that women were much less likely to be familiar with video games, and were therefore unlikely to fully appreciate the nature of video game norms. Consequently, they may have been more likely to react negatively to the gratuitous nature of the high-dominance conditions. As noted, the fact that men were more familiar with video games could not explain their more positive reactions to high levels of dominance, though—their familiarity would simply prevent them from finding such domination inappropriate. Consistent with our initial reasoning, we believe men's reactions to the domination stems from innate preferences to succeed in the domination of others.

In the second experiment, we specifically manipulated elements of the domination that we believed could affect its appropriateness—specifically, whether it was legitimate opponents or nonthreatening characters who were dominated. We argued that domination of nonthreatening characters would likely violate social norms related to acceptable domination, reducing the appeal of violent depictions that contained such behaviors. Such reactions should then crucially depend on the extent to which individuals subscribe to these norms. Individuals not frequently exposed to video games (disproportionately women) would apply broader norms of social interaction that would include standards that prohibit the domination of nonthreatening individuals. Regular gamers, in contrast, would be more likely to develop standards specific to appropriate in-game conduct that we hypothesized would permit the domination of nonthreatening individuals. We found evidence that was consistent with these ideas—gamers enjoyed violent portrayals of domination regardless of whether it was over legitimate opponents or nonthreatening individuals. Nongamers, on the other hand, found domination over nonthreatening individuals substantially less appealing, consistent with the notion that it violated their normative standards for appropriate domination.

When taken together, our experiments showed that physical domination in violent media lent to its appeal in men. Women, who found the violence less appealing than did men overall, reacted even more negatively when the violence contained high levels of domination. We also found evidence that norms that determine which targets can and cannot be dominated affected the appeal—an effect that we think may help explain the negative effect of domination within women. We should note that there were certain limits to the conclusions we were able to draw, however. In particular, we only ever manipulated domination or the type of domination *within* violent media depictions. In other words, we made no attempt to manipulate the level of violence. Thus, our conclusions are limited to the appeal of domination in violent contexts. We make no claims that violence without domination cannot be appealing, too. We would need a nonviolent control condition to investigate whether violence without domination is more appealing than comparable depictions that contain no violence. We do not, however, think that this detracts from the central point. Domination is inherent to most violent encounters, and as such, violent depictions where the protagonist dominates are more appealing than violent encounters where they do not. Consequently, the ability of violent depictions to satisfy men through vicarious domination may be one reason for their appeal.

Furthermore, there is some evidence to suggest that violence, without particular features that make it appealing, may not be inherently attractive. First, such a proposition has been implied or directly stated by a variety of scholars on the subject (e.g., Jansz 2005; Zillmann 1998). Second, studies examining the appeal of various violent media (in contrast to the effects of exposure) that have manipulated violent content have found that violence either detracted from or, at best, had no effect on attitudes (Hansen and Hansen 1990; Sparks, Sherry, and Lubsen 2005). While the current research does not relate directly to these findings, we do find that domination in violent media can increase its appeal, presumably in the same way that other factors, such as impression management (Zillmann et al. 1986), the justice motive (Zillmann 1998), and sensation seeking (Hoffner and Levine 2005), might as well. We should also add that in the context of video games, dominance is not restricted to the in-game experience. Multiplayer games are enormously popular, especially those with violent content (Au 2009). In this context, the physical domination of another character in the game corresponds to the domination of the person controlling that character outside of the game. As such, we would expect the possibility of these multiple sources of domination to enhance the overall appeal.

Domination—over both computer-controlled and player-controlled opponents—can certainly occur in the absence of violence. Violence-related domination is largely physical—one group or person uses force to physically suppress others in the game. Non–violence-related domination can either involve implied violence, as is the case in games that ostensibly involve conflict, but limit gameplay to strategic considerations (e.g., Star Wars: Rebellion, even board games such as Risk and Settlers of Catan fit into this category); or, games can be devoid of violence altogether, but nevertheless involve the prospect of domination along with some other ability (e.g., PGA Golf or Wii Puzzle). While superiority along such dimensions is also likely appealing (e.g., Wills 1981), we think there is something special about actual or implied *physical* domination—especially in men. It is likely rooted in evolved mechanisms that have developed specifically for the task of controlling con-specifics for the purpose of preferential access to mates and other fitness-related resources (Cummins 1996). Consistent with this, the phenotypical bases of physical domination, largely size and strength, seem to confer a variety of advantages on males (Buss 1988). In short, while domination, in the broad sense, does not necessarily involve violence, we suspect that the close relationship between violence and physical domination is one of the reasons violent media is particularly appealing to men.

Limitations

One of the key differences between violent video games and other violent media is that video games allow individuals to experience domination directly. In other media, the experience is vicarious. The current work focused exclusively on vicarious experiences. Our primary goal was to investigate whether domination in violent depictions would be sufficient to elicit the kind of positive reaction we would expect from the actual experience of domination. While our results did demonstrate that depictions of dominative violence were more appealing to men than nondominative violence, it is not clear that this would necessarily generalize to the actual experience of violent domination in interactive media, such as video games. On the one hand, violent domination entails harming or otherwise suppressing individuals, which is likely to be considered more counternormative than simply watching someone else engage in the same behavior. Of course, in video games, such actions are mere portrayals, which may mitigate such reactions, but the act is still one committed by the individual and not simply witnessed. On the other hand, actually dominating may well be more satisfying than merely witnessing domination. In short, it will be necessary to experimentally examine the role of domination in interactive media before conclusions can be made in this context.

There were a number of other limitations in the current work, too. First, a number of expected interactions did not reach significance. The pattern of results in these cases, however, was consistent with predictions, and more focused contrast analyses revealed significant differences where expected. Low power resulting from small sample sizes likely contributed to this problem. In the second study, we were also missing direct measures of the extent to which consumers' norms were violated by the advertisements—the mechanism by which certain types of domination were proposed to be more or less arousing. We did find that positive arousal mediated the appeal of the advertisements, although we did not have direct evidence that this was affected by violations of consumers' normative beliefs. We also found the predicted effect of gaming status, which at least provided evidence that these groups evaluated the depicted behavior differently, consistent with our proposed mechanism. Finally, we were able to conduct a brief follow-up experiment that showed that gamers found certain types of violent domination just as inappropriate as nongamers when they believed the act actually occurred, but found it significantly less inappropriate when they believe the act occurred in the context of a video game. Moreover, we found that gamers were significantly less likely to believe that it was wrong for video games to portray behavior that would be considered inappropriate in real life. Although not collected in the context of the second study, these results suggested that gamers were more likely than nongamers to hold norms that were specific to the gaming environment.

Implications

Perhaps the finding most directly relevant to marketers is that the portrayal of socially sanctioned domination in dramatic media, video games, and the advertisements that accompany them is likely to be broadly appealing to men. In the context of advertisements for violent media, such as video games, movies, or television shows, this suggests they should convey scenes that depict the protagonist dominating violent encounters rather than suffering at the hands of their foes. A cursory look at many popular video game advertisements and movie trailers suggests this may well be what marketers are currently doing anyway. It should be noted that such a focus, however, is only likely to turn women off further; not only did we find that they were less attracted to violent depictions than were men, but higher levels of protagonist domination decreased the appeal further. Fortunately for most marketers, it is men, and not women, who tend to be the consumers of violent media. While not directly explored in the current work, the results are also suggestive of the possibility that the ability to directly dominate opponents may be one reason for the appeal of violent video games among men. As such, games that allow for high levels of domination are likely to be more appealing than games that do not. As noted before, further research is required to investigate this idea more fully.

More broadly, the current research raises the possibility that vicarious experiences of domination in noninteractive media and actual domination in interactive media may be appealing outside of violent depictions. Given the overwhelming support for the negative effects of exposure to violent media, this suggests that marketers may be able to curb the level of violence in popular media while maintaining its appeal by focusing on the dominative elements of the drama, rather than those depicting harm. While the question of what makes dramatic media appealing is intensely complex, our research suggests that viewers, players, and possibly readers enjoy meaningful domination by the protagonist. Clearly, this effect should interact with a multitude of other elements in any drama, but it would seem that if each violent component of a dramatic medium was replaced by one that focused on the dominative core of the encounter, then it is possible that the medium would be substantially less violent while retaining its appeal.

Much of our discussion of violent media has been focused on media designed to entertain. Not all media, however, is designed with this goal in mind or, indeed, appreciated for this reason. News reports or documentaries featuring actual violence are clearly not designed to leave viewers feeling good. Similarly, fictionalized accounts of actual events as portrayed in films, television shows, and possibly even video games are not necessarily designed to be a positive experience per se. As noted before, reactions to depictions of actual physical harm may well be largely negative, and footage or depictions of real events often lacks the elements that might render the violence appealing (e.g., dominance or justice). In fact, perceptions that the harm is real, or based on reality, seem likely to only exacerbate negative reactions further (Zillmann 1998). Nevertheless, viewers do seem to be capable of appreciating such media, even if they are not able to enjoy it per se (e.g., extremely realistic war movies, such as *Saving Private Ryan*). In these cases, it is possible that the appeal of the media lies in perceptions that it can inform and educate consumers. Here, the prescription to substitute violent content for that which emphasizes dominative elements is misguided. Consumers' perceptions of the educational value of such media may even increase as their negative reactions to any violent or otherwise unpleasant content increases. In this way, positive reactions are, in a sense, a meta-reaction to judgments of the informational value of the media. Here, we might expect more realistic portrayals of violence to enhance appreciation, even as the violence is found to be increasingly more unpleasant. As such, this would suggest a quite different role for the appeal of violence in media—one that we think merits exploration in future research.

REFERENCES

Anderson, Craig A., and Brad J. Bushman (2001), "Effects of Violent Video Games on Aggressive Behavior, Aggressive Cognition, Aggressive Affect, Physiological Arousal, and Prosocial Behavior: A Meta-Analytic Review of the Scientific Literature," *Psychological Science,* 12 (5), 353–359.

———, and Karen E. Dill (2000), "Video Games and Aggressive Thoughts, Feelings, and Behavior in the Laboratory and in Life," *Journal of Personality and Social Psychology,* 78 (4), 772–790.

Au, Wagner James (2009), "The Top 10 Money-Making MMOs of 2008," *GigaOM* (February 1), available at http://gigaom.com/2009/02/01/top-10-money-making-mmos-2008/ (accessed June 10, 2009).

Bandura, Albert (1961), "Psychotherapy as a Learning Process," *Psychological Bulletin,* 58 (2), 143–159.

Baumeister, Roy F., and W. Keith Campbell (1999), "The Intrinsic Appeal of Evil: Sadism, Sensational Thrills, and Threatened Egotism," *Personality and Social Psychology Review,* 3 (3), 210–221.

Blanchard, Rashawn (2007), "Etiquette for the Virgin Gamer," Associated Content (February 8), available at www.associatedcontent.com/article/135740/etiquette_for_the_virgin_gamer.html?cat=19/ (accessed May 7, 2009).

Bushman, Brad. J., and Craig A. Anderson (2001), "Media Violence and the American Public," *American Psychologist,* 56 (6/7), 477–489.

———, and ——— (2002), "Violent Video Games and Hostile Expectations: A Test of the General Aggression Model," *Personality and Social Psychology Bulletin,* 28 (12), 1679–1686.

Buss, David M. (1988), "The Evolution of Human Intrasexual Competition: Tactics of Mate Attraction," *Journal of Personality and Social Psychology,* 54 (4), 616–628.

Carnagey, Nicholas L., Craig A. Anderson, and Brad J. Bushman (2007), "The Effect of Video Game Violence on Physiological Desensitization to Real-Life Violence," *Journal of Experimental Social Psychology,* 43 (4), 489–496.

Cialdini, Robert B., Raymond R. Reno, and Carl A. Kallgren (1990), "A Focus Theory of Normative Conduct: Recycling the Concept of Norms to Reduce Littering in Public Places," *Journal of Personality and Social Psychology,* 58 (3), 1015–1026.

———, Richard J. Borden, Avril Thorne, Marcus R. Walker, Stephen Freeman, and Lloyd R. Sloan (1976), "Basking in Reflected Glory: Three (Football) Field Studies," *Journal of Personality and Social Psychology,* 34 (3), 366–375.

Collier, Joel E., Pearson Liddell, Jr., and Gloria J. Liddell (2008), "Exposure of Violent Video Games to Children and Public Policy Implications," *Journal of Public Policy and Marketing,* 27 (1), 107–112.

Cummins, Denise D. (1996), "Dominance Hierarchies and the Evolution of Human Reasoning," *Minds and Machines,* 6 (4), 463–480.

Entertainment Software Association (2009), "Essential Facts About the Computer and Video Game Industry," available at www.theesa.com/facts/pdfs/ESA_EF_2009.pdf (accessed May 7, 2009).

Eron, Leonard D., L. Rowell Huesmann, Monroe M. Lefkowitz, and Leopold O. Walder (1972), "Does Television Violence Cause Aggression?" *American Psychologist,* 27 (4), 253–263.

Federman, Joel (1998), *National Television Violence Study,* vol. 3, Thousand Oaks, CA: Sage.

Haninger, Kevin, and Kimberly M. Thompson (2004), "Content and Ratings of Teen-Rated Video Games," *Journal of the American Medical Association,* 291 (7), 856–865.

Hansen, Christine Hall, and Ranald D. Hansen (1990), "The Influence of Sex and Violence on the Appeal of Rock Music Videos," *Communication Research,* 17 (2), 212–234.

Hoffner, Cynthia A., and Kenneth J. Levine (2005), "Enjoyment of Mediated Fright and Violence: A Meta-Analysis," *Media Psychology,* 7 (2), 207–237.

Huesmann, L. Rowell (2007), "The Impact of Electronic Media Violence: Scientific Theory and Research," *Journal of Adolescent Health,* 41 (6, Suppl.), S6–S13.

———, and Nancy G. Guerra (1997), "Children's Normative Beliefs About Aggression and Aggressive Behavior," *Journal of Personality and Social Psychology,* 72 (2), 408–419.

Jansz, Jeroen (2005), "The Emotional Appeal of Violent Video Games for Adolescent Males," *Communication Theory,* 15 (3), 219–241.

Linz, Daniel, Edward Donnerstein, and Steven M. Adams (1989), "Physiological Desensitization and Judgments About Female Victims of Violence," *Human Communication Research,* 15 (4), 509–522.

Lucas, Kristen, and John L. Sherry (2004), "Sex Differences in Video Game Play: A Communication-Based Explanation," *Communication Research,* 31 (5), 499–523.

McClelland, David C. (1985), *Human Motivation*, Cambridge: Cambridge University Press.
Meltzoff, Andrew N., and M. Keith Moore (2002), "Imitation, Memory, and the Representation of Persons," *Infant Behavior and Development*, 25 (1), 39–61.
Murray, John P. (2008), "Media Violence: The Effects Are Both Real and Strong," *American Behavioral Scientist*, 51 (8), 1212–1230.
Nielsen Media Research (2006), "Nielsen Media Research Reports Television's Popularity Is Still Growing" (September 21), available at www.thinktv.com.au/media/Articles/Nielsen_Media_Reports_TV%27s_Popularity_Is_Still_Growing.pdf (accessed October 26, 2010).
Ortutay, Barbara (2008), "Take-Two's 'Grand Theft Auto IV' Tops $500M in Week 1 Sales," Associated Press (May 8), available at www.usatoday.com/tech/gaming/2008-05-07-gta-iv-sales_N.htm (accessed May 8, 2008).
Paik, Haejung, and George Comstock (1994), "The Effects of Television Violence on Antisocial Behavior: A Meta-Analysis," *Communication Research*, 21 (4), 516–546.
Ryan, Richard M., C. Scott Rigby, and Andrew Przybylski (2006), "The Motivational Pull of Video Games: A Self-Determination Theory Approach," *Motivation and Emotion*, 30 (4), 347–363.
Savage, Joanne, and Christina Yancey (2008), "The Effects of Media Violence Exposure on Criminal Aggression: A Meta-Analysis," *Criminal Justice and Behavior*, 35 (6), 772–791.
Sparks, Glenn G., John Sherry, and Graig Lubsen (2005), "The Appeal of Media Violence in a Full-Length Motion Picture: An Experimental Investigation," *Communication Reports*, 18 (1), 21–30.
Toch, Hans (1993), "Good Violence and Bad Violence: Self-Presentations of Aggressors Through Accounts and War Stories," in *Aggression and Violence: Social Interactionist Perspectives*, Richard B. Felson and James T. Tedeschi, eds., Washington, DC: American Psychological Association, 193–206.
Uhlmann, Eric, and Jane Swanson (2004), "Exposure to Violent Video Games Increases Automatic Aggressiveness," *Journal of Adolescence*, 27 (1), 41–52.
Wills, Thomas A. (1981), "Downward Comparison Principles in Social Psychology," *Psychological Bulletin*, 90 (2), 245–271.
Zillmann, Dolf (1998), "The Psychology of the Appeal of Portrayals of Violence," in *Why We Watch: The Attractions of Violent Entertainment*, Jeffrey H. Goldstein, ed., New York: Oxford University Press, 179–211.
———, James B. Weaver, Norbert Mundorf, and Charles Aust (1986), "Effects of an Opposite-Gender Companion's Affect to Horror on Distress, Delight, and Attraction," *Journal of Personality and Social Psychology*, 51 (3), 586–594.

9

Celebrity Violence Outside the Ad Context
Synergies and Concerns

Nora J. Rifon, Karen Smreker, and Sookyong Kim

The use of celebrities in advertising is a long-standing marketing tactic, often employed to cut through advertising clutter and for the positive brand images that celebrities can create. Studies on the effects of celebrity endorsements have established several positive outcomes that can result from using a celebrity to advertise a brand. These outcomes include increased brand awareness, positive brand attitudes, enhanced message credibility, and the transference of a range of positive attributes from celebrity to brand.

Many celebrities are paid high fees for their appearance in advertisements, brand endorsements, and even for something as simple as tweeting about a brand; Khloe Kardashian and Tori Spelling each receive thousands of dollars for a single brand tweet (Associated Press 2011). As of 2010, it was estimated that $50 billion was spent on celebrity endorsements in traditional media (Crutchfield 2010) and another $35 billion on digital endorsements (Shayon 2011). Some of the highest paid celebrity endorsers include male athletes (David Beckham), entertainers (Jay Z), and female actors (Catherine Zeta-Jones) (CompareBusinessProducts.com 2010). By definition, celebrity status is achieved through notoriety and popularity, and celebrities have their own brand and equity that they can bring to endorsements. Desirable and effective endorsers are not only widely known, but are attractive and often aspirational figures, and their influence is attributed to the characteristics they embody and bring to a brand.

Celebrity is accompanied by widespread media coverage and scrutiny, with countless media outlets dedicated to celebrity news. PerezHilton.com and Gawker.com were recently ranked as two of the top ten blogs throughout the world and both focus on celebrity gossip (Aldred et al. 2008). Even The Huffington Post, which presents itself as an authoritative and serious news source, has a section dedicated to celebrity gossip (Aldred et al. 2008). Positive stories on celebrities are popular, but when a celebrity is involved in some type of scandal, the reporting of the news is typically not limited to gossip magazines and Web sites. Stories of celebrities drinking and driving, being aggressive and violent, and misbehaving in general are widely reported. While some endorsers lose their contracts, as was the case for celebrity chef Paula Deen, others appear to survive and sometimes thrive as some advertisers choose to continue their relationship with the celebrity, and sometimes spin the incident or reputation for bad behavior into profits, as in the case of Charlie Sheen.

While marketers are concerned with the backlash that can come from a celebrity scandal, perhaps a more pressing societal concern should be the message that is communicated to those who admire a celebrity who has engaged in frowned-upon behaviors. When that celebrity receives a pass from the judicial system, continued incentives, or is embraced by advertisers, the message is that negative behaviors do not yield negative consequences. For example, Fox Sports used Mike Tyson, who at the time had been convicted of rape, in an advertising campaign relying on his violent, criminal image to communicate what they intended to be a humorous message (Elliott 2002). Indeed, the increasing popularity of violence in advertising intended to reach and appeal to mass audiences, often with humorous intent, such as ads airing during the Super Bowl (Blackford et al. 2011), suggests the disturbing trend that violence is becoming more acceptable in mainstream advertising. As advertisers embrace celebrity icons who engage in violent behaviors, do they also send a signal of acceptance of the celebrity's negative behavior and indicate approval? Should we be concerned in particular for tweens and teens who seek role models and often find them in celebrity?

This chapter raises and reviews issues related to violent behavior of celebrities and the potential consequences of the synergy that comes from their presence in advertising and the press coverage of the violent behavior. Celebrities are brands themselves (Kowalczyk and Royne 2013), so even when they are not endorsing specific products, press coverage of their lives constitutes publicity, a form of promotion that celebrities rely on to maintain their own brand equity. When a celebrity is in the press for negative behavior, then the celebrity's own brand equity may suffer, as well as the equity of endorsed brands. We offer a short review of the use of celebrities in advertising, their value to advertisers, and what makes them influential. We present trends in celebrity misbehavior as reported in the press and offer details of some cases to illustrate the types of behaviors they display. In addition, we explore the consequences of their behaviors, such as loss of endorsements, prison time, or lack thereof, as a cue that signals the acceptability of their behaviors and to reflect the way their negative behaviors are framed by the press. Next, we review the role of celebrity in popular culture, and celebrities' potential influence on consumers, particularly adolescents who are likely to seek role models in celebrities. Finally, we raise issues for the future of celebrity in our society, and address the need to add the study of celebrities to our studies of media violence.

LITERATURE REVIEW

Celebrities as Endorsers

Research unequivocally indicates that celebrities can have positive outcomes for endorsed brands. A celebrity endorser can make an ad more memorable (Tantiseneepong, Gorton, and White 2012), can increase interest in a product (Maronick 2006), and can improve brand attitude (Doss 2011). In 2009 alone, $50 billion was spent on celebrities as endorsers (Crutchfield 2010). The CEO of Ad.ly, a firm that focuses on endorsements via social media, suggests that another $35 billion is spent on digital endorsements (Shayon 2011). Endorsers from the world of sports have been shown to increase stock prices on the day of the endorsement announcement, and increase sales within one week of winning a championship game (Elberse and Verleun 2012) or NASCAR title (Clark, Cornwell, and Pruitt 2009). Other benefits include memorability and cutting through ad clutter. Additionally, celebrity endorsers can improve attitudes toward the brand, and attitudes towards the ad, both of which can help reposition a brand (Tantiseneepong, Gorton, and White 2012). Celebrity endorsements are thought to be effective because the endorsement encourages the everyday consumer to associate the brand being endorsed with the celebrity endorsing it (O'Cass and Frost 2002) and to believe that the use of that brand may transform the consumer to become more like the endorser.

A celebrity is successful as an endorser when, in the eyes of the consumer, the positive images and meanings associated with the celebrity are transferred to the endorsed product. According to McCracken (1989), this occurs through a three-step process. In the first step, society develops a cultural meaning that becomes associated with a particular celebrity. Next, the celebrity transfers that meaning to the product they are endorsing. Finally, the meaning is transferred from the product to the consumer when the consumer purchases and uses the product (McCracken 1989). It has also been shown that a celebrity will have greater impact if the consumer views the celebrity image as desirable and aspirational; the celebrity will be more successful as an endorser because the consumer is hoping the use of the endorsed product will help the consumer achieve a desired trait (Choi and Rifon 2012). A blatant illustration of this phenomenon can be seen in the now classic Quaker Oats 1992 Gatorade campaign, "I Wanna Be Like Mike," which showed images of Michael Jordan's on-court basketball prowess accompanied by the sounds of children singing, "I wanna be like Mike" (bigwayne84 2006).

Social Cognitive Theory (SCT) posits that behavior can be learned through observing others receiving desirable consequences from performing that behavior (Bandura 1986). Furthermore, the likelihood of behavior changing depends on attention paid to and identification with the model (Berzonsky and Ferrari 1996). The greater the perceived similarity between the observer and the model, the greater the influence the model has on the observer's behavior (Bandura 1986; Schunk 1987). Choi and Rifon's (2012) findings suggest that this similarity should be based on an aspirational goal sought by the observer. The most successful celebrity endorsers are seen as attractive, familiar, and experts, but more importantly, trustworthy and likeable (Atkin and Block 1983). Thus, celebrities are role models who have the potential to influence those who know, watch, and admire them.

Reader's Digest dedicated an entire issue to reporting the results of a survey conducted with the Wagner Group that measured the most trusted people in the United States (Smith and Caporimo 2013). The researchers first identified 200 individuals from 15 professions considered to be "opinion shapers and headliners," then presented the list to "a representative sample" of 1,000 people and asked them to rank all 200 on the list for their trustworthiness. The three highest scorers were people from within the individual's personal circle, specifically one's own doctor, spiritual adviser, and child's current teacher. When the top three were removed from the list, the number one most trusted person was the actor Tom Hanks, and number two was actress Sandra Bullock. The findings indicate that within some professions, popular celebrities were more trusted than their real-world counterparts. People trust judges on TV more than they trust Supreme Court judges, with Judge Judy ranking 28th and Ruth Bader Ginsburg 36th. In general, do-gooders are more likely to earn trust, with doctors, philanthropists, and educators among the top five most altruistic professions. However, Dr. Oz (number 16) and Dr. Sanjay Gupta (number 17) were more trusted than the U.S. Surgeon General, Dr. Regina Benjamin (number 22) (Smith and Caporimo 2013). The results point to the appeal that many celebrities have developed, but also suggest that the repeated appearance of a celebrity in film, television, and other media is likely to create a sense of familiarity and trust that is not paralleled for other noted experts. The trust that the public has for celebrity imbues a persuasiveness to their words and behaviors. When a celebrity behaves in aggressive or violent ways, she/he receives extensive press coverage, and the potential influence on society has not been well studied. To begin, we offer a cross-sectional snapshot of celebrity negative behavior as reported in the press.

Reports of Negative Celebrity Behaviors

Do celebrities contribute to the violent landscape when they are involved in controversy, and engage in well-publicized aggressive or violent behavior? The authors recently performed a study of popular press coverage of celebrity antisocial behavior (Smreker et al. 2013). We highlight some of the findings here and also offer a review of recent cases of celebrity violence to describe the incidence and breadth of negative celebrity behaviors in recent years.

To assess the extent and type of celebrity negative behavior, a three-year span of *People* magazines from January 2009 to December 2011, covering 154 issues, was reviewed and analyzed for stories that reported on a range of celebrity transgressions (Smreker et al. 2013). Smreker et al. (2013) took a more liberal view of what constituted celebrity bad behavior, by considering what Cruz and Bushman label in this volume as aggressive behaviors in addition to those that they would consider violent. Based on Anderson and Bushman's (2001) definition, violent behavior is "aggression that has as its goal extreme physical harm, such as injury or death," (Cruz and Bushman, in this volume), and aggression is considered to be "behavior that is intended to harm another person who does not want to be harmed" (Cruz and Bushman, this volume). Smreker et al.'s (2013) content analysis looked for many types of harm and behaviors that had the potential to harm the celebrity and others. Types of harm included financial and property damage, and behaviors that created harm or had the potential to harm included violations of social norms and laws (for example, drinking and driving), indulgence in drugs and alcohol, using racial slurs, and discrimination, in addition to violent behaviors that created physical and sexual harm.

Over the three-year period, 87 celebrities were noted in 196 stories reporting on celebrity misdeeds. This represented 109 unique incidents, and translates to an average of 3.78 stories per week. Violent behavior was not the only behavior noted, and the behaviors that were the subject of the stories ranged from violations of social norms, indulgence in drugs and alcohol, harm to others through verbal, financial, and property damage, racial slurs and discrimination, as well as physical and sexual violence. The most common types of harms were physical bodily harm (non-sexual) and verbal injury. Nine celebrities were alleged to have engaged or did engage in violent behaviors accounting for 11 unique violent incidents during the three-year period. Of those nine celebrities, Mel Gibson was mentioned for more than one altercation and Lindsay Lohan was the only female to be mentioned. Additionally, out of the 11 instances, five involved drugs.

The study also examined the consequences to the celebrity, legal or social or professional, for having engaged in negative behaviors. For all infractions, celebrities accepted responsibility in only 14 of the 109 incidents reported, and furthermore, consequences such as fines, jail time, or rehabilitation were reported for only 17 out of the 109 total incidents. For the violent incidents, in only four cases was there a report that the celebrity responded by accepting responsibility. The most common consequence was jail, and the most common violent incident was domestic violence committed by a man against a woman. Charlie Sheen, Chris Brown, and Mel Gibson were all charged with abusing their partners. Sheen received mandatory rehabilitation and probation (Banda 2010), Brown was sentenced to five years of probation (Duke 2012), and Gibson received probation when he pled no contest (Cieply 2011) (see Table 9.1). Despite the fact that both Sheen and Brown were convicted of domestic violence, neither was sentenced to time in prison, a signal that perhaps violent behavior is acceptable or at least tolerated.

The content analysis represents three years of *People* magazine articles, but there are countless vehicles in print, television, and online that carry stories about celebrity behaviors. The stories identified by this study were likely to have been covered across a wide range of vehicles, and we can only speculate as to how many people were aware of these stories. Notwithstanding, the message that is sent by the stories is troublesome.

Case Studies of Recent Celebrity Violence

In 2010, Lindsay Lohan was accused of attacking an employee at her court-ordered treatment center. The victim, Dawn Holland, claimed that Lohan threw a cell phone at her and then pulled a phone out of Holland's hand, causing her to sprain her wrist. Holland later recanted her statement even though police determined Lohan had committed battery (Lee 2011a). Holland was fired from her job for discussing a patient with the tabloids and about six months later tried to sue Lohan for $1 million (Hughes 2011). The case was settled for an undisclosed amount (TMZ Staff 2012). Soon after settling the case with Holland, Lohan was again accused of assault, this time for punching a person in the face at a nightclub in New York City. While Lohan was initially charged with misdemeanor assault (Jacobs 2013), the case was eventually dropped when it was discovered the victim invented the assault (Jacobs and Dillon 2013). In this case, we see how a

Table 9.1

Violent Celebrity Behaviors Reported in *People* Magazine, 2009–2011

Celebrity	Number of Stories	Morality	Behavior	Response	Consequence
Charlie Sheen	8	Illegal	Violence	Accepted responsibility	Jail; Rehab
Chris Brown	15	Illegal	Violence	Accepted responsibility, apologized, showed remorse	
David Boreanaz	1	Illegal	Violence		
James Arthur Ray	2	Illegal	Violence; drugs	Apologized, showed remorse	Jail; Rehab
Keith Brown	2	Unethical	Violence; drugs	Accepted responsibility	Jail
Kiefer Sutherland	2	Illegal	Violence	Accepted responsibility, apologized, showed remorse	
Lawrence Taylor	2	Illegal	Violence; drugs		Jail
Lindsay Lohan	1	Illegal	Violence; drugs		
Mel Gibson	2	Illegal	Violence		
Mel Gibson	1	Illegal	Violence		
Mel Gibson	1	Illegal	Violence; drugs		Rehab

celebrity with a history of press coverage for behaviors that violate legal and social norms can also attract unwarranted accusations that create more press attention and speculation.

In 2009, Chris Brown beat his then girlfriend, singer Rihanna. Initially, he fled the scene of the crime, but turned himself in later that day. Brown apologized and was charged with making criminal threats and felony assault (Lee 2009). He pled guilty and was sentenced to community service, therapy, and five years of probation. As soon as news of the attack broke, "Got Milk" stopped running Brown's ads and Wrigley's Doublemint gum pulled his endorsement (Fisher 2009). Radio stations then began banning Brown's music from their airwaves (Kaufman 2009). In 2011, Brown appeared on *Good Morning America*, where he was repeatedly asked questions about the incident with Rihanna. He walked out of the interview and returned to his dressing room, where he threw a chair through a window (ABC News 2011). Then in January 2013, Brown was accused of attacking R&B singer Frank Ocean. Even though Ocean publicly forgave Brown and said he didn't want to press charges (Associated Press 2013), the district attorney's office was still trying to decide whether or not to file charges. Since Brown was under probation for his previous felony assault charges, the incident could be seen as a violation of his probation (TMZ Staff 2013b), however he was not charged with any violation.

In January 2010, Oksana Grigorieva accused her ex-boyfriend Mel Gibson of domestic violence. She stated than Gibson had punched her in the face multiple times and alleged that he had broken one of her teeth during one of the altercations. Just weeks after Grigorieva filed for a restraining order, pictures surfaced of her with a black eye, allegedly from one of the attacks. Gibson claims that the injury occurred when he tried to stop Grigorieva from harming their nine-month-old daughter (Oh 2010). After the photo was leaked, multiple audio recordings were also leaked in which Gibson is heard screaming and threatening his then girlfriend (Hammel 2010). Gibson eventually pled no contest to the domestic abuse and was sentenced to three years of probation (Lee 2011b), but no prison or fine.

In December 2009, Charlie Sheen was arrested and charged with third-degree assault, criminal mischief, and felony menacing for attacking his then wife with a knife (Khan 2010; Wang 2009). Sheen then had a very public meltdown, giving incoherent interviews saying things like he had "tiger blood" and was "winning." In addition, he began verbally attacking his costars as well as the executive producer of his hit TV show *Two and a Half Men* (Bosch 2011). Shortly after, Sheen was fired from *Two and a Half Men*, with producers citing the arrest, his meltdown, and an incident in which he caused $7,000 worth of damage at a hotel (Fleeman 2011). While Sheen did lose his endorsement deal with Hanes (Wang 2010), his comeback seems unprecedented. He capitalized on his meltdown by creating a nationwide comedy tour called "My Violent Torpedo of Truth/Defeat Is Not an Option," which sold out in only 18 minutes (TMZ Staff 2011). Only three months after being fired from *Two and a Half Men*, Sheen received a new show, *Anger Management* (Schwartz 2011). The show premiered on June 28, 2012, to record-breaking numbers (Ockenfels 2012).

NFL player Aaron Hernandez's legal trouble began in June 2013 when it was alleged that he was responsible for shooting a man in the face causing him to lose his right eye (TMZ Staff 2013a). The case was dismissed, but shortly thereafter, Hernandez was arrested and charged with several firearm offenses as well as first-degree murder. It was alleged that Hernandez killed the victim due to the victim's knowledge about double murder committed by Hernandez in 2012 (Rodak and Associated Press 2013). Hernandez is also being investigated for the unsolved double murder (Shoichet, Levitt, and Castillo 2013).

These cases illustrate the wide range of aggressive and violent behaviors by celebrities that are reported in the media. While some acts are more aggressive than others, all received substantial coverage in the press, and the coverage across the acts varies by person. For example, both Charlie Sheen and Chris Brown were convicted of physically abusing their female partners. Brown received almost twice as many stories as did Sheen.

Reality Television and the New Generation of Celebrity

Reality television has changed the face of celebrity and opened a door to 24/7 coverage of celebrity lives. Programs such as *Keeping Up with the Kardashians* and *Tori and Dean* follow celebrities through their everyday lives. Reality television has also created a new breed of celebrity, one who is unknown to the public prior to the programming, but after being followed through a "real" everyday life, the unknown emerges as a popular icon with blogs, Web sites, and extensive media coverage. Cable channel Bravo, owned by NBC Universal, is arguably the pioneering dominant force in the reality television programming world.

Bravo reaches over 95 million households (Bravo Media 2013) and is the home of several popular reality series, including *Top Chef, Inside the Actors Studio,* and the many programs that are part of the *Real Housewives* franchise. Included in the franchise are *The Real Housewives of Orange County, The Real Housewives of Atlanta, The Real Housewives of New Jersey, The Real Housewives of New York, The Real Housewives of Beverly Hills, The Real Housewives of Miami,* and the now defunct *The Real Housewives of DC*. Within each franchise, "housewives" are followed by cameras as they walk through their everyday lives, and each city typically focuses on five or six women, their careers and families. Perhaps what the shows are most known for is the high level of social aggression displayed among the women in the group (Anthes 2008). The aggression is fueled by Bravo through its hosting of blogs where housewives sling arrows and audience members post aggressively as well. According to Anthes (2008), Bravo suspended one of its blogs as a result of audience "vitriol."

Their highest ratings are typically for the end-of-season reunion shows, where all of the housewives, and sometimes friends and partners, appear and are encouraged by the host, Andy Cohen, to address the conflicts that have been brewing during the filming season. Cohen, who is the executive vice president of development and talent at Bravo, presents pointedly phrased questions designed to irk the cast and generate tension, and he is often successful. The ratings for the housewives shows may not compete with overall ratings for prime-time broadcast network programming, but they draw a substantial 18–49 demographic. *The Real Housewives of New Jersey* 2010 reunion show was watched by over 3.8 million households and received a 2.0 rating for the 18–49 demographic (Kempen 2013). Confronted for her behavior by Anderson Cooper on his talk show *Anderson,* New Jersey housewife Teresa Giudice is known for her temper tantrums, table flipping, and bullying of her castmates (HuffPost TV 2012). The last season of *The Real Housewives of Beverly Hills* witnessed the exposure of housewife Taylor Armstrong's domestic abuse by husband Russell Armstrong (Wihlborg 2011) and his subsequent suicide (Marikar 2011).

There is little research on this trend of social and physical displays of aggression in reality television, but one study examined the narcissistic tendencies of celebrities in general and those in reality television in particular (Young and Pinsky 2006). One of the researchers, Dr. Drew Pinsky, is a celebrity in his own right, with television and radio show programming, notably, *Celebrity Rehab with Dr. Drew*, which ran on VH1. The researchers compared scores on the Narcissism Personality Inventory from a convenience sample of celebrities who had appeared on Dr. Pinsky's radio show *Loveline* with a group of MBA students. They classified the celebrities into four groups—musicians, comedians, actors, and reality TV personalities—and compared them with each other and with the MBA students across the five component dimensions of narcissism: exploitiveness, authority, exhibitionism, superiority, and entitlement. They found that the celebrities were more narcissistic than the MBA students, and that both actors and reality TV personalities scored equally high for overall narcissism, but that reality TV personalities scored significantly higher than all other groups on the exploitiveness dimension. They regressed years of experience on narcissism scores and found no significant relationship, suggesting that celebrity must attract narcissism, and not the converse that celebrity creates it. Furthermore, they state that narcissists crave attention, are overconfident, and often lack empathy, a profile that is consistent with the levels of social aggression observed in many reality programs.

Violent Celebrity Endorser Behavior and Teens

Despite the significant body of literature on the use of celebrities for their positive influence, few studies have examined their potential negative effects. Those that address negative effects tend to focus on case studies rather than attempting to find any pattern in the bad behaviors and their effects (Erdogan and Drollinger 2008; Johnson 2005; Miller and Laczinak 2011; Thwaites et al. 2012; White, Goddard, and Wilbur 2009).

Damage to a marketer's brand may not be the only cause for concern. As advertisers embrace celebrity icons who engage in violent behaviors, do they also send a signal of acceptance of the celebrity's negative behavior and indicate approval? We suggest that the answer is yes. If advertisers embrace celebrity endorsers who engage in violent behaviors, it would serve as a signal of acceptance of the celebrity's negative behavior and indicate approval in society. Naïve consumers may theorize about the underlying reasons for the ad message featuring celebrity icons known for misbehaviors, and may view celebrity violence as one of the valuable resources for generating profits in society. Charlie Sheen's public firing from *Two and Half Men* was followed by Fox offering him a new sitcom. The tongue-in-cheek title of the show, *Anger Management*, played upon Sheen's negative and violent past, and the show's development can be seen as a reward for his behavior. Despite New Jersey housewife Teresa Giudice's social and physical aggression, she remains one of her show's stars and reaps profits from cookbooks and endorsements. It is possible that consumers view celebrity violence not as bad behavior, but as acceptable behavior that is rewarded by the media and advertisers.

Incidents of celebrity violence may have more widespread and profound effects on society. Celebrities represent ideals that people aspire to and this phenomenon is strong in the youth market. With 23.7% of the population under the age of 18, teenagers are one of the most heavily targeted consumer audiences (Sheehan 2003). Teens view celebrities as aspirational models whose traits should be emulated and imitated. Teens are even willing to change their appearance, values, attitudes, and behaviors in order to further align themselves with their celebrity idols (Boon and Lomore 2001), or to become a celebrity. For instance, a survey of 800 teenagers ages 16 to 19 found that one out of 10 teenagers would drop out of school if they had the chance to appear on television. Sixteen percent of the teens felt that they themselves would be celebrities one day and 9% thought that being famous is an easy way to become rich without needing any real skills (Cassidy 2006).

As noted in many of the chapters in this book, violence in the media comes in many forms, and appears to be increasing in its prevalence (see, for example, the chapters by Cruz and Bushman, and Fernandez and Richards). As noted by Cruz and Bushman, children will see 200,000 acts of violence on television before reaching their eighteenth birthday (Senate Committee on the Judiciary 1999). In the time since this hallmark Senate report, little has been done to determine if this number is increasing. Yet, concern for the effects of media violence on youth has not waned and studies of media violence have gone beyond television to platforms such as music, online and console games, as well as games for mobile devices such as smart phones and tablets (Cruz and Bushman, in this volume). Studies of video games, online games, and console games show that the most popular games are violent and often feature a first-person shooter and hand-to-hand combat (Becker-Olsen and Norberg 2010). The effects of exposure to media violence include increased aggression (Anderson et al. 2008; Lennings and Warburton 2011) and desensitization to violence (Becker-Olsen and Norberg 2010). Pagan and Wexlerf (1987) found that violence in and outside of the home is a predictor of future domestic violence and aggression toward strangers. They emphasized the role that social norms play in legitimizing and determining future aggressive and violent behavior, as modeling of violence and aggression appears to legitimize and encourage such behaviors. Thus, celebrity violence as reported in the media, including the reality series that portray the everyday lives of everyday people—such as the *Real Housewives* franchise—offers a vision of life that is dominated by social aggression, and has the potential to legitimize and influence violent and aggressive behaviors, particularly for teens.

Today social media offer various platforms for electronic aggression and there is great concern for its effects. Electronic social aggression, or harassment through mobile devices and computers, is increasing (David-Ferdon and Feldman Hertz 2007). With 74% of teens having a cell phone with Internet access (Madden et al. 2013), some are using text messages and social networking Web sites to bully and harass their peers. Cyberbullying includes sending or posting malevolent messages and/or images. These messages can be sent through social networking Web sites and emails, and/or through text messaging. With more teens and young adults spending so much time online, the likelihood of being exposed to or involved in cyberbullying increases (Madden 2010). Between 2008 and 2011, for example, cyberbullying has increased from a 6% instance rate to 16%. Past research showed that 88% of teens report having witnessed some form of cyberbullying in social media (Lenhart et al. 2011), yet 59% of teens don't view cyberbullying as a problem.

The dangers of cyberbullying have been well documented. When asked how cyberbullying made the victim feel, the top three responses were frustration, sadness, and anger (Patchin and Hinduja 2006). Victims of cyberbullying have increased feelings of loneliness, they are more likely to be depressed or anxious, and they are even more likely to miss or drop out of school. Extreme situations of cyberbullying may even lead to suicide or school shootings (U.S. Department of Health and Human Services 2013). However, victims are not the only ones to suffer the consequences of cyberbullying; the bullies and even bystanders can be affected too. Bullies are more likely to drop out of school, get into fights, engage in sexual activity at a younger age, and abuse drugs/alcohol as both a teen and an adult. The aggression often continues, with these bullies being abusive to their partners and children later in life. Even bystanders are more likely to have anxiety and abuse alcohol and drugs (U.S. Department of Health and Human Services 2013).

The increase in cyberbullying may also be a result of the ease with which one can engage in the behavior, but another speculation is that most teens believe that there are no consequences to their actions, and believe that they won't be caught (Moessner 2007). When asked, 81% of teens reported they engaged in cyberbullying simply because they think it's funny. Others said they either didn't like the victim or thought that person was a loser. Some teens cyberbullied others because their friends encouraged them to do it, and teens believe that everybody is cyberbullying (Moessner 2007). The motivation to cyberbully can be further fueled by the aggressive and violent behavior displayed by celebrities as reported in the general media. When a celebrity posts aggressive and hostile comments on Twitter or other venues, then teenagers have a direct experience of the behavior and often see no consequences to the celebrity who posted the comments. A recent example is Alec Baldwin's use of Twitter to ostracize reporter George Stark, using homophobic slurs and physically threatening him (Alsup and Karimi 2013).

CONCLUSIONS

Oscar Wilde wrote in *The Picture of Dorian Gray,* "[T]here is only one thing in the world worse than being talked about, and that is not being talked about." But is that the philosophy we should have when it comes to celebrities who model aggressive and violent behavior? This chapter examines issues related to violent behavior of celebrity endorsers, and the potential consequences of using them in advertising as well as the trends in press coverage of the violent behavior. The use of celebrities to endorse brands has been shown to be an effective strategy for advertisers because

Table 9.2

Potential Strategies for Marketers When a Celebrity Endorser Misbehaves, Based on Issue-Spreading Speeds and Audience Responses

		Audience responses		
		Negative	Negative but enjoyable	Accepting and forgiving
Issue-spreading speeds in media	Slow	Remove endorsement quietly	Only respond to audiences' questions	Keep endorsement but remain silent
	Fast	Issue immediate press release about endorsement withdrawal	Distraction tactics	Issue immediate press release about the firm's supporting and forgiving

the positive image of the celebrity endorser might be transferred to the product or brand image. Scandals or misbehavior of celebrity endorsers are harmful for advertisers because negative press coverage can also transfer to the product or brand image (White, Goddard, and Wilbur 2009). However, the coverage of celebrity bad behavior in the media, coupled with their endorsements, may create a synergy of effects when the celebrity behaves in aggressive or violent ways.

It is often the media (broadcast, print, Web) that spread the story of celebrity misbehavior to audiences. Stories of celebrities' misbehavior, such as drinking and driving, using drugs, being arrested, or committing acts of violence, are spread quickly to general audiences through various types of media. When the press become aware of a celebrity's misbehavior, they investigate and report many stories on the background of the behavior in a short period of the time. Thus, for marketers, it is important to understand the speed and the flow of the stories about the scandals so they can try to impede the speed of the massive media coverage and buffer the fallout. Marketers' early response to media coverage of an endorser's misbehavior is the best way to minimize the damage of the celebrity's own image as well as the endorsed brand images.

Advertisers cannot predict and control all of a celebrity's misbehavior after making a decision to use that individual as a product endorser. Factors such as personality, interaction with other people, media, and family issues each play a role that can lead to unexpected misbehavior of the celebrity endorser. Advertisers need to understand the celebrity's characteristics and prepare for the potential risks of using him or her as a product endorser. For example, advertisers can create a manual of celebrity misbehavior strategy based on the type of the infraction (mistakes, violation of social norms, unethical or illegal acts), issue-spreading speeds in media (slow vs. fast), level of damage (no harm, slight harms, or serious harms), or public responses (negative, negative but enjoyable, or accepting and forgiving) (see Tables 9.2 and 9.3). When the issue-spreading speed is slow with negative audience responses, marketers are better remaining silent and removing the endorsement to prevent any damage to the brand image. The most sensitive case for marketers would be the situation when the endorsers' misbehaviors spread fast in media, receiving negative audience responses. In this situation, marketers may need to send out a press release immediately to announce a firm's withdrawing its endorsement and emphasize that the firm is not related to any of endorsers' misbehavior. This prompt action would protect a firm from public criticism over the implication of accepting celebrities' misbehaviors.

Audience responses, however, are not always negative. Sometimes they enjoy the gossip, perhaps experiencing schadenfreude, and sometimes accept and forgive the celebrity's mistakes. If audience responses are negative toward the behavior, but there is pleasure about the celebrity's fall from grace and news of the issue spreads slowly in the media, marketers could limit their public response to audience questions about the firm's position. Perhaps the most spin-able situ-

Table 9.3

Potential Strategies for Marketers When Celebrity Endorsers Misbehave

Type of celebrity endorsers' misbehavior	Strategic action for advertisers	Description
Misbehaviors by mistake, without any harm	Keeping endorsement but remaining silent	Do not react or express any opinion regarding endorser's misbehavior
Violates social norms but no harms	Only respond to audiences' questions	Respond only if publics query a firm's position
Violates social norms with slight harms	Remove endorsement quietly	Remove endorsement without making any noise
Unethical with serious harms	Distraction tactics	Make media noise about the firm's consideration of withdrawing endorsement (position firm as one of the victims)
Illegal and unethical	Issue immediate press release about endorsement withdrawal	Send out a press release immediately to announce the firm's withdrawal endorsement, emphasizing that firm is not related to any of celebrity's misbehavior

ation of endorsers' misbehaviors for marketers would be the case of audience negative response toward the celebrity's behavior, with pleasure in witnessing the downfall, and with fast-speed media exposures. In this case, marketers could create some buzz around a firm's consideration of withdrawing an endorsement, and could position the firm as one of the victims of the endorser's misbehaviors, as well as having an open ear to public opinion. Marketers can demonstrate a moral persona to build up a personal relationship with their customers and fans via sharing their thoughts about the issue and solving the problem together. Lastly, if audiences are accepting and forgiving of the endorser's misbehavior, marketers can also express forgiveness.

The concerns presented in this chapter focus on the potential effects of celebrity negative behavior on youths. Teens are more sensitive to the images and messages that come from celebrities they look up to. The study of violence in media must now extend to advertising in its many forms and across many platforms. Celebrities, as endorsers and as their own brands, represent models for many young people, and the ubiquitous coverage of their behavior has fueled their influence. No longer confined to gossip shows and blogs, celebrity stories are broadcast on major news stations across the world (Aldred et al. 2008). For example, when news broke about Chris Brown's attack on then girlfriend Rihanna, the story appeared in major newspapers and on every major news channel (Lee 2009; Itzkof 2009). This crossover that has led to celebrity gossip being considered newsworthy may also be partially responsible for the normalization we appear to be seeing when it comes to violent behaviors.

Furthermore, the incidence of celebrities expressing remorse or receiving punishment for their behaviors is quite low, with news organizations focusing more on the act than the punishment. It is also typical for news stories to focus on the celebrity and not on the victim. For example, the media fail to cover the trauma and recovery that victims are forced to go through following a violent attack (Sgarzi and Fusfeld 1993). By glorifying the violence and not focusing on the victim, the media can create a numbing effect, which can lead to teenagers' identifying with the attacker (Osofsky and Osofsky 1998). Teenagers then see only the increased coverage the celebrity received, not the repercussions or the impact it had on the victim, and may even seek to mimic these behaviors in the hopes of achieving celebrity status themselves. Research has shown that TV shows that show empathy over aggression can actually improve behavior in children (Emmons 2013). Therefore it stands to reason that reporting on stories of celebrities showing remorse and receiving punishment for their actions could also lead to improved behavior. With more than 60% of children being exposed to violence on a yearly basis, the media should not add to this number by glamorizing violent acts perpetrated by celebrities (CBS News 2009).

Additionally, the explosion of social media brings the immediacy of celebrity via news, but also through celebrity tweets and a connectivity and synergy that society has not experienced to date. When a celebrity uses Twitter to transmit aggressive and violent messages, this behavior is modeled in an immediate and more intimate manner for the teen observer. Twitter allows for participation, retweeting, responding, and a viral spiral of electronic aggression. With social media use increasing each day, people are now able to get their news faster. And many of Twitter's 218 million active users (Constine 2013) now turn to that medium for their news instead of mainstream news outlets (Berfield 2012). Additionally, Twitter users, the majority of whom are under the age of 29 (Duggan and Brenner 2013), are able to receive unfiltered information that would often be censored in print or on a news program.

In summary, celebrities are often studied for their effects as endorsers on consumer perceptions of brands. We contend that it is time to take a closer look at the role of celebrity in shaping society's views of aggressive and violent behavior. Celebrities' influence on consumers, particularly young consumers, should not be overlooked, particularly as this influence is not limited to advertising, but flows through traditional and social media in ways that researchers have yet to study.

REFERENCES

ABC News (2011), "Chris Brown Storms Off Set of 'Good Morning America,'" ABC News, March 22, http://abcnews.go.com/Entertainment/chris-brown-storms-off-set-good-morning-america/story?id=13193040#.Ub880Pb71Jw.

Aldred, Jessica, Amanda Astell, Rafael Behr, Lauren Cochrane, John Hind, Anna Pickard, Laura Potter, Alice Wignall, and Eva Wiseman (2008), "The World's 50 Most Powerful Blogs," *Guardian News and Media Limited,* March 8, www.theguardian.com/technology/2008/mar/09/blogs.

Alsup, Dave, and Faith Karimi (2013), "Alec Baldwin Launches Twitter Rant Against Journalist," CNN Entertainment, June 29, www.cnn.com/2013/06/28/showbiz/alec-baldwin-twitter-war/.

Anderson, Craig A., Akira Sakamoto, Douglas A. Gentile, Nobuko Ihori, Akiko Shibuya, Shintaro Yukawa, Mayumi Naito, and Kumiko Kobayashi (2008), "Longitudinal Effects of Violent Video Games Aggression in Japan and the United States," *Pediatrics,* 122 (5), 1067–1072.

———, and Brad J. Bushman (2001), "Effects of Violent Video Games on Aggressive Behavior, Aggressive Cognition, Aggressive Affect, Physiological Arousal, and Prosocial Behavior: A Meta-Analytic Review of the Scientific Literature," *Psychological Science,* 12 (5), 353–359.

Anthes, Emily (2008), "Real Housewives: Contagious?" *New York Magazine,* April 21, 2008, http://nymag.com/arts/tv/features/46205/.

The Associated Press (2011), "Tweeting for Money: The Twitter Checks Cashed by Celebrities like Khloe Kardashian ($8,000), Charlie Sheen ($9,500) and Even Jailbird LiLo ($3,500)," *Mail Online,* November 3, www.dailymail.co.uk/news/article-2057268/Twitter-endorsements-Khloe-Kardashian-costs-8k-Charlie-Sheen-9-5k-Lindsay-Lohan-3-5k.html.

——— (2013), "Frank Ocean Forgives Chris Brown, Says 'No Charges' Against Him," The Huffington Post, February 3, www.huffingtonpost.com/2013/02/03/frank-ocean-forgives-chris-brown_n_2610412.html.

Atkin, Charles, and Martin Block (1983), "Effectiveness of Celebrity Endorsers," *Journal of Advertising Research,* 23 (1), 57–61.

Banda, P. Solomon (2010), "Charlie Sheen Pleads Guilty in Aspen as Part of Plea Deal," The Huffington Post, August 2, www.huffingtonpost.com/2010/08/02/charlie-sheen-pleads-guil_n_668120.html.

Bandura, Albert (1986), *Social Foundations of Thought and Action: A Social Cognitive Theory,* Upper Saddle River, NJ: Prentice-Hall.

Becker-Olsen, Karen, and Patricia Norberg (2010), "Caution, Animated Violence," *Journal of Advertising,* 39 (4), 83–94.

Berfield, Susan (2012), "For Many, Twitter Replaced Traditional News Sources During Storm," *Business Week,* October 30, www.businessweek.com/articles/2012–10–30/for-many-twitter-replaced-traditional-news-sources-during-storm.
Berzonsky, Michael D., and Joseph R. Ferrari (1996), "Identity Orientation and Decisional Strategies," *Personality and Individual Differences,* 20 (5), 597–606.
bigwayne84 (2006), "Be Like Mike Gatorade Commercial (ORIGINAL)," YouTube, October 23, www.youtube.com/watch?v=b0AGiq9j_Ak.
Blackford, Benjamin J., James Gentry, Robert L. Harrison, and Les Carlson (2011), "The Prevalence and Influence of the Combination of Humor and Violence in Super Bowl Commercials," *Journal of Advertising,* 40 (4), 123–124.
Boon, Susan D., and Christine D. Lomore (2001), "Admirer-Celebrity Relationships Among Young Adults," *Human Communication Research,* 27 (3), 432–465.
Bosch, Torie (2011), "Charlie Sheen Interviews: Tiger Blood, Adonis DNA and Charlie Sheen the Drug [VIDEOS]," AOL News, February 28, www.aolnews.com/2011/02/28/charlie-sheen-interviews-tiger-blood-adonis-dna-and-charlie-s/.
Bravo Media (2013), Bravo Media, NBCUniversal, www.nbcuni.com/cable/bravo/.
Cassidy, Sarah (2006), "Teenagers Beguiled by False Dreams of Instant Fame on Reality TV," *The Independent,* January 13, www.independent.co.uk/news/education/education-news/teenagers-beguiled-by-false-dreams-of-instant-fame-on-reality-tv-522770.html.
CBS News (2009), "U.S.: 60% of Kids Exposed to Violence," CBS News, October 7, www.cbsnews.com/2100–201_162–5369862.html.
Choi, Sejung Marina, and Nora J. Rifon (2012), "It Is a Match: The Impact of Congruence Between Celebrity Image and Consumer Ideal Self on Endorsement Effectiveness," *Psychology and Marketing,* 29 (9), 639–650.
Cieply, Michael (2011), "Mel Gibson in Plea Deal in Battering Case," *The New York Times,* March 11, www.nytimes.com/2011/03/12/business/media/12gibson.html?_r=0.
Clark, John M., T. Bettina Cornwell, and Stephen W. Pruitt (2009), "The Impact of Title Event Sponsorship Announcement on Shareholder Wealth," *Marketing Letters,* 20, 169–182.
CompareBusinessProducts.com. (2010), "12 Rich Celebrities Moonlighting as Expensive Spokespeople," Compare Business Products, March 29, www.comparebusinessproducts.com/fyi/12-rich-celebrities-moonlighting-expensive-spokespeople.
Constine, Josh (2013), "How Many Of Twitter's 218 Million Users Are Just Blind-Tweeting from Other Apps?" TechCrunch, October 3, http://techcrunch.com/2013/10/03/blindtweeting.
Crutchfield, Dean (2010), "Celebrity Endorsements Still Push Product: Why, in the Era of Social Media, the Rewards Continue to Outweigh the Risks," *AdAge,* September 22, http://adage.com/article/cmo-strategy/marketing-celebrity-endorsements-push-product/146023/.
David-Ferdon, Corinne, and Marci Feldman Hertz (2007), "Electronic Media, Violence, and Adolescents: An Emerging Public Health Problem," *Journal of Adolescent Health,* 41 (6), S1-S5.
Doss, Samuel (2011), "The Transference of Brand Attitude: The Effect on the Celebrity Endorser," *Journal of Management and Marketing Research,* 7 (1), 1–11.
Duggan, Maeve, and Joanna Brenner (2013), "The Demographics of Social Media Users—2012," Pew Research Center's Internet and American Life Project, February 14, www.pewinternet.org/2013/02/14/the-demographics-of-social-media-users-2012/.
Duke, Alan (2012), "Singer Chris Brown Clears Another Probation Hurdle," CNN, November 1, www.cnn.com/2012/11/01/showbiz/chris-brown-hearing/index.html.
Elberse, Anita, and Jeroen Verleun (2012), "The Economic Value of Celebrity Endorsements," *Journal of Advertising Research,* 52 (2), 149.
Elliott, Stuart (2002), "The Media Business: Advertising—A New Campaign on Fox TV Guarantees to Push the Envelope" *The New York Times,* September 19, www.nytimes.com/2002/09/19/business/media-business-advertising-new-campaign-fox-tv-guarantees-push-envelope.html.
Emmons, Sasha (2013), "Is Media Violence Damaging to Kids?" February 21, CNN.com, www.cnn.com/2013/02/21/living/parenting-kids-violence-media/index.html.
Erdogan, B. Zafer, and Tanya Drollinger (2008), "Death and Disgrace Insurance for Celebrity Endorsers: A Luxury or Necessity?" *Journal of Current Issues and Research in Advertising,* 30 (1), 71–77.
Fisher, Luchina (2009), "Could Chris Brown Still Be Kids' Choice?" ABC News, March 10, http://abcnews.go.com/Entertainment/WinterConcert/story?id=7042524&page=1#.ULlijZPjnEU.
Fleeman, Mike (2011), "Charlie Sheen Fired from Two and a Half Men," *People,* March 7, www.people.com/people/article/0,,20471718,00.html.
Hammel, Sara (2010), "Mel Gibson Blasts Oksana—Again—in Reputed New Rants," *People,* July 28, www.people.com/people/article/0,,20405875,00.html.

HuffPost TV (2012), "Anderson Cooper Calls Out Teresa Giudice for Bullying Behavior at Real Housewives of New Jersey Reunion," The Huffington Post, September 26 (video), www.huffingtonpost.com/2012/09/26/anderson-cooper-teresa-giudice_n_1917282.html.

Hughes, Sarah Anne (2011), "Lindsay Lohan Sued for Assault by Fired Betty Ford Worker," *The Washington Post,* July 22, www.washingtonpost.com/blogs/celebritology/post/lindsay-lohan-sued-for-assault-by-fired-betty-ford-worker/2011/07/22/gIQAgiiMTI_blog.html.

Itzkof, Dave (2009), "Chris Brown Pleads Not Guilty," *The New York Times,* April 7, www.nytimes.com/2009/04/08/arts/music/08arts-CHRISBROWNPL_BRF.html?ref=rihanna.

Jacobs, Shayna (2013), "Lindsay Lohan, Charged with Assault in Chelsea Nightclub Catfight, Set to Appear in Court Monday," *The New York Daily News,* January 6, http://www.nydailynews.com/entertainment/gossip/lohan-set-swing-court-article-1.1234073.

———, and Nancy Dillon (2013), "Lindsay Lohan Will Not Be Charged with Punching Psychic." *The New York Daily News,* March 22, www.nydailynews.com/new-york/lilo-charged-punching-psychic-article-1.1296533.

Johnson, Allison R. (2005), "When a Celebrity Is Tied to Immoral Behavior: Consumer Reactions to Michael Jackson and Kobe Bryant," *Advances in Consumer Research,* 32, 100–101.

Kaufman, Gil (2009), "Chris Brown's Songs, TV Appearances Yanked from Air," MTV News, February 11, www.mtv.com/news/articles/1604786/chris-browns-songs-tv-appearances-yanked-from-air.jhtml.

Kempen, Simon (2013), "Highest Rated Housewives Reunion Episode," Bravo Ratings, March 31, http://bravoratings.com/2013/03/31/highest-rated-real-housewives-reunion-episode/.

Khan, Amina (2010), "Charlie Sheen Charged with Felony in Alleged Assault on Wife in Aspen [Updated]," *Los Angeles Times,* February 8, http://latimesblogs.latimes.com/lanow/2010/02/charlie-sheen-charged-with-3-felonies-in-alleged-assault-on-wife-in-aspen.html.

Kowalczyk, Christine M., and Marla B. Royne (2013), "The Moderating Role of Celebrity Worship on Attitudes Toward Celebrity Brand Extensions," *Journal of Marketing Theory and Practice,* 21 (2), 211–220.

Lee, Ken (2009), "Chris Brown Under Investigation for Felony Battery," *People,* February 8, www.people.com/people/article/0,,20257693,00.html.

——— (2011a), "Police: Lindsay Lohan Committed Battery," *People,* January 4, www.people.com/people/article/0,,20454735,00.html.

——— (2011b), "Mel Gibson Sentenced to Counseling, Probation in Battery Case," *People,* March 11, www.people.com/people/article/0,,20473323,00.html.

Lenhart, Amanda, Mary Madden, Aaron Smith, Kristen Purcell, Kathryn Zickuhr, and Lee Rainie (2011), "Teens, Kindness and Cruelty on Social Network Sites," Pew Research Center's Internet and American Life Project, www.pewinternet.org/~/media/Files/Reports/2011/PIP_teens_Kindness_Cruelty_SNS_Report_Nov_2011_FINAL_110711.pdf.

Lennings, Heidi I. Brummert, and Wayne A. Warburton (2011), "The Effect of Auditory Versus Visual Violent Media Exposure on Aggressive Behavior: The Role of Song Lyrics, Video Clips and Musical Tone," *Journal of Experimental Social Psychology,* 47 (4), 794–799.

Madden, Mary (2010), "Cyberbullying 2010: What the Research Tells Us," Pew Internet and American Life Project, www.pewinternet.org/Presentations/2010/May/Cyberbullying-2010.aspx.

———, Amanda Lenhart, Maeve Duggan, Sandra Cortesi, and Urs Gasser (2013), "Teens and Technology 2013," Pew Internet and American Life Project, www.pewinternet.org/Reports/2013/Teens-and-Tech.aspx.

Marikar, Sheila (2011), "Real Housewives of Beverly Hills Husband Was $1.5 Million in Debt Before Apparent Suicide," ABC News, August 16, http://abcnews.go.com/Entertainment/husband-real-housewives-star-15-million-debt-suicide/story?id=14316572.

Maronick, Thomas J. (2006), "Celebrity Versus Company President as Endorsers of High Risk Products for Elderly Consumers," *Journal of Promotion Management,* 11 (4), 63–80.

McCracken, Grant (1989), "Who Is the Celebrity Endorser? Cultural Foundations of the Endorsement Process," *Journal of Consumer Research,* 16 (3), 310–321.

Miller, Felicia, and Gene Laczniak (2011), "The Ethics of Celebrity-Athlete Endorsement: What Happens When a Star Steps Out of Bounds?" *Journal of Advertising Research,* 51 (3), 499–510.

Moessner, Chris (2007), "Cyberbullying," HarrisInteractive: Trends and Tudes, 6 (4), 1–5, http://us.vocuspr.com/Newsroom/ViewAttachment.aspx?SiteName=NCPCNew&Entity=PRAsset&AttachmentType=F&EntityID=103393&AttachmentID=0f59e5b2-844e-41f2-b03e-11e5298fbce7.

O'Cass, Aron, and Emily Frost (2002), "Status Brands: Examining the Effects of Non-Product-Related Brand Associations on Status and Conspicuous Consumption," *Journal of Product and Brand Management,* 11 (2), 67–88.

Ockenfels, Frank (2012), "Charlie Sheen's 'Anger Management' Breaks Ratings Record," *Rolling Stone,*

June 29, www.rollingstone.com/culture/news/charlie-sheens-anger-management-breaks-ratings-record-20120629.

Oh, Eunice (2010), "Photo of Bruised Oksana Grigorieva Hits the Web," *People,* July 7, www.people.com/people/article/0,,20405605,00.html.

Osofsky, Joy D., and Howard J. Osofsky (1998), "Children's Exposure to Violence: A Critical Lens for Reporting on Violence," Nieman Reports, www.nieman.harvard.edu/reports/article/102284/Childrens-Exposure-to-Violence.aspx.

Pagan, Jeffrey, and Sandra Wexlerf (1987), "Crime at Home and in the Streets: The Relationship Between Family and Stranger Violence," *Violence and Victims,* 2 (1), 5–23.

Patchin, Justin W., and Sameer Hinduja (2006), "Bullies Move Beyond the Schoolyard: A Preliminary Look at Cyberbullying," *Criminolgy and Penology,* 4 (2), 148–169.

Rodak, Mike, and The Associated Press (2013), "Murder Charge for Aaron Hernandez," ESPN, June 28, http://espn.go.com/boston/nfl/story/_/id/9424056/aaron-hernandez-new-england-patriots-taken-police-custody.

Schunk, Dale H. (1987), "Peer Models and Children's Behavioral Change," *Review of Educational Research,* 57, 149–174.

Schwartz, Alison (2011), "Charlie Sheen Set to Return to TV in Anger Management," *People,* July 18, www.people.com/people/article/0,,20510995,00.html.

Senate Committee on the Judiciary (1999), "Children, Violence, and the Media: A Report for Parents and Policy Makers," Senate Committee on the Judiciary, September 14, www.indiana.edu/~cspc/ressenate.htm.

Sgarzi, Judith M., and Robert T. Fusfeld (1993), "The Media's Influence on Behavior and Violence," Meeting of American Society of Criminology, Phoenix, AZ.

Shayon, Sheila (2011), "Celebrity Endorsements a Mixed Blessing," Brandchannel, February 9, www.brandchannel.com/home/post/2011/02/09/Celebrity-Endorsements-a-Mixed-Blessing.aspx.

Sheehan, K. Brian (2003), *Controversies in Contemporary Advertising,* Thousand Oaks, CA: Sage.

Shoichet, Catherine E., Ross Levitt, and Mariano Castillo (2013), "Police Are Back at Hernandez Home," CNN.com, June 27, www.cnn.com/2013/06/27/us/nfl-hernandez/index.html?hpt=hp_t1.

Smith, Courtenay, and Alison Caporimo (2013), "The Most Trusted People in America," *Reader's Digest,* June, www.rd.com/slideshows/readers-digest-trust-poll-the-100-most-trusted-people-in-america/.

Smreker, Karen, Nora J. Rifon, Sookyong, Kim, and Jef I. Richards (2013), "Famous or Infamous? A Content Analysis of Celebrity Bad Behavior Reported in the Press," American Academy of Advertising Global Conference, Hawaii.

Tantiseneepong, Nisachon, Matthew Gorton, and John White (2012), "Evaluating Responses to Celebrity Endorsements Using Projective Techniques," *Qualitative Market Research: An International Journal,* 15 (1), 57–69.

Thwaites, Des, Ben Lowe, Lien L. Monkhouse, and Bradley R. Barnes (2012), "The Impact of Negative Publicity on Celebrity Ad Endorsements," *Psychology and Marketing,* 29 (9), 663–673.

TMZ Staff (2011), "Charlie Sheen Tour Sold Out in 18 Minutes!" TMZ, March 12, www.tmz.com/2011/03/12/charlie-sheen-tour-ticketmaster-detroit-chicago-tickets-sold-out-18-minutes.

——— (2012), "Lindsay Lohan Settles Beef with Betty Ford Worker," TMZ, May 7, http:/www.tmz.com/2012/05/07/lindsay-lohan-betty-ford-dawn-holland-settlement/.

——— (2013a), "Aaron Hernandez: Patriots Star Sued," TMZ, June 19, www.tmz.com/2013/06/19/aaron-hernandez-new-england-patriots-lawsuit-gun-shooting-miami-strip-club/.

——— (2013b), "Chris Brown: D.A. Could File Charges In Frank Ocean Fight," TMZ, June 10, www.tmz.com/2013/06/10/chris-brown-probation-hearing-frank-ocean-fight/.

U.S. Department of Health and Human Services (2013), "Effect of Bullying," stopbullying.gov, www.stopbullying.gov/at-risk/effects/.

Wang, Cynthia (2009), "Brooke Mueller's 911 Call: Charlie Pulled a Knife," *People,* December 28, www.people.com/people/article/0,,20333373,00.html.

——— (2010), "Hanes Suspends Charlie Sheen Commercials," *People,* January 6, www.people.com/people/article/0,,20334845,00.html.

White, Darin W., Lucretia Goddard, and Nick Wilbur (2009), "The Effects of Negative Information Transference in the Celebrity Endorsement Relationship," *International Journal of Retail and Distribution Management,* 37 (4), 322–355.

Wihlborg, Ulrica (2011), "Taylor Armstrong: My Marriage Was Abusive," about.com, July 28, http://marriage.about.com/gi/o.htm?zi=1/XJ&zTi=1&sdn=marriage&cdn=people&tm=10&f=10&su=p284.13.342.ip_&tt=11&bt=6&bts=6&zu=http%3A//www.people.com/people/article/0%2C%2C20513539%2C00.html.

Young, S. Mark, and Drew Pinsky (2006), "Narcissism and Celebrity," *Journal of Research in Personality,* 40 (5), 463–471.

PART V

SPECIAL CONCERNS FOR CHILDREN

10

Violence Is in the Ads, Too
Should Television Advertisements Be Rated?
Marla B. Royne and Alexa K. Fox

With 98% of U.S. households owning at least one television set, 60% of homes subscribing to cable television (PTC 2012a), and a growing number of households subscribing to satellite and wireless services (Desrochers and Holt 2007), children are increasingly being exposed to television programs and advertisements. Total television advertising expenditures grew from an estimated $29 billion in 1990 (U.S. Census Bureau 2006) to nearly $80 billion in 2012 (Goetzl 2013), and children ages 2 to 11 view about 25,600 advertisements per year (Desrochers and Holt 2007). At the same time, studies have long suggested that parents are concerned about the negative effects that advertising can have on their children (Grossbart and Crosby 1984; Laczniak, Muehling, and Carlson 1995).

In the early 2000s, most television sets began to come equipped with a V-chip, a device that can block designated television programs based on their content ratings. However, because television advertisements are not rated, the V-chip is unable to block commercials (TV Parental Guidelines 2012), meaning that children can still be exposed to violence in television ads. This is particularly troubling, considering that researchers have found positive associations between media violence and aggressive behaviors (i.e., Anderson and Bushman 2002; Lewis, Watson, and Tay 2007), and that a significant amount of television ads targeted at children age 12 and younger contain violent content (Shanahan, Hermans, and Hyman 2003).

Further, more than 105,000 Americans were injured or killed during a firearm-related incident in 2010 (Institute of Medicine 2013). These alarming statistics, along with widely publicized violent incidents such as school shootings in Chardon, Ohio, and Newtown, Connecticut, have led to increased public concern about violence. It is particularly disconcerting to note that young adults and even children are committing a number of these violent acts, especially because children view about 150,000 acts of violence on television by age 18 (Statistic Brain 2012). Given these findings, as well as a significant increase in violent media in recent years (Rifon, Royne, and Carlson 2010), it may be time to reevaluate the need for a television advertising rating system. Hence, the purpose of this chapter is to explore this issue. In doing so, we review research on violence in advertising and its effects on children. We then report results from an exploratory study to begin to understand how children feel about content in advertisements that are aired during programs they watch. We conclude with recommendations for advertisers and policymakers with regard to regulating television commercials.

VIOLENT CONTENT AND CHILDREN

Children's exposure to violent media is a significant public health concern (Kunkel 2007). In 1998, the National Television Violence Study concluded that violent portrayals are pervasive across television programming, and are found in a majority of programs. At the same time, research shows that children's learning of behavior can be facilitated by the media they consume just as easily as it is facilitated though real-life observation. The psychology and advertising literature proposes that, in general, media violence negatively affects children's behavior. Even brief exposures to violent content can lead to an increase in aggressive cognitions (Brocato et al. 2010), behaviors (Paik and Comstock 1994), and personality traits (Anderson and Bushman 2001). Such exposure can also lead to increased desensitization toward victims of violence and exaggerated fear of being victimized by violence (Kunkel 2007). These effects are heightened as a result of repeated exposure to violence (Anderson et al. 2008).

Effects are also heightened for particular aspects of violence. For instance, portrayals of violence that seem realistic are more likely to trigger aggression in viewers than unrealistic portrayals of violence (Seawell 1998). However, even fantastical depictions of violence can increase such behaviors in children, because kids generally find it difficult to distinguish fantasy from reality. The *National Television Violence Study* also found that attractive perpetrators of violence (i.e., heroes and characters portrayed as "good guys") tend to increase learning of aggressive behaviors, findings supported by the existing literature on source credibility. More specifically, research shows that the effectiveness of a message depends on a source's familiarity, likeability, similarity, and attractiveness to the viewer (McGuire 1985; Ohanian 1990). This is particularly relevant in an advertising context because advertisers often use likeable and attractive celebrity endorsers to persuade viewers. That is, if a perpetrator of violence resonates with a child, the child is more likely to mimic that individual's behavior. In short, it is clear that contextual effects of media violence can have a significant impact on children.

WHO'S RESPONSIBLE?

Researchers have long debated the responsibility of the regulation and monitoring of children's exposure to violence in advertising. Some scholars believe that schools should teach children how to cope with advertising and help develop a self-regulatory system (Armstrong and Brucks 1988). Although these programs may facilitate children's understanding that advertisements do not always promote acceptable behaviors, Armstrong and Brucks (1988) note that such programs may not be as effective as critiques of advertising that can occur at the "point-of-viewing."

Other researchers have suggested that parents should always be present when children watch television so they can control access to harmful content and promote tasteful viewing. Unfortunately, however, this is an impractical and improbable scenario, in part because children watch an average of 30 hours of television each week (McDonough 2009). Armstrong and Brucks (1988) suggest that parents develop household rules to guide their children's television exposure; it may be difficult, however, for children to follow these rules without parental supervision.

Still other researchers have proposed that the government should be responsible for monitoring children's exposure to violent advertising (Huston, Watkins, and Kunkel 1989). In fact, the U.S. Senate passed the Child Safe Viewing Act of 2007, which required the Federal Communications Commission (FCC) to examine parental control and rating systems, including technology "enhancing the ability of a parent to protect his or her child from indecent or objectionable programming, as determined by such parent" (Child Safe Viewing Act 2008). Despite such efforts and the development of television program industry standards by government agencies, most of these standards do not apply to advertisements. Advertising targeted toward children has been illegal in countries such as Sweden (Radio and Television Act 1996) and Norway (Jolly 2011) for more than 20 years, but the United States has never taken such an approach. Hence, literature has long debated a more extreme approach such as banning all advertisements directed at children, even though researchers argue that such tactics may have limited effectiveness (Armstrong and Brucks 1988); that is, if children watch television programs that are not explicitly directed at children, but are considered family friendly, opportunities may still exist for children to see inappropriate ad content.

The effect of violence on children continues to be debated outside of academia as well. An increase in violent societal events has prompted television networks to reconsider airing certain program content. Networks claim they want to be "respectful of the social climate we're [the United States] in right now" (Marechal 2013) by choosing not to air episodes of programs that depict children committing violent acts. However, many parental and educational organizations that advocate responsible entertainment believe that it should not require the occurrence of extreme violent acts for television networks and producers to reassess the airing of violent television content. There is also concern about the content of television advertisements, because even brief exposure to violent content can lead to aggression in children (Paik and Comstock 1994).

CURRENT RATINGS SYSTEMS

The Telecommunications Act of 1996 gave the television industry the first opportunity to establish voluntary ratings of television programs (FCC 2012). The National Association of Broadcasters, the National Cable Television Association, and the Motion Picture Association of America established the TV Parental Guidelines, which work in conjunction with the V-chip to block designated programs based on their content. The guidelines contain two basic components: audience and content label. The audience component indicates the appropriate audience for a particular television program. For example, "TV Y" stands for "Youth" and signifies that a program is appropriate for all children, including those ages 2 to 6. The content of a program with a "TV 14" rating is suggested as inappropriate for children below 14 years of age. This means that the television network and/or program producer urges parents not to allow children under 14 years old to watch the program for various reasons, which are denoted by the content label. For instance, a program could contain intensely suggestive dialogue (D), strong coarse language (L), intense sexual situations (S), or intense violence (V). Hence, a program can carry one of seven ratings, displayed for the first 15 seconds of the program and generally redisplayed after each commercial break (TV Parental Guidelines 2012).

Although the guidelines now apply to most television programs, news and sports programs are exempt from the ratings system (TV Parental Guidelines 2012). Moreover, television ads are exempt from the ratings system, indicating that even if a child is watching a program that may be age appropriate, the ad content aired during that program may not follow the same guidelines. And even if parents take precautions to monitor which programs their children watch, kids may still be exposed to violent content through advertisements (Blackford et al. 2011). Hence, a child's television viewing experience may not be completely safe. This can be especially problematic for younger children, who are less able to accurately process ad information than older children (Paik and Comstock 1994; John 1999).

ORGANIZATIONAL EFFORTS

Some organizations have made efforts to monitor advertising directed at children. One major force is the Parents Television Council (PTC), a nonpartisan educational organization that advocates responsible entertainment (PTC 2012b). The organization focuses primarily on monitoring television programs and movies that are rated as suitable for children but may still contain questionable content. In fact, the PTC found that of the 392 prime-time television programs aired on broadcast networks, 121 include at least one act of gun violence, yet are rated as appropriate for 14-year-old children (Bauder 2013). The organization tries to curtail the effects of violent content by writing program reviews so that parents are able to assess the type of content present in a given program.

In an effort to reduce the amount of violent content aired on broadcast networks, the PTC is currently focused on its Advertiser Accountability campaign, which calls advertisers' attention to the negative effects that can result from violent content. In April 2013, the PTC voiced its concerns at an AT&T shareholders' meeting, urging its advertisers "to make a commitment to do well by my fellow shareholders by also doing what is good for children" (PTC 2013). Since the current television ratings system does not apply to commercial spots, advertisers are not required to rate the commercials they create. Hence, while the PTC's efforts are noteworthy, involved parties may disagree on "what is good for children."

The Decency Enforcement Center for Television (Decent TV) is a nonprofit organization that advocates the defense and enforcement of decency laws related to television. The organization feels that "the broadcast airwaves, by law, are a public place, no different than streets, sidewalks, and parks, and people must be free to go to those places at any time without risk that children or unconsenting adults may risk being exposed to unwanted indecency" (Decency Enforcement Center for Television 2012). Unlike the PTC, Decent TV does not attempt to determine the appropriateness of a given television program; rather, the group advocates for existing laws restricting indecent broadcasting on television to late night hours, when children are less likely to be watching. Decent TV also works with the FCC to research improved technology for filtering indecent television content.

In 1974, the advertising industry and the Better Business Bureau created the Children's Advertising Review Unit (CARU) to evaluate child-directed advertising (Council of Better Business Bureau 2008). CARU offers a set of guidelines to follow when creating ads targeted at children under the age of 12 (Brocato et al. 2010). However, because the guidelines are optional and research indicates that violent content continues to be prevalent in television ads targeted at children (Ji and Laczniak 2007; Shanahan, Hermans, and Hyman 2003), advertisers do not seem to adhere regularly to these guidelines. Hence, it may be time to re-evaluate the regulation of television advertisements on programs that are generally appropriate for children. To gain preliminary insight on potential changes, we felt it was important to begin by listening to those individuals who would be directly affected by such changes: children.

EXPLORATORY STUDY

As an initial investigation into the perceptions of television advertising among children, 22 third-grade students from the southeast United States participated in an exploratory study. To begin to understand what potentially inappropriate content children notice in television advertisements, we asked the students to keep a television diary for one week. Specifically, they were instructed to record the names of all television programs they watched and if they saw any commercials that they did not like or made them feel uncomfortable. Half of the participants were boys, and all students were either 8 or 9 years old. Parental permission was required for student participation.

Results from the study indicated that some students were uncomfortable with the content of the advertisements they viewed; 70% of these students were boys. Eighteen of the 22 students reported watching television on both weekdays and weekends, while only four students watched television just on weekdays. Table 10.1 shows the breakdown of ratings for the programs that the students reported watching. As indicated, the majority of programs watched were rated Y7, G, and PG, all deemed age-appropriate by the TV Parental Guidelines for the sample of children in the study.

Many of the students watched television programs intended specifically for children, such as the Disney Channel's *Jessie* and Nickelodeon's *SpongeBob SquarePants*. Some students did not elaborate, but mentioned that the content of the advertisements made them feel uncomfortable,

Table 10.1

Number of Programs Viewed Categorized by TV Parental Rating

Program rating	Number of programs viewed with this rating
Y	2
Y7	16
G	12
PG	15
PG-13	3
Not rated	8

even though these commercials were aired during children's programs. Several other children described how advertisements for hospitals and direct-to-consumer advertisements for prescription drugs scared them because of the frightening portrayal of the consequences. Other students noted they were uncomfortable with advertisements for other children's programs because the characters exhibited emotions and behaviors such as jealousy, bullying, and anger. These findings suggest that children are indeed disturbed by some television advertisement content, even for commercials aired on programs that are deemed suitable for children.

Several students noted that they watched television programs that are rated TV-G, such as *How It's Made* and *Full House*. Television programs receive this rating if they are not targeted specifically for children, but are designed so that children can watch the program unattended. According to the TV Parental Guidelines, these programs "contain little to no violence, no strong language, and little or no sexual dialogue or situations." Interestingly, some students indicated they were uncomfortable with the commercial content because they knew that the programs were not technically created for their age group. One student even mentioned the use of a digital video recorder (DVR) to skip those commercials. Others found commercials aired on Cartoon Network programs made them uncomfortable because these spots included adult content, such as "adult stuff," "hospital commercials," and "people being mean to a girl." Such findings indicate that children watch programs that are not specifically designed for them, but under the current ratings, are acceptable for them to view unattended. More importantly, while the content of the programs made appropriately rated, the content of the ads aired during such programs may be intended for older audiences and inappropriate for children.

DISCUSSION AND IMPLICATIONS

Results of this exploratory study suggest that young children can easily be exposed to advertising content that makes them feel uncomfortable. The TV Parental Guidelines and the V-chip work together to regulate the violent content of television programs, but because the V-chips do not apply to television advertisements, children are still exposed to violence. Even more troubling is that some children expressed discomfort with the advertisements they saw while watching programs on the Disney Channel and Nickelodeon, channels targeted directly toward children. Other networks, such as the Cartoon Network, can be particularly deceiving because while they only air cartoons, many of these programs are rated TV-Y7-FV and TV-PG, denoting, respectively, the inclusion of intense fantasy violence and suggesting they should be watched with parental guidance. If parents cannot ensure their child's safety on such channels, they may find it difficult to trust other channels that air family-friendly programming but are not targeted specifically at children.

Based on the existing literature and results from our exploratory study, we argue that it is time for television networks, advocacy groups, advertisers, and academicians to work together to create standards for advertising content that work in conjunction with the TV Parental Guidelines. For example, during the airing of a program rated TV-Y7, the network should not air teasers for any shows that are rated for older audiences. Advertisements for products and services should adhere to the same guidelines. For example, a 2008 commercial for Doritos Nacho Cheese Flavored Tortilla Chips depicts a man setting up a mousetrap and eating Doritos while waiting for a mouse to emerge from its hole. Instead, a man in a mouse costume breaks down the wall, subsequently tackling and punching the man eating the Doritos. Although this depiction of violence is meant to be humorous, it may be inappropriate to air during programs that are rated TV-Y, TV-Y7, or TV-G. For networks that air only children's programs, these standards should apply without exception. For networks that air children's programming during certain hours and adult programming during other hours, the standards should apply whenever a children's or general audience program is being aired.

We recognize that advocating for such standards may generate resistance to the control of advertising content. Just a few years ago, the Association of National Advertisers (ANA) pressured the FCC to deny any potential regulations on commercial content, arguing that such restrictions would seriously undermine ad-supported media. The ANA also claimed that such regulations would go beyond the scope of the Child Safe Viewing Act and would be indicative of regulatory overkill because relatively few ads would be affected (ANA 2009).

However, with company and other organizational efforts beginning to take accountability for their advertisement content and creating their own standards, it may be the right time to revisit a standardized content rating system for television commercials, and such a system may be best developed through industry self-regulation. For example, starting in 2015, the Walt Disney Company will require that all television, radio, and Web site advertisements aired on the company's networks comply with a strict set of nutritional standards (Barnes 2012). The goal of such efforts is to promote healthier food and beverage choices among child viewers. The Disney Channel, as well as other networks, can take similar efforts to create network-specific standards for violence in advertisements. For instance, the content of the advertisements aired during a TV-Y rated program on the Disney Channel should comply with this rating.

But as other areas of the entertainment industry have shown, the mere existence of a ratings system may not necessarily be enough. The motion picture industry has implemented a ratings system since the enactment of the Motion Picture Production Code in 1930 (Shurlock 1947). This system has evolved over the years, but not without great debate and scrutiny from the government, concerned parents, and citizen organizations. In April 2013, the Motion Picture Association of America announced changes to its movie rating system. The new "Check the Box" campaign will require not only that the movie's rating be written in a larger font size, but also a list of the reasons why a movie received a particular rating (Associated Press 2013). However, citizen organizations such as the PTC question whether this campaign will truly decrease children's viewing of inappropriate content or whether it will simply draw children's attention to the reason the movie received a particular rating and, subsequently, increase their desire to watch it. Hence, it is recommended that researchers, advertisers, and policymakers work together to develop industry standards for violent content in television advertisements. In doing so, it is important to examine how much attention children and parents give to other entertainment ratings. Is simply increasing font size an effective way to increase awareness of a rating or should we be focusing on reforming the standards by which content is rated?

It may also be time to take yet another step back and reconsider the type of content that is assigned a particular rating. Consumer organizations have continually fought for the advertising industry to "maintain decency" on television, but as the entertainment industry continues to push the envelope on the type of content allowed on the air, we wonder if researchers, advertisers, and policymakers can agree on what should be defined as "decent" and "appropriate" content.

Children now spend less time with parents and more time with peers (Dotson and Hyatt 1994), and they are exposed to more television than ever before (Dotson and Hyatt 2005). They are also exposed to entertainment and advertisement content through other media such as the Internet, all of which may contribute to their increased desensitization. As such, scholars, practitioners, and policymakers should work together to reexamine the type of content that is available to children and to redefine what is deemed "decent" and "appropriate" for various age groups.

Further, the majority of students in our study reported watching television on both weekdays and weekends, while only a few students watched only on weekdays. This suggests that although research on children's exposure to television violence sometimes focuses on programs aired on Saturdays (e.g., Shanahan, Hermans, and Hyman 2003), policy changes should consider both weekday and weekend programming.

FUTURE RESEARCH

Much of the existing literature on violence focuses on children's interaction with television programs and video games (e.g., Bensley and Van Eenwyk 2001; Ferguson, San Miguel, and Hartley 2009; Olson et al. 2007). However, existing literature and our exploratory results offer considerable research opportunities on this topic in other environments. First, more research is needed to better understand children's attitudes and behaviors that result from exposure to violent television advertisements. Literature suggests that by age 4, most children can distinguish between a television program and an advertisement but do not understand the intent of advertising (Butter et al. 1981). By 7 or 8 years old, children tend to understand the persuasive nature of advertisements (Bever et al. 1975; Robertson and Rossiter 1974). Regardless of whether children are young enough to simply distinguish between television programs and advertisements or they are old enough to understand the intent of advertising, exposure to violence in advertisements is likely to enhance their attraction to violence and affect their subsequent behavior. Thus, additional empirical inquiry is needed to examine such effects.

More studies are also needed to examine the relationship between violence in television advertising and school bullying. School bullying is a serious issue that has received increasing media attention in recent years. While just 7% of students reported being bullied in 2003, 29% reported being bullied in 2009 (Dinkes et al. 2009). Although research has examined factors such as academic performance (Cook et al. 2010), exposure to domestic violence (Baldry 2003), exposure to television (Zimmerman et al. 2005), and their effects on bullying, little research has examined the relationship between children's exposure to violence in television advertisements and bullying attitudes/behaviors. Further, in our study, boys comprised the majority of the students who felt uncomfortable about certain ads. This finding is consistent with recent research reporting that pre-adolescent girls are more likely than boys to commit an act of violence (Orpinas et al. 2012). Future research should explore gender differences as well as whether violent advertisements contribute to the increase in school bullying.

Yet another area ripe for future research is the relationship between even brief exposure to violence in television advertisements and desensitization to violence. Cline, Croft, and Courrier (1973) found that consumers who are more exposed to violence tend to perceive violence as less intense, which can translate into reduced levels of sympathy for victims of violence and reduced negative attitudes toward violence (Carnagey, Anderson, and Bushman 2007). Thus, researchers should examine whether violence in television advertisements contributes to children's desensitization toward violence, which may also contribute to bullying behaviors. If such linkages are established, antibullying organizations such as StopBullying.gov and STOMP Out Bullying should consider joining forces with the television monitoring organizations (e.g., the PTC) to work toward policy implementation that creates standards for violence in advertising.

Although television advertising has existed for decades, it is clear that ample opportunities exist for increased regulation. If we concern ourselves only with the content of television programs and not the content of the advertisements aired during those programs, many of the existing efforts to regulate television program content may be negated. Because children can be negatively affected by even brief, repeated exposures to violence, it is time to take action to minimize these effects. We hope that scholars, advertisers, and advocacy organizations will continue to explore the ideas raised in this chapter and strive toward a set of guidelines for television advertisement regulation.

REFERENCES

Anderson, Craig A., and Brad J. Bushman (2001), "Effects of Violent Video Games on Aggressive Behavior, Aggressive Cognition, Aggressive Affect, Physiological Arousal, and Prosocial Behavior: A Meta-Analytic Review of the Scientific Literature," *Psychological Science,* 12 (5), 353–359.

——— (2002), "The Effects of Media Violence on Society," *Science,* 295 (5564), 2377–2379.

———, Akira Sakamoto, Douglas Gentile, Nobuko Ihori, Akiko Shibuya, Shintaro Yukawa, Mayum Naito, and Kumiko Kobayashi (2008), "Longitudinal Effects of Video Games on Aggression in Japan and the United States," *Pediatrics,* 122 (5), 1067–1072.

Armstrong, Gary M., and Merrie Brucks (1988), "Dealing with Children's Advertising: Public Policy Issues and Alternatives," *Journal of Public Policy & Marketing,* 98–113.

The Associated Press (2013), "Motion Picture Association Changing Its Rating System to Include More Information on Violence," Fox News, April 16, www.foxnews.com/entertainment/2013/04/16/motion-pictures-association-changing-its-rating-system-to-include-more/.

Association of National Advertisers (ANA) (2009), "ANA Urges FCC to Reject Content Ratings for TV Commercials," April 16, www.ana.net/content/show/id/1809 (accessed June 4, 2013).

Baldry, Anna C. (2003), "Bullying in Schools and Exposure to Domestic Violence," *Child Abuse & Neglect,* 27 (7), 713–732.

Barnes, Brooks (2012), "Promoting Nutrition, Disney to Restrict Junk-Food Ads," *The New York Times,* June 5, www.nytimes.com/2012/06/05/business/media/in-nutrition-initiative-disney-to-restrict-advertising.html?pagewanted=all&_r=0.

Bauder, David (2013), "TV Violence Still Prevalent, According to New PTC Study," HuffPost TV, May 1, www.huffingtonpost.com/2013/05/01/tv-violence-ptc-study_n_3193813.html.

Bensley, Lillian, and Juliet Van Eenwyk (2001), "Video Games and Real-Life Aggression: Review of the Literature," *Journal of Adolescent Health,* 29 (4), 244–257.

Bever, Thomas G., Martin L. Smith, Barbara Bengen, and Thomas G. Johnson (1975), "Young Viewers' Troubling Response to TV Ads," *Harvard Business Review,* 53 (November–December), 109–120.

Blackford, Benjamin J., James Gentry, Robert L. Harrison, and Les Carlson (2011), "The Prevalence and Influence of the Combination of Humor and Violence in Super Bowl Commercials," *Journal of Advertising,* 40 (4), 123–134.

Brocato, E. Deanne, Douglas A. Gentile, Russell N. Laczniak, Julia A. Maier, and Mindy Ji-Song (2010), "Television Commercial Violence," *Journal of Advertising,* 39 (4), 95–108.

Butter, Eliot J., Paula M. Popovich, Robert H. Stackhouse, and Roger K. Gamer (1981), "Discrimination of Television Programs and Commercials by Preschool Children," *Journal of Advertising Research,* 21 (April), 53–56.

Carnagey, Nicholas L., Craig A. Anderson, and Brad J. Bushman (2007), "The Effect of Video Game Violence on Physiological Desensitization to Real-Life Violence," *Journal of Experimental Social Psychology,* 43 (3), 489–496.

Child Safe Viewing Act of 2007 (2008), Public Law No. 110–452, 122 Stat. 5025.

Cline, Victor B., Roger G. Croft, and Steven Courrier (1973), "Desensitization of Children to Television Violence," *Journal of Personality and Social Psychology,* 27 (3), 360–365.

Cook, Clayton R., Kirk R. Williams, Nancy G. Guerra, Tia E. Kim, and Shelly Sadek (2010), "Predictors of Bullying and Victimization in Childhood and Adolescence: A Meta-Analytic Investigation," *School Psychology Quarterly,* 25 (2), 65–83.

Council of Better Business Bureau (2008), "About the Children's Advertising Review Unit (CARU)," www.asrcreviews.org/category/caru/about_caru/.

Decency Enforcement Center for Television (2012), "About Decent TV," www.decenttv.org/aboutdecenttv.htm.

Desrochers, Debra M., and Debra J. Holt (2007), "Children's Exposure to Television Advertising: Implications for Childhood Obesity," *Journal of Public Policy & Marketing,* 26 (2), 182–201.

Dinkes, Rachel, Jana Kemp, Katrina Baum, and Thomas D. Snyder (2009), *Indicators of School Crime and Safety: 2009* (NCES 2010–012/NCJ 228478), Washington, DC: National Center for Education Statistics, Institute of Education Sciences, U.S. Department of Education, and Bureau of Justice Statistics, Office of Justice Programs, U.S. Department of Justice, http://bjs.gov/content/pub/pdf/iscs09.pdf.

Dotson, Michael J., and Eva M. Hyatt (1994), "The Impact of Changes in the Household on the Consumer Socialization Process," *Proceedings of the Southern Marketing Association,* New Orleans, LA, November, 156–160.

——— (2005), "Major Factors in Children's Consumer Socialization," *Journal of Consumer Marketing,* 22 (1), 35–42.

Federal Communications Commission (FCC) (2012), "V-Chip: Viewing Television Responsibly," http://transition.fcc.gov/vchip/.

Ferguson, Christopher J., Claudia San Miguel, and Richard D. Hartley (2009), "A Multivariate Analysis of Youth Violence and Aggression: The Influence of Family, Peers, Depression and Media Violence," *Journal of Pediatrics,* 155 (6), 904–908.

Goetzl, David (2013), "TV Spending Nears $80 Billion, DVR Penetration Chasing 50%," TV Blog, April 22, www.mediapost.com/publications/article/198659/tv-spending-nears-80-billion-dvr-penetration-cha.html#axzz2ROdQaRpb?sc=P01000WW130426&utm_source=PTCWrap&utm_medium=email&utm_campaign=P01000WW130426.

Grossbart, Sanford L., and Lawrence A. Crosby (1984), "Understanding the Bases of Parental Concern and Reaction to Children's Food Advertising," *Journal of Marketing,* 48 (3), 79–92.

Huston, Aletha C., Bruce A. Watkins, and Dale Kunkel (1989), "Public Policy and Children's Television," *American Psychologist,* 44 (2), 424–433.

Institute of Medicine of the National Academies (2013), "Priorities for Research to Reduce the Threat of Firearm-Related Violence," Report brief, June, www.iom.edu/~/media/Files/Report%20Files/2013/Firearm-Violence/FirearmViolence_RB.pdf.

Ji, Mindy F., and Russell N. Laczniak (2007), "Advertisers' Implementation of the CARU Guidelines for Advertising Targeted at Children," *Journal of Current Issues and Research in Advertising,* 29 (Fall), 27–38.

John, Deborah Roedder (1999), "Consumer Socialization of Children: A Retrospective Look at Twenty-Five Years of Research," *Journal of Consumer Research,* 26 (December), 183–213.

Jolly, Rhonda (2011), "Marketing Obesity? Junk Food, Advertising, and Kids," Parliament of Australia Research Paper no. 9 2010–11, www.aph.gov.au/About_Parliament/Parliamentary_Departments/Parliamentary_Library/pubs/rp/rp1011/11rp09.

Kunkel, Dale (2007), "The Effects of Television Violence on Children," presented to the Hearing before the U.S. Senate Committee on Commerce, Science, and Transportation, June 26, www.apa.org/about/gr/pi/advocacy/2008/kunkel-tv.aspx.

Laczniak, Russell N., Darrel D. Muehling, and Les Carlson (1995), "An Investigation of Mothers' Attitudes Toward 900-Number Advertising Directed at Children," *Journal of Public Policy and Marketing,* 14 (1), 108–116.

Lewis, Ioni, Barry Watson, and Richard Tay (2007), "Examining the Effectiveness of Physical Threats in Road Safety Advertising: The Role of the Third-Person Effect, Gender, and Age," *Transportation Research Part F: Traffic Psychology and Behaviour,* 10 (1), 48–60.

Marechal, A.J. (2013), "NBC Pulls 'Hannibal' Episode in Wake of Violent Tragedies (EXCLUSIVE)," *Variety,* April 19, http://variety.com/2013/tv/news/nbc-pulls-episode-4-of-hannibal-in-wake-of-newtown-boston-bombings-1200390579/?utm_source=sailthru&utm_medium=email&utm_campaign=breakingnewsalert.

McDonough, Patricia (2009), "TV Viewing Among Kids at an Eight-Year High," Nielsen Company, October 26, www.nielsen.com/us/en/newswire/2009/tv-viewing-among-kids-at-an-eight-year-high.html.

McGuire, William J. (1985), "Attitudes and Attitude Change," in *Handbook of Social Psychology,* vol. 2, Gardner Lindzey and Elliot Aronson, eds., New York: Random House, 233–346.

Ohanian, Roobina (1990), "Construction and Validation of a Scale to Measure Celebrity Endorsers' Perceived Expertise, Trustworthiness, and Attractiveness," *Journal of Advertising,* 19 (3), 39–52.

Olson, Cheryl K., Lawrence A. Kutner, Jason B. Almerigi, Lee Baer, Armand M. Nicholi II, and Eugene V. Beresin (2007), "Factors Correlated with Violent Video Game Use by Adolescent Boys and Girls," *Journal of Adolescent Health,* 41 (1), 77–83.

Orpinas, Pamela, Lusine Nahapetyan, Xiao Song, Caroline McNicholas, and Patricia M. Reeves (2012), "Psychological Dating Violence Perpetration and Victimization: Trajectories from Middle to High School," *Aggressive Behavior,* 38 (6), 510–520.

Paik, Haejung, and George Comstock (1994), "The Effects of Television Violence on Antisocial Behavior: A Meta-Analysis," *Communication Research,* 21 (4), 516–546.

Parents Television Council (PTC) (2012a), "Facts and TV Statistics," http://w2.parentstv.org/main/Research/Facts.aspx#.

―――― (2012b), "About the PTC," http://w2.parentstv.org/main/About/Default.aspx.

―――― (2013), "PTC Statement from Today's AT&T Shareholder Meeting," press release, April 26, http://w2.parentstv.org/Main/News/Detail.aspx?docID=2793&sc=P01000WW130503&utm_source=PTCWrap&utm_medium=email&utm_campaign=P01000WW130503.

Radio and Television Act (1996), SFS No. 2010:696, Ministry of Culture, Sweden.

Rifon, Nora J., Marla B. Royne, and Les Carlson (2010), "Violence and Advertising," *Journal of Advertising,* 39 (4), 9–10.

Robertson, Thomas S., and John R. Rossiter (1974), "Children and Commercial Persuasion: An Attribution Theory Analysis," *Journal of Consumer Research,* 1 (June), 13–20.

Seawell, Margaret, ed. (1998), *National Television Violence Study,* vol. 3, London: Sage.

Shanahan, Kevin J., Charles M. Hermans, Michael R. Hyman (2003), "Violent Commercials in Television Programs for Children," *Journal of Current Issues & Research in Advertising,* 25 (1), 61–69.

Shurlock, Geoffrey (1947), "The Motion Picture Production Code," *Annals of the American Academy of Political and Social Science,* 254 (November), 140–146.

Statistic Brain (2012), "Television Watching Statistics," www.statisticbrain.com/television-watching-statistics/.

TV Parental Guidelines (2012), "The TV Parental Guidelines," www.tvguidelines.org/faqs.htm.

U.S. Census Bureau (2006), *Statistical Abstract of the United States: 2006,* Washington, DC: U.S. Government Printing Office.

Zimmerman, Frederick J., Gwen M. Glew, Dimitri A. Christakis, Wayne Katon (2005), "Early Cognitive Stimulation, Emotional Support, and Television Watching as Predictors of Subsequent Bullying Among Grade-School Children," *JAMA Pediatrics,* 159 (4), 384–388.

11

Television Commercial Violence
Potential Effects on Children

E. Deanne Brocato, Douglas A. Gentile,
Russell N. Laczniak, Julia A. Maier, and Mindy Ji-Song

For over 30 years there has been a considerable amount of research dealing with the broadly defined issue of advertising to children. In general, this research has led to two conclusions: Children's responses to ads depend on their developmental stage (older children demonstrate a greater ability to accurately process ad information compared to younger children; John 1999; Ward, Wackman, and Wartella 1977) and parents are concerned about the potentially negative effects that ads may have on their offspring (e.g., Grossbart and Crosby 1984; Laczniak, Muehling, and Carlson 1995). Apparently aware of these conclusions, the industry has responded in a proactive manner by developing (in conjunction with the Council of Better Business Bureaus) the Children's Advertising Review Unit (CARU). CARU is a self-regulatory unit that evaluates ads targeted at children and, if deemed necessary, requests changes through voluntary cooperation of advertisers (CARU 2003). Moreover, CARU developed a set of principles that advertisers can use when creating ads targeted at children under the age of 12. CARU suggests that if advertisers follow these guidelines, concerns that critics have levied against the industry will be minimized. At the heart of these guidelines is one principle that suggests that ads targeted at younger children should be limited to promoting prosocial products and behaviors. However, recent research questions the degree to which advertisers are complying with this principle (Ji and Laczniak 2007; Schor 2004; Shanahan, Hermans, and Hyman 2003). For example, a study by Shanahan, Hermans, and Hyman (2003) concluded that a significant amount of television ads targeted at children age 12 and younger contain violent content. In fact, this research reported that on Saturday mornings, commercials contained more violent content than did the programs.

These findings are noteworthy since other research provides evidence that there is a correlation between media violence and children's tendencies to behave in less than desirable ways. For example, a study using meta-analytic procedures (Paik and Comstock 1994) concluded that even *brief* exposures to violent content in television programming or films may make children more likely to engage in aggressive behaviors (than those who had not viewed similar subject matter). What is especially troubling, however, is the positive relation that has been identified between children's exposure to violent materials in the media and an increase in their aggressive behaviors over the longer term. A recent report published by the U.S. Surgeon General (U.S. Public Health Service 2001) concludes that exposure to violence on television has a significant statistical relationship with aggressive behaviors, and its cumulative effects may lead children to form aggressive personality traits. This conclusion is based on research that has demonstrated that repeated exposure to media violence influences children's knowledge structures regarding aggression, which in turn reinforces aggression-based knowledge structures so as to change personality traits (Anderson and Bushman 2001). Although personality traits are influenced by many factors such as genetics and parental influence, the report paints a more ominous picture in that it notes that youth who currently have aggressive personality traits are more prone to consume media violence (than those having less-pronounced aggressive traits), which creates a vicious cycle of consumption and knowledge-structure reinforcement. Repeated exposures to violence, in turn, are likely to make children even more aggressive in nature, further compounding the problem (termed a "downward spiral" by Slater et al. 2003). Longitudinal studies also provide evidence that early life exposure to media violence may lead children to use more aggressive behaviors over an extended period of time (Anderson et al. 2008; Huesmann et al. 2003). The evidence suggests that the consumption of media violence is one significant risk factor for the development of aggression in children. Given that children rely on ads as an important means of gathering marketplace information (Schor 2004), we feel that the presence of violent content in commercials may be in opposition to the CARU guidelines, which state a goal of promoting prosocial behaviors in children.

However, it is important to mention that some authors note that the effects of media violence are not monolithic. Media violence can provide a fantasy world in which children are able to express certain levels of anger and aggression without harming others (Jones 2002) and provide a safe place for children to experiment with activities that may be unacceptable in real life (Olson, Kutner, and Warner 2008). Other studies note that media violence is only one risk factor among many that lead to aggressive behaviors in children (Ferguson, San Miguel, and Hartley 2009; Ferguson et al. 2008). Furthermore, it is important to note that varying parental actions can protect children from engaging in aggressive and violent behaviors such as family meals (e.g., Fulkerson et al. 2006).

Nonetheless, given the evidence that exposure to violent media influences children's aggressive thoughts and behaviors, research on the possible negative consequences of violent commercials on youth is warranted. Thus, the purpose of the present investigation is to explore the potential effect of commercials containing violent content on children. First, this study briefly reviews psychological theories that suggest why and how media violence influences children's behaviors. Second, a series of focus groups that were conducted with both parents and children regarding violence in media and television advertising is discussed. Themes were extracted from these groups and integrated with prior research on media violence to develop a set of testable research hypotheses. To shed light on these hypotheses, results are reported from a preliminary investigation conducted to determine whether exposure to violent commercials has the potential to influence aggressive behaviors in children.

THE INFLUENCE OF MEDIA VIOLENCE ON CHILDREN

Definitions

To appropriately discuss the theoretical foundations of the effects of media violence on children, it is necessary to provide precise definitions of several key terms. "Violence" is defined by the World Health Organization as "the intentional use of physical force or power, threatened or actual, against oneself, another person, or against a group or community that either results in or has a high likelihood of resulting in injury, death, psychological harm, mal-development or deprivation" (Kug et al. 2002, p. 5). Consistent with this definition and prior research in psychology (Anderson and Bushman 2001), the present study defines "media violence" as media-based content that depicts *intentional* attempts by individuals to inflict harm on others. Commercial violence is another form of television content that includes intentional attempts by actors to inflict harm on others. It is important to note that these definitions suggest that a depiction of violence may be live action or animated, and scripted or real (Anderson and Bushman 2001). In addition to being intentional, the definition of violence specifies that the intended harm is to a target who would be motivated to avoid it if possible. Thus, this definition purposefully excludes accidents that lead to harm, but includes intentional acts that may be unsuccessful in causing harm.

Theory and Research

Many theories have been developed to understand and predict the development of aggressive tendencies in children. Most of these theories are domain specific and focus on neural substrates, specific emotions such as frustration, cognitive constructs, or how aggression is learned via observation. Although each of these specific theories has been tested and supported in specific contexts (see Table 11.1 for a summary of several studies), they have left the field somewhat fragmented because they focus on the issue of aggression at different levels of analysis. In an effort to integrate these specific ideas into an overarching theory of aggressive effects, Anderson and Bushman (2001, 2002) developed the General Aggression Model (GAM). The model includes individual difference variables (e.g., personality traits, genetics, history), situational variables (e.g., provocation, learning opportunities), and potential moderating variables (e.g., parental intervention, gender). This breadth is both the model's greatest strength and weakness—it is so broad that it lacks some of the individual-level details that many of the domain-specific models on which it is based included. However, it is important to note that the GAM has been recently supported in longitudinal studies in both the United States and Japan (e.g., Anderson et al. 2008).

In the short term, the GAM posits that exposure to media violence will lead children to engage in aggressive behaviors via a learning-activation-application mechanism. Specifically, the model suggests that exposure to media violence will likely lead individuals to generate aggressive cognitions that may eventually lead to arousal and other emotional reactions. The GAM further suggests that the child will use these aggressive cognitions to update memory-based knowledge structures regarding aggression and violence. Memory-based knowledge structures for aggression include aggressive behavior scripts (e.g., when provoked one should retaliate), aggressive perceptual schemata (e.g., people dressed in black are potential enemies), and aggressive beliefs (e.g., fighting is acceptable in certain instances). Aggressive behaviors are likely to result when aggressive script-like knowledge structures are cued to action.

According to the GAM, repeated exposures to violence are thought to be especially problematic in that the violent cognitions generated (in response to each exposure) serve as learning trials in which aggressive knowledge structures are rehearsed, reinforced, and updated. Because of this reinforcement, each trial (i.e., exposure to a violent depiction) makes the knowledge structures more automatic and more difficult to change. In other words, repeated exposures to media violence tend to lead children to formulate aggressive cognitions or thoughts that reinforce their existing knowledge structures regarding aggression, making them more resistant to change. Furthermore, once the knowledge structures become more solidified, they become more automatic, such that they become faster to access and act on. Once a person has well-formed knowledge structures regarding aggression, the child can eventually develop more aggressive personality traits. When activated via situational cues, these traits can lead children to act in a more aggressive manner than had they not been exposed to violent episodes in the first place. As noted above, there has been significant support for the GAM in the psychology literature (Anderson, Gentile, and Buckley 2007; Bushman and Anderson 2002; Gentile et al. 2004). Furthermore, it appears that the GAM predicts that even a brief exposure to a violent episode (such as one located within a 30-second television commercial) can lead children to formulate aggressive cognitions, since the violence could easily reinforce aggression-related memory structures. However, such a notion has yet to be tested empirically.

Table 11.1

Limited Review of Literature Dealing with Effects of Violence

Authors	Population	Type of media	Findings
Anderson and Bushman (2001)	Meta-analysis	Violent video games	Violent video games increased aggression in females and males, adults and children, in experimental and nonexperimental studies. Aggressive cognitions were also significantly higher across all areas.
Anderson et al. (2010)	Meta-analysis: cross-cultural comparison	Violent video games	Violent video game exposure was found to be a causal risk factor for aggressive cognition, aggressive behavior, aggressive affect, decreased prosocial behavior, and empathy.
Bensley and Van Eenwyk (2001)	Children	Violent video games	Overall findings: the studies that examined violent video games on young children's aggression were more likely to have consistent significant results compared to the teenage and college/young adult age groups.
Bushman (1998)	College students	TV programs/commercials	Nonviolent condition recalled, recognized more brands and more commercial details than violent condition. Higher anger ratings impaired memory.
Bushman (2005)	Adults	TV programs/commercials	TV programs that were violent or sexual in content reduced the viewers' recall, interest, and likelihood of selecting the advertised brand(s).
Bushman and Anderson (2001)	Meta-analysis: scientific evidence and news reporting	Media violence (general)	Scientific research has demonstrated a significant positive increase in the relationship between media violence and aggression over the past three decades.
Ferguson, San Miguel, and Hartley (2009)	Children	Violent video games	Depression, peer influences, antisocial personality, and parental aggression predicted youth violence, but violent media did not.
Gentile et al. (2004)	Adolescents	Violent video games	Exposure to more violence yielded more hostility, e.g., arguments with teachers, physical fights, and poor school performance.
Olson, Kutner, and Warner (2008)	Male children	Violent video games	Boys like to play electronic games, especially violent ones, for five main reasons: (1) explore/master different environments, (2) experience power/fame fantasies, (3) emotional regulation, (4) social tools, and (5) learning new skills (i.e., sports games).
Olson et al. (2007)	Children	Violent video games	More boys than girls play video games every day, and boys are more likely to play M (mature)-rated games frequently. More hours of play were correlated with more violent video game use.
Paik and Comstock (1994)	Meta-analysis	TV violence	A positive and significant correlation between TV violence and aggressive behavior was found.
Shanahan, Hermans, and Hyman (2003)	Children's commercials	Saturday morning commercials	The level of violence in commercials is higher than the level of violence in programming (commercials are created in isolation). Highest levels of violence are found in the "spots" for upcoming programs.
Wood, Wong, and Chachere (1991)	Meta-analysis children	Media violence	Media violence exposure resulted in a significant increase in the viewers' aggressive behavior. However, the results are not uniform across studies.

RESEARCH PHASE I: CHILDREN'S FOCUS GROUPS

The main purpose of the focus group studies was to investigate parents' and children's perception of media violence and explore how television commercial violence *might* influence children. Because there is a lack of research on children's reactions to violence in commercials, a more exploratory approach was deemed to be appropriate (Strauss and Corbin 1990). This is a unique type of media in that exposure can be very short and may not be viewed as potentially harmful. However, the GAM implies that a child's exposure to even short violent episodes (such as those contained in commercials) may lead to aggression. Given these conflicting possibilities, we felt a qualitative approach to explore perceptions of commercial violence was warranted. Focus groups were chosen as the qualitative method for several reasons, including the ability to leverage the benefits of peer interaction, time restrictions on collecting data, and the ability to assimilate information in a timely manner (Greenbaum 1998). Although there are limitations to focus group research, such as possible bias from peers and leading questions from the moderator, focus groups were chosen as the best method to explore our research questions. Careful consideration was taken in preparing a moderator for the studies to avoid these limitations. The focus groups were conducted with several questions in mind (and so to correspond with the parents' focus groups). These included: How do children classify and define violence? What is the level of parental involvement in the choice of media viewed by children?

Study Procedures

Participants were recruited from a list developed by researchers at a large Midwestern university (and ultimately consisted of 6 groups with a total of 42 participants). It is important to note that the potential participant list included both people who resided in the university town as well as many who lived in surrounding communities, allowing for a reasonably diverse subject pool. All participants had parental permission to participate in the 90-minute group discussions that were led by a professional moderator. To ensure a high level of objectivity, the moderator was a trained professional who was unaware of the specific aims of the research. The children ranged in age from 7 to 13, with 50% of the respondents being male. As an incentive for participation, each respondent was paid for his time.

Each focus group was audiotaped and transcribed verbatim, yielding 92 pages of single-spaced interview data. To ensure accuracy in the transcription, the tapes were reviewed by a different individual. The transcriptions were used to determine themes across all groups using open coding (Glaser and Strauss 1967; Strauss and Corbin 1990). Overall themes were evaluated separately by three individuals through an iterative process (Thompson 1997). Each researcher read through the transcripts and determined the overall themes using cross-case analysis and open coding (Beverland, Lindgreen, and Vink 2008). There was little disagreement between the initial proposed themes and the themes found by the two other researchers. All researchers were able to gain consensus on the emerging themes.

Resulting Themes

In general, two major themes evolved in the focus group discussions: the first was the role of blood and realism in defining violence and the second involved the perceived lack of parental concern with media (and commercial ad) violence. Each of these themes is discussed below.

Defining Violence

Many of the participants provided a definition of media violence that differed from that which guided this research (intentional harm to victims who would not wish to be harmed). Several conditions were deemed as necessary by the participants in order to classify media content as being violent. For example, when the participants were asked to define violence, their responses focused mainly on the realism and the depiction of blood and gore during the media event. These elements were found to be recurring in the definitions of many participants across all of the groups.

Realism was an important characteristic of violence in relation to the characters being used in a scene. For example, the use of cartoon characters was seen as more fantasy than violence, although the acts performed by the cartoon characters could be defined as violent. If an event occurred in a cartoon, children seemed to not be able to relate to it or believe that it could happen to them. As a young boy explained, cartoon violence differs from "real" violence:

> In cartoon violence you're not actually getting hurt. Most of it is silly. (Robbie, 9-year-old)

Many of the children made the association between blood and violence. Even though a televised scene might depict people getting shoved, pushed, thrown to the ground, or even shot, the participants did not view it as a violent episode unless there was blood. Actual blood was a driving force in the perception of violence, as noted by several participants when asked to define violence:

> Violence is fighting with weapons, with swords, blood, and gore. (Josh, 7-year-old)

> If you blow something up. Something with blood. (Alex, 11-year-old)

A number of the participants made the direct association between blood and violence without regard for the act that caused the blood to occur. In the case of accidents, if there was blood, it was deemed violent; this again differs for the formal definition that includes *intentional harm*. As another participant explains, tripping and falling can be violent:

> Violent is bleeding really bad. Sometimes it's when somebody falls down and they're scratched or bleeding really bad. (Nick, 13-year-old)

These finding suggests that the formal definitions used by researchers to determine violence in the media do not align with how children define it. It seems as though children may be unaware that some television content they are viewing is violent and, thus, there is a concern that since they are unaware of the violence they may not be able to psychologically resist its effects.

Parental Concern

Another emerging theme centered on the level of perceived parental concern for violence in media—especially commercials. Many of the children did *not* feel that their parents were concerned with media violence in general. However, when asked what media parents monitor or restrict because of violent content, participants noted that commercials were *not* included. While it was noted that some parents often had rules about movies, shows, or video games, no participants mentioned having any restrictions on commercials (because of violence). Participants did state that the only commercials parents discouraged them from viewing were trailers for movies (and, in particular, those that they did not want their children to see). According to many of the participants, parents were not really concerned with violence unless it was very bloody or graphic, as this comment from one child participant illustrates:

> My parents don't care about violence as long as it is not blood and gore. (Bobby, 9-year-old)

When there was parental control, parents often seemed to exercise differing levels of control. Several participants mentioned that their mothers seemed to be more concerned with what is acceptable to watch as compared to their fathers. The level of parental control seemed to align with what type of shows the parents liked to watch themselves. One explains:

> If I am watching TV with my mom, so she tries to make me avoid the bad commercials, but if I'm watching with my dad, he watches really gory shows and he doesn't mind if I'm watching them. (Nate, 10-year-old)

Others explain that their parents differ in regard to what they are able to watch:

> My mom doesn't want me to watch different things, and my dad doesn't care. (Stephanie, 12-year-old)

> Yeah, yeah, my dad isn't as tight about it as my mom. (Paul, 12-year-old)

This lack of consistency between mothers' and fathers' control was a common theme throughout the focus groups and may pose issues for defining media violence and for setting rules in the household. Overall, the children noted a lack of parental concern for commercials as compared to other media, and when control was enforced, there was a lack of consistency between parents about what children may or may not watch.

RESEARCH PHASE II: PARENTS' FOCUS GROUPS

Study Procedures

To explore parents' understanding of violence, and specifically the notion that parents perceive violent television commercials as a potential problem, 6 focus groups were conducted with a total of 40 adults. Parents (12 males and 28 females) were recruited at the same time as the children's focus group participants. Participants engaged in 90-minute group discussions led by a moderator. Generally, participants were the parents of the children who took part in the children's focus groups. Once again, to ensure a high level of objectivity, a professionally trained moderator was used. Parents were paid for their participation in the study. Similar to the children's focus groups, the parent studies were conducted with several broad questions in mind. These included: How do parents classify and define violence? Are parents concerned about commercial violence?

As with the children's focus groups, all sessions were audiotaped and transcribed verbatim, yielding 132 single-spaced pages of interview data, and to ensure accuracy in the transcription, the tapes were again checked by a different individual. The same procedures as the children's focus groups were followed with regard to reading and finding themes in the transcripts.

Resulting Themes

In general, three major themes evolved in the focus group discussions: the importance of realism in defining violence, a general disbelief that violence in commercials posed a problem, and an ability to handle media violence and mitigate any problems that it might cause children.

Defining Violence

The parent focus groups provided a definition of violence that differed from the formal definition used by Anderson and Bushman (2001). Similar to the children's focus groups, parents defined violence in terms of realism and the amount of blood or gore shown. The parents were more concerned with violence that was "realistic" as opposed to cartoon or animation violence. For example, when asked to define violence and state concerns about its effects on his children, a father of three clearly noted the importance of realism:

> Bloody body on the floor . . . clearly, animation doesn't bother me as much, but when it is very realistic, it is really disturbing to me. (Bill)

The parents also made a distinction between real and cartoon/animated violence. There was less concern for animated violence compared to the depiction of real people in violent acts. When referring to animated violence in commercials, a mother of two stated:

> Those don't bother me as much as the shooting of real people, you know, with blood that spills everywhere. (Jane)

Thus, the parents' definition of violence seemed to mirror the children's. Aggression and violence are defined by observable blood, gore, and realism. Parents seemed to disregard cartoon or animated violence because they felt their children knew the difference between it and reality. Again, this misalignment with scholarly definitions of violence could produce problems, as prior research demonstrates that media violence does not need to be bloody or realistic to have a negative effect on children (e.g., Anderson et al. 2003). Parents appeared to have a lack of concern for the *intent to harm* as a driving force in violent content. They seem to focus mainly on the *outcome* and the level of depicted injury.

Concern for Violence in Commercials

Another theme was the *lack* of parental concern with media violence in general and for violence in commercials as well. Parents were more concerned over the influence of the commercials in terms of what the products had to offer than they were over violent depictions in ads. As one father of three states:

> I don't think violence in commercials is the problem . . . the fact that it gets all of the advertisers . . . trying to influence them [children]. It's trying to make us think like we're not uncomfortable about what we do and why we do that. You know, you've got to drink a Miller beer or you won't get the girl. I think it's that stuff that's the real problem. (Dwight)

A mother of three also felt that violence was not the biggest issue in advertising:

> I don't see violence in commercials as the biggest problem. It is the stuff that you don't notice but that you're still influenced by. (Tracy)

Many parents made the comparison between television shows and movies compared to commercials, stating that commercials were less violent. The level of violence between the media types was evidenced throughout all the groups interviewed. A different mother of three states:

The TV shows are so much more violent than the commercials, I mean that, it's more the sexual stuff, you pick up the violence from the TV shows and it's a lot more extreme than the commercials I think, at least from what I've seen. (Michele)

Parents seemed to feel that if violence did exist in commercials, it was implied, but not actual. This is consistent with their position that aggression is defined by depicted blood. How marketers influence children through adult content, product, and usage situations seemed to be more of an immediate concern.

There was a reoccurring theme related to sexual or adult content in commercials, and this seemed to be of more concern than violence. Several parents mentioned this type of adult content:

I am more tolerant to violence than other forms of problematic issues on television such as provocative issues. (Dave)

I think I get more uncomfortable with sexual innuendos. (Joanne)

Although violence may be in commercials, parents felt they needed to protect their children more from sexual content. Sexual content was viewed as more of an immediate concern to parents when trying to protect their children.

Parents' Ability to Mitigate the Effects of Commercial Violence

A final theme that emerged was that parents felt that if violence was a problem in the media, they could handle the situation and mitigate its effects. Many of the parents spoke of watching television with their children. By being present, they felt that they could address any problems or concerns that might arise during the programming. Several parents viewed watching television as family time, and by coviewing, they could address any problems or concerns as they emerged. In order to educate their children, many parents felt they had talked to their children about the downside of television and what problems could arise. As one father of four states:

I'd stress to my kids that TV, their goal is not necessarily your betterment or your education ... it is what are they trying to get from you. (Alan)

The parents felt that talking to their children and explaining the influences of television gave their children the knowledge to evaluate problem situations that may occur. By explaining the problems and pitfalls of commercials specifically, several parents were confident that their children were given the tools to make good decisions and evaluations. As Melinda (mother of two) notes:

We have talked to him about these ads. That's the purpose of them. It's called persuasion. (Melinda)

OVERALL DISCUSSION OF FOCUS GROUP RESULTS

The focus groups yield four possible conclusions (regarding the focus group participants): (1) parents' and children's definitions of violence are inconsistent with those provided by aggression researchers (e.g., Anderson and Bushman 2001; Bushman and Anderson 2001); (2) parents and children have little, if any, concern with violent content in commercials; (3) parents felt that they could mitigate the effects of media violence if it became a problem; and (4) while mothers and fathers are inconsistent between themselves regarding concern about media violence in general, parents appear to be more troubled with other advertising aspects (such as sexual content) than they are with violence. The focus group data did not appear to suggest that parents have greater concerns about the potential effects of violent content on boys versus girls.

It is important to acknowledge that results of these focus groups should be interpreted with a certain degree of caution. Research techniques such as focus groups are typically used to generate ideas and insights into problems; they should not be used to generalize findings to those individuals who were not participating. Thus, while our focus groups suggested that child and parent concern with commercial violence was not widespread, more quantitative studies should be performed before concluding that this is the case for all.

EXPERIMENTAL STUDY

Given the findings that parents (in our focus groups) perceive that commercial violence is not a problem, and the results of Shanahan, Hermans, and Hyman (2003) that child-directed commercials contain more violence that similarly targeted programs, we felt it was important to determine whether children *could* be adversely affected by the presence of violent content in television ads. Such a notion is especially important given that the GAM suggests that children are likely to generate aggressive cognitions when exposed to even small doses of violent (versus nonviolent) content in the media. Consistent with the GAM, we hypothesize:

H1: *Children exposed to commercials with violent content are likely to generate more aggressive cognitions than those exposed to similar commercials that are void of violent content.*

There is an additional concern, however, that the presence of commercials paired with violent programming may be even more problematic. That is, violent programs may prime children's violence-based knowledge structures, potentially creating additive effects and eliciting more aggressive cognitions in response to violent commercials (as opposed to when violent commercials are paired with programs that do not contain violent scenes). Such thinking is consistent with the GAM in that violent programs could allow receivers to evoke violent-based knowledge structures that would put them in a mind-set to generate even more aggressive cognitions than they normally would. Thus, we hypothesize:

H2: *Children exposed to both commercials and programs containing violence are likely to generate more aggressive cognitions than those exposed to violent commercials contained in nonviolent programs.*

A recent study noted that boys are more likely to seek out violent media content than are girls (Christakis and Zimmerman 2007). These authors suggest that this may be due to socialization differences (regarding aggression), cultural norms, or genetic dispositions. Extending these results to the case of ad exposure, we expect that boys will be more likely to focus on ads that contain violent content than girls. Given this line of thinking, we hypothesize:

H3: *When exposed to violent content in commercials, boys will generate more aggressive cognitions than girls.*

Finally, based on the focus group data, it appears that both parents and children believe that parental intervention will temper the influence of violent content on kids' behaviors. It is important to note that such an influence is consistent with prior research in consumer socialization that suggests that parents' coviewing of television programs and commercials with their children is an effective means of socializing their offspring to appropriately deal with the media (Carlson and Grossbart 1988; John 1999). Previous research suggests that coviewing allows parents the opportunity to lessen the influence of advertising on children (Carlson, Grossbart, and Walsh 1990). With coviewing, parents and children are provided an opportunity to converse about violence in ads and its possible effects. Thus, coviewing is thought to provide parents with an opportunity to lessen advertising's effects on their children, not just at the time of the conversation but, because it has lasting effects, well into the future as well (Grossbart and Crosby 1984). Thus, we felt that if coviewing regularly occurred in the child's household, the effects of commercial violence could be lessened.

Although our experiment focused on children viewing ads in isolation from their parents, to determine the potential effects of parents' coviewing on children's responses to violent commercials, children were asked about the degree to which they typically coview television with parents. Given that research has suggested that coviewing will lessen the effects of media on children, we hypothesize:

H4: *When exposed to violent content in commercials, children who are more likely to coview television with their parents will generate fewer aggressive cognitions than those who are less likely to coview.*

RESEARCH PHASE III: EXPERIMENTAL STUDY

Method

Experimental Design

The study used a 2 (experimental ad: nonviolent vs. violent) × 2 (experimental program: violent vs. nonviolent) × 2 (sex: girl vs. boy) experimental design. Subjects were randomly assigned to one of the four experimental conditions (for the ad and program manipulation—sex obviously was not manipulated). The violent ad featured action figure toys (based on the comic book and movie for the "Fantastic Four"), while the nonviolent ad featured a remote-control car (Rewinder). Both ads were rated to be equal in a pretest of ad likability by subjects similar to (but not the same subjects as) those used in the main experiment. All subjects viewed excerpts of two experimental programs (which featured two shows, one targeted at girls—*Totally Spies;* the other targeted at boys—*GI Joe: Cobra*). Violent and nonviolent program conditions used differing parts of these same programs.

Experimental Stimuli

To test the hypotheses, eight 9-minute videos were created. All videos followed the format: commercial block 1 (30 seconds—target commercial), program segment 1 (3 minutes), commercial block 2 (30 seconds—cereal commercial), program segment 2 (3 minutes), and commercial block 3 (30 seconds—target commercial repeated). The two program segments included a section of children's shows, one targeted to boys (*GI Joe*) and one targeted toward girls (*Totally Spies*). One segment of each was shown to each child—therefore each child saw one section of a boy-directed show and one of a girl-directed show (in randomized order). The design was 2 (violent show or nonviolent show) × 2 (violent ad or nonviolent ad). In the nonviolent conditions, children saw two segments of the shows that did not include any aggression; the violent and nonviolent segments were from different parts of the same episodes. Regarding the commercials, there was one filler ad that was seen once, and one target ad that was seen in two of the commercial blocks. The violent

172 SPECIAL CONCERNS FOR CHILDREN

ad featured a set of action figure toys that attempted to harm each other. The nonviolent ad was for a remote-controlled vehicle (and contained no acts of harm). Both ads included age-appropriate (approximately 8- to 12-year-old) male and female actors.

Subjects

Children (ages 8–12) were recruited from a database of those who expressed interest in participating in research experiments. Graduate students called potential subjects based on their age. Potential participants were contacted in a random order. There were 165 total participants (55% male), each randomly assigned to a condition. For the most part, subjects resided within driving distance of a major Midwestern university (where the experiment was run). All subjects were paid for their participation in the experiment.

Procedure and Measures

Procedures

Subjects were greeted by an experimental assistant as they entered the research laboratory. Both subjects (children) and parents were provided with assent/consent forms and were asked to sign them before proceeding. Upon receiving the signatures, parents were asked to go to a waiting area. Children (subjects) completed a preliminary survey that included their age, media habits (including coviewing of television with their parents), and other general information. Subjects then viewed one of the experimental videos (randomly selected). After viewing the DVD, subjects were presented with another questionnaire, which assessed their violent cognitions and other information (e.g., postexposure ad and brand attitudes). Upon completion of the survey, subjects were debriefed and returned to their parents. At this point, the experimental procedures were explained to waiting parents and (child) subjects paid for their participation.

Measures

Consistent with previous research (e.g., Anderson et al. 2004), aggressive cognitions were measured via a word-completion task. Commensurate with their age, participants were presented with a series of four- and five-letter words that contained one or two blanks (for letters that they would formulate to complete a word). For example, children could have completed the word K I _ _ as "kill" or "kiss." The percentage of aggressive words formed from 15 possible words was used as the study's dependent variable. To address the level of coviewing between parents and the child, a single-item measure, was used: "How often do you watch TV with a parent?" anchored by 1 = "always" and 5 = "never."

Results

Overall Experimental Results

Means and standard deviations of aggressive cognitions generated by subjects in each experimental condition are reported in Table 11.2. As can be seen from the means, subjects viewing the violent ad (marginal mean = 1.55) appeared to generate more aggressive cognitions than those viewing the nonviolent ad (marginal mean = 1.43). Also, subjects viewing the violent program appeared to generate more violent cognitions (mean = 1.53) than those viewing the nonviolent program (mean = 1.45). Hypothesis test results are reported below.

Table 11.2

Means (and Standard Deviations) per Cell

Dependent variable = Aggressive cognitions

	Program		
Ad	Nonviolent	Violent	Total
Nonviolent	1.37	1.49	1.43
	(.83)	(.90)	(.86)
Violent	1.53	1.57	1.55
	(.77)	(.68)	(.72)
Total	1.45	1.53	1.49
	(.80)	(.79)	(.79)

Main Regression Results

H1–H3 were tested via dummy variable regression (with the percentage of aggressive cognitions serving as the dependent variable, and exposure to the violent ad [0 = not exposed; 1 = exposed], exposure to the violent program [0 = not exposed; 1 = exposed], and sex [0 = girl; 1 = boy] used as the independent variables). Results are reported in Table 11.3. Exposure to the violent ad ($\beta_{\text{violent ad}} = .059$; $p < .05$) and sex ($\beta_{\text{sex}} = -.088$; $p < .01$), but not exposure to the violent program ($\beta_{\text{violent program}} = .038$; $p > .10$), were significant indicators of the percentage of aggressive cognitions developed by participants. *All interactions (both two- and three-way) were not significant.* Thus, exposure to the violent ad increased the percentage of aggressive words generated by subjects, supporting H1. However, contrary to expectations, the regression results did not support H2, although they were in the predicted direction. Specifically, exposure to both commercials and programs containing violence did not result in the generation of more aggressive cognitions as compared to exposure to violent commercials paired with nonviolent programs. It is possible that this effect was not observed since parents might have previously expressed concerns with violence in programs—children might have been more vigilant to the potential consequences of violent programs. Finally, the main effect for sex only shows that boys have a stronger tendency to have violent cognitions but says nothing about the role of the commercial. Since the ad × sex interaction is not significant, no support was provided for H3.

H4 was tested via regression analysis (see Table 11.4). Participants' self-reported coviewing of television and the significant independent variables from the first regression equation (reported above) were used as the independent variables in this analysis. As expected, coviewing was negatively related to the percentage of aggressive words generated in response to the stimuli ($\beta_{\text{coviewing}} = -.051$; $p < .01$), after controlling for violent ad condition and sex, providing support for H4. No significant interaction terms were observed.

Discussion for Experimental Results

Results of the experiment suggest that children are susceptible to the negative influences of violence contained in television commercials. Children (regardless of their gender and the nature of the surrounding television program) generated more aggressive cognitions when exposed to commercials that contained violent content when compared to those who viewed television ads with no violent content. Although boys generated more violent cognitions than did girls,

Table 11.3

Regression Results

Dependent variable = Aggressive cognitions
$R^2 = .105$ ($F = 6.293$; $df = 3, 161$; $p < .001$)

Independent variable	Coefficient (SE)
Constant	.361
Violent ad	.059**
	(.026)
Violent program	.038
	(.026)
Sex	−.088*
	(.026)

Note: SE = standard error.
* $p < .01$.
** $p < .05$.

Table 11.4

Regression Results

Dependent variable = Aggressive cognitions
$R^2 = .137$ ($F = 8.439$; $df = 3, 161$; $p < .001$)

Independent variable	Coefficient (SE)
Constant	.235
Violent ad	.056**
	(.025)
Sex	−.088*
	(.025)
Coviewing	−.051*
	(.017)

Note: SE = standard error.
* $p < .01$.
** $p < .05$.

all participants generated more aggressive cognitions after viewing commercials with violent content (compared to those who viewed nonviolent ads). Thus, one may argue that violence in commercials has the potential to contribute to all children's development and reinforcement of knowledge structures regarding violence, regardless of their sex. This is consistent with other recent studies that have attempted to find interactions with child sex (e.g., Anderson, Gentile, and Buckley 2007).

It is interesting to note that given that parents participating in the focus groups appeared to have little concern with violence in commercials and expressed confidence in their ability to mediate its potentially negative effects on children, the results do support the notion that coviewing may help them accomplish this objective. Results of our experiment suggested that children of parents who regularly coview television generated less aggressive cognitions than those who came from households where mothers and fathers tended not to engage in this activity.

GENERAL DISCUSSION

Previous research suggested that a surprising number of ads targeted at children contain some type of violent content. This finding is particularly important as one considers the multitude of ads targeted at children. For example, prior to the deregulation of advertising to children in 1983, approximately $100 million was spent annually on such ads; in 2006, this amount was estimated to be $17 billion (Linn 2006). Thus, even a small percentage of ads containing violent themes or images could influence millions of children. Given that prior research has established a strong link between children's exposure to media violence and aggressive cognitions, feelings, and behaviors, there is potential for child-directed ads to contribute to this important societal issue. The present research, which reports on several empirical investigations, attempted to shed light on potential concerns that might emerge as children are exposed to violent television ads.

Results of the studies reported here paint a picture suggesting that violence in commercials targeted at children may pose a problem. Specifically, in the focus groups, parents expressed little concern with the effects of violent commercials on their children (parallel focus groups with children mirrored this lack of concern). Yet results of an experiment determined that exposure to ads containing violent content clearly increased the amount of violent cognitions that were generated by children. Thus, parents' lack of concern does not seem to be warranted—children may be affected by exposure to violence in commercials. As noted in the GAM (Anderson and Bushman 2002), the generation of violent cognitions may start a process whereby children reinforce aggressive knowledge structures and, as a result, may be more likely to engage in aggressive acts (as a result of viewing violent television ads). Repeated activation of aggressive knowledge structures (via the generation of violent cognitions in response to violent content in commercials) becomes more automatic with repetition and eventually may become a part of a child's personality, providing him or her with the potential to act more aggressively in some instances. Thus, there is potential that repeated exposure to commercials containing violence may lead children to act more aggressively than they would have otherwise.

One of the major motivations for our undertaking of this research centered on the CARU's guideline regarding the promotion of prosocial behaviors in ads targeted at children. Given that children appear to have the potential to generate more aggressive cognitions after exposure to violent ads, we feel it may be appropriate to strengthen the guidelines. Specifically, we recommend that the guidelines ask that advertisers refrain from including violent or aggressive content in ads directed at children (with violence defined as characters engaging in or threatening intentional harm to other characters).

Although we expected that there may be evidence of sex differences in the generation of aggression cognitions in response to violent ads, it was not observed in the present study. Boys generated more aggressive cognitions than did girls for all ads, yet they did not do so specifically for those containing violent content. These results suggest that the effects of media violence are not a problem that is unique to boys. Thus, public policy or self-regulatory efforts aimed at reducing the number or impact of ads containing violent contents needs to be enacted with respect to all children (not just boys).

Finally, results of the experimental study suggested that children who typically coview television with their parents are less likely to generate aggressive cognitions after exposure to violent ads. This finding is consistent with the notion suggested by Carlson and Grossbart (1988) that coviewing is an effective means of socializing children about the potentially harmful effects of advertising on children. Thus, results suggest that parents can lessen the potentially harmful effects of violent commercial content on their children via coviewing and discussion. However, such a conclusion should be interpreted with a degree of caution; focus group results suggested that parents had little understanding of what constitutes violence in ads. As a result, although it appears that coviewing and discussion (by parents with their children) of ads that contain obvious violence may mitigate potentially harmful effects, this may not occur. Given their lack of understanding of what constitutes aggression and violence, parents may not be as likely to note its presence in ads and, thus, would not be motivated to engage in discussions with their children. Moreover, it is important to note that our measure of parental coviewing may have been overly simplistic. Thus, it may not have captured the depth of this important concept.

Because parents play such a pivotal role in how media and advertising consumption affect children, additional research dealing with this topic is needed. While the present study investigated the influence of only a single behavior (coviewing) in attempting to better understand how parental involvement may mitigate the effects of media on children, recent research has identified three additional aspects of parental involvement that may be used to mediate media effects: limit setting on amount of time, limit setting on media content, and active mediation (where parents discuss media thoughtfully with children). Focusing on the present study, it is possible that our measure of coviewing served as a proxy for all of these aspects. Future research is needed to study each aspect separately, however, as it appears that active parental mediation rather than simply coviewing may be effective in mitigating the potential detrimental effects of media on children (Buijzen 2009; Buijzen and Valkenburg 2005; Nathanson 1999, 2002; Nikken and Jansz 2006). Nonetheless, the results of the present study and past research suggest that a potential fruitful avenue for public policy action would be to focus on parents and help them to understand their pivotal role in moderating the effects of violent media content on their children (Gentile, Saleem, and Anderson 2007).

STUDY LIMITATIONS

As with all empirical investigations, the present study had limitations (most of which can be addressed in future research studies). All data gathered (in both the focus groups and the experiment study) were gathered with subjects who resided in or near a single city in the Midwestern United States. Thus, as is the case with any empirical study, the generalizability of the results could be questioned. Certainly, results should be replicated in other parts of the country with more economically and socially diverse samples. For the experiment, results were generated from a set of two commercials that were embedded in two differing scenes from two animated television programs. Thus, results could differ for other ads (that feature different products) and other programs. Moreover, it is important to note that results were based on subjects' exposure to television commercials in a lab setting, and results are based on children's generation of aggressive cognitions (and not actual behaviors). Finally, since parental coviewing was not manipulated in the experiment, it is important to note that alternative explanations (other than those posed in H4) may not be ruled out. For example, it may be that the group of children who indicated that they coviewed with their parents more simply watched less television and were therefore exposed to less violence in the past. Thus, the generation of less-violent cognitions might be due to their having less well-developed violence-based cognitive structures. As a result of these limitations, future research regarding this important issue is needed before definitive public policy or self-regulatory actions could be recommended.

REFERENCES

Anderson, Craig A., and Brad J. Bushman (2001), "Effects of Violent Video Games on Aggressive Behavior, Aggressive Cognition, Aggressive Affect, Physiological Arousal, and Prosocial Behavior: A Meta-Analytic Review of the Scientific Literature," *Psychological Science*, 12 (5), 353–359.

———, and ——— (2002), "Violent Video Games and Hostile Expectations: A Test of General Aggression Model," *Personality and Social Psychology Bulletin*, 28 (12), 1679–1686.

———, Douglas A. Gentile, and Katherine E. Buckley (2007), *Violent Video Game Effects on Children and Adolescents: Theory, Research, and Public Policy*, New York: Oxford University Press.

———, Leonard Berkowitz, Edward Donnerstein, L. Rowell Huesmann, James D. Johnson, and Daniel Linz (2003), "The Influence of Media Violence on Youth," *Psychological Science in the Public Interest*, 4 (3), 81–110.

———, Nicholas L. Carnagey, Mindy Flanagan, Arlin J. Benjamin, Janie Eubanks, and Jeffery C. Valentine (2004), "Violent Video Games: Specific Effects of Violent Content on Aggressive Thoughts and Behavior," in *Advances in Experimental Social Psychology*, vol. 36, Mark Zanna, ed., New York: Elsevier, 199–249.

———, Akira Sakamoto, Douglas Gentile, Nobuko Ihori, Akiko Shibuya, Shintaro Yukawa, Mayum Naito, and Kumiko Kobayashi (2008), "Longitudinal Effects of Video Games on Aggression in Japan and the United States," *Pediatrics*, 122 (5), 1067–1072.

———, Akiko Shibuya, Nobuko Ihori, Edward L. Swing, Brad Bushman, Akira Sakamoto, Harold R. Rothstein, and Muniba Saleem (2010), "Violent Video Game Effects on Aggression, Empathy, and Prosocial Behavior in Eastern and Western Countries," *Psychological Bulletin*, 136 (2), 151–173.

Bensley, Lillian, and Juliet Van Eenwyk (2001), "Video Games and Real-Life Aggression: Review of the Literature," *Journal of Adolescent Health*, 29 (4), 244–257.

Beverland, Michael B., Adam Lindgreen, and Michiel W. Vink (2008), "Projecting Authenticity Through Advertising," *Journal of Advertising*, 37 (1), 5–15.

Buijzen, Moniek (2009), "The Effectiveness of Parental Communication in Modifying the Relation Between Food Advertising and Children's Consumption Behaviour," *British Journal of Developmental Psychology*, 27 (1), 105–121.

———, and Patti M. Valkenburg (2005), "Parental Mediation of Undesired Advertising Effects," *Journal of Broadcasting and Electronic Media*, 49 (2), 153–165.

Bushman, Brad J. (1998), "Effects of Television Violence on Memory for Commercial Messages," *Journal of Experimental Psychology: Applied*, 4 (4), 291–307.

——— (2005), "Violence and Sex in Television Programs Do Not Sell Products in Advertisements," *Psychological Science*, 16 (9), 702–708.

———, and Craig A. Anderson (2001), "Media Violence and the American Public: Scientific Facts Versus Media Misinformation," *American Psychologist*, 56 (5/6), 477–489.

———, and ——— (2002), "Violent Video Games and Hostile Expectations: A Test of the General Aggression Model," *Personality and Social Psychology Bulletin*, 28 (12), 1679–1686.

Carlson, Les, and Sanford Grossbart (1988), "Parental Style and Consumer Socialization of Children," *Journal of Consumer Research*, 15 (June), 77–94.

———, ———, and Ann Walsh (1990), "Mothers' Communication Orientations and Consumer Socialization Tendencies," *Journal of Advertising*, 19 (3), 27–38.

Children's Advertising Review Unit (CARU) (2003), *Self-Regulatory Guidelines for Children's Advertising*, 7th ed., New York: Council for Better Business Bureaus.

Christakis, Dimitri A., and Frederick J. Zimmerman (2007), "Violent Television Viewing During Preschool Is Associated with Antisocial Behavior During School Age," *Pediatrics*, 120 (5), 993–999.

Ferguson, Christopher J., Claudian San Miguel, and Richard D. Hartley (2009), "A Multivariate Analysis of Youth Violence and Aggression: The Influence of Family, Peers, Depression, and Media Violence," *Journal of Pediatrics*, 155 (6), 904–908.

———, Stephanie M. Rueda, Amanda M. Cruz, Diana E. Ferguson, Stacey Fritz, and Shawn Smith (2008), "Violent Video Games and Aggression: Causal Relationship or Byproduct of Family Violence and Intrinsic Violence Motivation?" *Criminal Justice and Behavior*, 35 (3), 311–332.

Fulkerson, Jayne A., Mary Story, Alison Mellin, Nancy Leffert, Dianne Neumark-Sztainer, and Simone A. French (2006), "Family Dinner Meal Frequency and Adolescent Development: Relationships with Developmental Assets and High-Risk Behaviors," *Journal of Adolescent Health*, 39 (3), 337–345.

Gentile, Douglas A., Muniba Saleem, and Craig A. Anderson (2007), "Public Policy and the Effects of Media Violence on Children," *Social Issues and Policy Review*, 1 (1), 15–61.

———, Paul J. Lynch, Jennifer R. Lindner, and David A. Walsh (2004), "The Effects of Violent Video Game Habits on Adolescent Hostility, Aggressive Behaviors, and School Performance," *Journal of Adolescence*, 27 (1), 5–22.

Glaser, Barney G., and Anselm L. Strauss (1967), *Discovery of Grounded Theory: Strategies for Qualitative Research*, New York: Aldine de Gruyter.

Greenbaum, Thomas L. (1998), *The Handbook for Focus Group Research*, Thousand Oaks, CA: Sage.

Grossbart, Sanford L., and Lawrence Crosby (1984), "Understanding the Bases of Parental Concern to Children's Food Advertising," *Journal of Marketing*, 48 (Summer), 79–92.

Huesmann, L. Rowell, Jessica Moise-Titus, Cheryl-Lynn Podolski and Leonard D. Eron (2003), "Longitudinal Relations Between Children's Exposure to TV Violence and Their Aggressive and Violent Behavior in Young Adulthood: 1977–1992," *Developmental Psychology, Special Issue: Violent Children*, 39 (2), 201–221.

Ji, Mindy F., and Russell N. Laczniak (2007), "Advertisers' Implementation of the CARU Guidelines for Advertising Targeted at Children," *Journal of Current Issues and Research in Advertising*, 29 (Fall), 27–38.

John, Deborah Roedder (1999), "Consumer Socialization of Children: A Retrospective Look at Twenty-Five Years of Research," *Journal of Consumer Research*, 26 (December), 183–213.

Jones, Gerard (2002), *Killing Monsters: Why Children Need Fantasy, Super Heroes, and Make Believe Violence*, New York: Basic Books.

Kug, Etienne G., Linda L. Dahlberg, James A. Mercy, Anthony B. Zwi, and Rafael Lozano (2002), *World Report on Health and Violence*, Geneva: World Health Organization.

Laczniak, Russell N., Darrel D. Muehling, and Les Carlson (1995), "An Investigation of Mothers' Attitudes Toward 900-Number Advertising Directed at Children," *Journal of Public Policy and Marketing*, 14 (Spring), 108–116.

Linn, Susan (2006), "Commercializing Childhood: The Corporate Takeover of Kids' Lives," *Multinational Monitor*, 30 (August 25), available at www.multinationalmonitor.org/mm2008/072008/interview-linn.html (accessed October 2, 2010).

Nathanson, Amy I. (1999), "Identifying and Explaining the Relationship Between Parental Mediation and Children's Aggression," *Communication Research*, 26 (2), 124–143.

——— (2002), "The Unintended Effects of Parental Mediation of Television on Adolescents," *Media Psychology*, 4 (3), 207–230.

Nikken, Peter, and Jeroen Jansz (2006), "Parental Mediation of Children's Videogame Playing: A Comparison of the Reports by Parents and Children," *Learning, Media, and Technology*, 31 (2), 181–202.

Olson, Cheryl K., Lawrence A. Kutner, and Dorothy E. Warner (2008), "The Role of Violent Video Game Content in Adolescent Development: Boys' Perspectives," *Journal of Adolescent Research*, 23 (1), 55–75.

———, ———, ———, Jason B. Almerigi, Lee Baer, Armand M. Nicholi II, and Eugene V. Beresin (2007), "Factors Correlated with Violent Video Game Use by Adolescent Boys and Girls," *Journal of Adolescent Health*, 41 (1), 77–83.

Paik, Haejung, and George Comstock (1994), "The Effects of Television Violence on Antisocial Behavior: A Meta-Analysis," *Communication Research*, 21 (4), 516–546.

Schor, Juliet B. (2004), *Born to Buy*, New York: Scribner.

Shanahan, Kevin J., Charles M. Hermans, and Michael R. Hyman (2003), "Violent Commercials in Television Programs for Children," *Journal of Current Issues and Research in Advertising*, 25 (1), 61–69.

Slater, Micael D., Kimberly L. Henry, Randall C. Swaim, and Lori L. Anderson (2003), "Violent Media Content and Aggressiveness in Adolescents: A Downward Spiral Model," *Communication Research*, 30 (6), 713–736.

Strauss, Anslem, and Juliet Corbin (1990), *Basics of Qualitative Research: Grounded Theory Procedures and Techniques*, Newbury Park, CA: Sage.

Thompson, Craig J. (1997), "Interpreting Consumers: A Hermeneutical Framework for Deriving Marketing Insights from the Texts of Consumers' Consumption Stories," *Journal of Marketing Research*, 34 (4), 438–455.

U.S. Public Health Service (2001), "Youth Violence: A Report of the Surgeon General," available at www.surgeongeneral.gov/library/youthviolence/ (accessed October 2, 2010).

Ward, Scott, Daniel B. Wackman, and Ellen M. Wartella (1977), "The Development of Consumer Information Processing Skills: Integrating Cognitive Development and Family Interaction Theories," in *Advances in Consumer Research*, vol. 4, William D. Perreault, Jr., ed., Atlanta: Association for Consumer Research, 166–171.

Wood, Wendy, Frank Y. Wong, and Gregory J. Chachere (1991), "Effects of Media Violence on Viewers' Aggression in Unconstrained Social Interaction," *Psychological Bulletin*, 109 (3), 371–383.

12

Caution, Animated Violence
Assessing the Efficacy of Violent Video Game Ratings
Karen L. Becker-Olsen and Patricia A. Norberg

The controversy surrounding violent video games persists, as top ten lists for 2009 include titles such as Street Fighter, Resident Evil, and Kill Zone 2 (www.cnbc.com/id/30948057/?slide=1/), and half the March 2009 Nielsen-ranked top ten games were labeled as having violent content (http://en-us.nielsen.com/content/nielsen/en_us/insights/rankings/video_games.html). Microsoft's shooting game Gears of War was the best-selling console game in December 2006, selling 815,700 copies and finishing third in sales for the year (Associated Press 2007). Three years later, the game continues to perform well, with Gears of War II taking the top-selling video game spot in November 2008 at over 1.5 million copies sold (Reuters 2008). Clearly, the idea of simulating real-world violence is a huge commercial success, especially in the youth through young adult markets. However, the success comes with increasing scrutiny from consumer advocacy groups calling for greater government intervention and monitoring, stricter retailer oversight, and stronger parental controls.

Games such as Mortal Kombat and Resident Evil, which feature explicit violence with hand-to-hand combat and first-person shooting as central components of game play, continue to fuel the controversy. A November 2007 decision by Target and other retail outlets to pull Manhunt 2 a week after its release exemplifies the conundrum faced by retailers. This particular game, initially rated mature (M), was shrouded in debate even before its release because of the extremely violent story line (a patient escapes from a mental hospital and either kills or must be killed, forcing the player to engage in sadistic acts of murder). Youth advocacy groups appealed to the Entertainment Software Ratings Board (ESRB) on behalf of parents and successfully secured an adult-only (AO) rating. However, the game manufacturer then blocked some game content and was able to reverse the decision just before launching to maintain the mature rating. In this case, even with the mature rating, retailers were skeptical, and many chose not to sell the game. Thus, both retailers and parents count on the ESRB to appropriately rate video games and clearly note where questionable content exists.

Extant research suggests that repeated exposure to this questionable violent content contained in video games can serve to engender violent, aggressive, and antisocial behaviors (Anderson and Bushman 2001; Anderson and Dill 2000; Ballard and Weist 1996; Van Schie and Wiegman 1997). Thus, the ESRB was created in 1994 to rate video games and to help parents manage their children's video game consumption. Currently, the organization rates most video games on an age scale beginning at EC (early childhood) and ending at AO (adults only), with additional content descriptors to further explain the age ratings (e.g., cartoon violence, fantasy violence, animated blood, or strong language). Ratings and content descriptors together serve as a guidepost for the level and intensity of profane language, sexual content, and violence. Hence, just as traditional advertising and packaging provide product information to help consumers make more informed choices, ratings systems provide similar cues and information. Theoretically and quite ideally, video game and other electronic content rating systems should help parents understand what kind of content is contained in the video game before they allow the purchase and play of the game.

It is important to note that it is not our purpose to debate or advocate for or against violent video game content, but rather to suggest that the current rating system and its related parental communication is perhaps ineffective in terms of informing parents. Fifteen years after the creation and nearly a decade since the Federal Trade Commission (FTC) praised the ESRB for its efforts in informing parents about questionable video game content (www.ftc.gov/reports/violence/appendicesviorpt.pdf), we find that parents are still relatively uninformed about and miscomprehending of both the rating system's age breakdowns and more recent content descriptors. These findings mirror previous work that called into question the validity of the age rating system (Cantor 1998; Haninger and Thompson 2004; Walsh and Gentile 2001; Wartella, O'Keefe, and Scantlin 2000). Thus, the primary purpose of this paper is to explore the efficacy of ESRB-assigned ratings and content descriptors as related to violent video games.

It is interesting to note that little research has emerged regarding parental perceptions and cognitive processing related to the rating system, though several large-scale studies were conducted in the late 1990s (Cesarone 1998) and early 2000s (FTC 2000; Walsh et al. 2003) with a focus on awareness and intended usage. These studies show that parents realize that video games are rated, and increasing numbers report an interest in using the ratings (FTC 2000). The research focus now needs to shift from awareness and intended usage to understanding actual usage, parental processing of the ratings information, and the system's ability to adequately inform parents, especially in light of current perspectives on parental control and intervention. The Supreme Court affirms that parents not only have the right and authority to control the activities of their children but also the responsibility to do so for activities that pose potential risk of harm to the child (Davidson 1996). Yet this assumes that parents are aware of the risks and are able to understand and enforce standards. In that one of the key roles of the ESRB is to help parents manage their children's video game consumption via ratings, it is important that parents do not miscomprehend the ratings. Thus, the need for research on parental processing and understanding of the rating system is further warranted.

Through two studies, we help address the dearth of research on ratings efficacy, specifically focusing on the gap in parent-child ratings perceptions and factors that might lead to differences in perceptions. Our findings suggest that youth may be desensitized to violence, and such desensitization may remain unchecked due to lack of parental use or miscomprehension of ratings information. Thus, we argue that changes are needed in the rating system and that communication about ratings needs to take into account parental perceptions of violence and age appropriateness.

In our first study, we investigate both parental and teen perceptions of video game violence and ratings associated with games. By addressing both sets of consumers, we are able to understand the potential dual nature of the game choice decision as well as better understand varying perceptions of violence contained in the video games. We show that parents and youth perceive video game violence differently (and therefore assign game-related ratings differently), and that this difference may be driven by desensitization in the latter group as compared to the former group. In our second study, we continue to explore parental perception, arguing that the content descriptors used in the current rating system do not foster a sense of parental understanding of the actual violence contained in video games, and in some cases may lead to miscomprehension on the part of the parent. Our findings suggest this may be due to parental reliance on outdated exemplars (e.g., Wile E. Coyote as cartoon violence) that bias perceptions of game content. Thus, we provide evidence that current video game content descriptors and associated age ratings are not effective in meeting the objectives of informing the parental consumer about potentially harmful or inappropriate content.

SENSITIVITY TO VIOLENCE

Researchers have discussed two different outcomes of repeated exposure to violent media/video games—one associated with aggressive behavioral manifestations and the other associated with desensitization to violence. In line with the latter, we argue here that individuals who are repeatedly exposed to violent media will become desensitized to it, though they may not overtly engage in violent behaviors.

Carnagey, Anderson, and Bushman define desensitization to violence as "a reduction in emotion-related physiological reactivity to real violence" (2007, p. 490). Cline, Croft, and Courrier (1973) define desensitization in a similar way, equating it to "psychological blunting," "turning off," "tuning out," and "habituation." This second definition corresponds to concerns about the effects of heavy violent video game use in that habituation reflects the process by which stimuli, in this case, the video game violence, is perceived as less intense. Their research showed that test participants who were *less* exposed to violence were more aroused and took greater time to recover from the emotional state (as measured by galvanic skin response [GSR] and blood volume pulse) than those with higher levels of exposure. Thomas et al. (1977) also suggest that desensitization occurs when an initial arousal to violent stimuli is reduced and thus changes an individual's present internal state. Likewise, systematic desensitization has been shown to reduce avoidance behavior, and when there is no direct adverse consequence of fear-provoking behavior, there is an opportunity for fear extinction (Bandura, Blanchard, and Ritter 1969). The concerns associated with desensitization are that individuals may not notice aggressive events, may perceive resulting injuries as less severe, may feel less sympathy for victims, and may have less negative attitudes toward violence (Carnagey, Anderson, and Bushman 2007).

Correspondingly, how or what people perceive as violent has been shown to be a function of the rates and types of exposure to violent stimuli (Carnagey, Anderson, and Bushman 2007). Thus, differences across cultures, age cohorts, and generations are likely to exist. According to a report issued by the American Academy of Pediatrics (2001), today's younger audiences are more desensitized to violence not solely because of video games but because of their total media diet. They consume news, video games, music videos, and television programming that all contain more violent content today than 30 years ago, suggesting a higher threshold and tolerance level for violent stimuli.

More recent research points specifically to violent video games as key agents for the desensitization process (Carnagey, Anderson, and Bushman 2007; Staude-Muller, Bliesener, and Luthman 2008), such that violence and aggression are increasingly seen as being normal (Huesmann, Moise, and Podolski 1997). Thus, we expect that young people who consume more violent video games than their parents will be more desensitized to the violent content, thereby rating games lower (more leniently) than parents who have minimal or no exposure to these games. We examine the perceptions of video game ratings (warnings) in a parent-child decision context in Study 1 (desensitization effects) and provide exploratory evidence that ratings may not be utilized as intended by the ratings board and the FTC.

STUDY 1: EXPLORING THE RATING SYSTEM

In this study, our goals were threefold: (1) to understand what parents and young people know about the rating system, (2) to examine perceptions of video game violence across various age cohorts as related to differences in perceptions of violence, and (3) to examine the extent to which ratings correspond to these violence perceptions. As Robert Bork (1996) wrote in *Slouching Toward Gomorrah*, society can tolerate only so much deviation from the mean until the mean itself becomes redefined. We believe that the mean for "acceptable violence exposure" is shifting.

Sample

A total of 160 people participated in the study without compensation. The sample was divided into four equal age groups: middle school, high school, college, and parent of a child at least 10 years old. The first group, middle school, comprised students in grades 6 through 8 with ages in the range of 10 through 14 and an average age of 12. The high school group comprised students in grades 9 through 12 with ages in the range of 14 through 18 and an average age of 15. The third group, college, comprised students ages 18 to 22 and an average age of 20. The last group, parents, comprised adults ages 36 and up, with an average age of 45. All respondents in the parent group had at least one boy at home between the ages of 10 and 18 and owned at least one video game console. Although both boys and girls engage in video game play, boys are more likely to play violent games and play for more hours than girls (Gentile 2009); thus, all of the nonparent subjects were male (54% of the parent group were male). All subjects were from upper-middle-class Northeastern suburban communities.

Procedure

Subjects were told they were participating in a video game rating study and asked to fill out a survey as well as watch four 10- to 15-second promotional clips for four different highly successful video games: Street Fighter, Super Mario World, Viva Piñata, and Gears of War. These games were chosen in that they represented top sellers and covered a range of violence from "not at all" to "violent." First, subjects were asked how involved parents were in video game selection in their household (with 1 = not at all involved and 7 = highly involved). Then they were asked to provide information regarding prior video game consumption, including hours played and types of games played. Next, subjects were asked how involved they thought parents should be in video game choice for various age groups (responses were scaled and anchored with 1 = "not at all" and 7 = "very"). In the next section, subjects were asked about their familiarity with the ESRB rating system and where they could get rating information. Then they were shown box art (with the rating stripped out) and asked to rate the perceived violence level of the video games—Street Fighter (violent), Super Mario World (not very violent), Viva Piñata (not violent), and Gears of War (very violent)—on a 1 = "not violent at all" to 7 = "very violent" scale and with the ESRB ratings. Last, each subject watched a promotional clip of the video games and then again assigned each of the four games one of the ESRB ratings. Game order was randomized to reduce carryover effects from previous clips.

Results

As expected, we found significant differences across the age groups for all of the variables evaluated.

Hours Played

Not surprisingly, hours of play varied significantly across the age groups, $F(3, 159) = 45.52$, $p < .001$, with middle school boys playing more hours of video games than adults or even older teens. See Table 12.1 for details on hours played.

Parent Role in Selection

As we might expect, differences existed across the groups regarding the role that respondents believe parents *should* play in video game selection, $F(3, 159) = 45.52, p < .001$. Middle school boys felt that parents should have a limited role in which games they select ($M = 2.30$), but that

Table 12.1

Descriptive Statistics: Hours Played, Parental Involvement, and ESRB Knowledge

	Middle school	High school	College	Parent
Weekly play (answers per person with n = 40 in each age cohort)				
0	0	0	4	26
1–5	1	4	10	13
6–10	8	26	20	1
10–12	16	10	5	0
More than 12	15	0	1	0
How much should parents be involved? (1–7 scale, with 1 = not involved and 7 = very involved)				
Elementary	4.58	5.48	5.62	5.98
Middle school	2.30	4.32	5.07	5.85
High school	1.12	1.15	1.89	5.52
How much are parents actually involved?	2.67	2.87	1.36	2.89
ESRB knowledge (1–7 scale, with 1 = no knowledge and 7 = high knowledge)	6.17	3.42	3.61	2.41

Note: ESRB = Entertainment Software Ratings Board.

parents should play a larger role in the selection of games for elementary and younger children ($M = 4.58$). The high school and college groups felt that parents should assist with the selection of games for middle school students ($M = 4.32$) and younger children ($M = 5.48$), but not high school or above ($M = 1.15$). In contrast, parents felt that they should have a role in video game selection through high school, $M_{elementary} = 5.98$, $M_{middleschool} = 5.85$, $M_{highschool} = 5.52$; $F(3, 40) = 2.45$, $p > .05$. It is interesting to note that these results are in conflict with what *actually* happens in the sample group. At the middle school and high school levels, parents are only moderately involved in the selection of video games and not involved at the college level; this is confirmed by low means reported by parents. Thus, although parents express that they should be involved, the reality is most are, at best, moderately involved. See Table 12.1 for means.

Ratings System

Respondents were asked how much they knew about the rating system and the ESRB. Although actual knowledge was never tested or confirmed, we did find significant differences across age groups for self-reported knowledge, $F(3,159) = 8.21$, $p < .001$. Middle school students reported the highest level of knowledge of the ESRB ($M = 6.17$), whereas parents reported relatively little knowledge ($M = 2.41$) and high school and college students were in the middle ($M = 3.42$ and $M = 3.61$, respectively). Respondents were also asked where they might find rating information, and unaided responses showed that greater than 80% of middle school, high school, and college students knew the information was on the box cover and in advertisements. The remaining 20% of students noted the Internet as a source for rating information, with some noting specific sites such as gamebox.com. In contrast, 30% of parents did not know where to find the information, while of the remaining 70%, only 5% noted that the information was on the box cover or in advertisements. The others all noted "online" but did not specify any particular Web site.

Rating the Games

For the groups' ratings on the four video games, we found fewer discrepancies for the two less-violent games. In fact, all groups rated the less-violent games relatively consistent with the ESRB rating of E (Everyone) both before and after viewing the promotional clip. Thus, the discrepancies in ratings seem to exist in the more violent or Teen (T) end of the spectrum. Middle school respondents tended to rate both Street Fighter and Gears of War as E10+ (Everyone 10 and older)—one and two levels, respectively, below the ESRB rating, with no significant differences between pre- and postexposure to the clip ($\chi^2 = .46$, $p > 1$). High school students tended to rate Street Fighter as an E10+ game and Gears of War as a Teen game (both one rating below the ESRB). College students were split on Street Fighter, assigning mostly E10+ and Teen ratings preexposure. Postexposure, some college students changed their rating from E10+ to Teen, although not a significant number ($\chi^2 = 2.18$, $p > .05$). For Gears of War, college students were less likely to alter their ratings after exposure and tended to rate the game as a Teen game, again one rating below the ESRB. As expected, parents showed significant differences in ratings pre- and postexposure for both Street Fighter and Gears of War ($\chi^2 = 8.74$, $p < .05$, $\chi^2 = 14.37$, $p < .01$, respectively). The pattern of results suggests that before previewing the clip, parents rated the game as did the ESRB, while postexposure they tended to rate the game more harshly than did the ESRB (see Table 12.2 for full details). This change in ratings suggests that the box art and title might signal a response different from the actual game. Given that few of the parental respondents had a history of playing video games, it is likely that the content was not what they were expecting.

Discussion

As expected, students of all ages were playing more video games than their parents and had a greater knowledge of the games and the rating system. It is interesting to note that although parents believe children's video game consumption should be monitored, most were not actually doing this. Our findings are suggestive of the desensitization hypothesis in that we found strong differences across the three student groups and parents, such that middle school students rated games most lenient and also interact with video games the most in our study as measured via number of hours of play per week. Thus, it appears that students who are experienced with video games are less likely to perceive the games as violent. Although this could be a function of a demand effect (middle school students simply want to play Teen-rated games), it is likely that violence desensitization is at least partially responsible for the results. This idea is supported by the data, which shows significant video game exposure of high school and college students who also rate the games lower, again suggesting they perceive the games as less violent than do the parents. It is reasonable to assume that both high school and college students are free to play and purchase Teen- and even Mature-rated games; thus, they have little to gain by rating the games more liberally than the ESRB. In addition, it is reasonable to believe that most of the students in the sample were knowledgeable about the games before exposure to the promotional clip since there were few changes in ratings after exposure to the clip for these groups.

In summary, we suggest that our exploratory evidence shows that parents demonstrate greater sensitivity to violence, manifested in more stringent ratings assignments, than their younger counterparts. Although we do not directly test desensitization via traditional mechanisms used in lab experiments, such as skin reaction, heart rate monitoring, and so forth, the choice measures here indicate that desensitization may be present in accordance with the habituation definitions suggested by Cline, Croft, and Courrier (1973) and Huesmann, Moise, and Podolski (1997). Future tests could seek to demonstrate a more direct link between frequency of interaction with games and desensitization.

Table 12.2

Video Game Ratings Before and After Viewing Promotional Clip

	Middle school		High school		College		Parents	
	Before	After	Before	After	Before	After	Before	After
Viva Pinata	**E–90%** EC–10%	**E–80%** EC–20%	**E–90%** EC–10%	**E–90%** EC–10%	**E–80%** EC–20%	**E–80%** EC–20%	**E–90%** EC–10%	**E–90%** EC–10%
Super Mario World	**E–90%** EC–10%	**E–85%** EC–15%	**E–90%** EC–10%	**E–90%** EC–10%	**E–90%** EC–10%	**E–85%** EC–15%	**E–90%** EC–10%	**E–90%** EC–10%
Street Fighter	E10+–87.5% **T–10%** M–2.5% AO–0%	E10+–90% **T–10%** **M–0%** AO–0%	E10+–62.5% **T–35%** M–2.5% AO–0%	E10+–62.5% **T–35%** M–2.5% AO–0%	E10+–40% **T–45%** M–15% AO–0%	E10+–32.5% **T–55%** M–12.5% AO–0%	E10+–7.5% **T–65%** M–22.5% AO–5%	E10+–2.5% **T–45%** M–30% AO–22.5%
Gears of War	E10–92.5% T–7.5% **M–0%** AO–0%	E10–95% T–5% **M–0%** AO–0%	E10–5% T–57.5% **M–37.5%** AO–0%	E10–10% T–60% **M–30%** AO–0%	E10–10% T–55% **M–30%** AO–5%	E10–10% T–55% **M–30%** AO–5%	E10–0% T–15% **M–75%** AO–10%	E10–0% T–5% **M–45%** AO–50%

Notes: Rows in boldface represent the actual ESRB (Entertainment Software Ratings Board) rating of the game; indicating in the first row that the game was rated as E by the ESRB and 90% of middle school subjects gave it the same rating. E = Everyone; EC = Early Childhood; E10+ = Everyone 10 and older; T = teen; M = mature; AO = Adults Only.

Our evidence also suggests that the ESRB ratings on violent content are more lenient than our parental respondents' ratings once they "learned" the extent of violent content by watching the video clips. This suggests that some type of parental miscomprehension is taking place. Although box art and game titles might also trigger cognitions about game age appropriateness, we find that this may be very different from how parents would rank games if they were exposed to the actual content.

Last, there are myriad reasons as to why parents may not be monitoring their children's video game consumption, including time pressure, trust, a disbelief that exposure to violent video games is harmful, or simply limited knowledge about video games. If parents are not monitoring video game consumption because their knowledge about video games/ratings/ESRB is so low that they rely solely on their children's preferences or because they do not necessarily understand the effects that violent video games can have or even because the rating systems prove too cumbersome to use (see Cantor 1998; Gentile and Walsh 2002), then parents need resources to help them easily overcome these obstacles. Given these insights, we turn to further examining why parents are not monitoring video game consumption and how age and content ratings can influence parental perceptions of game appropriateness. Specifically, we are interested in whether the ESRB age ratings and content modifiers are effective in helping parents comprehend the content or lead to further miscomprehension.

CATEGORIZATION AND PERCEPTUAL BIAS

Rooted in social cognition theory, the idea that previously learned information is stored in memory and called upon during a perceived relevant decision context (Wyer and Radvansky 1999; Wyer and Srull 1986) is widely accepted. Thus, past experiences can affect how individuals classify and interpret new information. The theory further suggests that categorical representations, prototypes, or exemplars form the basis for judgment of new or unfamiliar objects or stimuli and how that stimuli should be interpreted and classified (Fiske 1982; Snyder 1992; Van Auken and Adams 1998). However, the classification of new or unfamiliar stimuli is not always accurate, as perceptual biases can influence interpretation and lead to miscomprehension. For example, when past categorical learning is incomplete or sparse, the matching of new stimuli with existing categories might not be optimal while nonetheless influencing how the new stimuli are interpreted (Waldmann and Hagmayer 2006). Often, miscomprehension leads to confusion or even discounting of information; thus, comprehension is critical for ensuring that a piece of information is received and made diagnostic (Jacoby and Hoyer 1987).

Because inferred meaning on the part of the receiver of a message (see Jacoby, Nelson, and Hoyer 1982) is likely to influence (mis)comprehension and is typically based on an individual's past experiences and expectations (Harris and Monaco 1978; see also Waldmann and Hagmayer 2006), we suggest that the interpretation of video game ratings information by parents might be biased. Consider that each parent filters rating information through their own past experiences in forming individual expectations for their child. Through years of exposure to age-based movie ratings and the movies themselves, parents are likely to have reference points for age-based standards and may therefore more concretely process age ratings of video games. Thus, the meaning of E (Everyone) and T (Teen) ratings on games (Haninger and Thompson 2004) is likely to be perceived as equivalent to G-rated movies and PG13-rated movies. In other words, a video game rating of Teen may automatically trigger thoughts of PG13 movies. These same past experiences can also bias perceptions in that parents might use outdated movies as their guidepost. For example, in the case of less-concrete terms such as "cartoon," perceptual bias may ensue if in fact animation is associated with past imagery and actions that do not reflect the images and actions in the current video game context. In fact, Walsh and Gentile (2001) found that only half the parents understood the age ratings on video games.

In essence, miscomprehension is likely to stem from reliance on outdated exemplars in the absence of current exposure to video games on the part of parents. Therefore, differences in perceptions of the words "violent," "fantasy," or "cartoon" are likely to exist. For example, a rating that indicates "cartoon violence" might be associated with a parent's exemplar of Wile E. Coyote getting blown up by TNT, when in fact cartoon violence in the video game can be much more realistic. In this case, the judgment of risk associated with cartoon violence would be biased downward because it is classified as having similar attributes as this earlier exemplar. This misapplied classification may then lead to over-/underutilization of rating information by the parent. As evidenced in our study and other research, most parents are not playing video games and thus would not have an intuitive or learned understanding of the content that might otherwise act as an interrupt to the misclassification of video content. Although one might argue that the phenomenon observed here is merely one of classifying stimuli differently, with parents classifying based on a system that is different than their children (and perhaps the ESRB), we suggest that actual miscomprehension ensues on the part of the parents. As Jacoby, Nelson, and Hoyer (1982) suggest, when a message/medium (in this case, the content qualifier) evokes a meaning different than the source intended, or when it evokes more than one thought, then miscommunication or ambiguous communication occurs (see also Harris and Monaco 1978). We believe this is what occurs with video game ratings.

In Study 2, we examine parental perceptions of violence content descriptors and age ratings, hypothesizing that parental perceptions are based on past experiences, and as such, are likely to vary across age cohorts, as shared experiences (e.g., key events, cultural references, and media exposure) are likely to change. As discussed above, social cognition theory and categorization in part help explain how perceptual biases are formed based on an individual's prior knowledge and experiences in that outdated exemplars may drive how parents process rating information in the absence of experience that might trigger category updating or recategorization.

STUDY 2: UNDERSTANDING AGE AND CONTENT RATINGS

In this study, we conducted an experiment with parents to better understand parental perceptions of video games, violence, and rating scales. Prior to the actual experiment, a series of focus groups were conducted as a pretest to identify where ratings might be creating misperceptions about video game content and to verify that parents often do not participate in the game choice process or regularly supervise game play.

Pretest

As in Study 1, participants were from an upper-middle-class community in the Northeastern United States. All participants were parents with boys ages 10 to 18 who own at least one video game console. There were few discrepancies across the groups, thus the following discussion is reflective of all groups. Half the respondents were male, and the average age was 45.

Three key findings arose that are then further explored in the main study:

1. *Parents believe games can be harmful when played in excess or if they are very violent, even though they do not seem to preview the games played or understand the content.* Parents were asked whether they believed that engagement in video games promoted antisocial or aggressive behavior. All the participants agreed that playing video games could lead to antisocial behavior; however, they did not believe that the effect would be

significant for their children given the hours they played. Even after sharing some of the existing research on the detrimental effects of video game play, parents were still skeptical that their children would experience antisocial behavioral effects. Consistent with the findings of The Entertainment Software Association 2006 annual report, parents remained relatively positive about their children's video game entertainment (www.theesa.com/facts/pdfs/ESA_EF_2006.pdf).

2. *Parents believe their children choose games wisely and there is a great sense of expressed trust between parents and their children.* Parents were also asked to discuss video game selection, and in general they reflected that young people chose the games they were interested in without parental involvement. As in Study 1, in which parents reported that they were only minimally involved in game selection, parents in the focus groups noted that their children often used their own money to purchase the games, leaving parents out of this decision phase. Asked if they checked the types of games their children played or knew of the games, most could not name three games their children owned, and a few could not name any games. Generally, parents believed their children made good choices and were "not problem children." Some commented that they had no reason to not trust their children's decisions.

3. *Unless the content descriptor states realistic or sexual violence, parents do not perceive the game as very violent or inappropriate for middle school age children. This perception was altered when parents were shown clips of games marked as animated violence.* Most parents felt that as long as the game was not listed as realistic violence or sexual violence, it was appropriate for children as young as age 10. When asked about the animated violence, cartoon violence, fantasy violence, or animated blood descriptors, parents noted cartoons of their era or violence depicted in *Star Wars* movies, which they felt was appropriate for young people age 10 or older. As an example, Wile E. Coyote and Bugs Bunny were noted as being quite violent cartoons and still appropriate for young children. Clearly, the reference point for animated violence for parents seems to be cartoons of their childhood rather than current titles. After parents were shown clips of videos marked as animated violence, animated blood, and fantasy violence, they were surprised at the intensity of the violence and were quick to note that the clips did not match their expectations. Thus, as in Study 1, we find that parents' past experiences are fueling the miscomprehension.

Given the parental feedback in the focus groups, it is likely that various content descriptors and even age ratings will significantly influence violence perceptions of parents. In this study, we experimentally examine two content descriptors and two age ratings. Of particular interest is the content descriptor "animated violence" (see also Haninger and Thompson 2004, and Gentile 2008 for similar concern). As noted, the word *animation* seems to invoke animated images of traditional cartoon and Looney Tunes characters engaged in slapstick-style mischief. Thus, we expect that parents will perceive a game rated with animated violence as less violent (in terms of intensity and frequency of violent episodes) than one rated with realistic violence.

Design

In a 2 (games) × 5 (ratings) completely randomized study, we experimentally examined the impact of age ratings and content descriptors on parental perceptions of violence across two different games.

Sample

Two hundred parents were recruited at a large sporting event in the Northeastern United States and participated without compensation. Only one parent per household participated. All households had children between the ages of 8 and 17 who regularly played video games and owned at least one game console or a computer. Sixty-eight percent of the participants were female, and the average age was 46.

Procedure

Participants were shown a picture of the cover of the box for either Gears of War or Street Fighter with no rating information, an age rating of Teen or E10+, or a content descriptor of Animated Violence[1] or Realistic Violence. The same game titles were used in this study as in Study 1 to provide a replication of the findings, as well as to further understand the discrepancy in perceived ratings from the first study. After exposure to the box cover, participants were asked to rate the appropriateness of the game for two age brackets, the amount or frequency of violent content they thought would be in the game, and the perceived intensity of the violence. All variables were measured on a 1 to 7 scale, with 1 being not at all violent or inappropriate for the given age group and 7 being very violent.

Results

Because there were significant differences between the two games in the violence ratings, $F(1, 198) = 26.58$, $p < .01$, the game analyses are reported separately, whereas the results are collapsed across the two games when examining age appropriateness, $F(1, 198) = 1.67, p > .01$. There are no significant differences across gender, $F(1, 198) = 3.02, p > .05$.

Age Appropriateness

As expected, there were significant differences across the appropriateness ratings for teens, $F(4,195) = 66.88, p < .001$, and 9- to 12-year-olds, $F(4,195) = 100.25, p < .001$. Most interesting, as is shown in Table 12.3, parents were most critical when there were no ratings on the boxes. As expected, the Animated Violence descriptor had the strongest impact in terms of signaling appropriateness for both 9- to 12-year-olds, $F(1, 78) = 26.78, p < .001$, and teens, $F(1, 78) = 28.24, p < .001$, when compared to the No Rating condition. In fact, the Animated Violence descriptor had a stronger appropriateness impact than the E10+ rating for 9- to 12-year-olds, $F(1, 78) = 6.24, p < .05$, and was equally effective in signaling appropriateness for teens, $F(1, 78) = 12.16, p < .01$. The Teen rating led to only a moderate increase in appropriateness for the 9- to 12-year-old groups, $F(1, 78) = 7.73, p < .05$, while significantly increasing appropriateness for teens, $F(1, 78) = 8.95, p < .01$. In contrast, the Realistic Violence descriptor was not significantly different than the control of No Rating for the 9- to 12-year-olds, $F(1, 78) = 1.26, p > .1$, and only moderately increased perceptions of appropriateness for teens, $F(1, 78) = 6.35, p < .05$. See Table 12.3 for all means.

Violence Perceptions by Game

It is interesting to note that for Gears of War, the amount of perceived violence was unchanged by the age group rating and the content descriptors, $F(4, 95) = 1.26, p > .01$. However, the perceived intensity of violence was diminished for the content descriptor Animated Violence,

Table 12.3

Perceptions of Age Appropriateness

Rating	9–12	Teen
No rating	1.58	1.93
E10+	4.73	6.12
Teen	2.85	3.75
Animated violence	5.39	5.81
Realistic violence	1.78	2.20

Note: scale anchors: 1 = not at all appropriate; 7 = appropriate.

Table 12.4

Parental Perceptions of Violence Across Age Ratings and Content Qualifiers

	Amount of violence	Intensity of violence
Gears of War		
No rating	6.53[a]	6.48[a]
Teen	6.41[a]	6.37[a]
E10+	6.01[a]	5.98[a]
Animated violence	6.31[a]	4.37[b]
Realistic violence	6.57[a]	6.23[a]
Street Fighter		
No rating	5.78[a]	5.95[a]
Teen	5.63[a]	5.87[a]
E10+	5.42[a]	5.24[a]
Animated violence	4.79[b]	3.98[b]
Realistic violence	5.58[a]	5.57[a]

Notes: Means in the same column with different superscripts are significantly different.
Scale anchors: 1 = not at all violent/intense; 7 = very violent/intense.

$F(4, 95) = 16.86$, $p < .01$. For Street Fighter, the pattern was slightly different. The Animated Violence descriptor diminished both perceptions of the amount of violence and the intensity of violence, $F(4, 95) = 8.36$, $p < .05$; $F(4, 95) = 21.30$, $p < .01$. All other ratings appeared to leave perceptions of the amount of violence or the intensity of violence unchanged. See Table 12.4 for means related to violence perceptions.

Discussion

In this study, we were able to demonstrate that age ratings and content qualifiers act as signals for parents suggesting appropriateness of game content. In addition, we were able to demonstrate that the descriptor "animated violence" is perhaps one signal that leads to miscomprehension in that this descriptor may suggest to parents "cartoon-type" violence of an era gone by. It is interestingly to note that parents seemed to understand that the games have significant amounts of violence, yet many still seemed to find the games appropriate. The results further suggest that it is the perceived intensity of violence that drives appropriateness more than frequency of violence. For both games, the frequency of violence was relatively constant, yet when the descriptor Animated Violence was used, age appropriateness increased significantly, indicating that the game was more appropriate when it was rated/qualified with "animated violence," irrespective of frequency of violent acts.

Also interesting is the effect of "no rating" on the games. Here, parents were the most vigilant in assigning appropriateness to the game, suggesting that without any cues, parents are more conservative in their assessment. This may be because the process of matching content to existing cognitive categories/classifications is modified or is not possible. Alternatively, in the absence of a rating, parents may use the box art and title to determine age appropriateness. This is somewhat counter to the argument that the ratings help parents make better decisions. Of course, the underlying assumption in both cases is that parents actually look at and are somewhat involved in the video game decision.

GENERAL DISCUSSION

Given that the evidence across these two studies shows (1) there are significant differences in ratings processing among parents and children, (2) parents do not always monitor or control video game choice, and (3) even if they do monitor choice via rating on box covers, they do not necessarily understand the various ratings and content descriptors, it is important to reevaluate the rating system and ensure that it meets the needs of parents as well as younger consumers.

In the studies reported herein, participants were forced to assign an appropriateness value to a game based on the rating or descriptor. In reality, most parents may not attend to the game as carefully as they did in this experiment, since they believe their children make good choices and will not be affected by violent games from a behavioral standpoint (as suggested by our pretest participants). It should also be noted that many parents today believe that they have so many demands on their time that they simply do not have the time to monitor everything their children are doing. Our findings and the related considerations emphasize the need to address two important and underlying issues: (1) convincing all parents that repeated exposure to violent video games can affect even their children (e.g., via consequences of desensitization as suggested by Carnagey, Anderson, and Bushman 2007 and others, and emphasized in our Study 1), and (2) making the rating system clear, accurate, and easy to use (as emphasized in our Study 2).

We show that there is a vast discrepancy between what youth and adults/parents perceive as violent content and that parents' miscomprehension of ratings is in part explained by ambiguity in rating information, especially in the content descriptors. Moreover, our results suggest that parents may have different reference points (use outdated exemplars) for some content descriptors than what is intended by the ESRB, and they have difficulty assigning meaning to them. If parents do not process animated violence or fantasy violence accurately, they may remain unconcerned about games containing such violence where they should be concerned. This further supports the idea that the system needs to be revamped so it can more adequately meet parents' needs. Previously, the policy issue has centered around whether the expressed detrimental effects of exposure to violent video games are great enough to warrant government intervention. We alternatively/additionally would argue that parental confusion may be strong enough to warrant government or industry intervention.

Parents are the gatekeepers of what their children can or cannot have, and they need to take responsibility for the consumption habits of their children. It is their responsibility to be informed and monitor the hours and types of games played. This process becomes easier and more effective when industry associates partner with parents and provide clear information and guidelines. Thus, the burden does not fall completely on the parent. The campaign initiated in 1998 by the ESRB in conjunction with the Parent-Teacher Association (PTA) to educate parents on video games and ratings in the form of handbooks that were distributed to PTA parents (www.esrb.org/about/news/downloads/ESRB_PTA_Brochure-web_version.pdf) is a step in the right direction. However, such materials may not reach parents, may be ignored based on the volume of materials already distributed via schools, and do not reach non-PTA members. This last point is critical since parents who join the

PTA are probably already some of the most involved and informed parents. The guidebooks clearly identified the age ratings, locations of ratings on game boxes, and the parental controls on the various consoles; however, the detail on rating system content descriptors was largely absent.

We suggest that in light of the complexity of the issue and busy life schedules of parents, in addition to these PTA-supported instructional materials, multiple touch points for information access will be necessary going forward. For example, regulators might (1) incent retailers who sell games or consoles to post information about ratings at the point of purchase to reach at least those parents who are present at the time of purchase, and (2) incent manufacturers to include rating system information in game packaging and console packaging. Moreover, regulators might force manufacturers to run a public service campaign similar to the drinking and driving campaigns that alcohol manufacturers are required to support.

Other non–communication-based strategies might also be considered. For example, public policy efforts might include incenting retail establishments to take a stand against selling Mature or Adult Only games to minors and working with manufacturers to reduce the violent content on Teen-rated games. Moreover, and as suggested previously (Walsh and Gentile 2001), devising a common rating system across media (television, music, video games, movies) with uniquenesses only where needed could potentially reduce the confusion about ratings on the part of all constituents. Most important, and regardless of which strategies are employed to motivate parents to "get involved," a cleaning up and periodic review of rating labels (especially content descriptors) that takes into account the perceptual biases that are likely to influence interpretation is needed.

FUTURE RESEARCH

There are several areas that warrant future research. First, a better understanding of how previous exposure to violent content shapes processing of age and content descriptors is necessary. As noted, social cognition theory addresses the comprehension acquired in daily life about people and events for which an individual has prior knowledge and argues that previously learned information is called upon during a decision context (Wyer and Radvansky 1999; Wyer and Srull 1986). As applied to the topic of ratings, recognizing what constitutes a semantically congruent exemplar is important. Is exposure to cartoon violence as in Wile E. Coyote getting blown up by TNT related to animated video game violence, or is news footage of street fighting related to violence in the game Street Fighter? Similarly, an understanding of what acts trigger specific previous experiences needs further exploration. Is it the game title, the box art, the rating, or some combination of these factors? Further, identifying which previous experiences are diagnostic is important. Again, if both news images and cartoon images are triggered, individuals will need to reconcile which is more diagnostic for the given decision. Research on how we might prompt parents to revise perception about/recategorize new information by creating updated, more relevant, and accessible exemplars might be a productive next step. With this in mind, considering an initiative whereby policymakers and ratings boards "work with" the type of heuristic processing that is most likely to be used in this decision context instead of attempting to change the degree to which parents directly attend to information via more traditional inform-the-consumer campaigns might be reasonable.

Second, evaluating risk assessment as related to parents and video game play is important and may help to explain why parents are not more involved in the process of monitoring video game play. Slovic, Fischoff, and Lichtenstein (1982) demonstrate that consumers in general believe they are adept at evaluating risk, but in actuality, they undervalue less concrete risks while overvaluing concrete risks. Because of the difficulties linking video game play to actual behavior, parents are likely to undervalue risk and therefore ignore or at best cursorily consider rating information on video games. Future research might be focused on examining these issues and developing better solutions.

Third, in our studies, we focused on boys given the current state of play of traditionally violent video games. However, we do not wish to suggest that girls are immune to the effects of violence in video games or media, and the examination of the effects of violent media on females continues to need attention (Buchanan et al. 2002 is a notable exception). How violence is defined in the context of girls is likely to be much more subtle, such as psychological bullying and verbal abuse. It is likely that we need an expanded definition of violence to truly capture violent acts of females. In addition, we need to consider the examination of nontraditional violent "games," such as those associated with Internet games, social networking, and so forth.

Last, because video game ratings not only appear on game packaging but in the advertisements for games (at minimum on the game boxes pictured in the ads), the potential for youth to use ratings as a signal might actually trigger a boomerang effect. In other words, if youth process the ratings in game advertisements (e.g., in gamer magazines) in such a way that the violent content identified by a rating is perceived to be attractive, then they may develop strategies to manage the perceptions of parents in arguing to play or purchase the game prior to the parent ever seeing the game or game ads. More simply, children may develop strategies of their own to limit the amount of parental involvement in the purchase decision. Research in this area is important, as the question of degree to which video game rating information should be contained in advertisements is yet to be addressed.

NOTE

1. Note that at the time of the study, "animated violence" was listed as a descriptor in the ESRB rating system. This has now been changed to "cartoon violence," which we believe would trigger an equal if not greater perceptual bias.

REFERENCES

American Academy of Pediatrics, Committee on Public Education (2001), "Media Violence," *Pediatrics,* 108 (5), 1222–1226.

Anderson, Craig A., and Brad J. Bushman (2001), "Effects of Violent Video Games on Aggressive Behavior, Aggressive Affect, Physiological Arousal, and Prosocial Behavior: A Meta-Analytic Review of the Scientific Literature," *Psychological Science,* 12 (5), 353–359.

———, and Karen E. Dill (2000), "Video Games and Aggressive Thoughts, Feelings, and Behavior in the Laboratory and in Life," *Journal of Personality and Social Psychology,* 78 (4), 772–790.

Associated Press (2007), "Video Game Sales Post a Record: Sales of Games, Game Consoles and Accessories Top $12.5B in '06" (January 15), available at www.msnbc.msn.com/id/16597649/ (accessed October 25, 2010).

Ballard, Mary E., and J. Rose Weist (1996), "Mortal Kombat: The Effects of Violent Video Game Play on Males' Hostility and Cardiovascular Responding," *Journal of Applied Social Psychology,* 26 (8), 717–730.

Bandura, Albert, Edward B. Blanchard, and Brunhilde Ritter (1969), "Relative Efficacy of Desensitization and Modeling Approaches for Inducing Behavioral, Affective, and Attitude Changes," *Journal of Personality and Social Psychology,* 13 (3), 173–199.

Bork, Robert (1996), *Slouching Toward Gomorrah: Modern Liberalism and the American Decline,* New York: Regan Books.

Buchanan, Audrey M., Douglas A. Gentile, David A. Nelson, David A. Walsh, and Julia Hensel (2002), "What Goes In Must Come Out: Children's Media Violence Consumption at Home and Aggressive Behaviors at School," paper presented at the International Society for the Study of Behavioural Development Conference, Ottawa, August 2–6.

Cantor, Joanne (1998), "Ratings for Program Content: The Role of Research Findings," *Annals of the American Academy of Political and Social Science,* 557 (May), 54–69.

Carnagey, Nicholas L., Craig A. Anderson, and Brad J. Bushman (2007), "The Effect of Video Game Violence on Physiological Desensitization to Real-Life Violence," *Journal of Experimental Social Psychology,* 43 (5), 489–496.

Cesarone, Bernard (1998), "Video Games: Research, Ratings, Recommendations," *ERIC Digest* (November), available at www.ericdigests.org/1999-2/video.htm (accessed October 25, 2010).

Cline, Victor B., Roger G. Croft, and Steven Courrier (1973), "Desensitization of Children to Television Violence," *Journal of Personality and Social Psychology,* 27 (3), 360–365.

Davidson, Howard (1996), "No Consequences—Re-examining Parental Responsibility Laws," *Stanford Law and Policy Review,* 7 (1), 23–25.

Federal Trade Commission (FTC) (2000), "Marketing Violent Entertainment to Children: A Review of Self-Regulation and Industry Practices in the Motion Picture, Music Recording and Electronic Game Industries," Federal Trade Commission, Washington, DC (September), available at www.ftc.gov/reports/violence/vioreport.pdf (accessed October 27, 2010).

Fiske, Susan T. (1982), "Schema-Triggered Affect: Applications to Social Perception," in *Affect and Cognition: The 17th Annual Carnegie Symposium on Cognition,* Margaret S. Clark and Susan T. Fiske, eds., Hillsdale, NJ: Lawrence Erlbaum, 55–78.

Gentile, Douglas A. (2008), "The Rating Systems for Media Products," in *Handbook of Children, Media, and Development,* Sandra L. Calvert and Barbara J. Wilson, eds., Oxford: Blackwell, 527–551.

——— (2009), "Pathological Video Game Use Among Youth 8 to 18: A National Study," *Psychological Science,* 20 (5), 594–602.

———, and David A. Walsh (2002), "A Normative Study of Family Media Habits," *Applied Developmental Psychology,* 23 (2), 157–178.

Haninger, Kevin, and Kimberly M. Thompson (2004), "Content and Ratings of Teen-Rated Video Games," *Journal of the American Medical Association,* 291 (7), 856–865.

Harris, Richard J., and Gregory E. Monaco (1978), "Psychology of Pragmatic Implication: Information Processing Between the Lines," *Journal of Experimental Psychology,* 107 (1), 1–22.

Huesmann, L. Rowell, Jessica F. Moise, and Cheryl-Lynn Podolski (1997), "The Effects of Media Violence on the Development of Antisocial Behavior," in *Handbook of Antisocial Behavior,* David M. Stoff, James Breiling, and Jack D. Maser, eds., New York: Wiley, 181–193.

Jacoby, Jacob, and Wayne D. Hoyer (1987), *The Comprehension and Miscomprehension of Print Communications: An Investigation of Mass Media Magazines,* New York: Advertising Educational Foundation.

———, Margaret C. Nelson, and Wayne D. Hoyer (1982), "Corrective Advertising and Affirmative Disclosure Statements: Their Potential for Confusing and Misleading the Consumer," *Journal of Marketing,* 46 (1), 61–72.

Reuters (2008), "UPDATE 2-US Video Game Sales Up 10 Percent in Nov—Report" (December 11), available at www.reuters.com/article/idUSN1141365020081212/ (accessed October 1, 2010).

Slovic, Paul, Baruch Fischoff, and Sarah Lichtenstein (1982), "Facts Versus Fears: Understanding Perceived Risk," in *Judgment Under Uncertainty: Heuristics and Biases,* Daniel Kahneman, Paul Slovic, and Amos Tversky, eds., Cambridge: Cambridge University Press, 463–489.

Snyder, Rita (1992), "Comparative Advertising and Brand Evaluation: Toward Developing a Categorization Approach," *Journal of Consumer Psychology,* 1 (1), 15–30.

Staude-Muller, Frithjof, Thomas Bliesener, and Stefanie Luthman (2008), "Hostile and Hardened? An Experimental Study on (De-)Sensitization to Violence and Suffering Through Playing Video Games," *Swiss Journal of Psychology,* 67 (1), 41–50.

Thomas, Margaret Hanratty, Robert W. Horton, Elaine C. Lippincott, and Ronald S. Drabman (1977), "Desensitization to Portrayals of Real-Life Aggression as a Function of Exposure to Television Violence," *Journal of Personality and Social Psychology,* 35 (6), 450–458.

Van Auken, Stuart, and Arthur J. Adams (1998), "Attribute Upgrading Through Across-Class, Within-Category Comparison Advertising," *Journal of Advertising Research,* 38 (2), 6–16.

Van Schie, Emil G. M., and Oene Wiegman (1997), "Children and Videogames: Leisure Activities, Aggression, Social Integration, and School Performance," *Journal of Applied Social Psychology,* 27 (13), 1175–1194.

Waldmann, Michael R., and York Hagmayer (2006), "Categories and Causality: The Neglected Direction," *Cognitive Psychology,* 53 (1), 27–58.

Walsh, David A., and Douglas A. Gentile (2001), "A Validity Test of Movie, Television, and Video-Game Ratings," *Pediatrics,* 107 (6), 1302–1308.

———, ———, Jeremy Gieske, Monica Walsh, and Emily Chasko (2003), "Video Game Report Card," National Institute on Media and the Family, Minneapolis, December 8.

Wartella, Ellen, Barbara O'Keefe, and Ronda Scantlin (2000), "Children and Interactive Media: A Compendium of Current Research and Directions for the Future," Report to the Markle Foundation, available at www.aeforum.org/aeforum.nsf/88e10e9813be5a4780256c5100355eb1/0bdab430721f11f680256f8f004b0680/$FILE/markle_final_2000.pdf (accessed October 1, 2010).

Wyer, Robert S., Jr., and Gabriel A. Radvansky (1999), "The Comprehension and Validation of Social Information," *Psychological Review,* 106 (1), 89–118.

———, and Thomas K. Srull (1986), "Human Cognition in Its Social Context," *Psychological Review,* 93 (3), 322–359.

PART VI

PUBLIC SERVICE CAMPAIGNS

13

Using Mass Media Domestic Violence Campaigns to Encourage Bystander Intervention

Magdalena Cismaru, Gitte Jensen, and Anne M. Lavack

Intimate partner violence is a critical problem—one that occurs along many dimensions, takes many forms, and arises under a range of different conditions (Mears and Visher 2005; Stephens, Hill, and Gentry 2005). Previous research suggests that bystanders witness up to one-third of the incidents involving intimate partner violence (Planty 2002). Bystanders can play an important role in ensuring that domestic violence is reported to the authorities, and that victims of domestic violence receive help (Felson and Paré 2005). However, bystanders are often uncertain how to react or what their role should be (Latané and Darley 1970; Liz Claiborne Inc. 2006).

The purpose of this paper is to identify ways that mass media campaigns can encourage bystander intervention in situations of domestic violence against partners. We first review the literature on intimate partner violence, and we examine the role of bystanders using theory developed by Latané and Darley (1970). We outline the search methodology we utilized to identify existing campaigns aimed at encouraging bystander intervention against intimate partner violence, and we analyze 12 existing campaigns in terms of their fit with the Latané and Darley (1970) model. Finally, we provide 10 recommendations for practitioners involved in developing campaigns to persuade bystanders to intervene against intimate partner violence.

INTIMATE PARTNER VIOLENCE AND THE ROLE OF BYSTANDERS

Also known more generally as *domestic violence, intimate partner violence* includes four types of spousal abuse—physical, sexual, property, and psychological (Carden 1994; Ganley 1981; Sonkin, Martin, and Walker 1985). Physical violence includes acts such as shoving, slapping, punching, kicking, choking, throwing, scalding, cutting, smothering, or biting (Koss et al. 1994). Sexual abuse involves forcing an intimate partner, through the use of verbal or physical threats or intimidation, to participate in sexual activities against his or her own will. Property violence includes breaking some symbolically meaningful or favored possessions, punching holes in walls, breaking down doors, or throwing things (Carden 1994). Psychological violence consists of verbal and nonverbal behaviors to isolate, humiliate, demean, or control an intimate partner (Carden 1994; Stephens, Hill, and Gentry 2005). Some have suggested that property violence and psychological violence have become more common in recent years because perpetrators believe that these are less likely to be reported than physical abuse (Stephens, Hill, and Gentry 2005).

According to the World Health Organization (WHO), 10% to 50% of women worldwide are physically assaulted by their partners at some point during their lifetime (Rothman, Butchart, and Cerdá 2003). Data from the U.S. National Violence Against Women Survey show that close to 1 in 4 women and 1 in 13 men report being "raped and/or physically assaulted by a current or former spouse, cohabiting partner, or date at some time in their lifetime" (Tjaden and Thoennes 2000, p. iii).

Intimate partner violence is a crime, yet the majority of this violence is not reported to authorities. Data from the 2005 Personal Safety Survey in Australia show that 63% of women who experienced physical assault and 81% of women who experienced sexual assault by their partner did not report it to the police (Government of Australia 2005). According to the Statistics Canada (2005) Family Violence report, only 27% of Canadian victims of domestic violence report the incidents to the police.

Bystanders play an important role in intervening in domestic violence. Berk et al. (1984) found that half the calls to the police in the United States regarding domestic violence incidents were made by bystanders. In an analysis of U.S. National Crime Victimization Survey data from 1993 to 1999, Planty (2002) found that 36% of violent incidents occurred in the presence of bystanders, and that the presence of bystanders drastically increased the likelihood of the violent incidents being reported to the police.

A public survey commissioned by Liz Claiborne Inc. and *Redbook* on bystanders to domestic violence found two-thirds of respondents were unsure of the signs of domestic violence, with over 90% failing to regard emotional, verbal, and sexual abuse as signs of domestic violence (Liz Claiborne Inc. 2006). Moreover, the majority of the respondents were unsure about what to do when confronted with domestic violence. Of the 52% of respondents who said they suspected that a close acquaintance was involved in domestic abuse, only 69% took action. Half of those who got involved talked to the victim, a family member, or mutual friends, 40% talked to the abuser, 35% contacted the police, and 19% contacted domestic violence groups.

Given high prevalence rates of domestic violence and low rates of police reports by victims of abuse, efforts have been made to increase reporting by third parties. Government and not-for-profit organizations use advertising and social marketing components such as mass media campaigns, educational kits, and community events to convey the message that domestic violence is unacceptable. These campaigns range from small community-based programs to nationwide advertising campaigns sponsored by multinational corporations. Campaigns have a variety of objectives, including (1) raising awareness about domestic violence and available help services; (2) combating social attitudes and beliefs that normalize and trivialize domestic abuse; and (3) providing advice for victims, perpetrators, professionals, and bystanders on how best to combat domestic violence. Campaigns that specifically focus on bystander intervention are the focus of this paper.

LATANÉ AND DARLEY'S MODEL OF BYSTANDER INTERVENTION

Bystander behavior has been widely researched by social psychologists following the highly publicized murder of Kitty Genovese in 1964, a murder reputedly witnessed by 38 neighbors who failed to help. Following Rosenthal's (1964) landmark book detailing the tragic death of Kitty Genovese, Darley and Latané (1968) and Latané and Darley (1970) conducted several psychological experiments, considered seminal for later research on bystander intervention in emergencies in general (Carlson 2008). Hoefnagels and Zwikker (2001) empirically tested Darley and Latané's (1968) and Latané and Darley's (1970) work in a domestic violence context.

Latané and Darley's (1970) model of bystander intervention as applied to the area of domestic violence (Hoefnagels and Zwikker 2001) outlines five steps that determine whether a bystander renders aid in an emergency situation. First, the bystander must notice the incident; this sometimes requires a shift of attention to an unusual event. Second, the bystander must interpret the incident as an emergency and realize that someone needs help. The interpretation of what is often an ambiguous situation depends on a number of personal and social factors, such as the person's willingness to believe that an emergency is actually happening and the reactions of other bystanders by which the individual is influenced. Third, after the interpretation of an event as an emergency, the bystander must decide that it is his or her responsibility to intervene. Several variables such as bystander characteristics, victim characteristics, situational factors, and characteristics of the relationship between the bystander and the victim determine whether the bystander will feel this responsibility. Fourth, when the bystander has decided to help, the form of intervention must be chosen. The most important choice to be made at this point is whether the intervention will be direct (e.g., jumping into the fight oneself) or indirect (e.g., calling the police). Finally, the bystander must act and the planned intervention must be implemented; this involves making practical choices. At this point, the bystander may begin to undertake actions that are not difficult to perform under normal circumstances; however, the stress generated by the situation may make even a potentially simple task much more difficult (Hoefnagels and Zwikker 2001; Latané and Darley 1970).

Bystander intervention may fail when any of these five steps fall short. A bystander can fail to notice the event, can fail to interpret it as an emergency, can fail to assume the responsibility to take action, can fail to identify what type of action can be taken, or can simply fail to act (Latané and Darley 1968). Understanding how to improve the success of bystander intervention is important in the context of reducing domestic violence. Some of the campaigns against domestic violence have been developed with the specific aim of encouraging appropriate bystander intervention. In the following section, we outline the methods used to identify 12 such campaigns.

METHODOLOGY

We began our examination of domestic violence campaigns promoting bystander intervention by gathering relevant English-language communication and program materials posted on the Internet. Specifically, the first two authors independently conducted a Google search for campaigns using key words such as "victims of domestic violence," "antiviolence," "abuse," "abused women," "domestic violence campaign," "intimate partner violence campaign," and "family violence campaign." Using a snowball search methodology, additional key words were identified and added during the search process. Links were followed from initially accessed Web sites to locate additional Web sites of interest. Health-related government Web sites such as the U.S. Department of Health and Human Services, National Institutes of Health, Health Canada, and similar Web sites from other English-speaking countries were also searched. Scholarly articles referring to campaigns against intimate partner violence were located through a variety of databases such as Blackwell-Synergy, JSTOR, PsycINFO, and ABI/INFORM. These scholarly databases were used not only to identify relevant campaigns but also to locate information about the theory, design, strategy, and evaluation of relevant campaigns.

We included all campaigns targeting bystanders of intimate partner violence that had mass media components such as television, radio, magazine ads, posters, Web sites, postcards, and so forth. We did not include the many Web sites that simply provided links to other Web sites or links to campaigns already located. Nor did we include campaigns targeting only social attitudes toward domestic violence (without directly addressing bystanders) or targeting victims of domestic violence or campaigns concerning child abuse or elder abuse. We included major campaigns running at the national and international level, and therefore did not include solely local initiatives. The recency or currency of the campaign did not affect inclusion; if it was a relevant mass media campaign whose components were available on the Internet, we included it.

While there are dozens of campaigns more generally directed at the issue of intimate partner violence, we were able to identify only 12 mass media domestic violence campaigns that specifically encouraged bystander intervention. The 12 campaigns were from five countries: the United States, the United Kingdom, Australia, New Zealand, and India. Of these five countries, India is an outlier, as the other four are reasonably similar culturally; however, we included the campaign from India to illustrate cultural differences in what is considered acceptable behavior with respect to bystander intervention. Although domestic violence is a global phenomenon, its prevalence and related norms vary greatly around the world (Stephens, Hill, and Gentry 2005; WHO 2002).

For the 12 campaigns included in our analysis, the first two authors conducted a content analysis and assessed the salient components, including title and Web address, initiator, and target group. The objectives of each campaign were determined by looking for information about what the campaign was trying to achieve. While some campaigns had only one behavioral objective (i.e., encouraging bystanders to report incidents of intimate partner violence), the majority of campaigns had multiple objectives (e.g., raising social awareness, providing help services to victims and perpetrators, fund-raising). Our focus was solely on bystander intervention; therefore, for multifaceted campaigns, only the campaign elements addressing bystander intervention were analyzed. In the course of the campaign search, no theories or background documents guiding the development, implementation, and evaluation of these 12 existing campaigns were identified, in spite of a careful search for this type of information. Formal research data, such as pretesting of campaign materials with focus groups and postevaluations of campaign effectiveness, were not publicly available for any of the 12 campaigns. Therefore, we propose Latané and Darley's (1970) model of bystander intervention as an appropriate framework to guide and analyze campaigns aimed at encouraging bystander intervention. All components of each campaign were evaluated and campaigns were categorized in terms of their adherence to Latané and Darley's (1970) model of bystander intervention.

Disagreements regarding campaign coding between the authors were managed through discussion. The analysis was based solely on the information found on the Internet; the campaign designers were not contacted to obtain additional materials, and no attempt was made to contact campaign designers in order to discuss the target audience, establish the validity of this coding, or ask whether theory had affected the campaign design. Based on the coding and analysis, the Appendix was developed to list the salient components of each of the 12 relevant campaigns, including campaign title and year, campaign description and Web address, initiator of the campaign, campaign materials, target audience, and adherence to the Latané and Darley (1970) model.

LINKING THE 12 BYSTANDER CAMPAIGNS TO THE LATANÉ AND DARLEY MODEL

Of the 12 campaigns we located, 11 were concerned primarily with physical violence and one campaign (Tell a Gal P.A.L. [www.clicktoempower.org]) was concerned specifically with financial abuse and how financial concerns can deter women who want to leave abusive relationships. All 12 bystander intervention campaigns presented the victims of domestic violence as female and the perpetrators as male. Campaigns consisted of a wide variety of materials, including Web sites, radio and television ads, and print materials such as posters, brochures, and guidelines. Some of the identified campaigns featured celebrity spokespersons or authorities (primarily police). Other campaigns included testimonials from bystanders, victims, or perpetrators of domestic violence.

The following sections describe the steps a bystander follows when considering intervening in a domestic violence situation, as proposed by Latané and Darley's (1970) model of bystander intervention. The 12 identified campaigns are analyzed in terms of their adherence to the five steps proposed in this model.

Step 1: The Bystander Must Notice the Incident

To date, little research has been conducted to evaluate how spousal abuse taking place in the privacy of a home influences bystander intervention (Hoefnagels and Zwikker 2001). The majority of people suspect or know someone who they believe has been the victim of spousal abuse (Sorenson and Taylor 2003). Most bystanders to domestic violence are in close physical proximity or are intimately acquainted with the victim or the perpetrator. In a study of calls to a child abuse helpline, Hoefnagels and Zwikker (2001) discovered that the majority of bystanders to child abuse were neighbors to the abused child (30.4%), parent figures (16.8%), or peers/friends (15.8%). Similar empirical studies have not been carried out to examine the characteristics of bystanders to spousal violence, but according to the Statistics Canada (2005) Family Violence report, the most frequently relied on sources of informal support for both male and female victims of spousal violence were family members (67% of female victims/44% of male victims) and friends/neighbors (63% of female victims/41% of male victims). Other sources of informal help include doctors, nurses, lawyers, and members of the clergy. Overall, 73% of victims of spousal violence stated that they had confided in someone close to them.

Consistent with the literature, most of the 12 campaigns encouraging bystander intervention were directed at individuals intimately acquainted with either the victim or the perpetrator. The most popular target audiences in these campaigns were friends and family (Crimestoppers Domestic Violence [www.crimestoppers-uk.org]; Family Violence: It's Not OK. Are You OK? [www.areyouok.org.nz/family_violence.php]; Tell a Gal P.A.L.; Reducing the Risk [www.reducingtherisk.org.uk]; See It and Stop It! [www.seeitandstopit.org]; There's No Excuse for Domestic Violence [http://endabuse.org]; Violence Against Women—Australia Says No [www.fahcsia.gov.au/sa/women/progserv/violence/Pages/default.aspx]) and neighbors and coworkers (Bell Bajao [http://bellbajao.org]; Family Violence: It's Not OK. Are You OK?; There's No Excuse for Domestic Violence). One campaign (CUT IT OUT [www.cutitout.org]) focused on educating hairdressers on the signs of domestic violence and where to go for help. The rationale for this campaign was that many women see their hairdressers as confidants and form close personal relationships with them. Two campaigns (White Ribbon Day [www.whiteribbonday.org.au]; Don't Ignore It [www.refuge.org.uk]) targeted broad audiences by criticizing the implicit social acceptance of domestic violence and hegemonic masculine norms. One campaign (Norfolk Constabulary Domestic Violence Campaign [www.mediaoutcomes.co.uk/casestudies/7/]) did not appear to be targeted at any specific audience but was simply aimed at the general public.

In terms of the actual "incident" being noticed, almost all of the Web sites for the 12 campaigns described domestic violence, types of violence, as well as warning signs of an abusive relationship, thereby making it possible for a bystander to identify abuse (i.e., Don't Ignore It; See It and Stop It; Tell a Gal P.A.L.; Violence Against Women—Australia Says No; White Ribbon Day). Some also contrasted characteristics of a healthy, respectful relationship with an abusive one (i.e., White Ribbon Day). However, most of the public service announcements (PSAs) focus on physical abuse. Some ads depicted neighbors hearing yelling, screaming, and other noises consistent with a physical assault (i.e., White Ribbon Day). Other ads showed people (victims, abusers, or bystanders) stating what physical or sexual abuse is, or is not (i.e., Violence Against Women—Australia Says No). However, few dealt with other forms of domestic violence, such as psychological abuse. One exception was the Family Violence: It's Not OK. Are You OK? campaign, which mentioned emotional abuse, name calling, as well as abusers making victims feel "worthless." The Bell Bajao campaign also had a PSA in which a female designer talks about verbal abuse. To better represent the full spectrum of potential abuse, future campaigns should broaden their focus to include psychological abuse. Most researchers agree that abusive behavior is likely to escalate over time from verbal to physical aggression (Worden and Carlson 2005), so it is important for bystanders to be aware of the signs of all types of abuse.

None of the 12 domestic violence campaigns depicted male victims. Because domestic abuse against men is less common, it is often trivialized. This trivialization is not only detrimental to facilitating bystander intervention, but the lack of male victims in public domestic violence campaigns may also result in bystanders being less likely to notice abuse involving male victims or to interpret such abuse as an emergency. Depicting men as victims might also make male bystanders more likely to pay attention and sympathize with victims of domestic abuse in general. Therefore, future domestic violence campaigns should broaden their conceptualization of victims/perpetrators to include male victims and female perpetrators.

Step 2: Interpret the Situation as an Emergency

Spousal abuse provides a very ambiguous situation, even for those most likely to detect it. Neighbors may have a hard time differentiating a loud argument from a violent assault (Paquin 1994). Therefore, detailing signs of abuse is a must in helping bystanders to evaluate a situation and decide if it is necessary to intervene. However, bystanders' attitudes toward domestic violence influence the degree to which they will perceive a domestic dispute as an emergency. Several studies show that many people attribute domestic abuse to women actively seeking, provoking, and tolerating violence, and this attribution may make bystanders less likely to interpret the incident as an emergency. Indeed, a survey conducted by Worden and Carlson (2005) showed that bystanders' assessments of an incident depends in part on what they believe are the causes of violence; if bystanders believe some level of violence is normal or justifiable, they are less likely to intervene in violent incidents. Nearly half the respondents indicated that women's treatment of men accounts for "some violence." Nearly one in four agreed that some women want to be abused, and nearly two-thirds believed that women could leave violent relationships "if they really wanted to." Similarly, Shotland and Straw (1976) found that participants in bystander intervention experiments were likely to regard domestic violence as a "private matter," "none of my business," and not particularly serious. Felson, Messner, and Hoskin (1999) found that bystanders are less likely to report domestic violence if the offender and the victim are a couple and if the abuse does not involve physical violence. However, bystanders generally do not view more serious assaults as private matters, regardless of the relationship between the victim and the perpetrator. Therefore, one could expect bystanders to be more likely to intervene when witnessing a serious assault.

The Family Violence: It's Not OK. Are You OK? campaign was one that targeted the social belief that domestic violence is a private matter by having a former abuser testify that his friends cared enough about him and his partner to threaten to call the police if he did not get help. Several other campaigns also targeted this belief (e.g., Bell Bajao). However, more work needs to be done to discredit the belief that the victim causes the abuse or wants it. This belief is clearly addressed in domestic violence campaigns targeting the victim; nevertheless, bystanders also need to fully understand that nobody deserves to be abused. Domestic violence campaigns using slogans that urge bystanders to intervene might also consider including components portraying children as witnessing violence. While many people believe women have some responsibility and agency in violent relationships, children are perceived as far more helpless (Hastings, Stead, and Webb 2004) and thus may be a stronger impetus to encourage intervention.

Only two of the 12 bystander intervention campaigns explicitly appealed to a sense of emergency: the campaign entitled There is No Excuse for Domestic Violence and the Bell Bajao campaign. The campaign called There Is No Excuse for Domestic Violence included posters with the slogan "While you are trying to find the right words, your friend may be trying to stay alive," while the Bell Bajao campaign stated, "domestic violence will lead to a disaster." However, other campaigns, such as Family Violence: It's Not OK. Are You OK? and Violence Against Women—Australia Says No, warned against hasty intervention with statements like the following: "Some things we want abused people to do may put them in more danger.... What you consider reasonable action may be deadly for her. Keeping quiet may be less dangerous." While all these campaigns had sound reasons for recommending a particular behavior and all had the victim's well-being in mind, such conflicting messages may make it difficult for bystanders to decide whether a domestic dispute is an emergency that requires immediate intervention. Therefore, future domestic violence campaigns should provide clarification regarding when it is appropriate to consider intervening (as well as the best way to intervene) and when it might be wiser to abstain.

Step 3: Responsibility to Intervene

Bystander passivity fosters an implicit atmosphere of social tolerance of domestic violence. Latané and Darley (1970) identified several factors that influence whether a bystander feels responsibility to intervene: (1) bystander characteristics, (2) victim characteristics, (3) characteristics of the relationship between bystander and victim, and (4) situational factors. Other researchers have identified myriad personal and social factors that influence helping behavior in incidents of domestic violence, including cost-benefit analyses of helping and nonhelping, stereotypes, prejudice against women, and victim blaming (Garcia and Herrero 2007).

Bystander Characteristics

Although the social inhibition of helping was found to be a consistent phenomenon (Latané and Nida 1981), in general, the influence of bystanders' sociodemographic characteristics on helping behavior has yielded inconsistent results, in part due to the type of intervention needed in a particular situation.

For example, some researchers have found that men are more likely to help women, whereas women are more likely to help children (Levine et al. 2002); females and elderly people may be less likely to intervene if there is a high risk of physical confrontation, but may be more likely to intervene if the intervention involves calling authorities or talking to the victim. Other researchers have found no association between sociodemographic factors and bystander intervention in incidents of domestic violence (e.g., Frye 2007).

Nevertheless, bystander competence has been found to be of key importance in determining if a bystander will offer to help. Piliavin, Rodin, and Piliavin (1969) found that bystanders are less likely to intervene directly if the intervention appears to have an unwanted physical or psychological consequence, such as exposing oneself to danger or verbal harassment. In addition, given that more than half the women served by women's shelters eventually return to their abusive partners (Aguirre 1985; Giles-Sims 1983; Snyder and Scheer 1981; Stone 1984), bystander feelings of efficacy (or especially lack of efficacy) may constitute another factor affecting the likelihood that one bystander will intervene. Specifically, if one bystander chooses to intervene and observes that his or her efforts are in vain, it is likely that this person will abstain from intervening in the future. Therefore, future campaigns should emphasize the beneficial effects of bystander intervention.

While the 12 campaigns we reviewed generally portrayed domestic violence as an important social issue that requires intervention, most of the campaigns did not explicitly target the bystander's sense of competence and the bystander's safety. Because most bystanders are neighbors, friends, and family members who might also be well acquainted with the perpetrator, these bystanders may be hesitant to get involved if they fear for their own safety, are worried about the future of their relationship with the victims' family, or are concerned about the victim's or the abuser's well-being. The Bell Bajao campaign recommended intervening without an explicit confrontation (e.g., ringing the doorbell to borrow a cup of milk), thereby not providing reasons for the aggressor to get angry. Other campaigns, such as Crimestoppers, encouraged bystanders who do not want to get personally involved to call the police. More campaigns should highlight possible interventions that protect the safety of bystanders, such as an anonymous call to police or social services. Mass media campaigns could assist in increasing bystanders' feelings of competence by including explicit references to helplines, where bystanders can talk to domestic violence counselors who can help them decide if an intervention is appropriate and what type of intervention is recommended.

Victim Characteristics

Male aggression toward female victims is seen as less acceptable, more injurious, and more criminal than female aggression toward male victims (Bethke and DeJoy 1993). However, as discussed earlier, bystanders are much less willing to intervene in an assault on a woman when they perceive the perpetrator to be her husband or male partner. Shotland and Straw (1976) conducted a series of experiments in which a man physically attacked a woman in the presence of a bystander. In these experiments, bystanders intervened more frequently when led to believe the couple were strangers (65%) than married (19%). Furthermore, when bystanders were unsure about the relationship between perpetrator and victim, they were likely to infer an intimate connection and did not intervene. Hence, the perceived relationship between those involved in the violent incident can serve to legitimize the violence. None of the evaluated campaigns addressed this issue. Future domestic violence campaigns should point out that a preexisting relationship does not make violence acceptable, and it should not deter bystanders from intervening.

Characteristics of the Relationship Between Bystander and Victim

The literature concerning the personal relationship between bystander and victim/perpetrator is scarce. Evidence indicates that in most cases of domestic violence, the bystander knows the victim or the perpetrator intimately through family ties, friendship, or physical proximity (e.g., neighbors/coworkers). Indeed, in Hoefnagels and Zwikker's (2001) study of bystanders to child abuse, 96.7% were personally acquainted with either the victim or the perpetrator. However, the participants in experimental research concerning helping behavior (e.g., Latané and Darley 1968; Shotland and Straw 1976) typically were strangers to the victim and perpetrator (e.g., confederates hired by the researcher). Likewise, survey research often uses vignettes to examine what participants would do in a particular situation. In these vignettes, the participant does not have a personal relationship with the people described, which might influence their self-reported helping behaviors. Therefore, more research is needed to explore how the intimate relationships between bystander, victim, and perpetrator influence the likelihood of intervention.

Situational Factors

It is important to consider the influence of situational factors in the community, such as poverty, social isolation, lack of social cohesion, social disorganization, and community violence, on helping behaviors. Social disorganization theory (Hurley 2004) suggests that in neighborhoods characterized by social disorder (e.g., drug dealing, prostitution, crime, vandalism), residents feel there is a lack of social control or the neighborhood is a dangerous place (Garcia and Herrero 2007). Social disorder also signals neighbors' unwillingness to intervene against criminal behavior or to call the police (Sampson and Raudenbush 1999). Social disorder produces feelings of fear that weaken neighborhood cohesion and facilitate more crime and disorder (Markowitz et al. 2001). Collective efficacy (e.g., whether neighbors undertake actions such as breaking up fights on the streets or scolding disrespectful children) is an important predictor of violence rates at the neighborhood level as well as violent victimization at the individual level (Sampson, Morenoff, and Gannon-Rowley 2002).

Little empirical research has examined the relationship between social disorganization and reporting of domestic violence to authorities. Garcia and Herrero (2007) analyzed data from a national survey in Spain and found that respondents who perceived high neighborhood disorder were considerably less likely to report incidents of domestic violence than respondents who perceived low or moderate neighborhood disorder. Therefore, community campaigns should target feelings of social disorder and the resistance of residents to get involved in domestic disputes by fostering feelings of shared identity in the community and highlighting collective efficacy with regard to combating violence. Campaign efforts to target social disorder must be backed by law enforcement and the justice system through legislation, such as mandatory arrest laws or public campaigns that portray the police as being intolerant of domestic violence incidents.

Indeed, those U.S. states that have implemented mandatory proarrest policies in domestic violence cases have reported positive changes in attitudinal norms toward intimate partner violence since these policies went into effect (Salazar et al. 2003). In addition, studies show that arrest reduces reassault by the same perpetrator (Maxwell, Garner, and Fagan 2001), and reporting of partner violence to police by victims or third parties decreases repeat offenses (Felson and Paré 2005). Although further research is needed to clarify the effect of mandatory arrest policies on bystander intervention, Frye (2007) suggests that mandatory arrest policies may also increase the likelihood of informal responses, including reporting to police by third parties. None of the identified bystander intervention campaigns addressed community factors such as poverty and crime rates. However, police services in various communities have launched campaigns to promote new mandatory arrest laws and deliver a stern warning to perpetrators that the police do take domestic violence seriously (London Metropolitan Police Service Domestic Violence Campaign [www.met.police.uk/campaigns/domestic_violence_2010/index.htm]). Consequently, future domestic violence campaigns targeting bystanders should consider addressing the mandatory arrest issue in their communications.

The 12 domestic violence campaigns we examined used widely different methods to shape perceptions of the victim and perpetrator and induce a sense of responsibility to act. The Violence Against Women—Australia Says No campaign focused on debunking the sense of impropriety associated with interference in a private dispute by using statements such as "It is OK to get involved—you could save a life." Crimestoppers UK uses fear to encourage bystander intervention. Their Web site states: "Two women are killed every week as a result of domestic violence in England and Wales. If you suspect a friend or family member is experiencing abuse you can call the charity Crimestoppers anonymously on 0800 555 111." The Don't Ignore It campaign, the Norfolk Constabulary Domestic Violence campaign, and the Reducing the Risk campaign all used a similar approach. The Bell Bajao campaign also points out that the lack of intervention might lead to a "disaster."

In contrast, the hard-hitting There Is No Excuse for Domestic Violence campaign used posters with slogans such as "It is hard to confront a friend who abuses his wife. But not nearly as hard as being his wife." Their television ad featured a young child sitting alone and frightened on the stairs as his angry father screams and threatens his mother. The child cringes as his father hits his mother. The words appear: "Children have to sit by and watch. What's your excuse?" Both the television ad and the poster slogan convey the message that bystander intervention makes a difference and that nonintervention is inexcusable. The Family Violence: It's Not OK. Are You OK? campaign shows a man who is grateful to friends who intervened. This approach relieves bystander fears that an intervention might be unwelcome.

The CUT IT OUT campaign encourages hairstylists to enroll as a facilitator. The See It and Stop It campaign encourages bystanders to "recognize abuse, say something at the first sign of abuse and take it a step further," by doing things such as hanging a poster in one's school. The Tell a Gal P.A.L. campaign uses an indirect approach to convince bystanders to intervene by explaining in detail the negative consequences of experiencing abuse, by pointing out that the bystander can make a difference, and by providing advice on how to help.

The White Ribbon Day television ad uses a sarcastic approach to show that nonintervention makes the bystander an accomplice in the violent dispute. The television ad features a couple eating supper while overhearing a man next door abusing his wife. The husband picks up a baseball bat, walks across the hall, and knocks on the neighbor's door. When the abusive man opens the door, he hands him the baseball bat, saying, "You might be needing this." The concluding text reads: "Do nothing and you may as well lend a hand." A somewhat similar approach was taken by the campaign called There's No Excuse for Domestic Violence, which created an ad showing people overhearing a violent dispute and doing nothing about it.

Step 4: Appropriate Intervention

The research literature has little to say about what constitutes appropriate bystander intervention or how bystanders decide among multiple options for intervention. The 12 bystander intervention campaigns we examined provided many different interpretations of what is appropriate intervention. The Norfolk Constabulary Domestic Violence campaign encouraged victims and bystanders to report incidents of domestic violence to the police. The CUT IT OUT campaign encouraged hairdressers to talk to their clients about abuse and refer them to sources of professional help (helplines, shelters, women's centers). The Tell a Gal P.A.L. campaign encouraged women to talk to their girlfriends about planning a financially secure future as a way to alleviate financial concerns if they have to leave a relationship.

The majority of the domestic violence campaigns stressed the primary role of the bystander as being a supportive ally. The Reducing the Risk campaign and the Family Violence: It's Not OK. Are You OK? campaign provided guidelines for friends and family members to open up a dialogue about current domestic violence with the clear aim of referring victims to a specialist in domestic violence. The latter campaign stressed that professional services are better equipped to help the victim than the bystander himself or herself: "There may be limits to what you can offer. New Zealand research shows that women feel best served and supported by specialist domestic violence intervention organizations and women's centres." The Violence Against Women—Australia Says No campaign also emphasized the role of bystanders as sympathetic and supportive. In their brochure, "What do you do when she tells you?" the bystander is encouraged to "Listen to her, believe her, support her whether her decision is to stay or leave." The bystander is also advised to make a safety plan and to find out about available help services. The Don't Ignore It campaign acknowledges that intervention can be dangerous for the bystander as well as the victim. The Crimestoppers Domestic Violence campaign suggested that bystanders who do not want to get personally involved can contact Crimestoppers and file an anonymous report to the police. This is one of the few campaigns that provided bystanders with the option of helping the victim without getting personally involved in the domestic dispute.

The See It and Stop It campaign was directed at youth ages 13 to 18 and included recommendations on how to talk to a friend who is suspected of being a victim of dating violence. Although the Web site advised the bystander to encourage the abused peer to contact a counselor, talk to their parents, and seek medical attention for physical injuries, it did not mention reporting the incident to the police. The campaign also did not provide any information regarding the potential danger for the teenager who decides to intervene.

Both the There Is No Excuse for Domestic Violence campaign and the White Ribbon Day campaign used strong slogans to encourage bystander intervention, but neither provided suggestions for appropriate intervention or action. Instead, their educational materials were focused on prevention. The campaign Web site for There Is No Excuse for Domestic Violence offered educational booklets for organizing community events to raise awareness about domestic violence. The White Ribbon Day campaign Web site included a list of helplines, but otherwise was concerned with promotion of social attitudes that defy the normalization of violence against women. Hence, their mass media advertising encouraged intervention without specifying a particular course of action, whereas other materials focused solely on prevention efforts.

The Bell Bajao campaign from India was the only campaign that depicted concrete examples of bystander intervention. Several television ads featured a male neighbor and a group of neighborhood boys, each ringing the doorbell to the house where a woman is being abused by her husband. The subtext to the television ads reads: "Asking for a small cup of milk is all you need to do to bring domestic violence to a halt." This television spot asks men to challenge men who engage in violence.

Sometimes, in the 12 campaigns that were reviewed, it was unclear whether a bystander should resort to immediate intervention (i.e., get physically involved or call the police) or proactive intervention (i.e., talk to the victim and devise a safety plan, but ultimately leave it up to the victim when to get help). It is also unclear how the bystander should decide on the appropriate intervention for the situation. This ambiguity can result in a bystander abstaining from intervening. Therefore, future domestic violence campaigns should consider clarifying appropriate courses of intervention in particular situations. These clarifications could be achieved by providing a helpline for bystanders, or a Web site to assist them in determining the best course of action, or by presenting campaigns that show examples of domestic violence situations and the appropriate course of action in each situation.

Step 5: Finally, the Bystander Must Act

After having decided on a preferred course of action, the bystander must then actually implement that action. One of the major deterrents of action at this stage is perceived danger. Piliavin and Piliavin (1972) have proposed that bystanders are less likely to help a victim if they feel helping may place them in danger, irrespective of how many other bystanders are present. Paquin (1994) conducted a study of bystander intervention by neighbors and found that in those cases where the bystander had called the police or physically intervened, the relationship with the violent family had subsequently deteriorated. Therefore, if bystanders are encouraged to report violence, it is important to enable bystanders to maintain their anonymity. Victim support is less likely to lead to deterioration of the relationship and could potentially provide critical assistance to the victim in a time of crisis. However, more research involving measures of actual bystander behavior is needed to further explore this topic.

As shown while discussing the appropriate intervention, most of the campaigns encouraging bystander intervention in domestic violence disputes include a call for action, ranging from simply encouraging people to donate, volunteer, or call the police to physically going to the place where the abuse takes place. Indeed, the White Ribbon Web site has a "Get involved" section that asks people to buy a ribbon, make a donation, or volunteer. In addition to asking for donations and volunteers, the Crimestoppers UK campaign encourages bystanders to "Give information anonymously" online or by calling a phone number. One of the ads for the Australia Says No campaign says to bystanders who witness abuse and believe they cannot say anything, "Yes, you can," thereby encouraging action. In addition, the Family Violence: It's Not OK. Are You OK? campaign depicts a man who is given an ultimatum by his friends the day after he assaulted his wife: "Get some help or we'll call the police." Finally, the Bell Bajao campaign message "Bring domestic violence to a halt, ring the bell" encourages bystanders to go to the door of the neighbor where domestic violence is taking place and ask to borrow something or invite the perpetrator for a ball game, thereby interrupting abuse and possibly ending it at least temporarily.

CONCLUSIONS

In common with many types of social marketing campaigns, mass media campaigns designed to combat domestic violence are often developed with relatively limited funding. The result is a lack of theory incorporated within the design, implementation, and campaign evaluation, as well as a lack of formal research with the target audience (including a failure to pretest campaign materials or conduct postevaluations of the campaigns). This lack of research makes it difficult to judge which campaign strategies are most effective at increasing bystander intervention. This review examined 12 domestic violence campaigns encouraging bystander intervention. Although the individual campaigns draw on important aspects of bystander intervention, such as challenging social norms, emphasizing bystander responsibility, implying bystander capability, and stressing the need for intervention, collectively they are contradictory in many respects.

Latané and Darley's (1970) model of bystander decision making implies that campaigns should identify where and why a bystander might fail to intervene during the five steps in the decision-making process (i.e., notice a situation, identify the situation as an emergency, realize that the bystander has a responsibility to intervene, identify a clear option for intervention, and act). Campaigns that help bystanders move through these five steps of the decision-making process are more likely to promote action than those campaigns whose ambiguity or lack of consistency might cause a bystander to fail to intervene. As shown in the Appendix, the second step (i.e., "identifying the situation as an emergency") is the step least addressed by the 12 evaluated campaigns. Any type of domestic violence or domestic abuse should be considered socially unacceptable and wrong, and bystanders should be urged to intervene in some way, even when the bystander is not entirely certain that it looks like "an emergency."

It is clear that campaigns aimed at encouraging bystanders to intervene in situations of domestic violence can have a positive and beneficial effect by increasing the likelihood of intervention. To help improve such campaigns in the future, 10 key recommendations are offered:

1. The target audience for the campaign should include neighbors and friends, family members, teachers, doctors, nurses, lawyers, and members of the clergy.
2. The campaign's depiction of abuse should be expanded to include verbal and emotional abuse.
3. Men should be depicted as potential victims of domestic violence, and women should be depicted as potential abusers.
4. The various forms of abuse and signs of abuse should be described in detail.
5. Campaigns should emphasize that nobody deserves to be abused, that no form of abuse should be tolerated, and that abuse is socially unacceptable.
6. Campaigns should emphasize that a prior or existing relationship does not justify abuse, and that domestic violence is not a private matter.
7. Bystanders should be made aware of the positive effects of the mandatory arrest policies.
8. Campaigns should point out that bystanders should always intervene and, to help them do so, campaigns should provide a confidential phone line where bystanders can call and be advised of the appropriate course of action.
9. Bystanders should be provided with examples and clarifications regarding what they could or should do in particular situations.
10. Bystanders who intervene should be given positive reinforcement by praising them and showing testimonies of abusers and victims who are grateful to them.

The above set of recommendations is theory based and provides concrete and realistic advice for improving domestic violence campaigns aimed at encouraging bystander intervention. Following these 10 steps can help to create more effective campaigns.

REFERENCES

Aguirre, Benigno E. (1985), "Why Do They Return? Abused Wives in Shelters," *Social Work*, 30 (4), 350–354.

Berk, Richard A., Sarah Fenstermaker Berk, Phyllis J. Newton, and Donillen R. Loseke (1984), "Cops on Call: Summoning the Police to the Scene of Spousal Abuse," *Law and Society Review*, 15 (3), 317–346.

Bethke, Teresa M., and David M. DeJoy (1993), "An Experimental Study of Factors Influencing the Acceptability of Dating Violence," *Journal of Interpersonal Violence*, 8 (1), 36–51.

Carden, Ann D. (1994), "Wife Abuse and the Wife Abuser: Review and Recommendations," *Counseling Psychologist*, 22 (4), 539–582.

Carlson, Melanie (2008), "I'd Rather Go Along and Be Considered a Man: Masculinity and Bystander Intervention," *Journal of Men's Studies*, 16 (1), 3–17.

Darley, John M., and Bibb Latané (1968), "Bystander Intervention in Emergencies: Diffusion of Responsibility," *Journal of Personality and Social Psychology*, 8 (4), 377–383.

Felson, Richard B., and Paul-Phillippe Paré (2005), "The Reporting of Domestic Violence and Sexual Assault by Nonstrangers to the Police," *Journal of Marriage and Family*, 67 (3), 597–610.

———, Steven F. Messner, and Anthony Hoskin (1999), "The Victim–Offender Relationship and Calling the Police in Assaults," *Criminology*, 37 (4), 931–948.

Frye, Victoria (2007), "The Informal Social Control of Intimate Partner Violence Against Women: Exploring Personal Attitudes and Perceived Neighborhood Social Cohesion," *Journal of Community Psychology*, 35 (8), 1001–1018.

Ganley, Anne L. (1981), *Participant's Manual: Court Mandated Therapy for Men Who Batter—A Three-Day Workshop for Professionals*, Washington, DC: Center for Women Policy Studies.

Garcia, Enrique, and Juan Herrero (2007), "Perceived Neighborhood Social Disorder and Attitudes Toward Reporting Domestic Violence Against Women," *Journal of Interpersonal Violence*, 22 (6), 737–752.

Giles-Sims, Jean (1983), *Wife Battering: A Systems Theory Approach*, Beverly Hills, CA: Sage.

Government of Australia (2005), "ABS Personal Safety Survey: User Guide," available at www.ausstats.abs.gov.au/ausstats/subscriber.nsf/0/A14E86B98435CC54CA2571C50074B17C/$File/4906055003_2005.pdf (accessed October 2, 2010).

Hastings, Gerard, Marine Stead, and John Webb (2004), "Fear Appeals in Social Marketing: Strategic and Ethical Reasons for Concern," *Psychology and Marketing*, 21 (11), 961–986.

Hoefnagels, Cees, and Machteld Zwikker (2001), "The Bystander Dilemma and Child Abuse: Extending the Latané and Darley Model to Domestic Violence," *Journal of Applied Social Psychology*, 31 (6), 1158–1183.

Hurley, Dan (2004), "On Crime as Science (A Neighbor at a Time)," *New York Times* (January 6), D1–D2.

Koss, Mary P., Lisa A. Goodman, Louise F. Fitzgerald, Nancy Felipe Russo Gwendolyn Puryear Keita, and Angela Browne (1994), *No Safe Haven: Male Violence Against Women at Home, at Work, and in the Community*, Washington, DC: American Psychological Association.

Latané, Bibb, and John M. Darley (1968), "Group Inhibition of Bystander Intervention in Emergencies," *Journal of Personality and Social Psychology*, 10 (3), 215–221.

———, and ——— (1970), *The Unresponsive Bystander: Why Doesn't He Help?* New York: Appleton-Century-Crofts.

———, and Steve Nida (1981), "Ten Years of Research on Group Size and Helping," *Psychological Bulletin*, 89 (2), 308–324.

Levine, Mark, Clare Cassidy, Gemma Brazier, and Stephen Reicher (2002), "Self-Categorization and Bystander Non-Intervention: Two Experimental Studies," *Journal of Applied Social Psychology*, 32 (7), 1452–1463.

Liz Claiborne Inc. (2006), "Bystander Survey," New York, available at www.loveisnotabuse.com/web/guest/search/journal_ content/56/10123/84924?search_key=/web/guest/search/?p_ p_id=content_search_key_p_p_lifecycle=0_key_p_p_state= maximized_key_p_p_mode=view_key_p_p_col_id= column-1_key_p_p_col_count=1_key__content_search_struts_action=%2Fext%2Fcontent_search%2Fsearch_key__content_search_keywords=survey+results_key_redirect=http%3A%2F%2Fwww.loveisnotabuse.com%2Fweb%2Fguest%2Frelationshipabuseoverview_key_keywords=survey results/ (accessed October 22, 2010).

Markowitz, Fred E., Paul E. Bellair, Allen E. Liska, and Jianhong Liu (2001), "Extending Social Disorganization Theory: Modeling the Relationship Between Cohesion, Fear, and Disorder," *Criminology*, 39 (2), 293–319.

Maxwell, Christopher, Joel H. Garner, and Jeffrey Fagan (2001), *The Effects of Arrest on Intimate Partner Violence: New Evidence from the Spouse Assault Replication Program*, Washington, DC: National Institute of Justice.

Mears, Daniel P., and Christy A. Visher (2005), "Trends in Understanding and Addressing Domestic Violence," *Journal of Interpersonal Violence*, 20 (2), 204–211.

Paquin, Gary W. (1994), "A Statewide Survey of Reactions to Neighbor's Domestic Violence," *Journal of Interpersonal Violence*, 9 (4), 493–502.

Piliavin, Irving M., Judith Rodin, and Jane Allyn Piliavin (1969), "Good Samaritanism: An Underground Phenomenon?" *Journal of Personality and Social Psychology*, 13 (4), 289–299.

Piliavin, Jane A., and Irving M. Piliavin (1972), "Effect of Blood on Reactions to a Victim," *Journal of Personality and Social Psychology*, 23 (3), 353–361.

Planty, Mike (2002), "Third-Party Involvement in Violence Crime, 1993–1999," Bureau of Justice Statistics, Special Report, Washington, DC (July), available at http://bjs.ojp.usdoj.gov/content/pub/pdf/tpivc99.pdf (accessed March 2, 2009).

Rosenthal, Abraham M. (1964), *Thirty-Eight Witnesses: The Kitty Genovese Case*, Berkeley: University of California Press.

Rothman, Emily F., Alexander Butchart, and Magdalena Cerdá (2003), *Intervening with Perpetrators of Intimate Partner Violence: A Global Perspective*, Geneva: World Health Organization.

Salazar, Laura F., Charlene K. Baker, Ann W. Price, and Kathleen Carlin (2003), "Moving Beyond the Individual: Examining the Effects of Domestic Violence Policies on Social Norms," *American Journal of Community Psychology*, 32 (3/4), 253–264.

Sampson, Robert J., and Stephen W. Raudenbush (1999), "Systematic Social Observation of Public Spaces: A New Look at Disorder in Urban Neighborhoods," *American Journal of Sociology*, 105 (3), 603–651.

———, Jeffrey D. Morenoff, and Thomas Gannon-Rowley (2002), "Assessing 'Neighborhood Effects': Social Processes and New Directions in Research," *Annual Review of Sociology*, 28 (August), 443–478.

Shotland, R. Lance, and Margret K. Straw (1976), "Bystander Response to an Assault: When a Man Attacks a Woman," *Journal of Personality and Social Psychology*, 34 (5), 990–999.

Snyder, Douglas K., and Nancy S. Scheer (1981), "Predicting Disposition Following Brief Residence at a Shelter for Battered Women," *American Journal of Community Psychology*, 9 (5), 559–566.

Sonkin, Daniel J., Del Martin, and Lenore E. A. Walker (1985), *The Male Batterer: A Treatment Approach*, New York: Springer.

Sorenson, Susan B., and Catherine A. Taylor (2003), "Personal Awareness of Domestic Violence: Implications for Health Care Providers," *Journal of the American Women's Medical Association*, 58 (1), 4–9.

Statistics Canada (2005), "Family Violence in Canada: A Statistical Profile," Ottawa (July 14), available at www.statcan.gc.ca/daily-quotidien/050714/dq050714a-eng.htm (accessed December 1, 2008).

Stephens, Debra L., Ronald P. Hill, and James W. Gentry (2005), "A Consumer-Behavior Perspective on Intimate Partner Violence," *Journal of Contemporary Ethnography*, 34 (February), 36–67.

Stone, Lorene H. (1984), "Shelters for Battered Women: A Temporary Escape from Danger or the First Step Toward Divorce?" *Victimology: An International Journal*, 9 (2), 284–289.

Tjaden, Patricia, and Nancy Thoennes (2000), "Extent, Nature, and Consequences of Intimate Partner Violence," National Institute of Justice, Washington, DC, available at www.ncjrs.gov/pdffiles1/nij/181867.pdf (accessed January 12, 2010).

Worden, Alissa P., and Bonnie E. Carlson (2005), "Attitudes and Beliefs About Domestic Violence: Results of a Public Opinion Survey: II. Belief About Causes," *Journal of Interpersonal Violence*, 20 (10), 1219–1243.

World Health Organization (WHO) (2002), "Prevention of Intimate Partner Violence and Sexual Violence," Geneva, available at www.who.int/violence_injury_prevention/violence/activities/intimate/en/index.html (accessed January 12, 2010).

Appendix 13.1

Domestic Violence Campaigns Encouraging Bystander Intervention

Campaign/year/ initiator	Campaign description and Web address	Objectives	Campaign components	Target group	Adherence to Latané and Darley's model
Australia					
White Ribbon Day—November 25 (2005) by the United Nations	Promotes culture change around the issue of domestic violence. Encourages men and boys to wear a white ribbon on November 25 and urges men to speak out against violence against women. http://theinspirationroom.com/daily/2005/white-ribbon-day-tv-ads/ www.whiteribbonday.org.au www.youtube.com/watch?v=AvBKIBhfgPc	To change social norms by challenging social acceptance of domestic violence. To encourage victims to seek help.	Events, Web site, TV ads.	Everyone, primarily males and bystanders	Step 1 Step 3 Step 4
Violence Against Women—Australia Says No (2004–2007) by the Australian Government Office for Women	Increases community awareness of the issues of domestic violence and sexual assault and provides professional consultation (via helpline) to victims, family and friends, and perpetrators. www.fahcsia.gov.au/sa/women/progserv/violence/Pages/default.aspx http://theinspirationroom.com/daily/2007/australia-says-no-to-violence-against-women/	To change social norms. To negate the excuses of men abusing their partners. To encourage bystander intervention.	TV ads, helpline for victims, perpetrators, friends and family, publications (no longer available online), brochure, poster, Web site.	Victims, perpetrators, friends, and family	Step 1 Step 2 Step 3 Step 4
India					
Bell Bajao (2008) by the Breakthrough (international human rights organization) and Indian Ministry of Women and Child Development	Aims to change the zeitgeist and to encourage people to speak up about domestic violence (bystander intervention). In particular, it seeks men as direct partners ready to "ring the bell" and intervene in situations of abuse. www.bellbajao.org	To encourage bystander intervention.	TV ads, posters, radio ad debunking stereotypes about women's mobility (English and Hindi), mobile video van, Web site.	Neighbors, primarily men and boys	Step 1 Step 2 Step 3 Step 4

(continued)

Campaign/year/ initiator	Campaign description and Web address	Objectives	Campaign components	Target group	Adherence to Latané and Darley's model
New Zealand					
Family Violence: Is Not OK. Are You OK? (2008) by the Government of New Zealand	Aims to increase the understanding of family violence and to promote changes in violent behaviors. www.areyouok.org.nz/home.php	To encourage bystander intervention. To change social norms.	Community Action Fund (provides financial support for community activities), community action tool kit, TV ads, helpline, Web site.	Neighbors/ coworkers, friends, and family	Step 1 Step 2 Step 3 Step 4
United Kingdom					
Crimestoppers Domestic Violence Campaign (2008) by Crimestoppers UK	Encourages bystanders to take action by supporting the victim or calling the police/Crimestoppers. This is the only campaign that addresses options for people who do not want to get personally involved. www.crimestoppers-uk.org/how-we-help/our-partners/ community-partners/making-communities-safer/domestic-violence	To encourage bystander intervention.	Web site, posters.	Everyone, in particular friends and family	Step 3 Step 4
Don't Ignore It (2003–2005) by the Refuge and Women's Aid	Criticizes the implicit acceptance of domestic violence in the United Kingdom. The central message is that domestic violence is unacceptable and everyone has a part to play in preventing the problem. www.refuge.org.uk/about-us/prevention-and-education/ campaigns/dont-ignore-it/	To encourage people who witness incidents of domestic violence to "step in" and "take action."	Cinema advertising campaign, national poster campaign, billboards in the London Underground, Web site.	Everyone	Step 1 Step 3 Step 4

Norfolk Constabulary Domestic Violence Campaign (2004) by the Norfolk Police and the Eastern Daily Press	Assists the police in increasing reporting of domestic violence by victims and their friends and families. www.mediaoutcomes.co.uk/casestudies/7/ www.norfolk.police.uk/safetyadvice/personalsafety/domesticabuse/aspx	To encourage bystander intervention.	Radio ads, newspaper ads, campaign posters, Web site.	Not specified	Step 1 Step 3 Step 4
United Kingdom					
Reducing the Risk (2008) by the Thames Valley Police/Oxfordshire Domestic Violence Steering Group	Aims at increasing early reporting of domestic abuse and reducing repeat victimizations. www.thamesvalley.police.uk/crprev/crprev-domabu.htm	To provide advice to family members and friends on how to help victims of domestic abuse (men or women).	Web site, brochures, domestic abuse helpline.	Friends and family members	Step 1 Step 3 Step 4
United States					
CUT IT OUT (2001–ongoing) by the Salons Against Domestic Abuse Fund, National Cosmetology Association, Southern Living at Home	Mobilizes salon professionals and trains them to recognize warning signs and safely refer clients to local resources and the National Domestic Violence Hotline (based on the belief that many women will form close relationships with their salon professionals). www.cutitout.org/adopt.html	To encourage bystander intervention. To provide services for victims.	Educational seminars, awareness materials (posters, safety card kits), Adopt-a-Shelter program, Web site.	Salon professionals	Step 1 Step 3 Step 4

(continued)

Campaign/year/ initiator	Campaign description and Web address	Objectives	Campaign components	Target group	Adherence to Latané and Darley's model
See It And Stop It! (2008) by the Family Violence Prevention Fund, the Advertising Council, and Teens in Massachusetts	Offers information on how to recognize the signs of dating violence and how to stop it. Created by and for teens. www.seeitandstopit.org/pages/	To offer information on how to recognize the warning signs of dating violence and how to stop it.	Posters, online tool kit, and Web site.	Teens between 13 and 18, victims, perpetrators, and bystanders	Step 1 Step 3 Step 4
Tell a Gal P.A.L. (2008) by the Allstate Foundation	Encourages men and women to overcome the taboo and talk openly about domestic violence. P.A.L. stands for Pass It On—spread the word about domestic abuse; Act—plan for a secure financial future; and Learn—about resources available and protect personal and financial safety. www.clicktoempower.org	To encourage bystander intervention and to provide services for victims.	Celebrity spokesperson, Web site where the Allstate Foundation will donate $1 to the cause every time people click on a banner, links to specific information about rebuilding a financial future.	Friends, predominantly women (the Web site has a designer purse competition)	Step 1 Step 3 Step 4
There's No Excuse for Domestic Violence (2008) by the Family Violence Prevention Fund	Encourages people to question their tacit acceptance of domestic violence. www.endabuse.org/section/_get_help	To encourage bystander intervention to prevent domestic violence.	TV public service announcements, education materials (neighbors/ person to person), posters, Web site.	Neighbors, friends, family members close to victims of domestic violence	Step 1 Step 2 Step 3 Step 4

14

Unintended Effects of a Domestic Violence Campaign

Sarah N. Keller, Timothy Wilkinson, and A.J. Otjen

A nascent body of literature has documented the occurrence of unintended effects in health communication and, recently, a great deal of attention has been paid to the potential for audiences to react unpredictably to fear appeal messages (Cho and Salmon 2007; Witte, Meyer, and Martell 2001). Specifically, Witte, Meyer, and Martell (2001) propose that audiences who feel unable to change their current behaviors may respond with denial, defense-avoidance, or reactance (undermining a messenger) to health messages that elucidate the risks of their current behavior in an attempt to promote health behavior change. Simultaneously, a growing body of literature documents the gender-specific nature of domestic violence with recommendations leading toward tailoring interventions by gender. This study describes the development of a campaign designed to increase the perceived threat of abuse and the corresponding reactions of men and women.

Given previous research indicating widespread audience denial of abuse, the campaign described here focused on increasing the public's perception of domestic violence as a severe community problem. Offenders frequently minimize the severity of their offense or completely deny incidents of abuse. Most (83%) convicted offenders in one study felt that their situation was blown out of proportion and that police made the incident sound worse than it really was (Henning, Jones, and Holdford 2005). Health educators have long indicated that increasing an audience's perception of a health risk is the first step in promoting preventive action (Witte, Meyer, and Martell 2001).

In spring 2006, students and faculty at a state university introduced the "Open Your Eyes" mass media campaign to increase perceived severity of abuse, perceived response efficacy of domestic violence hot lines, and awareness of services (Keller and Otjen 2007). Because the campaign used negative and highly emotionally charged ads and employed gender stereotypes to confront a highly sensitive issue, it might have triggered some backlash reactions.

One purpose of this paper is to look at the different effects of the campaign on men and women and to explore why such differences might have occurred. A second purpose is to examine the overall effectiveness of the campaign using components of the Health Belief Model as an analytical tool (Becker et al. 1977). First, we review prior domestic violence interventions, unintended effects of health communication and relevant behavior change communication theories. Next, we describe the campaign project and outline results. This is followed by a detailed discussion of findings, the drawing of conclusions, acknowledgment of limitations, and suggestions for future research.

BACKGROUND

Domestic Violence Interventions

Domestic violence interventions typically take one of three primary forms: shelters for survivors, hot lines for survivors and perpetrators, or information services for both survivors and perpetrators

(Gosselin 2010). Responses to domestic violence have focused to date primarily on interventions after a problem has been identified and harm has occurred. A particular challenge for those working in domestic violence prevention involves finding strategies for informing both survivors and perpetrators about available services. Often, neither audience is reached until the issue has entered the legal system.

There are, however, new domestic violence prevention strategies emerging, and prevention approaches from the public health field can serve as models for further development of these strategies (Wolfe and Jaffe 1999). Among these are social marketing campaigns aimed at reaching both perpetrators and victims of abuse in order to educate individuals about the severity of the issue and the availability of services. The goal of these campaigns is to empower victims to escape abusive situations and to encourage perpetrators to seek assistance in changing their behaviors. Through public service announcements and advertisements, such campaigns typically provide information regarding warning signs of domestic violence as well as community resources for victims and perpetrators.

A review of intimate partner violence prevention programs from 1991 to 2001 found that most were clinic based, and of the few interventions involving public education, few had been systematically evaluated. Most interventions targeted at women attempted to increase physician screening for victims or refer clients to counseling and shelters. Of the interventions designed for male batterers (either alone or with partners), not many have been associated with effective outcomes (Wathen and MacMillan 2003). One comprehensive public education campaign, developed by the Family Violence Prevention Fund (FVPF) in collaboration with the Advertising Council, employed television advertisements to deliver the message that there is no excuse for domestic violence, and to make referrals to local domestic violence services. Results of a telephone survey evaluation from 1994 to 1996 showed significant decreases over the two years in the number of people who said they (1) did not know what to do about domestic violence, (2) did not believe it was necessary to report incidences of domestic violence, (3) felt that it was no one else's business when a husband beats his wife, and (4) believed that the media exaggerated the problem of domestic violence (Wolfe and Jaffe 1999).

Unintended Effects of Health Communication

Health communication campaigns, as outcomes of and inputs into the social process, can create both unintended and intended effects (Cho and Salmon 2007). Starting with the notion of noise (Shannon and Weaver 1949), communication scholars have long been mindful of the potential of a communication outcome to deviate from intention. Campaign designers, as senders of messages, can only control inputs while outcomes are influenced by multiple forces (Schramm 1961). Westley and MacLean (1957) observed that, unlike interpersonal settings, mass communication limits feedback from the receiver, minimizing opportunities to detect audience reactions. Here, we present a typology of potential unintended effects of health communication and then discuss the dissonance and boomerang effects that appear to have occurred in our advertising campaign.

Unintended or Excluded Audiences

It is typically recommended that evaluators of health communication campaigns assess changes only in intended audiences. Doing so, however, may not provide a complete or objective understanding of campaign effects. In fact, the third-person effect hypothesis (Davidson 1983) is based on this very phenomenon. Confining evaluation to the scope of the planner's intended audience will not provide a proper understanding of the function that health communication campaigns play in society. Messages intended for a subset of the population might produce misunderstanding among members of the nontargeted subset. For example, breast cancer prevention messages emphasizing the need for women with a family history of breast cancer to have regular mammography created a false sense of security among women who did not have a family history (Lerman et al. 1990). Health communication campaigns, perhaps due to their manifest intent to promote social good, have been underexamined for their potential to cause undesirable effects.

Boomerang Effects

Health messages have been associated with boomerang effects. Research has reported that exposure to fear appeals resulted in intentions to increase smoking (Rogers and Mewborn 1976), drinking (Kleinot and Rogers 1982), and a self-reported increase in unsafe sex (Witte 1992). Witte, Meyer, and Martell (2001, p. 27) suggest that when a person's perceived threat begins to exceed their perceived sense of self-efficacy, the person will focus on how frightened he or she feels and try to eliminate fear through denial (e.g., "It's not that big a problem" or "It'll never happen to me"), defense-avoidance (e.g., "This is just too scary; I'm simply not going to think about it"), or reactance (e.g., "They're just trying to manipulate me; I'm going to ignore them").

Culpability

Health messages may also increase an individual's guilt about a poor health behavior, because most health messages are based on the presumption that individuals have the potential to change their behaviors. Individuals taking action to prevent and manage their risk might be celebrated. Individuals who feel incapable of changing their risk behaviors may experience an elevated sense of guilt, which may, in turn, reduce their ability or motivation to change (Guttman 1997; Minkler 1999; Ryan 1976). Models of behavior change postulate that in addition to the motivation to change, individuals must also have the internal resources to carry out the recommended behavior (Ajzen 1991; Strecher et al. 1986). Therefore, when individuals desire to change but lack the needed abilities or necessary environmental supports, they can end up in psychological distress (Festinger 1957). This intransigence may be particularly relevant in circumstances of domestic violence that typically occur in long-term, enmeshed psychological and family relationships that are not easily ended.

Johnson and Leone (2005) describe two types of abuse perpetrators: the Intimate Terrorism abuser is typically male, very controlling, and resistant to change, whereas the Situational Couple abuser could be either gender, wants to change, and can even be treated. Men typical of the Intimate Terrorists described by Johnson and Leone would likely experience feelings of dissonance when confronted with messages urging prevention of domestic violence. Such dissonance could lead to boomerang effects.

Social Reproduction

Health communication may also reinforce existing social distributions of knowledge, attitudes, and behaviors. An evaluation of the television program *All in the Family* indicated that the program, designed to dispel ethnic biases, reinforced existing biases among some viewers (Vidmar and Rokeach 1974). Similarly, the Open Your Eyes campaign might have simultaneously educated those who were already aware of the need for prevention and education while reinforcing stigmas among those who were in favor of the status quo, and possibly antagonizing those who perceived the campaign as anti-male.

Social Norming

Campaigns, via social norming, can render individuals vulnerable to shame and isolation. Social norms demand compliance and forge conformity. A person who is out of alignment with implicit and explicit social expectations becomes even more vulnerable to shame and isolation in a campaign atmosphere (Piers and Singer 1953). For those who are able to adapt to majority social norms, normative messages may lead to a healthier lifestyle. Those who cannot or will not conform are marginalized; the attitudes of the nonmarginalized toward the marginalized can become increasingly negative (Goffman 1963).

Gender-Specific Responses

Only a few studies look at gender-specific responses to advertising. Ford and LaTour (1996) present a model in which purchase or boycott intention is a function of both gender role resistance and negative corporate image. A comparison can be made with this study insofar as purchase intent can be equated with increased awareness (or use) of domestic violence services, and negative corporate image can be equated with the intransigence of commonly held domestic violence–related myths, which the campaign attempted to debunk.

Studies of gender portrayals in advertising rarely link gender portrayals to gender-specific effects. Women are typically shown in advertising as passive, submissive, deferential, unintelligent, shy, dreamy, gentle, likely to be manipulated, and helpless. In contrast, men have often been portrayed as constructive, powerful, dominant, autonomous, and achieving (Artz, Munger, and Purdy 1999; Browne 1998). Sexist advertising has been associated with sexual harassment, violence against women, negative self-evaluations, distorted body images, eating disorders, and stereotyped perceptions of, and behavior toward, men and women (Gulas and McKeage 2000; Lavine, Sweeney, and Wagner 1999). Audiences that frequently view television portrayals of violent sex, objectified women, and irresponsible men may gradually become cultivated to adopt similar beliefs about sex in the real world. This recognition that popular media may serve as a poor vehicle for sexual socialization should not prevent media from being used as a positive health educator. However, if gender stereotypes in advertising increase stereotypical behaviors, then it is possible that media depictions of men as violent and women as provocative or submissive may encourage abusive behavior in real life.

THEORY AND HYPOTHESES

The goals of many domestic violence awareness campaigns, including the one discussed here, are to call attention to the severity of abuse, increase perceived susceptibility to the risk of abuse, educate potential victims about support services, and change public acceptance of myths that tacitly blame victims or deny abuse. Similar beliefs are laid out by the Centers for Disease Control and Prevention as important targets for public policy, domestic violence prevention, and public health campaigns (CDC 2006).

In the current campaign, attitudinal objectives were based on both formative research and what has been called the "grandmother" theory of health behavior change (Becker et al. 1977). The Health Belief Model (HBM) suggests that individuals weigh the potential benefits of a recommended response against the psychological, physical, and financial costs of an action before considering change. Becker et al. (1977) believed that a combination of perceived susceptibility (e.g., "I am at risk for X") and severity (e.g., "X is a serious problem that causes harm") provides the motivation for action, while the perceived cost/benefit ratio provides the pathway for action.

Similarly, the Heuristic-Systematic Model (HSM) postulates that individuals are more likely to change their behaviors in response to a message when their comprehension of an issue is high (Eagley and Chaiken 1984). According to HSM, comprehension *mediates* persuasion and can influence persuasion by its impact on attention to and comprehension of message content. Systematic processing is conceptualized as an analytic orientation in which people take all (or most) relevant information into account in forming their attitudinal judgments. It implies, as does the Elaboration Likelihood Model's "central route," that attitudes are mediated by recipients' understanding and cognitive elaboration of incoming information (Petty and Cacioppo 1986).

Building on this theoretical background, the campaign was designed to increase audience understanding of the threat and prevalence of domestic violence, as well as increase belief in the effectiveness of emergency response services (e.g., hot lines and services). In this paper, both perceived severity of a health risk and perceived response efficacy of a solution are conjectured to contribute to comprehension.

Although the rates of abuse are high, the percentage of victims who access support services is consistently reported to be low (Carlson and Worden 2005). Of 240 respondents in this study who reported knowing someone who was assaulted, only 28 (11%) reported contacting local domestic and sexual violence centers. Health educators have also made clear that audience awareness of services is a preliminary step to increasing use. Therefore, domestic violence hot line numbers were referred to in every ad (Appendix 14.1). This leads to the first hypothesis:

H1: Campaign exposure increased awareness of domestic violence services.

According to HBM, individuals appraise hazards by determining whether they think the threat is severe and whether they think they are susceptible to it. Extensive denial of abuse uncovered by the formative research conducted for this campaign (focus groups with men and women and in-depth interviews with survivors) further prompted campaign organizers to focus on increasing public recognition of the severity of domestic violence (Henning, Jones, and Holdford 2005).

Message comprehension, which, in this case, is partly comprised of perceived severity of a threat, is considered to be an important prerequisite for systematic processing (Eagley and Chaiken 1984). Greenwald and Leavitt (1984) suggest that persuasive impact and attitudinal effects are greater when message analysis, comprehension, and motivation for systematic processing are high. Thus, this campaign specifically targeted audience perceived severity and comprehension of the threat. We hypothesize that:

H2: Campaign exposure increased perceived severity of domestic violence.

Witte, Meyer, and Martell (2001), who built on HBM, argue that the greater the threat perceived, the more motivated individuals are to evaluate the efficacy of the recommended response. Witte, Meyer, and Martell argue that it is essential for the threat to be counterbalanced with a strong positive message that will instill in audiences a belief that there is an effective solution. For people who feel unable to change their behaviors, perceptions of threat become perceptions of fear (Witte, Meyer, and Martell 2001). At such a point, people shift to a fear control process, bypassing all thoughts of the threat.

Thus, a repeated theme of the campaign was to recommend that people call a hot line, with the intention of increasing audience perceptions that an effective solution was available. The concept of response efficacy (e.g., "Will I get accurate and useful information from calling a domestic violence hot line?") was promoted through cues to action for hot lines and one television ad that demonstrated a phone call to services. Therefore, we hypothesize that:

H3: Campaign exposure increased beliefs about the response efficacy of domestic violence services.

Many scholars have argued that domestic violence results from larger gender inequalities in society. Viewed through this lens, the perpetration of abuse by men against women can be conceptualized as the interpersonal enactment of larger cultural forces (Connell 1995). In particular, the physical and economic power of men, achieved through a gendered division of labor, combine with women's powerful emotional commitment to a cultural script about the importance of marriage and motherhood, and work to disempower individual women in unhealthy heterosexual relationships (Davies, Ford-Gilboe, and Hammerton 2009; Wolfe and Jaffe 1999).

This gender relations paradigm has been adopted in domestic violence prevention strategies with mixed results. For example, the "Duluth Model" (the Duluth Domestic Abuse Intervention Projects) sought to achieve "attitude adjustment" among violent men, encouraging them to cultivate a more feminist, and therefore egalitarian, view of their relationships (Dutton and Sonkin 2003; Milner 2004). Dutton and Sonkin conclude that the Duluth campaign placed too much blame on men, causing shame among clients and exacerbated "tendencies to externalize blame, reject feedback and experience chronic levels of high anger" (2003, p. 2). These critics assert that campaigns that focus on dominant gender ideology can foster a backlash reaction among abusive men, undermining the goal of reducing domestic violence. Given the highly gendered nature of the issue, and the highly stereotypical gender roles portrayed in the Open Your Eyes ads, H4, H5, and H6 predict that audience reactions to the campaign will vary by gender:

H4: The relationship between campaign exposure and awareness varies by gender.
H5: The relationship between campaign exposure and beliefs about response efficacy of domestic violence services varies by gender.
H6: The relationship between campaign exposure and beliefs about severity varies by gender.

METHODS

Message Design

The Open Your Eyes campaign was successfully launched in April 2006 and ran through the summer on local television stations, billboards, newspapers, and posters. Television and billboard ads were re-run for three months in winter 2008, immediately before the follow-up survey (see Appendix 14.2).

Three print ads were produced (see Appendix 14.1). Four television ads were created to communicate the beliefs listed above. "Barbecue" showed a man hitting his wife with a spatula during a family barbecue and being put in jail (addressing perceived severity). "Brain injury" showed a man freaking out as an ambulance arrives after he has apparently hit his wife so hard her head is bleeding on the floor (addressing perceived severity). "Teddy bear" showed a young boy shaking his teddy bear after seeing his parents have a violent argument (addressing perceived susceptibility and perceived severity). And "MP3" shows a young woman listening to headphones while jogging in an upscale neighborhood, with a voice-over echoing her husband's emotional abuse (addressing perceived susceptibility). Each ad was followed by a fact about the prevalence of domestic violence, with a prompt to call a hot line for domestic violence services (addressing response efficacy).

Data Collection and Sample

Surveys

Two cross-sectional surveys with random stratified samples (using all mailable addresses as the sample frame) of 2,500 men and women in two Montana counties were mailed before and after the campaign. The questionnaires were nearly identical in content. Accompanying the survey was a letter of introduction on university letterhead urging respondents to fill out the survey because the results would be used for an educational campaign. Also included were instructions on how to fill out the instrument and a self-addressed prepaid mailing envelope. No incentives were offered. Reminder notices were sent after the first month to increase response rates. The instructions explained that this was an anonymous survey.

The sample size was calculated from the available project budget, an estimate of response rate, and the estimated percentage of invalid mailing addresses. The addresses were purchased from Dunn & Bradstreet Small Business Services, with 175 of the addresses coming from Carbon County and the remainder from Yellowstone County, proportionate to the populations of the two counties. Time constraints required researchers to cut off accepting usable surveys on March 9, 2006, for the baseline survey, and June 1, 2008, for the follow-up survey.

The overall response rate for usable responses to the baseline was 17% and 15% for the follow-up (or "posttest") survey. Each response was given a tracking number and entered into a database. This tracking number allowed researchers to review a specific survey to reconcile data input errors. Comments listed on each survey were also captured.

Research Design

The research design used in this study is similar to the One Group Pretest-Posttest design except that the before and after groups were obtained through random samples rather than the same sample at two points in time. This approach has been used extensively in previous research, particularly in the field of health communications (Figueroa, Bertrand, and Kincaid 2001; Vaughan and Rogers 2000; Westoff and Bankole 1997, 1999). Although popular in the social sciences, this design is subject to several threats to validity (Garson 2010).

Presser, in a study examining social change as portrayed through Louis Harris surveys, states:

> Sample comparability is one obvious factor that can distort inferences about change in the population. If respondent background characteristics differ between surveys, and if these characteristics are related to the variable of interest, then one might observe an apparent shift in the focal variable that is actually due to differences in the composition of the samples. (1982, p. 408)

While acknowledging the limitations and difficulties of this design, evaluation scholars at the Carolina Population Center have published recommendations on the proper use of statistical controls to ameliorate its shortcoming. In this paper, we make use of these recommendations by controlling for self-selection, testing for maturation effects, and minimizing the time between the interval between time 1 and time 2 to curtail possible history bias (the impact of related, intervening events). This is discussed thoroughly in the "Limitations and Future Research" section.

Measures

The survey instrument had been employed in a previous study and was redrafted after further testing on small samples of both populations. The survey was designed to include multi- or single-item measures of the four beliefs believed to be critical to the success of the campaign (Appendix 14.3).

Survey questions consisted of the following types: attitudes toward domestic violence were measured on a five-point "strongly disagree/strongly agree" scale for each theme, and the items used to measure each theme showed an acceptable level of intercorrelation. We used campaign exposure ("Do you recall having seen any TV or print advertisements from the Open Your Eyes campaign to prevent domestic violence?") as the independent variable in our initial analyses. The dependent variables included awareness of services and attitudes about the issue. Items were drawn from Witte, Meyer, and Martell (2001) for perceived severity and response efficacy. Perceived severity was measured with a four-item scale (Cronbach's $\alpha = .61$) (e.g., "Domestic violence is a serious issue that requires government or police involvement") (Witte, Meyer, and Martell 2001). Response efficacy was measured with a single item (i.e., "Domestic violence counseling and support services are good ways to help victims of domestic violence"). A paper by Bergkvist and Rossiter states:

> a single-item measure is sufficient if the construct is such that in the minds of raters (e.g., respondents in a survey), (1) the object of the construct is "concrete singular," meaning that it consists of one object that is easily and uniformly imagined, and (2) the attribute of the construct is "concrete," again meaning that it is easily and uniformly imagined. (2007, p. 176)

Limited sociodemographic information was also captured through the first part of the questionnaire (Appendix 14.3).

RESULTS

Data Analysis

The main steps in the analysis were as follows:

1. Descriptive statistics for the sample were derived, and a cross-tabulation of the attitudinal items by sex was performed.
2. Independent t-tests were used to compare means of women before and after the campaign, and men before and after the campaign.
3. Independent t-tests were used to compare women to men at pretest, and women to men at posttest.
4. Analysis of covariance (ANCOVA) was used to examine the variance in dependent variables explained by campaign exposure, and by gender.

A total of 430 usable survey responses were available for analysis from the precampaign survey, and 374 usable survey responses were available from the postcampaign survey.

This study used a multiwave cross-sectional approach similar to past studies conducted to evaluate mass media interventions (Booth-Butterfield and Reger 2001; Kirby 1999; Westoff and Bankole 1997, 1999).

Both samples were randomly drawn from the counties exposed to campaign messages, and included different individuals. The two cross-sectional samples were theoretically representative of the populations from which they were drawn, matching each county in demographic distribution (age, gender, etc.), and therefore are compared for the purposes of this study. Charles Westoff, a senior demographer at the Office of Population Research at Princeton University, is well known for his use of multiwave, cross-sectional surveys for demonstrating the impact of communication programs, as illustrated by his research on family planning communication using the Demographic and Health Surveys.[1] He has used repeated independent cross-sectional sample surveys to demonstrate program effect. He found a consistent positive association between campaign exposure and family planning use in all countries, an association he could not remove by statistical controls (Figueroa, Bertrand, and Kincaid 2001).

As modeled by Westoff, this study inserted a variable to control for self-selection bias. Based on the likelihood that individuals with prior domestic violence experience might be more likely to attend to campaign messages and participate in the study, a question was asked regarding domestic violence experience (Appendix 14.3). No significant differences were found in responses to dependent variable questions between participants with and without prior domestic violence experience.

The statistics presented are based on the usable answers to each question. For the purposes of this analysis, all respondents to the posttest survey were considered to be "exposed" to the campaign, based on the mass media used (extensive TV airtime and billboard postings) and social contamination bias (Figueroa, Bertraind, and Kincaid 2001).

The data for each outcome were analyzed using two-factor ANCOVA with before and after campaign exposure as one between-groups factor, and gender as a second. Three covariates were included to control for any possible differences: age, experience with domestic violence, and number of children.

Exposure and Self-Reported Effects

Twenty-one percent ($n = 78$) of respondents said "yes" in response to the question "Do you recall having seen any TV or print advertisements from the Open Your Eyes campaign to prevent domestic violence?" Self-reported exposure was equal for men and women. Twenty-one percent ($n = 42$) of women reported having seen the ads, as did 21% ($n = 36$) of men.

The most common channel for exposure was television. When asked where the ad was seen (TV, billboards, newspaper, or posters), 15% ($n = 55$) marked television, 7% ($n = 25$) marked billboards, and the remaining categories were unmarked.

Of the 78 respondents who recalled having seen an ad, 10% ($n = 7$) reported taking some kind of action as a result. Five percent ($n = 4$) said they tried to help others, 2.5% ($n = 2$) said they left a relationship, 6.4% ($n = 5$) recommended someone else leave a relationship, 3.8% ($n = 3$) intervened in an abusive situation, and 2.5% ($n = 2$) said they called the police.

The bulk of the survey asked the respondent to signify his or her answer using categorical responses. The following questions were answered using a five-point Likert scale. The majority of respondents (72%) strongly agreed with the statement "Domestic violence is a serious issue that our community should focus on preventing," and over 92% were in overall agreement ($M = 1.38$).

Eighty-two percent *did not* agree that domestic violence should be settled within the family ($M = 4.27$). Only 9% agreed in general with the statement "Domestic violence should be settled within the family rather than involving the police or government officials." Over 84% of the respondents agreed that domestic violence was a serious crime worthy of jail time for the abuser ($M = 1.63$).

Nearly 88% of the respondents agreed with the statement "Physical, sexual, emotional, spiritual, and economic harassment are all forms of domestic violence" ($M = 1.54$). Eighty-four percent of the respondents disagreed that abuse may be provoked and deserved ($M = 4.38$). Over 80% of the respondents agreed that "Domestic violence advocacy and support services are effective ways of helping victims of domestic violence" ($M = 1.75$).

Gender Differences in Domestic Violence Attitudes

Segmentation by gender resulted in stark differences in the responses.

Awareness of Services

A comparison of means showed that campaign exposure (i.e., membership in the posttest group of respondents) was significantly different among women at pre- vs. posttest, but not men (Table 14.1). Women in the posttest group tended to have greater awareness of domestic violence services compared to women at pretest, while men did not show significant differences. This finding supports H1 for *women only;* campaign exposure increased awareness of domestic violence service. It also supports H4: The relationship between campaign exposure and awareness varies by gender.

A comparison of women and men at pretest shows no significant differences in mean levels of awareness, while a comparison of women to men at posttest indicates that women were significantly more aware of services than men.

Table 14.2 displays ANCOVA results for the variable awareness of services by campaign exposure and gender, as well as an F-test for each of the variables, the number, mean, and standard deviation for pre- and posttest men and women. The campaign exposure variable was significant at the .10 level ($F = 3.02, p < .10$). Gender was not significant ($F = .32, p < .574$). The interaction variable, gender × campaign exposure, was significant at the .10 level ($F = 3.33, p < .10$). Of the control variables, only Age was significant ($F = 6.36, p < .05$).

A post hoc Tamhanes test (used when variances are unequal) shows the mean score for awareness of services increased significantly for women after the campaign, from .5769 to .6946 ($p = .062$). In contrast, the mean score for men was essentially unchanged after the campaign, from .6205 to .6257.

These findings support H1 and H4, which posited that campaign exposure would increase awareness of services (for women but not men) and that this awareness varies by gender.

Response Efficacy

A comparison of means (Table 14.1) showed that posttest women had greater perceived response efficacy compared to pretest women, while the male perceived response efficacy did not change significantly. Table 14.3 shows no significant difference between male and female attitudes toward response efficacy at pretest, but a significant difference between genders at posttest.

Table 14.4 displays the ANCOVA results for response efficacy by campaign exposure and gender. The campaign exposure variable was significant ($F = 10.12, p < .01$). Gender was significant ($F = 5.81, p < .05$). The interaction variable, gender × campaign exposure, was not significant ($F = 1.41, p > .10$). Of the control variables, only age was significant ($F = 4.93, p < .05$).

Campaign exposure was associated with increased response efficacy for women (but not men) only in t-test analysis, giving limited support to H3, that campaign exposure would increase response efficacy beliefs, and H5, that this relationship would vary by gender.

Perceived Severity

Figure 14.1 illustrates the divergence between mean perceived severity among men and women before and after exposure to the advertising campaign. Women's perception of severity increased after the campaign while perceived severity dramatically decreased for men.

Table 14.1 shows that male-perceived severity decreased from pre- to posttest on almost every dimension, while female-perceived severity increased from pre- to posttest on every dimension.

Table 14.1

Pre- Versus Posttest Mean Domestic Violence Attitudes for Men and Women

Constructs	Variables	Group	Pretest Mean	Pretest SD	Posttest Mean	Posttest SD	Significance
Awareness services	Awareness of services	Male	.62	.49	0.63	0.49	—
		Female	.58	.50	0.69	0.46	**
Perceived severity	Domestic violence is a serious problem	Male	4.67	.66	4.46	0.90	*
		Female	4.59	.71	4.72	0.68	*
	Police should help settle disputes	Male	4.31	1.05	3.92	1.24	***
		Female	4.20	1.13	4.51	0.98	**
	Perpetrators should go to jail	Male	4.39	1.03	3.98	1.27	***
		Female	4.29	1.00	4.29	1.20	—
	Abuse can be economic, emotional, or physical	Male	4.48	1.05	4.22	1.49	*
		Female	4.37	1.08	4.70	0.91	***
Response efficacy	Domestic violence services are effective	Male	4.10	1.21	4.30	1.01	—
		Female	4.23	1.03	4.54	0.99	***

* Significant difference at the .05 level.
** Significant difference at the .01 level.
*** Significance at the .001 level.

Figure 14.1 **Perceived Severity by Gender**

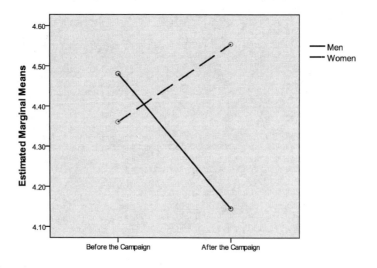

Table 14.2

Awareness of Services by Campaign Exposure, by Gender

Variable	n	M	SD	F	df	Significance
Intercept				68.48		.000
Age				6.36	1	.012
Past abuse				.15	1	.697
Number of children				.28	1	.596
Campaign exposure				3.02	1	.083
Gender				.32	1	.574
Gender × campaign exposure				3.33	1	.069
Pretest men	195	.62	.49			
Posttest men	171	.63	.49			
Pretest women	234	.58	.50			
Posttest women	203	.69	.46			

Table 14.3 shows that male and female attitudes regarding severity were not significantly different on any dimension at pretest, while they were significantly different at posttest.

Table 14.5 displays an F-test for each of the variables as well as the number, mean, and standard deviation for pre- and posttest men and women. The campaign exposure variable was not significant. Gender was significant ($F = 7.77, p < .00$) as was the gender × campaign exposure interaction variable ($F = 27.27, p < .00$). The control covariates were not statistically significant.

A post hoc Tamhanes test showed the mean score on the perceived severity variable increased significantly for women after the campaign, from 4.36 to 4.55 ($p = .010$). In contrast, the mean score for perceived severity decreased significantly for men after the campaign, from 4.48 to 4.15 ($p = .000$).

These findings support H2, which posited that campaign exposure increased perceived severity, and H6, which posited that the relationship between campaign exposure and beliefs about severity varies by gender.

Results obtained to examine the relationship between campaign exposure and self-reported behavior changes were not significant. However, frequency analysis showed that 10% of respon-

Table 14.3

Pre- and Posttest Mean Domestic Violence Attitudes of Men Versus Women

			Pretest		Posttest		
Constructs	Variables	Group	Mean	SD	Mean	SD	Significance
Awareness of services	Awareness of services	Pretest	.62	.49	.58	.50	—
		Posttest	.63	.49	.69	.46	**
Perceived severity	Domestic violence is a serious problem	Pretest	4.67	.66	4.59	.71	—
		Posttest	4.46	.90	4.72	.68	***
Perceived severity	Police should help settle disputes	Pretest	4.31	1.05	4.20	1.13	—
		Posttest	3.92	1.24	4.51	.98	***
Perceived severity	Perpetrators should go to jail	Pretest	4.39	1.03	4.29	1.00	—
		Posttest	3.98	1.27	4.29	1.20	*
Perceived severity	Abuse can be economic, emotional, or physical	Pretest	4.48	1.05	4.37	1.08	—
		Posttest	4.22	1.49	4.70	.91	***
Response efficacy	Domestic violence services are effective	Pretest	4.10	1.21	4.23	1.03	—
		Posttest	4.30	1.01	4.54	.99	*

* Significant at the .05 level.
** Significant at the .01 level.
*** Significance at the .001 level.

Table 14.4

Response Efficacy by Campaign Exposure, by Gender

Variable	n	M	SD	F	df	Significance
Intercept				1,027.05	1	.000
Age				4.93	1	.027
Past abuse				1.70	1	.193
Number of children				1.80	1	.18
Campaign exposure				10.12	1	.002
Gender				5.81	1	.016
Gender × campaign exposure				1.41	1	.236
Pretest men	194	4.12	1.18			
Posttest men	171	4.30	1.00			
Pretest women	235	4.23	1.03			
Posttest women	203	4.54	.99			

Table 14.5

Perceived Severity by Campaign Exposure, by Gender

Variable	n	M	SD	F	df	Significance
Intercept				2,620.92	1	.000
Age				.003	1	.953
Past abuse				1.54	1	.216
Number of children				.58	1	.449
Campaign exposure				2.23	1	.136
Gender				7.77	1	.005
Gender × campaign exposure				27.27	1	.000
Pretest men	194	4.48	.68			
Posttest men	171	4.15	.81			
Pretest women	235	4.36	.68			
Posttest women	203	4.55	.60			

dents who recalled the campaign reported some type of behavior change (see Appendix 14.3 for types of behavior).

DISCUSSION

This paper reports findings from a media intervention designed to raise awareness about domestic violence and to prevent abuse. A quasi-experimental, in-field approach was used to assess campaign effects. The project had four key research objectives that are now related to the evaluation findings.

Results showed that 21% of the target audience, irrespective of gender, recalled seeing messages from the campaign; 10% of those exposed reported taking some kind of action. This degree of audience recall is impressive given the nonprofit nature of the project and the fact that most of the media were obtained through donations, pro bono rates, or public service announcements. This degree of audience recall is also impressive because the advertisements were all creatively and strategically designed by undergraduate marketing and communication students (albeit with professional help).

H1 predicted increased awareness of domestic violence services and H3 suggested increased belief in response efficacy of such services. Independent t-tests demonstrated support for both hypotheses. H4, H5, and H6 suggested that these effects would vary by gender. Independent t-test and ANCOVAs showed that awareness of services increased significantly for women (but not men) from pretest to posttest, lending support for H4. A t-test (but not ANCOVAs) showed increased belief in the effectiveness of services among women, lending limited support for H5.

H3 predicted campaign exposure would increase perceived severity, and H6 predicted this relationship would vary by gender. Women (but not men) increased their perceived severity of domestic violence from pretest to posttest, according to both types of analysis. The campaign appeared to have effectively reached women.

What is perhaps startling about the above results is that male perceived severity of domestic violence moved in the opposite direction intended by the campaign. Several possible explanations are offered. First, it may be that the two cross-sectional samples were not comparable (see more on this in the "Limitations and Future Research" section). Second, it may be that men responded to the campaign with a fear control response, resulting in defense-avoidance of the issue, thus leading to reduced recognition of the problem. In a meta-analysis of fear appeals, Witte and Allen (2000) found that fear messages that were not accompanied by efficacy messages were more likely to trigger a defensive reaction, and that the more defensive one becomes, the less likely one is to make attitudinal or behavioral changes toward reducing a health risk. Although Witte, Meyer, and Martell (2001) found no difference by gender across the studies of fear appeals, it may be that gender acted as a mediator here because of the highly gender-sensitive nature of the subject matter.

It is not hard to imagine how this campaign might have triggered a backlash reaction among some men. Given that the campaign primarily targeted women, who were identified by formative research as the primary victims of abuse in 85% of reported cases by the Bureau of Justice Statistics (2003), a second possible interpretation is that the campaign effectively reached women but not men because they were not a target audience (or at least not a primary one). Overall, men actually grew more resistant to government involvement in abuse prevention and reduced their perceived severity of the issue over time. A third explanation is that the backlash was a reaction to unflattering gender stereotyping. Commenting on these findings, domestic violence scholar Jackson Katz said, "The ads may have unintentionally angered some men because the ads repeatedly portrayed women as victims and men as perpetrators, without any other men on screen who a man who's not abusive could identify with."[2] Indeed, the indirect audience of men in this campaign may have increased their sense of injustice and outrage at being unfairly blamed for the crimes of other men.

Feminist scholar Judith Milner writes that interventions that view men through a judgmental lens are likely to predispose men to denial and deceit, leading to further male dishonesty about their violence (Milner 2004). According to Katz (2000), mass media has created a masculine stereotype that glorifies dominance, power, control, and violence. Violent masculinity has thus become a "cultural norm" (Katz 2000). In fact, Milner and Katz both argue that public health attempts that engage violent men through confrontation will actually reduce women's choices. By using fear appeals (including violent reenactments of abuse in TV and portrayals of consequences in print art), this campaign may have been too confrontational.

A fourth possibility is that the response to our survey generated a self-selected sample of involved men. Such men may be more likely to have strong attitudes about domestic violence, possibly in the negative direction. Similarly, female respondents, if biased by self-selection, might have been more likely to have had direct experience with abuse and therefore may have been more likely to perceive the issue as severe. However, since both the pre- and posttest surveys were conducted in similar manners, with random samples of the population, such biases would be expected to affect both rounds of data collection similarly. Further, a comparison between respondents who reported knowing someone with prior domestic violence experience and those who did not resulted in no significant differences.

LIMITATIONS AND FUTURE RESEARCH

The results reported in this paper are limited to measurements of attitude change. While our data seemed to show that domestic violence ads can be effective at changing attitudes, such as perceived severity, further data collection is required to measure behavior changes in association with campaign exposure among the same individuals over time. In addition, determining whether these results are applicable to other social marketing campaigns requires additional research.

An obvious limitation of this study, as with much advertising research, is the difference between natural and forced exposure. Maintaining external validity by measuring audience exposures in a real-world setting naturally limits the researchers' ability to control exposure intensities and settings. Audience involvement and perceived risk might have been higher than among the general public because respondents to the randomized mail survey were self-selected. It clearly would have been superior to have used a panel design to be able to compare changes among the same individuals from time 1 to time 2. However, even with this approach, we would have faced several limitations to conducting experiments in a field setting.

In October 2001, the Population Communication Services Project (PCS), from the Johns Hopkins University and the MEASURE Evaluation Project at the Carolina Population Center convened an expert meeting to discuss methodological issues regarding the evaluation of applied communication programs:

> Although evaluators recognized that the experimental design (e.g., the pre-test–post-test control group design with randomization of subjects) provides the most compelling evidence of program effectiveness, it was deemed impractical for evaluating programs with a radio or TV component for several reasons: (1) impossibility of randomly assigning individuals or other units, such as villages or regions, to the experimental groups, (2) difficulty in getting a comparable population to serve as a control group, (3) contamination of the communication intervention into the control areas when they are used, and (4) intervening events ("history") unrelated to the intervention that altered the outcome, especially when programs last for several months or years. (Figueroa, Bertrand, and Kincaid 2001, p. 5)

To remedy these pitfalls, evaluation scholars at the Carolina Population Center recommend utilizing statistical controls to measure self-selection, dose-response relationships, and pathways for interaction. We have followed the recommendations by measuring theoretical constructs of how people might change, and controlling for self-selection. Although not ideal, these types of multiwave studies have been used in previous research, particularly in the field of health communications (Figueroa, Bertrand, and Kincaid 2001; Vaughan and Rogers 2000; Westoff and Bankole 1997, 1999).

Because the present study focused exclusively on perceived severity, awareness, and response efficacy, further research should explore how this campaign affected the other constructs of the HBM, specifically with reference to perceived susceptibility (the other dimension of health threat) and both dimensions of efficacy. While defense-avoidance was a primary tenet of this report, no data were collected to specifically determine whether the measured attitude changes actually represented defense-avoidance, or whether other phenomena were responsible. Qualitative data about the reasons for the audience's reaction to the Open Your Eyes campaign could give a fuller understanding.

Domestic violence is an important social, criminal, and cultural issue that needs to be addressed. Efforts to minimize domestic violence have traditionally included specialized shelters, clinic-based outreach and crisis intervention, with interventions typically occurring only after an incident has occurred. Mass media has been underutilized as a vehicle for reducing the incidence of domestic violence. This study provides support for the argument that mass media can be used to successfully educate people about this social problem. At the same time, the content of the media message must be carefully considered in order to best reach the targeted audiences.

NOTES

1. Demographic and Health Surveys (DHS) are nationally representative household surveys with large sample sizes. DHS surveys provide data for a wide range of evaluation indicators in the areas of population, health, and nutrition (MEASURE, *DHS+,* ORC Macro).

2. Author interview with Jackson Katz, May 23, 2009.

REFERENCES

Ajzen, Icek (1991), "The Theory of Planned Behavior," *Organizational Behavior and Human Decision Processes,* 50 (2), 179–211.

Artz, Nancy, Jeanne Munger, and Warren Purdy (1999), "Gender Issues in Advertising Language," *Women and Language,* 22 (2), 20–26.

Becker, Marshall H., Lois A. Maiman, John P. Kirscht, Don P. Haefner, and Robert H. Drachman (1977), "The Health Belief Model and Prediction of Dietary Compliance: A Field Experiment," *Journal of Health and Social Behavior,* 18 (4), 348–366.

Bergkvist, Lars, and John R. Rossiter (2007), "The Predictive Validity of Multiple-Item Versus Single-Item Measures of the Same Constructs," *Journal of Marketing Research,* 64 (2), 175–184.

Booth-Butterfield, Steven, and Bill Reger (2001), "The Message Changes Belief and the Rest Is Theory: The 1% or Less Milk Campaign and Reasoned Action," paper presented at the International Communication Association meeting, Washington, DC, May.

Browne, Beverly A. (1998), "Gender Stereotypes in Advertising on Children's Television in the 1990s: A Cross-National Analysis," *Journal of Advertising,* 27 (1), 83–96.

Bureau of Justice Statistics (2003), "Statistics Crime Data Brief, Intimate Partner Violence, 1993–2001," U.S. Department of Justice, Washington, DC, available at http://bjs.ojp .usdoj.gov/content/pub/pdf/ipv01.pdf (accessed October 2, 2010).

Carlson, Bonnie E., and Alissa Pollitz Worden (2005), "Attitudes and Beliefs About Domestic Violence: Results of a Public Opinion Survey," *Journal of Interpersonal Violence,* 20 (10), 1197–1218.

Centers for Disease Control and Prevention (2006), *Preventing Violence Against Women: Program Activities Guide,* Atlanta, GA: CDC.

Cho, Hyunyi, and Charles T. Salmon (2007), "Unintended Effects of Health Communication," *Journal of Communication Campaigns,* 57 (2), 293–317.

Connell, R. W. (1995), *Masculinities,* Berkeley: University of California Press.

Davidson, W. Phillips (1983), "The Third-Person Effect in Communication," *Public Opinion Quarterly,* 47 (1), 1–15.

Davies, Lorraine, Marilyn Ford-Gilboe, and Joanne Hammerton (2009), "Gender Inequality and Patterns of Abuse Post Leaving," *Journal of Family Violence,* 24 (2), 27–39.

Dutton, Don, and Daniel Sonkin (2003), *Intimate Violence: Contemporary Treatment Innovations,* New York: Haworth Trauma and Maltreatment Press.

Eagley, Alice H., and Shelly Chaiken (1984), "Cognitive Theories of Persuasion," in *Advances in Experimental Social Psychology,* vol. 17, Leonard Berkowitz, ed., New York: Academic Press, 268–359.

Festinger, Leon (1957), *A Theory of Cognitive Dissonance,* Stanford: Stanford University Press.

Figueroa, Maria E., Jane T. Bertrand, and D. Lawrence Kincaid (2001), *Evaluating the Impact of Communication Programs,* Chapel Hill, NC: Carolina Population Center, University of North Carolina at Chapel Hill.

Ford, John B., and Michael S. LaTour (1996), "Contemporary Female Perspectives of Female Role Portrayals in Advertising," *Journal of Current Issues and Research in Advertising,* 18 (1), 81–95.

Garson, G. David (2010), "Research Designs," *Statnotes: Topics in Multivariate Analysis,* available at http://faculty.chass.ncsu.edu/garson/PA765/manova.htm (accessed May 12, 2010).

Goffman, Erving (1963), *Stigma: Notes on the Management of Spoiled Identity,* Englewood Cliffs, NJ: Prentice Hall.

Gosselin, Denise K. (2010), *Heavy Hands: An Introduction to the Crime of Family Violence,* 4th ed., Boston: Prentice Hall.

Greenwald, Anthony G., and Clark Leavitt (1984), "Audience Involvement in Advertising: Four Levels," *Journal of Consumer Research,* 11 (June), 581–592.

Gulas, Charles S., and Kim McKeage (2000), "Extending Social Comparison: An Examination of the Unintended Consequences of Idealized Advertising Imagery," *Journal of Advertising,* 29 (2), 17–28.

Guttman, Nurit (1997), "Beyond Strategic Research: A Value-Centered Approach to Health Communication Interventions," *Communication Theory*, 7 (2), 95–124.
Henning, Kris, Angela R. Jones, and Robert Holdford (2005), "'I Didn't Do It, but If I Did I Had a Good Reason': Minimization, Denial and Attributions of Blame Among Male and Female Domestic Violence Offenders," *Journal of Family Violence*, 20 (3), 131–139.
Johnson, Michael P., and Janel M. Leone (2005), "The Differential Effects of Intimate Terrorism and Situational Couple Violence," *Journal of Family Issues*, 26 (3), 322–349.
Katz, Jackson (2000), *Tough Guise: Violence, Media and the Crisis in Masculinity*, Amherst, MA: Media Education Foundation.
Keller, Sarah, and Agnes J. Otjen (2007), "In-Class Experiential Service Learning: A Domestic Violence Campaign," *Journal of Marketing Education*, 29 (3), 234–244.
Kirby, Douglas (1999), "Reducing Adolescent Pregnancy: Approaches That Work," *Contemporary Pediatrics*, 16 (1), 83–94.
Kleinot, Michael C., and Ronald W. Rogers (1982), "Identifying Effective Components of Alcohol Misuse Prevention Programs," *Journal of Studies on Alcohol*, 43 (7), 802–811.
Lavine, Howard, Donna Sweeney, and Stephen H. Wagner (1999), "Depicting Women as Sex Objects in Television Advertising: Effects on Body Dissatisfaction," *Personality and Social Psychology Bulletin*, 25 (8), 1049–1058.
Lerman, Caryn, Barbara Rimer, Bruce Trock, Andrew Balshem, and Paul F. Engstrom (1990), "Factors Associated with Repeat Adherence to Breast Cancer Screening," *Preventive Medicine*, 19 (3), 279–290.
Milner, Judith (2004), "From 'Disappearing' to 'Demonized': The Effects on Men and Women of Professional Interventions Based on Challenging Men Who Are Violent," *Critical Social Policy*, 24 (1), 79–101.
Minkler, Meredith (1999), "Personal Responsibility for Health? A Review of the Arguments and the Evidence at Century's End," *Health Education and Behavior*, 26 (1), 121–140.
Petty, Richard E., and John T. Cacioppo (1986), "The Elaboration Likelihood Model of Persuasion," *Advances in Experimental Social Psychology*, vol. 19, Chicago: Academic Press, 123–205.
Piers, Gerhart, and Milton Singer (1953), *Shame and Guilt: A Psychoanalytic and a Cultural Study*, Springfield, IL: Charles C. Thomas.
Presser, Stanley (1982), "Studying Social Change with Survey Data: Examples from Louis Harris Surveys," *Social Indicators Research*, 10 (4), 407–422.
Rogers, Ronald W., and C. Ronald Mewborn (1976), "Fear Appeals and Attitude Change: Effects of a Threat's Noxiousness, Probability of Occurrence, and the Efficacy of Coping Responses," *Journal of Personality and Social Psychology*, 34 (1), 54–61.
Ryan, William (1976), *Blaming the Victim*, New York: Random House.
Schramm, Wilbur (1961), "How Communication Works," in *The Process and Effects of Mass Communication*, Wilbur Schramm, ed., Urbana: University of Illinois Press, 3–26.
Shannon, Claude, and Warren Weaver (1949), *The Mathematical Theory of Communication*, Urbana: University of Illinois Press.
Strecher, Victor J., Brenda M. DeVellis, Marshall H. Becker, and Irwin M. Rosenstock (1986), "The Role of Self-Efficacy in Achieving Health Behavior Change," *Health Education Quarterly*, 13 (1), 73–91.
Vaughan, Peter, and Everett M. Rogers (2000), "A Staged Model of Communication Effects: Evidence from an Entertainment-Education Radio Soap Opera in Tanzania," *Journal of Health Communication*, 5 (3), 203–228.
Vidmar, Neil, and Milton Rokeach (1974), "Archie Bunker's Bigotry: A Study in Selective Perception and Exposure," *Journal of Communication*, 24 (2), 36–47.
Wathen, C. Nadine, and Harriet L. MacMillan (2003), "Interventions for Violence Against Women: Scientific Review," *Journal of American Medical Association*, 289 (5), 589–600.
Westley, Bruce H., and Malcolm MacLean (1957), "A Conceptual Model for Mass Communication Research," *Journalism Quarterly*, 34 (Winter), 31–38.
Westoff, Charles F., and Akinrinola Bankole (1997), "Mass Media and Reproductive Behavior in Africa," Demographic and Health Surveys Analytical Report no. 2, Macro International Inc., Calverton, MD.
———, and ——— (1999), "Mass Media and Reproductive Behavior in Pakistan, India, and Bangladesh," Demographic and Health Surveys Analytical Report no. 10, Macro International Inc., Calverton, MD.
Witte, Kim (1992), "The Role of Threat and Efficacy in AIDS Prevention," *International Quarterly of Community Health Education*, 12 (December), 225–249.
———, and Mike Allen (2000), "A Meta-Analysis of Fear Appeals: Implications for Effective Public Health Campaigns," *Health Education and Behavior*, 27 (5), 591–615.
———, Gary Meyer, and Dennis Martell (2001), *Effective Health Risk Messages: A Step-by-Step Guide*, Thousand Oaks, CA: Sage.
Wolfe, David A., and Peter G. Jaffe (1999), "Emerging Strategies in the Prevention of Domestic Violence," *Future of Children*, 9 (3), 133–144.

APPENDIX 14.1

Appendix 14.2

Timeline for Open Your Eyes Campaign and Data Collection

Time:	Fall 2005	January–March 2006	April–August 2006	January–March 2008	March–June 2008
Activity:	Formative research	Baseline survey	Campaign aired (TV, billboard, print ads)	Campaign relaunched (TV, billboard)	Follow-up survey

Appendix 14.3

List of Variables

Variables	Items
Awareness of services	Are you aware of services available for domestically abused victims?
Behavior change	Reported taking some kind of action as a result of seeing an ad:
	Helped others
	Left relationship
	Called police
	Intervened
	Recommended someone else leave
Perceived severity	Domestic violence is a serious problem that our community should focus on preventing.
	Domestic violence should be settled within the family rather than involving the police or government officials. (inversely related)
	Domestic violence is a serious crime and the abuser should go to jail.
Perceived severity	Physical, sexual, emotional, spiritual, and economic harassment are all forms of domestic violence.
Response efficacy	Domestic violence advocacy and support services are effective ways of helping victims of domestic violence.
Campaign exposure	Do you recall having seen an ad from the Open Your Eyes campaign?
Demographics	Marital status
	Gender
	Age
	County
	Number of children
Self-selection	Has anyone you know ever been domestically abused?

PART VII

REGULATORY ISSUES

15

Violence, Advertising, and Commercial Speech

Leleah Fernandez and Jef I. Richards

As long as marketing has existed, so too has violence in advertising. Depictions of slavery and conquest appeared in ads throughout the colonial American era (O'Barr 2010). Images of tanks and soldiers populated magazines, billboards, and newspapers during the Great Depression and World War II (O'Barr 2010). Over time, advertising continues to test the threshold of community standards, resulting in ads that are sometimes considered dangerous, obscene, unethical, and/or offensive. At the same time, most ads are guaranteed a considerable amount of protection under the First Amendment, as commercial speech. At times this dynamic creates conflict between freedom of speech and consumer interests.

An act of violence refers to an action that causes, or intends to cause, harm. Violence can be directed to oneself (Gerbner et al. 2002), toward another individual or group (Kunkel et al. 1995; Kunkel et al. 2001), toward animals, or even at inanimate objects. Acts of violence can be physical or psychological, meaning implied threats, nonverbal communication, outbursts, and/or rage (Mustonen and Pulkien 1997, p. 173). In recent years, some argue that media violence has not just increased in quantity, but that images are increasingly more graphic, sexual, and the messages more sadistic (Media Education Foundation 2005; Reichert et al. 1999). Contemporary advertising uses violent images, messages, and depictions for marketing appeal and artistic purposes. Violence is often eroticized, adding novelty or aesthetics (Jhally 2002; Stankiewicz and Rosselli 2008).

The strategic reasoning for violence in advertising and the potential harm of media violence creates a growing tension between consumer advocates and marketing professionals. The goals of marketing and the interest of the public are seemingly at odds. Ads seek to draw attention and influence buying behaviors or belief systems. When complaints arise, marketers generally defend their decisions to use shock tactics. Marketers cite protection of commercial speech and/or defend their decisions as a form of artistic expression or cultural discourse. For example, the brand Benetton often incorporates violent images in its ads (see Figure 15.1). Some of these ads resulted in product bans and organized protests. Luciano Benetton, who is notorious for running these taboo advertising campaigns, responds to criticism, claiming the ads are intended to develop citizen consciousness (Tinic 1997).

Aggression, hostility, anger, and violence can all be seen as a legitimate and even necessary cultural expression (Gerbner et al. 1994). Violent content can indeed be used to draw attention to taboo, gritty, or unpopular social issues. Violence is often used explicitly to raise public awareness. Nonprofits and citizen groups routinely use shocking images and messages to earn attention for their cause (e.g., Murray 2012). For example, in 2013 New York City transit workers passed out blood-splattered Metro cards to commuters with a picture of the Grim Reaper on the back as part of a campaign to slow the speed requirements for trains when they approach stations (see Figure 15.2).

238 REGULATORY ISSUES

Figure 15.1 **Benetton Controversy Ads**

THE APPEAL OF VIOLENCE

Ads have a defined purpose: to link consumers and products and to sell these products. Like other forms of mass-mediated communication, advertising has the potential to reach large segments of various populations. Global expenditures on advertising exceeds half a trillion dollars each year. The United States is currently the largest contributor to the worldwide advertising market, spending nearly $161 billion in 2012 (ZenithOptimedia 2012). Due to the pervasive nature of advertising—and the amount of money dedicated to marketing communications—advertising can reinforce and cultivate unhealthy or destructive behaviors, particularly with repetitive messages and images over time.

There are several reasons to use violent content in ads and commercials. First, violence captures attention in a short period of time. Use of violence in advertising has been found to be effective in stimulating attention and processing the messages in an ad (LaTour, Snipes, and Bliss 1996). A common tactic is the eroticizing, romanticizing, or glamorizing of what might otherwise be considered risky or unhealthy behaviors. In order to incite purchase and consumption, violence is often portrayed in ads for otherwise inoffensive products (e.g., sports footwear, cereals, and soft drinks). For example, in 2008 PepsiMax ran a series of print ads featuring a cute but sad cartoon personification of a calorie. The ads illustrated the chubby blue calorie committing suicide in a variety of ultraviolent ways, including a gunshot to the head while holding a bottle of poison with a rope noosed around the neck (see Figure 15.3). Other ads show the calorie strapped to a warhead while cutting his wrist, or feature the calorie drenched in gasoline while lighting a match. The copy on these ads read "one very, very, very lonely calorie" (Creamer 2008).

Second, violence is easy to understand and has a somewhat universal appeal. Action appeals to young people (Sparks and Sparks 2000) and transcends language and cultural boundaries (Zillmann

Figure 15.2 **2013 Transit Cards**

1998). Advertising is needed to expand markets from local to global, and secure new brand loyalists, in order to prevent market saturation. At the same time, this globalization of marketing incurs costs, as various cultures and languages require additional investments in messaging modification. Amid the expanding market, advertising naturally gravitates toward the most cost-effective mechanism to reach across language and cultural boundaries. Action and violence are considered a universal language (Kellner and Cvetkovich 1997; Rockett 1988). Everyone can understand a battle, explosion, kick, or shot. At times these pursuits are at the expense of the brand reputation, for example, a series of Mentos ads (see Figure 15.4) was pulled after an international subsidiary of Ogilvy and Mather ran a series of ads depicting men committing suicide (Edwards 2011).

Third, as media violence becomes more prevalent and far reaching, so does advertising violence. Violence has been a key part of media since the birth of literature. Greek poetry often centered on themes such as murder and suicide. Shakespearean dramas portrayed rape, torture, and revenge. Stories of violence reach across all forms of media, from novels to computer games, music videos, and movies (Potter 2008). In recent years, violence across media has increased in the form of video games and popular films. From 1995 to 2012, the top-grossing movie for each year was a violent movie (Nash Information Services 2013). Violent films, and consequently advertising for these films, are often based on fights, explosions, and special effects. The top-selling video games in 2013 were action games, accounting for more than 23% of all sales, followed by shooter games, with over 21% of all sales (NPD Group 2013).

240   REGULATORY ISSUES

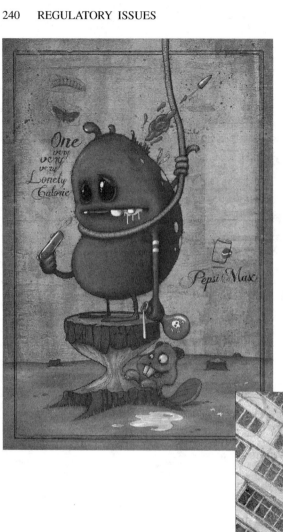

Figure 15.3   **Pepsi Magazine**

Figure 15.4   **Mentos Ad**

As entertainment-oriented media becomes more violent, so does the advertising for popular entertainment. Films, television, and video games portray a much more violent world than what actually exists (Lent 2002). Broadcast media, notably television, tend to portray violent content to a greater extent than nonviolent content (Van der Voort, 1986). The National Television Study (1998) reports that violent content accounts for 60% of television broadcasts, which is then reinforced by ads containing violence airing in the same time segment. Television stations in the United States subsist partially or entirely on advertisement revenue (Bushman 2005). Bushman (2005) points out how this broadcast advertising model creates a symbiotic relationship linked by the common thread of displays of violence. That is to say, television shows bring viewers' attention to the advertisements in order to assist in the sale of products.

TYPES OF ADVERTISING VIOLENCE

Media violence is notoriously hard to define and measure (Media Smarts n.d.). Violence is sometimes masked in humor or simply implied through gestures or innuendo. Aggression comes in many different forms (competition, conflict, contempt, rejection, envy, etc.) and categories (contrast, humor, irony, exaggeration, showiness, etc.) (Martínez, Prieto, and Farfán 2006, p. 275). In some cases, violence is broadly defined as the act (or threat) of injuring or killing someone, independent of the method used or the surrounding context (Lent 2002). Physical or psychological violence can refer to a spectrum of actions, ranging from nonverbal or implied threats to outbursts or rage (Mustonen and Pulkien 1997, p. 173). Some studies of mass media violence use a more specific definition. For example, the National Television Violence Study (quoted in Potter 1999, p. 68) defines violence as an "overt depiction of a credible threat of physical force or the actual use of such force intended to physically harm an animate being or group of beings" (p. 21). Violence can be described in many different ways, ranging from the mere mention of an act, to graphic elaborations on how it was conducted (Huesmann and Taylor 2006).

All ads are designed to influence consumer attitudes or behaviors, generally to prompt purchase. While the aim is similar across advertising campaigns, the marketing tactics can be quite different. Appeals and approaches designed to influence consumers are often crafted based on the nature of the product, brand, or service. The target audience and/or the medium of communication similarly vary depending on the nature of the product and specific goals of the campaign. Some approaches and media have a higher tendency toward violent content. For instance, advertising for entertainment-oriented media, such as films, video games, and some music labels tends to be especially violent. Magazines tend to use sexualized violence (Kilbourne 1999). Commercials targeting parents will often use violence to induce fear (Soderlund and Dahlen 2009), whereas viral ads tend to use violent comedy (Stone 2006).

Visual Violence in Print Ads

Some credit the trend toward violence in print advertising to Italian clothing company Benetton (Andersson et al. 2004; Tinic 1997). Benetton produced a series of ads in 1996 based on a collection of horrific images resulting from war and genocide. The magazine campaign included mutilated bodies, human limbs, land mines, and machetes, among other graphic depictions of weapons, victims, and injuries (Andersson et al. 2004). The graphic nature of these images was compounded by the fact that magazine ads tend to have very high visual quality and thus have the opportunity to create visual appeal or interest in the product (Wells, Burnett, and Moriarty 1998).

Violence can add novelty, focusing on capturing audience interest and maximizing the impact of the message. Violent appeals are particularly prevalent in ads that target boys and young men. For example, the use of military or sports tends to appear in ads for traditional male products,

Figure 15.5 **Game Boy**

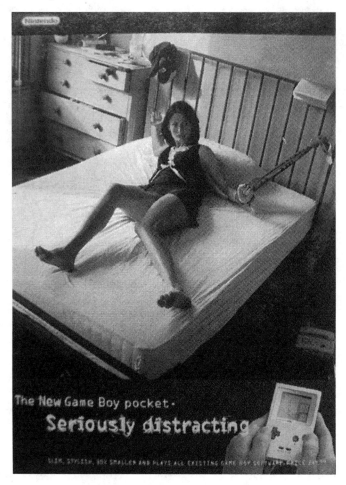

such as beer, running shoes, or deodorant, or to enhance the masculine appeal of more feminine products such as "lite" beer (Katz 2011).

Advertisements, particularly those targeting boys and young men, portray a chronic struggle for dominance. Sex is often used as a demonstration of power, emphasizing female submission rather than mutual pleasure (Kilbourne 1999). For instance, ads for video games tend to focus on sexualized violent content. The Game Boy ad in Figure 15.5 serves as an illustration of the implied violence, female submission, and sexualized advertising frequently used for marketing gaming devices. The ad features a woman tied to a bed, wearing lingerie.

Gender stereotypes prevalent in print ads often show men as violent, physically aggressive, hypersexual, or participating in "dangerous" activities for the thrill of it all (Katz 2011). The perpetuation and reinforcement of aggressive sexual appeals are thought to contribute to rape culture (Kilbourne 1999). For example, a Dolce and Gabbana ad that showed a woman pinned to the ground by the wrists by a bare-chested man while several other men looked on was banned in several countries (see Figure 15.6). Activists argued that the ad depicted a gang rape scenario, reinforcing the idea that men can take what they want from women (AFP 2007).

Another, albeit similar, criticism of advertising effects holds that eroticized displays of aggression may prompt victimization or feelings of vulnerability. Women and minorities are often

Figure 15.6 **Dolce & Gabbana**

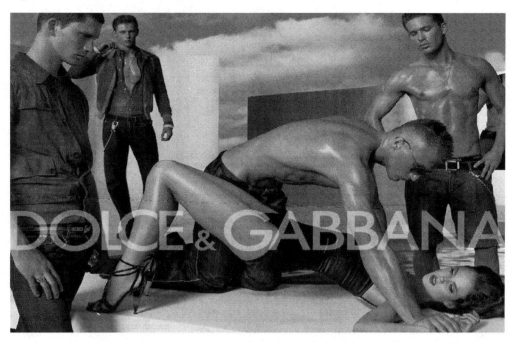

portrayed as victims of violence. Some argue that persistent messages of eroticized violence increase and normalize violence toward women, reminding women about their subservient position (Kilbourne 1999). From this perspective, depictions of violence cultivate an exaggerated sense of insecurity, mistrust, and anxiety. Research suggests that women and minorities develop a sense of vulnerability and dependence related to repeated exposure to violent content, including advertising (Kilbourne 1999). For example, an ad distributed by Bitch Skateboards and published in *Big Brother* magazine shows a male figure pointing a gun at the female figure. The founder of the company, Sal Rocco Jr., described the ad as harmless, claiming the female figure in the photo represents their rival company, Girl.

Violence coupled with stereotypes represents a chronic feature of advertising, particularly print advertising, and one that is the subject of social criticism. Advertising characteristically portrays a stereotypical "pecking order," an imbalance between those acting aggressively and those suffering from violence. Women, children, young people, the lower class, people with disabilities, and Asian Americans are at the bottom of the general violence pecking order (Kilbourne 1999). Men are generally portrayed as the perpetrators of violence (Katz 2011). Some media scholars argue that marketing appeals extend to race segmentation. For example, Katz (2011) postulates that the idea that men of color in particular need to adopt a hyper-masculine posture in order to gain credibility and respect because they historically have been marginalized by white culture. From this perspective, ads often tell boys of color that respect is linked to physical strength and the threat of violence. In other words, advertising reinforces messages that masculinity equates to the ability to scare people (Jhally et al. 1999).

Realistic Violence and Fear Appeals

Fear appeals refers to emotional rhetoric designed to frighten rather than enlighten; they are used to threaten or arouse fear in an audience in order to stimulate attitude change (Severin and

Tankard 2001). The use of violence to induce fear is an effective tool for increasing salience and thus motivation to buy. Products with an orientation toward safety will often appeal to fears; examples are cars, alarm systems, and cell phones or other communication products and services.

Media violence scholars have noted significant correlations between age and individual response to violence (Gerbner et al. 2002). For example, when compared to other age groups, three-to-five-year-olds are most frightened by things that appear scary; the fear is heightened by the fact that this age group cannot distinguish fact from fiction (Cantor 2002). From approximately six to eight years old, children tend to seek and watch violent material intended for older audiences. Despite their curiosity, children at this age are still frightened by depictions of violence, yet they see more violence, heightening their natural fears.

Pre-teens are less frightened by violent depictions, but are more fearful for personal safety. Depictions of parents in danger can be especially upsetting for pre-teens as they consume more adult-oriented media. Lastly, teens and adults tend to fear for personal safety, as well as fearing ostracism and embarrassment. They tend to be heavier media consumers, which leads to fears about crime and distrust of others—and beliefs that violence occurs to a much greater extent than in reality (Lent 2002). This effect is more powerful when the violence is portrayed realistically (Soulliere 2003). It is difficult to define or measure exactly how and to what extent fear impacts attitudes or behaviors. However, there is some relationship between viewing violence and feelings of fear and aggression (Ferguson 2008).

Over the past decade, video games have become almost synonymous with violence, depicting acts with movie-like realism (Montag, Weber, Trautner, Newport, Markett, et al., 2011). Realistic violence strengthens attitude toward the story, attitude toward the ad, and attitude toward the advertised product (Soderlund and Dahlen 2009, p. 1811). Video games are highly visual in nature, and purchases are generally driven by visual features such as realistic graphics and interesting story lines (NPD 2013). Ads often depict the most exciting, stimulating, potentially provocative, and attention-grabbing elements or representations of the game. However, the level of violence portrayed in video game advertising has occasionally triggered public backlash. For example, in 2008, ads for the release of Grand Theft Auto IV were removed from public transportation terminals and bus stops in some cities due to complaints about their violent content (Ferguson et al. 2010).

Happy Violence and Humor

Aggressive humor is broadly defined as comedy intended to ridicule, deprecate, or injure (Hetherington and Wray 1966). "Happy violence," frequently portrayed in video games and advertisements, refers to messages suggesting that all problems can be solved by violence. It sends the message that aggression resolves conflict, rather than perpetuating it. Media scholars say that such messages increase aggression, by making violence seem like a reasonable response to everyday conflicts (Anderson et al. 2008; Gerbner 1999).

Violence used in funny or novel contexts is an especially effective marketing tool, particularly ads that surprise viewers while simultaneously violating expected norms (Dahl, Frankenberger, and Manchanda 2003). For example, Super Smash Bros. launched an ad campaign in 2001 that showed the characters Donkey Kong, Yoshi, Mario, and Pikachu holding hands and skipping, suddenly segueing into multi-player violence. Humor results in increased attention to ads (Madden and Weinberger 1982; Stewart and Furse 1986; Weinberger and Campbell 1991). As such, much of the violent content in advertising is embedded in humor, thereby disguising the violent content as humor, a tactic known as the "comedic cloak" (Brown, Bhadury, and Pope 2010).

Comedic Appeals and Viral Violence

More viral ads use violence than do television ads (Porter and Golan 2006); generally these ads use comedic violence (Stone 2006). Viral advertising refers to "unpaid peer-to-peer communication of provocative content originating from an identified sponsor using the Internet to persuade or influence an audience to pass along the content to others" (Porter and Golan 2006). Brown, Bhadury, and Pope (2010) report that humorous ads that are high in violence are more likely to be passed on to third-party viewers in a viral manner. These types of comedic yet violent portrayals seemingly benefit when consequence severity is coupled with a comedic act of violence; these ads are the most likely to be passed from peer to peer. One example is the Ford SportKa campaign. One of the most widely shared SportKa viral ads begins with an orange tabby who, while strolling through a suburban neighborhood, comes across a small blue automobile parked in a driveway. The curious cat pokes its head into the open sunroof only to have the sunroof trap it by its neck. The scene ends with the cat's decapitated body falling to the ground. Often, such ads are shared exclusively online, skipping television or print media entirely (Brown, Bhadury, and Pope 2010).

RESPONSE TO VIOLENCE

One overarching criticism is that media violence causes real-world violence. This argument holds that exposure to media violence has both short- and long-term effects on viewers. In the short term, exposure can lead to aggression or a favorable attitude toward violence. In the long term, exposure can lead to desensitization or fear (see Cantor 2002). A 2003 study found that nearly half of the parents with children between the ages of four and six reported that their children had imitated aggressive behaviors from TV (Rideout, Vandewater, and Warfella 2003). However, it is not clear whether violent media cause more aggression or whether those who are already more aggressive are drawn to violent media (Bushman 1995). It is also possible that the two reinforce one another, so that those who are prone to aggression choose more violent media, which in turn encourages their aggressiveness.

Aggressive attitudes depicted in ads featuring warriors tend to illustrate a mean and nasty world, glorifying vigilante violence. Huesmann (1982) argues that exposure to heroic images coupled with violent content can be especially harmful for children. He argues that children develop "cognitive scripts" that guide their own behavior in imitation of the actions of media heroes; therefore, children begin to believe that the use of violence is an appropriate method of problem solving. Ads for the video game Halo 3 "Believe" are a prime example of this advertising tactic. The ads feature a series of narratives of veterans recalling their service, calling on players to join them in the final battle for survival. The ads depict live-action scenes of the "historic" war and celebrate aggressive retaliations. Previous research suggests that among adults, violence presented as real appears to promote aggression when compared to violence described as fictional. Still, fictional violence also seems to make aggression more likely than programming without violent content (Atkin 1983).

It is largely agreed that at the individual level, violence is the result of an interaction among personal, social, and environmental factors (Huesmann 1982). Few critics suggest that advertising violence is the *sole* cause of violent actions. How individuals interpret and respond to violent content is complex and difficult to define, let alone measure. However, there seems to be a relationship between violent media and aggression. Violent imagery has been linked to measurable physiological changes such as increased heart rate, faster respiration, and higher blood pressure (Bandura and Walters 1963). Some argue that this simulated "fight-or-flight" response predisposes people to act aggressively in the real world (Media Smarts n.d.).

Numerous media-effect studies suggest that children who see high levels of violence are more likely to become violent, hostile adults (e.g., Bushman and Anderson 2001; see also Huesmann et al. 2003). Some argue that advertisements can cultivate and reinforce tendencies toward violence or trigger pre-existing aggressive thoughts and feelings. From this perspective, an individual's desire to strike out is justified by media images in which both the hero and the villain use violence to seek revenge, often without consequences. There is some evidence to suggest a connection between viewing and aggression. In general, this research indicated that children are more likely to imitate aggression when the perpetrator of the violence is rewarded or at least not punished, and when the violence is presented as justified (e.g., Bandura and Walters 1963; Bandura, Ross, and Ross 1963). A recent study found that children don't associate media violence with its natural consequences; the author asserts that the lack of understanding represents a desensitization process that begins at an early age (Webb et al. 2007).

Violent images intended to appeal to children as future buyers often appear in ads for products such as computers, alcoholic drinks, tobacco, sports footwear, and mobile telephones (Martínez, Prieto, and Farfán 2006). Marketing tactics that leverage children as influential agents have a set of unique potential harms. Children tend to be easier to persuade than their parents, and children in turn lobby parents (Kapoor 2003, p. 14; Wadley 1993; McNeal 1992), even when the product is for adult use. In recent years, the entertainment industry has been scrutinized for targeting children for adult-oriented entertainment (American Academy of Pediatrics 2000; Buckler and Wilson 2010).

The use of media violence has received significant criticism from some scholars, concerned parents, and, more recently, public health organizations. In 2000, representatives of the American Medical Association, American Academy of Pediatrics, American Psychological Association, American Psychiatric Association, American Academy of Family Physicians, and the American Academy of Child and Adolescent Psychiatry jointly signed a statement delivered to the Congressional Public Health Summit. The petition stated that "television, movies, music, and interactive games are powerful learning tools and highly influential media" (American Academy of Pediatrics 2000). To better understand the significance of the public health claims, the following section provides a review of the legal environment concerning violence and advertising.

ADVERTISING PROTECTION AND REGULATION

Advertising frequently is scrutinized for tactics designed to shock, entertain, or gain attention. Advertising agencies and other companies, much like individual citizens, are guaranteed the right to speak freely. This right is protected under the U.S. Constitution. The First Amendment, passed in 1791, says, "Congress shall make no law . . . abridging the freedom of speech, or of the press." Considering that companies use advertisements as a form of speech, ads are regarded as a form of speech protected by the Constitution.

Despite First Amendment protection, some ads endure enough public scrutiny to prompt regulatory considerations. For example, in the 1970s a series of lawsuits called attention to the potential harm of advertising prescription drugs and abortion services in public spaces. In response to attempted state-level regulations, the U.S. Supreme Court essentially invalidated state regulations designed to limit or censor advertising (*Virginia Board of Pharmacy v. Virginia Citizens Consumer Council* 1976; *Bigelow v. Virginia* 1975). More specifically, the Supreme Court noted that the First Amendment encompasses protections to receive information as well as protections of speech. The Court later specified that any attempts to regulate must support a substantial state interest, unless the ads are deceptive or promote illegal products and services (*Central Hudson Gas & Electric v. Public Service Commission of New York* 1980). Today, any decision concerning regulatory reach is guided by a set of terms outlined in "The Central Hudson Test." The test requires that the government show that the regulation directly advances an important state interest and requires that any regulation be narrowly tailored to that purpose. It was also during this time that the Federal Trade Commission (FTC) looked at, but eventually dropped, providing some regulatory rules regarding children's advertising.

Some ads are called into question thanks to the nature of the product (e.g., tobacco) or the mechanisms for marketing (e.g., billboards), requiring a public discussion about the potential harm of particular advertisements and the acceptable regulatory reach to prevent identified harms. The Supreme Court recognizes that some specific circumstances warrant regulation when in the best interest of consumers and the state. Since the 1930s, both the Federal Communications Commission (FCC) and FTC have attempted to regulate communications of various forms, in order to prevent, mitigate, or minimize potential harm to consumers—particularly children. Obscenity is a prime example. In terms of obscenity, the Court has said repeatedly that, regardless of the strength of the government's interest in protecting children from harmful material, the government cannot reduce adults to seeing only what is fit for children (*Janet Reno v. American Civil Liberties Union* 1997). Thus, any FTC efforts toward protecting children against unfair or deceptive practices have involved practices that parents cannot prevent or control. To determine what is or is not obscene, the FCC relies on *community standards* to adhere to federal regulations prohibiting content viewable by children.

School shootings, such as the one at Sandy Hook Elementary School in Newtown, Connecticut, in December 2012, renewed public interest and action aimed at regulating broadcast violence. Following the Sandy Hook incident, President Barack Obama called on Congress to reexamine gun control, as well as the need to "rethink the way violence is often glorified in entertainment offerings" (Stelter 2013). The Children's Advertising Review Unit (CARU) holds that PG-13 films should not be advertising in shows targeted to young kids, because the rating means that some of the content may not be appropriate for them. The Motion Picture Advertising Association (MPAA) has countered that there should be no line drawn in the sand because "PG-13 does not necessarily mean you can't take a younger child to it." In response to growing public and political scrutiny of film and television violence, industry representatives (e.g., lobbying groups for filmmakers, theater owners, broadcasters, and cable operators) initiated a campaign intended to make parents more aware about ways to limit exposure to violent entertainment.

The marketing of adult entertainment to children has been, and continues to be, an ongoing issue between government regulators and various media industries. In a report released in 2000, the Federal Trade Commission called on the movie, music, and video game industries to stop using tactics that blatantly market violent entertainment to children. A more recent report recommended revamping and disclosing the rating system for violent content and restriction of marketing toward children (FTC 2009). Currently, state and federal governments are attempting to pass laws that punish retailers for selling violent video games to minors; such laws are then challenged as unconstitutional by video game producers.

Ads consume public spaces, print media, and broadcast time. Advertising is responsible for nearly all television and radio revenue, nearly half of all magazine revenue, and 80% of newspaper revenue (Jhally 1997). Professional sports, schools, and the Internet have all been integrated into the advertising system. Films, video games, and music labels occupy their respective media, meaning that violent content in films, games, and music can arguably be contained. To some extent, an individual can choose whether to view violence or to minimize or filter the level of violent content viewed within a household. However, advertising is often indiscriminate. Exposure to violent content in advertising is not a choice when promotions for violent films and games are featured in public spaces and advertised across various other media (e.g., billboards, television, and the Internet).

THE FUTURE OF REGULATION

The First Amendment to the Constitution says that Congress shall make no laws abridging the freedom of speech, press, religion, and so forth. U.S. policy has historically taken a hands-off approach. Regulatory action to minimize, restrict, or censor violence in advertising is further complicated by emerging forms of media and the nature of globalization. The Internet makes content widely available to adults and children, almost indiscriminately. The globalization of the marketplace favors a private-sector governing authority rather than public-sector governance. That is to say, the role of public governance is lost in an economically driven market that reaches far beyond national regulatory powers. In the instance of telecommunication, and in combination with the global expansion of U.S. entertainment, regional authorities and elected officials are far outside their governing boundaries. This shifting of cultural and market power represents a unique challenge for minimizing violent content under a market model, which profits from violence.

Marketing in the United States is inherently tied to the national economic paradigm; a successful economy depends on the production and sales of products and services. Advertising is necessary to facilitate those sales, meaning that marketing drives the economy. Globalization is the expansion of this economically driven model, and private-sector transnational companies are currently serving as the authoritative decision makers concerning global economic affairs. Such bodies are exempt from the prohibitions of the First Amendment. Gerbner argues that these transnational corporations use the protections of the First Amendment as a shield for privilege and for monopoly by which they claim the freedom to censor everybody else (Lent 2002). From this perspective, the current economic power system and existing protections system actually increase violence as a function of market-driven content created and distributed by relatively few, but powerful, global organizations.

Some argue that censorship fails to address the underlying problem—the economic motive behind increasing representations of mass media violence. From this perspective, a level playing field among content creators (and media owners) is necessary to minimize violent content. Antitrust laws were intended to reduce violence by admitting new entries and a greater diversity of ownership, employment, and representation (*Wired Magazine* 1997). Gerbner suggests that this problem of concentrated economic power can be addressed only by "diversifying, freeing, liberating production" (Gerbner 1999, p. 11). This approach is polarized from attempts to censor; greater liberties rather than restrictions could potentially liberate expression and representation from the existing restraints.

Some other alternatives to censorship might be more feasible, such as educational requirements emphasizing media literacy. Schools would be responsible for teaching analytical and critical viewing. Another approach would be government-subsidized programs devoted to something other than mindless, transitory entertainment. For example, Canada subsidizes public broadcasting through taxes. In Great Britain, television sets are taxed to reduce exposure to violent media. Notably, the British Board of Film Classification (BBFC) also censors some U.S. films for violence (for both adult and child viewers), and partially cuts them, even though they have already been edited for the U.S. censors (Burton 2010). Other alternatives might include charging fees to networks. The current U.S. broadcast model facilitates consolidated media ownership across broadcast networks, local stations, cable companies, and the studios that produce most of the programming. This vertical integration occurs either through direct ownership or long-term programming supply contracts that lock out potential competitors. In 2013, the network cable industry's top four players made up nearly 65% of industry revenue. These "media giants" continue to buy up and consequently control a majority of the media outlets.

Opening the market by buying and selling licenses to smaller companies could minimize immense profits resulting from the current broadcast models in the United States (*Wired Magazine* 1997).

Internationally, the problem of advertising-specific violence has been tackled more directly (e.g., European Union, Television Without Frontiers directive in 2008). In France, the Kriegal Report on the study of violence in television content has proposed radically vetting violent content on TV using technology to block the reception of violent images. In Sweden, following the launch of private television companies, the country totally prohibited child-focused advertising on television. In Spain, child protection concerning advertising is regulated by the constitution, which protects the citizen's right to truthful information and includes the obligation of honesty by professionals and companies involved in advertising (Section 20.1, paragraph d, General Advertising Act 1996, as cited in Volz, Handschuh, and Poshtakova 2005).

> In addition to that which is contained in section 3 of the General Law on Advertising, such television advertising that foments behaviour which is detrimental to health or the safety of people or for the protection of the environment . . . shall be considered illicit. Likewise, advertisements which incite violence or anti-social behaviour, which resort to fear or superstition or which can foment abuse, imprudence, negligence or aggressive behaviour shall also be considered illicit. Advertising which incites cruelty or ill treatment to people or to animals, or the destruction of cultural or environmental heritage shall likewise be considered illicit. (Act 22/1999, amending Act 25/1994, of 12 July, transposing the revised "Television Without Frontiers" into Spanish law)

ONLINE VIOLENCE: ACCESSIBILITY AND ABUNDANCE

Due to the pace of the emerging technologies, accessibility of digital content through the Internet, and existing standards of protected speech, regulating violent content on the Internet is particularly challenging (Tuthill 2013). New media forms are everywhere and interactive, unlike traditional narrative forms of advertising (e.g., print, film, and TV). Further, the Internet is part of youth culture. Children are growing up with the Internet as a daily and routine part of their lives. This creates more challenges for behavior modification due to the cultural significance and media use differences among digital natives and their parents.

Buzz marketing that relies on peer-to-peer sharing is further facilitated through social media platforms. Empirical research suggests that using violence in buzz marketing increases the spread of viral ads (Brown et al. 2010) find that violence increases the likelihood of an ad's being shared, particularly when the violence is embedded in humor. The violence in some viral ads has not gone unnoticed. For example, viral ads for the Ford SportKa (wherein a pigeon is violently dispatched), the Dodge Nitro (wherein a dog gets maliciously electrocuted by the car), and the video game Mortal Kombat have resulted in formal objections. Although advertisers were asked to remove a particular ad from circulation, the nature of the Internet is such that a campaign can be difficult to pull and may even result in more attention being directed to the advertisement.

Many Web hosting services and Web sites have user agreements, or company policies, that prohibit certain kinds of violent content. For example, Facebook recently banned ads with especially violent content. The decision was reached after the activist group Women, Action, and the Media (WAM!) urged an advertising boycott to protest grisly photos and mottos that encouraged rape, abuse, and other violence against women on Facebook. Further, self-regulatory bodies are currently attempting to create guidelines for the distribution and marketing of violent content online.

SELF-REGULATING ONLINE VIOLENCE

Self-regulatory guidelines concerning violence in interactive marketing have their own set of challenges. For example, the American Association of Advertising Agencies (AAAA) holds that the entertainment and video industries strive to market responsibly. However, professional associations cite a number of limiting factors, such as shifting societal norms, changing consumer tastes, and the rapid changes in information technologies. Adonis Hoffman, senior vice president and counsel for the AAAA, suggests that consumers lead action toward change in combination with enforceable industry standards. More specifically, Hoffman notes "we should not underestimate the power of pressure on these companies to conform to industry-developed and industry-enforced guidelines and standards, especially when combined with pressure from parents' groups and the power of competition in the market" (Parents Television Council 2009). However, any future or existing ethical or self-regulatory guidelines regarding violence are inconsequential to some content providers and independent marketers.

Notably, there is some evidence that the current culture of violence and, relatedly, the current emphasis on violence in advertising may come as a result of the industry's "conventional wisdom" rather than consumer preference. Recent research on television violence has shown that while images of violence are effective in getting people to watch, most viewers report preferences for less violent media content compared to more violent content (Weaver and Kobach 2012). This research warrants consideration of individual motivations that could be driving selective exposure to violent content.

VIOLENCE AS AN INDIVIDUAL CHOICE

New and emerging media forms increase consumer access and choice. With advancements in access to all types of media and media content, the possibility of limiting access—let alone censoring violent content—becomes more remote. In general, marketing professionals argue that changing standards and ethical guidelines should be industry-driven, and that parents should be provided the necessary tools to regain control of the violent content that enters the home. More specifically, the AAAA argues that shifting societal standards are putting pressure on marketers to cut down on violent content, while the pace of technological change and changing consumer tastes create a seemingly insurmountable challenge for content creators.

Overall, professional organizations maintain that parents have the tools for determining the level and nature of exposure to media violence. Organizations such as the Interactive Digital Software Association, a U.S. professional association of video and computer game publishers, and the Entertainment Software Ratings Board (ESRB) provide some mechanisms for minimizing exposure to violent content. For example, the ESRB uses a letter rating system to provide general guidelines for choosing age-appropriate games.

The board also writes content descriptors about the nature of the violence, sexual themes, and language of entertainment software and provides a searchable database to look up the ESRB ratings of video games. Similarly, the Internet Content Rating Association (ICRA) is a nonprofit, independent organization that seeks to empower the public, particularly parents, to make informed decisions about the material children view on the Internet by means of a content advisory system. From this site parents can activate a filter that restricts access to certain Web sites based on ICRA's standards.

DISCUSSION

The main point emerging from the preceding discussion should be that media violence is not a single thing, or of a single type. Violence comes in a variety of facades, and is used for a variety of purposes. It is a complex story, and the truth is that too little is known about its impact on society. Various theories suggest we have good reason for concern. And perhaps the most bothersome aspect is that even the youngest, most vulnerable developing minds in our civilization are being exposed repeatedly to this potential hazard. Whether or not an advertiser's reason for reliance on violence is strategically sound from a marketing communication perspective, it nonetheless contributes to a culture of violence.

Violence is not the only tool used to garner attention or convey product/service information in advertising, nor is it even one of the most common techniques. But it is not uncommon, either. Its uses are many and varied, and what we know of human behavior and cognitive processes leads to reasonable concerns about the effects of repeated exposure to violent appeals. There is no doubt that children are raised in a media surround that is inculcated with aggressive, and even horrific, themes. And advertising is a significant part of the fabric of that surround. Even if a single violent advertisement cannot be proved to have negative effects on an audience, that ad as a piece of the whole constituting a person's media environment might, in fact, be the one final catalyst for the resultant violent behavior.

Even so, the First Amendment of the U.S. Constitution stands as a firewall against well-intentioned regulatory efforts to curb such violence. It is a well-established principle that speech—commercial or otherwise—can be regulated if it threatens harm to any citizen, but only if that threat is real. "Mere speculation" is not sufficient (e.g., *44 Liquormart v. Rhode Island* 1996). While there is growing evidence that violence in media can be harmful, more evidence is needed if the use of violence in advertising, or any part of the media atmosphere, is to be legally contained. In the meantime, of course, nothing prevents advertisers from adopting an ethics-grounded policy of condemning the use of violence as an acceptable technique, at least where the product or service is not inherently related to violence (e.g., self-defense products like pepper spray and home alarms).

REFERENCES

Agence France-Press (AFP) (2007), "'Gang Rape' Dolce and Gabbana Advert Banned," News.com.au, March 7, www.news.com.au/breaking-news/gang-rape-dolce-and-gabbana-advert-banned/story-e6frfkp9-1111113111890.

American Academy of Pediatrics (2000), "Joint Statement on the Impact of Entertainment Violence on Children," Congressional Public Health Summit, July 26, www.aap.org/advocacy/releases/jstmtevc.htm.

Anderson, C.A., A. Sakamoto, D.A. Gentile, N. Ihori, A. Shibuya, S. Yukawa, M. Naito, and K. Kobayashi (2008), "Longitudinal Effects of Violent Video Games on Aggression in Japan and the United States," *Pediatrics*, 122 (5), e1067–e1072.

Andersson, S., A. Hedelin, A. Nilsson, and C. Welander (2004), "Violent Advertising in Fashion Marketing," *Journal of Fashion Marketing and Management*, 8 (1), 96–112.

Atkin, C. (1983), "Effects of Realistic Television Violence vs. Fictional Violence on Aggression," *Journalism Quarterly*, 60 (4), 615–621.

Bandura, A., D. Ross, and S.A. Ross (1963), "Imitation of Film-Mediated Aggressive Models," *Journal of Abnormal and Social Psychology*, 66, 3–11.

Bandura, A., and R. Walters (1963), *Social Learning and Personality Development*, New York: Holt, Rinehart and Winston.

Bigelow v. Virginia, 421 U.S. 809 (1975).

Brown, M.R., R.K. Bhadury, and N.K. Pope (2010), "The Impact of Comedic Violence on Viral Advertising Effectiveness," *Journal of Advertising*, 39 (1), 49–66.

Buckler, K., and S. Wilson (2010), "Media Violence Effects," in *Encyclopedia of Criminological Theory*, F. Cullen, and P. Wilcox, eds., Thousand Oaks, CA: Sage, 599–603.

Burton, G. (2010), *Media and Society: Critical Perspectives*, 2nd ed., Berkshire: Open University Press, 126–135.

Bushman, B.J. (1995), "Moderating Role of Trait Aggressiveness in the Effects of Violent Media on Aggression," *Journal of Personality and Social Psychology*, 69 (5), 950–960.

——— (2005), "Violence and Sex in Television Programs Do Not Sell Products in Advertisements," *Psychological Science*, 16 (9), 702–708.
Bushman, B.J., and C.A. Anderson (2001), "Media Violence and the American Public: Scientific Facts Versus Media Misinformation," *American Psychologist*, 56, 477–489.
Cantor, J. (2002), "The Psychological Effects of Media Violence on Children and Adolescents," presented at the Colloquium on Television and Violence in Society, Centre d'Études sur le Media, HEC Montréal, Montréal, Canada, April 19.
Central Hudson Gas & Electric v. Public Service Commission of New York, 447 U.S. 557 (1980).
Creamer, M. (2008), "Pepsi Opens a Vein of Controversy with New Suicide-Themed Ads," *Advertising Age Global,* December 2, http://adage.com/article/global-news/pepsi-opens-vein-controversy-suicide-themed-ads/132952/.
Dahl, D., K.D. Frankenberger, and R.V. Manchanda (2003), "Does It Pay to Shock? Reactions to Shocking and Nonshocking Advertising Content Among University Students," *Journal of Advertising Research,* 43 (3), 268–280.
Edwards, J. (2011), "What Were They Thinking? Mentos Ad Features Cyanide Suicide Joke," CBS News Moneywatch, April 18, www.cbsnews.com/news/what-were-they-thinking-mentos-ad-features-cyanide-suicide-joke/.
European Union (2008), "Television Broadcasting Activities: 'Television Without Frontiers' (TVWF) Directive," http://europa.eu/legislation_summaries/audiovisual_and_media/l24101_en.htm#AMENDINGACT.
Federal Trade Commission (FTC) (2009), "FTC Renews Call to Entertainment Industry to Curb Marketing of Violent Entertainment to Children," press release, December 3, www.ftc.gov/news-events/press-releases/2009/12/ftc-renews-call-entertainment-industry-curb-marketing-violent.
Ferguson, C.J. (2008), "The School Shooting/Violent Videogame Link: Causal Relationship or Moral Panic?" *Journal of Investigative Psychology and Offender Profiling,* 5 (1–2), 25–37.
———, A.M. Cruz, D. Martinez, S.M. Rueda, and D.E. Ferguson (2010), "Violence and Sex as Advertising Strategies in Television Commercials," *European Psychologist*, 15 (4), 304–311.
44 Liquormart v. Rhode Island, 517 U.S. 484 (1996).
Gerbner, G. (1999). "The stories we tell," *Peace Review*, 11(1), 9–15.
———, and L. Gross (1976), "Living with Television: The Violence Profile," *Journal of Communication*, 26, 173–199.
———, L. Gross, M. Morgan, and N. Signorielli (1994), "Growing Up with Television: The Cultivation Perspective," in *Media Effects*, J. Bryant and D. Zillmann, eds., Mahwah, NJ: Lawrence Erlbaum, 17–42.
———, L. Gross, M. Morgan, N. Signorielli, and J. Shanahan (2002), "Growing Up with Television: Cultivation Processes," in *Media Effects: Advances in Theory and Research,* 2nd ed., J. Bryant and D. Zillmann, eds., Mahwah, NJ: Lawrence Erlbaum, 43–67.
Hetherington, E.M., and N.P. Wray (1966), "Effects of Need Aggression, Stress, and Aggressive Behavior on Humor Preferences," *Journal of Personality and Social Psychology,* 4 (2), 229–230.
Huesmann, L.R. (1982), "Television Violence and Aggressive Behavior," in *Television and Behavior: Ten Years of Scientific Progress and Implications for the Eighties,* D. Pearl, L. Bouthilet, and J. Lazar, eds., Rockville, MD: National Institute of Mental Health, 126–137.
——— (1988), "An Information Processing Model for the Development of Aggression," *Aggressive Behavior*, 14, 13–24.
———, J. Moise-Titus, C.L. Podolski, and L.D. Eron (2003), "Longitudinal Relations Between Children's Exposure to TV Violence and Their Aggressive and Violent Behavior in Young Adulthood: 1977–1992," *Developmental Psychology*, 39 (2), 201–221.
———, and L.D. Taylor (2006), "The Role of Media Violence in Violent Behavior," *Annual Review of Public Health*, 27, 393–415.
Janet Reno, Attorney General of the United States, et al. v. American Civil Liberties Union et al. 521 U.S. 844 (1997).
Jhally, S. (1997), *Codes of Gender: Identity and Performance in Pop Culture* (video), Northampton, MA: Media Education Foundation.
——— (2002), *Killing Us Softly 3* (video), Northampton, MA: Media Education Foundation.
———, S. Ericsson, S. Talreja, J. Katz, and J. Earp (1999), *Tough Guise: Violence, Media, and the Crisis in Masculinity* (video), Northampton, MA: Media Education Foundation.
Kaiser Family Foundation (1996), *The Entertainment Media as "Sex Educators?" And, Other Ways Teens Learn About Sex, Contraception, STDs and AIDS*, Menlo Park, CA: Kaiser Family Foundation.
——— (1999), *Kids & Media @ The New Millennium,* Menlo Park, CA: Kaiser Family Foundation.

Kapoor, Neeru (2003), *Television Advertising and Consumer Response*, Mohan Garden, New Delhi: Mittal Publications.
Katz, J. (2011), "Advertising and the Construction of Violent White Masculinity: From BMWs to Bud Light," in *Gender, Race and Class in Media: A Critical Reader,* 2nd ed., G. Dines and J. Humez, eds., Thousand Oaks, CA: Sage, 261–269.
Keith, T. (2011), *The Bro Code: How Contemporary Culture Creates Sexist Men* (video), Northampton, MA: Media Education Foundation.
Kellner, D., and A. Cvetkovich, eds. (1997), *Articulating the Global and the Local*, Boulder, CO: Westview Press.
Kilbourne, J. (1999), *Deadly Persuasion*, New York: Free Press.
Kunkel, D., K. Cope-Farrar, E. Biely, W. Farinola, and E. Donnerstein (2001), *Sex on TV 2: A Biennial Report to the Kaiser Family Foundation Chart Pack,* Menlo Park, CA: Kaiser Family Foundation.
Kunkel, D., B. Wilson, E. Donnerstein, D. Linz, S. Smith, T. Gray, E. Blumenthal, and W.J. Potter (1995), "Measuring Television Violence: The Importance of Context," *Journal of Broadcasting and Electronic Media*, 39, 284–291.
LaTour, M., R. Snipes, and S. Bliss (1996), "Don't Be Afraid to Use Fear Appeals: An Experimental Study," *Journal of Advertising Research*, 36 (2), 59–67.
Lent, J.A. (2002), "Interview with George Gerbner," in *Against the Mainstream: The Selected Works of George Gerbner,* M. Morgan, ed., New York: Peter Lang, 21–33.
Madden, T.J., and M.G. Weinberger (1982), "The Effects of Humor on Attention in Magazine Advertising," *Journal of Advertising,* 11 (3), 8–14.
Martínez, J.I., M. Prieto, and J. Farfán (2006), "Childhood and Violence in Advertising: A Current Perspective," *International Communication Gazette*, 68, 269–289.
McNeal, J. (1992), *Kids as Customers*, Lexington, MA: Lexington Books.
Media Education Foundation (2005), "Media Violence: Facts & Statistics," www.jacksonkatz.com/PDF/ChildrenMedia.pdf.
Media Smarts (n.d.), "What Do We Know About Media Violence?" http://mediasmarts.ca/violence/what-do-we-know-about-media-violence.
Montag, C., B. Weber, P. Trautner, B. Newport, S. Markett, N.T. Walter, A. Felten, and M. Reuter (2011), "Does Excessive Play of Violent First-Person-Shooter-Video-Games Dampen Brain Activity in Response to Emotional Stimuli?" *Biological Psychology*, 89 (1), 107–111.
Murray, R. (2012), "PETA's 'Boyfriend Went Vegan' Ad Features Young Woman Who Appears to Have Been Abused," *The New York Daily News*, February 14, www.nydailynews.com/life-style/peta-controversial-new-tongue-in-cheek-ad-touting-vegan-diet-features-young-woman-appears-abused-article-1.1022655.
Mustonen, A., and L. Pulkien (1997), "Television Violence: A Development of a Coding Scheme," *Journal of Broadcasting and Electronic Media*, 41 (2), 168–189.
Nash Information Services, LLC (2013), "Domestic Movie Market Summary from 1995 to 2012," www.the-numbers.com/market/.
National Television Study (1998), ed. Margaret Seawell. Thousand Oaks, CA: Sage.
NPD Group (2013), "Group/Retail Tracking Service; Games Market Dynamics: U.S.," www.npd.com/latest-reports/video-games-consumer-purchasing-behavior-brief/.
O'Barr, W.M. (2010), "A Brief History of Advertising in America," *Advertising and Society Review,* 11 (1).
Parents Television Council (PTC) (2009), *Women in Peril: A Look at TV's Disturbing New Storyline Trend,* Los Angeles, CA: PTC.
Porter, L., and G.J. Golan (2006), "From Subservient Chickens to Brawny Men: A Comparison of Viral Advertising to Television Advertising," *Journal of Interactive Advertising*, 6 (2), 30–38.
Potter, W. James (1999), *On Media Violence*, Thousand Oaks, CA: Sage.
——— (2008), *Media Literacy*, Los Angeles: Sage.
Reichert, T., J. Lambiase, S. Morgan, M. Carstarphen, and S. Zavoina (1999), "Cheesecake and Beefcake: No Matter How You Slice It, Sexual Explicitness in Advertising Continues to Increase," *Journal of Mass Communication Quarterly*, 76, 7–20.
Rideout, V.J., E.A. Vandewater, & E.A. Wartella. (2003), *Zero to six: Electronic media in the lives of infants, toddlers and preschoolers.* Menlo Park, CA: Kaiser Family Foundation.
Rockett, W.H. (1988), *Devouring Whirlwind*, New York: Greenwood Press.
Severin, Werner J., and James W. Tankard Jr. (2001), *Communication Theories: Origins, Methods, and Uses in the Mass Media,* 5th ed., New York: Addison Wesley Longman.
Soderlund, M., and M. Dahlen (2009), "The 'Killer' Ad," *European Journal of Marketing*, 44 (11/12), 1811–1838.

Soulliere, D. (2003), "Prime-Time Murder: Presentations of Murder on Popular Television Justice Programs," *Journal of Criminal Justice and Popular Culture,* 10 (1), 12–38.

Sparks, G., and C. Sparks (2000), "Violence, Mayhem, and Horror," in *Why We Watch: The Attractions of Violent Entertainment,* J. Goldstein, ed., New York: Oxford University Press, 73–91.

Stankiewicz, J.M., and F. Rosselli (2008), "Women as Sex Objects and Victims in Print Advertisements," *Sex Roles,* 58, 579–589.

Stelter, B. (2013), "Media Companies, on Defensive About Violence, Plan Campaign on Parental Control," *New York Times,* February 27, http://mediadecoder.blogs.nytimes.com/2013/02/27/media-companies-on-defensive-about-violence-plan-campaign-on-parental-control/?_r=0.

Stewart, D.W., and D.H. Furse (1986), *Effective Television Advertising: A Study of 1000 Commercials,* Lexington, MA: Lexington Books.

Stone, B. (2006), "Killer Ads," *Newsweek* (January 25), http://msnbc.msn.com/id/11011419/site/newsweek/.

Tinic, S.A. (1997), "United Colors and Untied Meanings: Benetton and the Commodification of Social Issues," *Journal of Communication,* 47 (3), 3–26.

Tuthill, J.P. (2013), "'Protected Speech' Should Be Rethought," *San Francisco Chronicle,* January 3, www.law.berkeley.edu/14919.htm.

Van der Voort, T.H. (1986), *Television Violence: A Child's Eye View,* Amsterdam: Elsevier.

Virginia Board of Pharmacy v. Virginia Citizens Consumer Council, 425 U.S. 748 (1976).

Volz, Gerhard W., Felipe Bances Handschuh, and Dora Poshtakova (2005), "Advertising to Children in Spain," *Young Consumers,* 6 (2), 71–76, www.gala-marketlaw.com/pdf/LegalSpainfinal.pdf.

Wadley, Carma (1993), "Selling It to Kids," *Deseret News,* March 1, www.deseretnews.com/article/277993/SELLING-IT-TO-KIDS.html?pg=all.

Weaver, A.J., and M.J. Kobach (2012), "The Relationship Between Selective Exposure and the Enjoyment of Television Violence," *Aggressive Behavior,* 38 (2), 175–184.

Webb, T., L. Jenkins, N. Browne, A.A. Afifi, and J. Kraus (2007), "Violent Entertainment Pitched to Adolescents: An Analysis of PG-13 Films," *Pediatrics,* 119 (6), 1219–1229.

Weinberger, M.G., and L. Campbell (1991), "The Use and Impact of Humor in Radio Advertising," *Journal of Advertising Research,* 30 (6), 44–52.

Wells, W., J. Burnett, and S. Moriarty (1998), *Advertising: Principles and Practice,* Upper Saddle River, NJ: Prentice Hall.

Wired Magazine (1997), "Is Media Violence Free Speech?" *Hot Wired,* June, http://mediagovernance.univie.ac.at/fileadmin/user_upload/p_mediagovernance_industriesresearchgroup/Ressourcen/Is_Media_Violence_Free_Speech.pdf.

ZenithOptimedia (2012), "Global Advertising Spending Percentage Growth Rate 2013 vs 2012 by Media Type (graph)," December 3.

Zillmann, D. (1998), "The Psychology of the Appeal of Portrayals of Violence," in *Why We Watch: The Attractions of Violent Entertainment,* J. Goldstein, ed., New York: Oxford University Press, 179–211.

16

Violence in Advertising

A Multilayered Content Analysis

Tim Jones, Peggy H. Cunningham, and Katherine Gallagher

Most people in the developed world are routinely exposed to violence in television and film, video games, music, the Internet, and advertising. Public concern about media violence, particularly with "excessive quantity, graphic detail, interactive nature (in video and computer games), and gratuitous fictional and non-fictional violence" is growing (Cooper 2008, p. 23).

The effects of exposure to violent media content are well established. Positive associations between media violence and aggressive thoughts, hostile emotions, and aggressive or violent behavior have been found repeatedly, in both children and adults, in studies using a variety of methods, including laboratory and field experiments, cross-sectional studies, and longitudinal research (Anderson and Bushman 2002; Anderson et al. 2003).

Violence in advertising has received much less research attention than has violence in other types of media. This may be understandable given the relatively small amount of time people are exposed to advertising compared to the amount of time they spend consuming content from television, films, video games, music, and the Internet. However, because advertising executions are intended specifically to get and keep audience attention, to persuade, and to be memorable, the power of advertising to affect audience thoughts, emotions, and behaviors, both intended and unintended, is likely to be disproportionate to its share of audience viewing time. In addition, public concern about violence in advertising is persistent and increasing, prompting greater scrutiny by authorities responsible for responding to complaints about advertising (e.g., Advertising Standards Canada 2006).

If one were to ask audience members their general opinion about violent advertising, most would respond that "violent advertising is bad." Our research focuses on the question of whether violent advertising executions are always unethical. We propose that the use of violence in advertising may not be unequivocally bad, and that it may be appropriate in some contexts. Our research goal is to identify a set of normative recommendations for the use of violence in advertising. To this end, we use a multilayered analysis to assess the forms of violence used in advertising, the factors that might justify the use of violence in an advertisement, and the circumstances under which a violent advertisement might be considered appropriate within an ethics paradigm.

Our literature review and subsequent multilayered content analysis addresses these questions. Our normative marketing ethics approach identifies when violence in advertising might be an ethical marketing practice. We hope that this approach will provide advertisers with clear, actionable criteria to guide them in deciding whether and how to use violent content in advertising, to help policymakers and regulators determine whether violent content in an advertisement is ethical, to offer advocates for better advertising practice the basis for a set of benchmarks upon which to measure progress, and to give researchers a framework for measuring and analyzing the possible effects of violent content in advertising. In addition, our approach avoids the common pitfalls of prevailing approaches to marketing ethics that separate marketing and ethical decision making (Abela and Murphy 2008) by integrating previous research on media violence and empirical observations of violence in advertising with a normative ethical framework.

We begin by reviewing the literature on violence in media and in advertising, its prevalence, impact, and effectiveness. This is supplemented by an analysis of the observable features (manifest content) of a sample of violent advertisements. We then classify a sample of print advertisements and television commercials into themes (latent content). This procedure permits a systematic approach to analyzing violent content in advertisements. Finally, using this classification scheme, we use normative ethical theory to develop guidelines for the use of violence in advertising.

LITERATURE REVIEW

Concern about violence in society—domestic violence, bullying and violence in schools, road rage, media violence, workplace violence, violence-related products such as guns and video games, and violence in sports—has been growing. Media violence has long been an area of concern and has been thoroughly researched since 1952 (Smith 2002). The National Television Violence study (Debling 1998), a content analysis of over 8,000 hours of broadcast and cable television, found that over 60% of the programming aired in the United States contained violence. With the Internet allowing consumers to view content from around the world, consumer exposure to violent content may increase. Furthermore, such content is often beyond the regulatory domain of any single country.

The effects of media violence have been hotly debated. (See Freedman 2002 for an overview of the research contributing to the controversy.) While Freedman concludes that the negative effects of violent media content are questionable, Bushman and Anderson (2001) point to over 1,000 studies, both qualitative and quantitative, that show a consistent link between violent programming and increased aggression, especially among children. To counteract concerns about media violence, some voluntary codes have been developed and implemented (e.g., the Voluntary Code Regarding Violence in Television Programming developed by the Canadian Association of Broadcasters [www.cab-acr.ca/english/social/codes/violencecode.shtm], and the Czechoslovakian code, which prohibits linking violence with the advertisement of alcoholic products [www.eucam.info/eucam/czech_republic/]).

The rich literature on media violence indicates that, first, violent content is prevalent in television programs and many other forms of media, and second, violent content is multifaceted, nuanced, and complex. There are a variety of forms of violence, contexts in which violence occurs, and varying levels of intensity of violence. Such complexity makes accurate counts of violence in media difficult and conclusions from research into the effects of exposure to such violence tenuous. Some content analyses have attempted to overcome these difficulties by specifically examining the nature of violent content and the frequency in which it occurs in a variety of media (Gerbner and Gross 1976; Gosselin et al. 1997; Mustonen and Pulkkinen 1997; Paik and Comstock 1994; Wilson et al. 1997; Wilson et al. 2002).

Research on the frequency of violent content in advertising is surprisingly sparse, particularly given concerns about its effects (e.g., increased tolerance for aggression, increased violent behavior). Table 16.1 summarizes the samples and sample sizes, dependent variables, and findings of 13 studies. Estimates of the prevalence of violence in television advertising vary widely, ranging from about 3% in general programming (Maguire, Sandage, and Weatherby 2000) to 62% in food ads aimed at children (Rajecki et al. 1994). Caution should be used in comparing rates of violence found due to differences in definitions of violence and aggression, but it does seem that the frequency of violent content in advertising aimed at children is at least as high as and perhaps higher than that in advertising intended for a wider audience.

Table 16.1

Studies Pertaining to Violent Advertising

Study	Focus	Sample	Sample size	Dependent variable	Frequency of violence
Maguire, Sandage, and Weatherby (2000)	TV commercials during general programming	Representative TV commercials from eight American networks in 1996 and 1997	1,699 TV commercials	Violent content	2.8%
Scharrer et al. (2006)	TV commercials during general programming	One week of TV commercials in prime-time programming on American broadcast networks in 2004	4,347 TV commercials	Aggression	12.3%
Jones and Cunningham (2008)	TV commercials during general programming	Advertisements extracted from 200 hours of Canadian prime-time television over two weeks across five channels in 2005	7,717 TV commercials	Ads containing violence	12.9%
Anderson (1997)	TV commercials during sporting events	TV commercials aired during the 1996 Major League Baseball Playoffs	1,528 TV commercials	Violent content	6.8%
Anderson (2000)	TV commercials during sporting events	TV commercials aired during the 1998 Major League Baseball Playoffs	1,550 TV commercials	Violent content	8.8%
Tamburro et al. (2004)	TV commercials during sporting events	TV commercials aired during major sporting events aired before 9:00 P.M. for one year beginning September 1, 2001	1,185 TV commercials	Violence	6%
Macklin and Kolbe (1984)	Advertising aimed at children	TV commercials shown on the major American television networks on Saturday mornings in 1982	64 TV commercials	Aggressive content	12.5%
Rajecki et al. (1994)	Advertising aimed at children	Food ads aimed at children	92 TV commercials	Violence as a surface theme	62%
Larson (2001, 2003)	Advertising aimed at children	TV commercials featuring children in children's programming on Saturday mornings and weekday afternoons	595 TV commercials	Aggression	62%

(*continued*)

Table 16.1 (continued)

Study	Focus	Sample	Sample size	Dependent variable	Frequency of violence
Shanahan, Hermans, and Hyman (2003)	Advertising aimed at children	Minutes of children's TV programming	1,110 minutes of children's programming	Acts of violence per minute	3.46 per minute of commercials; 2.25 per minute of programming
Ji and Laczniak (2007)	Advertising aimed at children	TV commercials aired in programs children were most likely to watch	297 TV commercials	Violent or aggressive behaviors or scenes	10%
		TV commercials aired in programs younger children were most likely to watch			13%
		TV commercials aired in programs older children were most likely to watch			4.8%
Oliver and Kalyanaraman (2002)	Violence in movie previews on video rentals	Randomly selected 1996 Billboard Top-20 rental movies	47 movie previews	Acts of aggression per minute	2.52
				Gun scenes per minute	2.37
				Explosions per minute	.83
				At least one scene of aggression	75.7%
				At least one gun scene	45.8%
				At least one explosion	28%
Scharrer (2004)	Violence in print advertising	Print advertisements for video games appearing in large-circulation video game magazines	1,054 print advertisements for video games	Violence	55.8%

Many people find violence in advertising offensive (Christy and Haley 2007; Lawson 1985), but violent executions have been used for positive ends as well (e.g., antidrinking and driving campaigns). Violence has also been associated with different types of advertising appeals such as fear appeals (e.g., for self-defense products), informational appeals (e.g., for products that have a violent component, such as certain video games), and shock appeals (e.g., some fashion advertisements).

Fear appeals attempt to frighten target audience members in order to motivate them to take appropriate precautionary, self-protective action (Ruiter, Abraham, and Kok 2001). This approach is based on the belief that some form of arousal is required for behavior change (Henthorne, LaTour, and Nataraajan 1993). Violent executions have been used to instill fear in viewers (LaTour, Snipes, and Bliss 1996; Schoenbachler and Whittler 1996). Fear arousal has been found to enhance interest in the ad (LaTour, Snipes, and Bliss 1996); attitude toward the ad (LaTour, Snipes, and Bliss 1996); persuasion (Henthorne, LaTour, and Nataraajan 1993); and behavioral intentions (LaTour, Snipes, and Bliss 1996; Lewis, Watson, and Tay 2007). However, fear is a complex emotion that is not fully understood in the context of advertising, so results have been inconsistent (see, e.g., LaTour 2006; LaTour and Zahra 1989).

Informational appeals focus on consumers' practical, functional, or utilitarian needs. The content of informational advertising emphasizes facts, learning, and logical persuasion. In general, this appeal assumes that target audience members are open to the information provided in the advertisement, and that they will then use the information to make a decision about the subject of the advertising (Shimp 2003). Finally, some products, services, or ideas have a violent component. For instance, some video games are violent, as are some sporting events. In addition, some social marketing campaigns are concerned with violent issues such as domestic violence or cruelty to animals. In such cases, a violent execution may be used simply to provide information.

Shock appeals deliberately startle and upset audiences. One of the ways this can be accomplished is through gratuitous violence (Dahl, Frankenberger, and Manchanda 2003). The practitioner literature suggests several motives for using shock appeals: to capture audience attention (Croft 2002; deChenecey 2000; Garrett 1999; Jones 2002; Tomblin 2002; Woodward 2005), to attract media interest that will result in free publicity (Croft 2002; Garrett 1999; Jones 2002; Woodward 2005), to raise awareness (Croft 2002), to affect attitudes (Guria and Leung 2004), to enhance recall (Jones 2002), to influence behaviors (Guria and Leung 2004), and ultimately, to increase sales and profits (FrenchConnection 2008) or to achieve other mission-related goals. Dahl, Frankenberger, and Manchanda (2003) found that shocking content is superior to nonshocking content in its ability to attract attention and facilitate memory for the advertisement.

Only a few studies have examined the effectiveness of advertising with violent content. In a semiotic analysis of three violent fashion advertisements appearing in magazines, Andersson et al. (2004) found that respondent interpretations of the violent content were different and more negative than advertisers expected. Gunter, Furnham, and Pappa (2005) found that the violent version of a target advertisement was much better remembered than the nonviolent version when it appeared in a violent film clip. However, Bushman's (2007) study showed that violent ads were no more memorable than were neutral ads. Lewis, Watson, and Tay (2007) found that females were more likely than males to change their behavioral intentions in response to a violent social marketing advertisement.

In sum, estimates of the prevalence of violence in advertising vary widely. Advertisers seem to use violence for a variety of reasons: to capture attention, raise awareness, provide information, affect attitudes, enhance recall, and influence behavior. It is unclear, though, whether violence in advertising is actually effective for two reasons. First, only a few dependent variables have been tested (i.e., interpretation, recall, and behavioral intentions). Second, the results of the effectiveness studies have been inconsistent. We propose that one reason for these equivocal results is that varying definitions of violence have been used in previous research. The presence or absence of other factors might also have affected results. We conducted our content analysis as a way of identifying these other factors.

A MULTILAYERED CONTENT ANALYSIS

We used a multilayered content analysis approach in this research. In general, content analysis involves creating categories (or themes) from the data and then developing rules for assigning instances into these categories. Boyatzis (1998) defines a theme as a pattern in the phenomenon of interest that describes and organizes observations of the phenomenon and may also interpret aspects of it. Themes may be identified at the manifest level, in which they are directly observable (e.g., the number of violent acts per commercial), or at the latent level, in which they underlie the phenomenon (e.g., the meaning, causes, or consequences of violent content). In this study, to focus on more meaning-based understandings of violent content in advertising, we examined manifest content at the level of the advertisement and generated latent themes at two additional levels (see Table 16.2).

In the first layer of our analysis, we examined manifest content—the easily observable features of the advertisement that are salient for categorization. This included content such as words, visuals, pictures, specific behaviors, and sex of participants. We began by reviewing previous content analyses of violent content in media and programming to uncover commonly observed phenomena. Then, we examined a selection of violent advertisements to confirm the existence of the same phenomena as well as to identify other violent features unique to advertising.

In the second layer, we focused on latent content or themes. The classification of "latent pattern" content relies on the identification of themes relevant to the manifest content. These themes or latent patterns are implicit rather than directly observed. They may be constructed either deductively (based on theory or prior research) or inductively (directly from the phenomenon) (Boyatzis 1998, p. 4). We used both approaches. We read content analyses in media violence research (e.g., Mustonen and Pulkkinen 1997) that used similar approaches to get insight into the themes that appear in research on violence in media. In addition, we examined violent advertisements and made judgments about whether each was inappropriate, offensive, or unethical. We approached the analysis in this manner because of the prevailing belief that "violent advertising is bad."

In the third layer, we examined violent advertising from a normative ethical perspective. Our approach in this layer was deductive: we used existing normative ethical theory to uncover situations in which the use of violent content in advertising might be considered either ethical or unethical. In essence, we applied ethical principles to the themes uncovered in the latent content analysis in layer 2 to better understand when and if the use of violent content in advertising is ever ethical.

The result of this multilayered approach is a set of guidelines for use by practitioners and policymakers as well as a set of potential variables that can be used to guide future research on violent advertising.

Data Collection

To aid in our analysis, we amassed a collection of violent advertisements using a selective sampling procedure (Draucker et al. 2007). This approach is useful for situations in which sampling for proportionality is not the primary concern (Trochim 2006) and in situations such as latent content analyses where the purpose of the sampling approach is to find exemplars of a certain phenomena.

For this research, the population of interest was advertisements with violent content in consumer magazines available in Canada. The sampling site was a university library and advertisements

Table 16.2

Multilayered Content Analysis

Layer	1	2	3
Type of content	Manifest content	Latent content	Normative content
Level of analysis	Advertisement	Audience member	Societal
Type of data	Observable	Interpretations by researcher	
Research approach	Inductive (from advertisements) and deductive (from violent media research)	Inductive (from advertisements) and deductive (from violent media research)	Deductive (from ethical principles)
Descriptions	• Mode of violence (physical, psychological) • Seriousness (realization of violence, consequences) • Dramatization (duration, atmosphere, clarity and vividness)	Intensity	Nonmaleficence Autonomy
	• **Consistent with product category*** • **Consistent with main message of ad—brand/issue***	Congruence	Autonomy
	• Authorial or sponsor intent—social commentary versus attention tactic*	Perceived intention	Utility
	• Justification (intentionality, motivation, planned) • Legality • **Correspondence with genre/context***	Legitimacy	Utility
	• Realism (cultural distance) • Realism (temporal distance) • Realism (fictionality)	Identification	Honesty
	• Power of aggressor (sex, age of aggressor, characteristics) • Power of victim (sex, age, characteristics) • Glamorization (nature of aggressor/victim) • Efficacy of violence/depicted outcomes (profitability)	Power balance	Respect

*Represents manifest content unique to violent advertisements. Boldface added for emphasis.

were selected by two undergraduate students, one male and one female, who each spent 20 hours over three months identifying ads for coding. They identified violent advertisements according to the operational definition: "any explicit act of force destined to injure or kill, or the expression of any serious threat to injure or kill a character, whether human or human-like, regardless of the context in which the act occurred" (Gosselin et al. 1997, p. 143). Some magazines sampled were general interest (e.g., *Maclean's, Time*) and some were women's magazines (e.g., *Vogue*), men's magazines (e.g., *Esquire, GQ*), and special interest magazines (e.g., *Ski Canada, Sportsnet*). The students looked at each page of every magazine they chose. The library chosen as the data source typically displayed current copies of magazines for two to five years (depending on the popularity of such magazines) before they were discarded. Thus, all of the advertisements collected for this study were published within an approximate five-year period, between 2000 and 2005. This procedure resulted in a data set of 98 magazine advertisements.

We also collected a second set of violent advertisements, video advertisements found on the Web site www.adcritic.com, to validate the magazine ad content analysis. A graduate student selected commercials with violent content using the same operational definition. She dedicated 20 hours to scanning the Web site for commercials on the Web site for violent content. This procedure resulted in a 36-commercial data set.

Layer 1: Manifest Content Analysis

Content analysis, at a manifest level, has frequently been used to study violence in advertising (Anderson 1997; Scharrer 2004; Scharrer et al. 2006; Tabburro et al. 2004). This method has provided valuable insight into the number of occurrences of violence in advertising; however, few of these studies have gone beyond simple counts of violent advertisements or acts of violence. The content analyses of television violence conducted in the communications field, however, are much further developed. These studies have developed coding schemes for use in future research on the audience-level effects of exposure to media violence (Gosselin et al. 1997; Huesmann et al. 2003; Mustonen and Pulkkinen 1997; Wilson et al. 1997; Wilson et al. 2002). Such coding schemes have allowed research to capture some of the complexities of violent content.

A review of the coding schemes used in media research revealed a number of content variables relevant to the study of violent advertising. In this research, we adopted and adapted the coding scheme used by Mustonen and Pulkkinen (1997). Our initial review of the print sample identified content unique to advertisements: the link between violence to the purpose of the advertisement and the authorial intention for the use of the violence.

The first area of unique content is the issue of the link between the violence and other aspects of the advertisement such as the category (e.g., product, service, television program, event), the specific brand, or the genre or context of the advertisement (e.g., slice of life, slapstick comedy, sports). For example, an advertisement about a video game might depict violence because the game itself is violent (see Appendix 16.1, Figures 1–3). Another advertisement might present its appeal in the context of a sport, such as ice hockey or football—games that include some violence.

The second area of unique content is the issue of authorial intent. A number of the advertisements included violence specifically for the purpose of social commentary or providing an antiviolence message (see, e.g., Appendix 16.1, Figures 1–5). While it could be argued that there are television programs with the same goal of social commentary, they have not been the focus of content analyses of violent television programming. Because one of our purposes is to ascertain the ethicality of violent advertisements, such content is relevant since a violent advertisement with a positive intention may be ethical.

Our final coding scheme consisted of 30 content variables relevant to the analysis of violent advertisements (see Appendix 16.2). Each content variable includes several categories. For example, the content variable "primary mode of physical violence" includes eight different categories, such as "hitting with weapons or tools" and "strangling." We used this coding scheme to assess the violent content used in the magazine advertisement sample. Four trained undergraduate students independently coded each of the 98 magazine advertisements on each of the 30 content variables. The training session consisted of a detailed explanation of each of the content variables as well as a four-advertisement practice set that included extensive discussion among the coders and the research team.

In Appendix 16.2, we also report interrater reliabilities (IRR) and the frequencies of each category of each content variable. We assessed interrater reliabilities using the Perreault and Leigh (1989) reliability formula. The interrater reliability was 75% on average for all content variables, ranging from 53% to 91%, which for exploratory work such as this is acceptable. For some content variables (e.g., Purpose of the advertisement: to promote a product/service, to raise awareness of a social issue, to promote an upcoming program/movie, to promote an upcoming event, other), there was substantial interrater agreement (i.e., IRR > 80%). On the other hand, for content variables that required coders to make more subjective judgments (e.g., Efficacy: extent that the aggressor profits by violence: cannot code; not at all, a little bit, a lot), as might be expected, strength of agreement was only fair (IRR = 53%). In addition, the coding scheme we used was relatively unrefined; we identified several content variables in which categories could be combined to enhance reliability. For example, in the category Seriousness: aggressor's intent, 61% of the advertisements were coded for physical harms (to injure or to kill) as opposed to more psychological harms (to have fun, to threaten, or to insult). Such fine-grained distinctions among harms required the coders to make attributions about the violence and thereby depressed interrater reliabilities. The depiction of violence in advertisements when compared with media violence in general is less straightforward because advertising faces both time and space constraints. For example, a television commercial may not have the time to show a complete violent act, thus making the coding of its consequences a subjective opinion. The implication of this is that coding advertisements for violent content should emphasize agreement at the latent level (e.g., intensity, legitimacy) rather than the manifest level, since agreement at the latent level is acceptable (IRR = 66% to 80%).

Our frequency analysis began with the calculation of the reliabilities of the decisions made by all six pairs of coders for each content variable (recall that four coders assessed the 30 content variables for each of the 98 advertisements). To maximize reliability, we selected the pair of coders with the highest level of agreement within a given content variable across all 98 advertisements. If the two coders agreed on the category for a content variable for a particular advertisement, we used this pair's decision. If this pair did not agree, we resolved the disagreement by using the decision of the coder with the next highest level of agreement with the first pair. If there was still disagreement, we used the remaining coder's decision to resolve the disagreement. Of 2,940 coding instances, there were only 19 occurrences (<1%) when there was disagreement among all four coders. Only two of the 98 advertisements (~2%) had two content variables in which the coders could not agree. The remaining advertisements were either fully coded ($n = 81$; 83%) or had one content variable in which the coders could not agree ($n = 15$; 15%). In other words, the sample does not contain any advertisements that defied coding on more than two of the 30 content variables.

According to our frequency analysis (Appendix 16.2), this sample contained many different forms of violence consistent with the coding scheme developed by Mustonen and Pulkkinen (1997). For example, we found instances of both physical and psychological violence and of every type of consequence (e.g., harm to property/objects; mild, moderate, and severe injuries to people/living things; and death). Thus, all the content variables found in studies of violent media also appear in violent advertisements. We found one exception within content variable categories: there were no instances in which the aggressors included people of several age groups. We speculate that this exception is a result of a deficiency in the representativeness of our sample, as there is no obvious reason to expect that violent advertisements could not contain instances of groups of aggressors.

In addition to the forms of violent content found in media research, we confirmed that violent advertisements have some unique characteristics. First, we found advertisements in which the violence was both consistent (44%) and not consistent (56%) with the product category, the product category was clear (13%) and not clear (87%) to the audience member, and the inclusion of violence was consistent (54%) and not consistent (46%) with the positioning of the brand. Second, we found advertisements in which the purpose of the advertisement was to promote a product/service (80%), to raise awareness of a social issue (5%), to promote an upcoming program/movie (11%), and to promote an upcoming event (2%). Attributions for the inclusion of violence in the advertisement included the following: to enhance viewer interest/attention to the ad (74%), to make a social commentary about violence (7%), or to realistically depict a product category or context (16%).

Because violence in advertising occurs in many different forms, under several different contexts, with varying underlying motivations, and because it may be directed at various entities, research directed at uncovering the effects of exposure to violence is difficult. The natural question that arises from identification of all of these different characteristics of violence in advertising is as follows: "Are there common elements that will allow us to make generalizations about the nature of violent advertising?" Such generalizations require a latent content analysis, which we present next.

Layer 2: Latent Content Analysis

The purpose of this second layer of analysis was to organize the manifest content in Layer 1 into a number of higher-level abstractions or conceptual categories. We used a blended grounded theory approach (see Locke 2001) that uses both the data and the existing substantive theory on violence to inform our latent content development.

Two of the researchers generated latent content/themes based on their observations of the entire print advertisement data set ($n = 98$). We approached the analysis with the intention of finding examples of violent advertisements that could be considered not unethical. We then sought to explain why these particular advertisements that had violent content were not unethical.

Boyatzis (1998) warns against the natural tendency to project researcher values, thoughts, feelings, and competencies onto the data. To lessen contamination from projection, our research team came to the data with different perspectives. First, because the experience and interpretation of violence may differ across genders, we thought it important to have a mixed-gender team. In addition, the two researchers who performed the latent content analysis are focused in different areas of marketing. One has a background in ethics, the other in consumer behavior. Both have training in advertising. Each researcher examined the violent advertisements and made notes on what underlying themes might be present. We then met to compare notes and negotiate a common set of themes.

We identified six themes that might influence the appropriateness of an advertisement depicting violence: intensity of the violent depiction, congruence between violent content and the product or message, perceived intention behind the use of violence in the advertisement, legitimacy of the violence given the context, identification with the victim, and the extent of power imbalance between victim and aggressor. For each theme, we looked for similar themes in violence-in-the-media research. We uncovered three similar themes in the violent media research area and identified three themes unique to violent advertising.

We validated these themes by examining the television commercial data set. Two of the researchers looked for exemplars in the commercial data set that represent both high and low versions of each theme (see Appendix 16.3). For example, to validate the *intensity* theme, we identified one commercial that was considered by the researchers to be high in intensity and one commercial that was considered by the researchers to be low in intensity. We found exemplars of the extreme levels of all six themes in this data set (e.g., high/low intensity, congruent/incongruent, legitimate/illegitimate, positive/negative intention, realistic/fictional, empowerment/victimization). Because we were able to identify the six themes in this independent data set, we inferred that the themes were valid.

Theme 1: Intensity

We define "intensity" as the extent to which an advertisement displays violence as the powerful, forceful, explicit, and graphic presentation of violence. For example, depicting murder would be high in intensity, whereas showing a person shoving in a crowded place would be considered low in intensity. This theme stems from the manifest content of mode, seriousness, and dramatization aspects of the violence. This same theme has been identified in media research as extent and graphicness (Mustonen and Pulkkinen 1997).

This notion of intensity stems from research in psychology on stimulus and object valence. Events, objects, or situations may possess intrinsic attractiveness or aversiveness (Frijda 1986). Positive or negative emotions are said to be elicited by positive or negative stimuli such as pictures or words (Cacioppo and Berntson 1994), events (Bradley and Lang 2000), or film clips (Lang, Davis, and Ohman 2000). Viewers often perceive advertisements containing intense violence as a negative stimulus (Barnes and Dotson 1990).

The intensity of the violence depicted in the advertisements in our samples varied. An advertisement for plastic wrap (see Appendix 16.4 and Appendix 16.1, Figures 1–2) contains low levels of violence. This and similar ads use violence or references to violence as a metaphor for an attribute of the product (e.g., built tough). In contrast, an ad for sunglasses (see Appendix 16.4 and Appendix 16.1, Figure 1) and an ad for an advertising firm (see Appendix 16.3) show disturbing levels of physical violence (through depictions of blood and gore) and emotional violence (the threat of violence to a vulnerable victim), respectively. The "chain saw" commercial by a leading athletic shoemaker (see Appendix 16.3) is so intense that it was withdrawn from television after complaints from viewers.

Theme 2: Congruence

We define "congruence" as the extent to which the violent content in an advertisement is consistent with the product category or, in the case of social marketing messages, the main message in the ad. The idea of executional congruence (or relatedness) has appeared in a number of advertising studies on the use of humor (e.g., Zhang and Zinkhan 1991), with the central argument being that related humor can serve as issue-relevant arguments, thereby helping to provide benefit claims. Similarly, we suggest that issue-relevant violence may help to provide benefit claims about a particular violent product or marketing issue.

Our samples contained examples of both high- and low-congruence advertising violence. Some advertised products, such as many video games, television programs, movies, and sports, are inherently violent. The use of violence in advertisements intended to promote these products is consistent with their nature. For example, an advertisement for a program on the A&E network (see Appendix 16.4) shows a dead body covered in a white sheet. Viewers can infer from this advertisement that the show includes violence. Similarly, an advertisement for a video game (see Appendix 16.4 and Appendix 16.1, Figures 1–3) depicts characters in the game using violence. The viewer can infer from this advertisement that the game itself is violent. Yet in some advertisements, violent content is simply an executional element designed to garner viewer attention. For instance, the "Trunk Monkey" commercial for an automobile sales group (see Appendix 16.3) shows two episodes of violence: an angry driver verbally abusing another driver and the "Trunk Monkey" assaulting the angry driver with a tire iron. The violence in this commercial is not naturally connected to the automotive product category.

Theme 3: Perceived Intention

We define "perceived intention" as the viewer's attributions about the sponsor's purpose for including violence in an advertisement. The Persuasion Knowledge Model (Friestad and Wright 1994) suggests that people are aware of advertisers' goals and tactics, and that they can use this knowledge actively and skillfully. Perceived intention, therefore, is a judgment made by the viewer/reader about authorial intent—the intended meaning (Ahuvia 1998). Here, attributions of intent are based on the assessment of the violence and the corresponding inferences about intentions made by the viewers (B. Phillips 1997).

Violent advertising that might be perceived to have positive intentions would include advertising aimed at raising awareness of a social issue that involves violence (e.g., capital punishment, domestic violence, war, torture), and social marketing advertising campaigns designed to persuade target audience members to alter a harmful behavior (e.g., drive less aggressively). Violent advertising that might be perceived to have negative intentions would include the depiction of violence merely to increase attention to the advertisement and motivation to process and remember it.

A fashion advertisement (see Appendix 16.4 and Appendix 16.1, Figures 1–6) in our sample depicts explicit violent content with no text other than the brand name. This tactic seems to be used only to increase attention to the advertisement. In contrast, an advertisement for a community charity (Appendix 16.4) shows the disturbing results of violence, but the intent of the advertisement is to raise awareness of a social issue, namely, abuse of women and children. Similarly, Benetton advertisements (see Appendix 16.4 and Appendix 16.1, Figures 1–5) have often been used as a form of social commentary against violence.

Theme 4: Legitimacy

We define "legitimate violence" as behavior that is legal or appropriate given the context. The idea of "legitimacy" in this context has its roots in sociology and criminal justice, specifically the work done in the creation of the Violence Approval Index (Baron, Straus, and Jaffee 1988), which is based on directly expressed attitudes about when it is appropriate to use physical force. While the index finds regional variations in the approval of some forms of violence, there is consensus on a number of legitimate forms of violence. For example, activities such as hunting, the playing of contact sports, or the use of reasonable force in self-defense or in the protection of others are considered legitimate violence. Violent activities that are criminal or illegal in the context are considered illegitimate violence. The theme of legitimacy has also appeared in the research on media violence under the term "justified violence" (e.g., Mustonen and Pulkkinen 1997).

Note that legitimate violence differs from congruent violence. While congruent violence refers to a violent product (e.g., a violent video game, a violent movie, a gun), legitimate violence refers to the violent act depicted in the advertisement (e.g., a police officer using force to restrain a criminal or a hockey player body checking an opponent).

Many violent advertisements in our samples incorporate legitimate scenes from sports, connecting the advertised product with the lifestyle, behaviors, and attitudes associated with that sport (see Appendix 16.4 and Appendix 16.1, Figures 1–7), which would be deemed legitimate in that context. Or the advertisement may depict legitimate use of force defined by an aggressor's role. For example, an advertisement for a news program shows a scene involving police in riot gear (see Appendix 16.4 and Appendix 16.1, Figures 1–10). The police are exhibiting a legitimate use of force. In contrast, the advertisement for a brand of snowboards shows what appears to be a violent and presumably illegal interrogation of a prisoner (see Appendix 16.4). Similarly, an advertisement for a handbag brand displays a woman being held at gunpoint (see Appendix 16.1, Figures 1–8). Both are examples of illegitimate violence.

Theme 5: Identification

We define "identification" as the extent to which viewers have a natural connection or association with the characters in the advertisement. The idea of association with the characters in the advertisement has its roots in Social Identity Theory (Tajfel and Turner 1986), which asserts that group membership creates feelings of belongingness and association with other group members. Thus, if a viewer identifies with the victim of a violent act, the violence will be perceived as more harmful than if the viewer does not identify with the victim. The theme of identification has appeared in research on media violence as "realism" (Mustonen and Pulkkinen 1997) and the "nature of the perpetrator" (Wilson et al. 2002).

In some cases, advertising violence occurs in what is clearly a fictional or imaginary setting such as cartoons or fantastic settings, inhibiting identification. For example, the chocolate bar advertisement in our sample (see Appendix 16.4 and Appendix 16.1, Figures 1–9) shows physical bullying, but uses two characters from an animated television series. This act of bullying may be relatively less offensive because the characters are obviously not real. While we may recognize the two characters in the advertisement, we see this execution as fictional. Fictionalized executions may thus lessen the impact of the violence they contain.

In contrast, some ads use realistic or documentary-type scenes of violence. For example, an advertisement encouraging people to subscribe to a newspaper (see Appendix 16.4) shows a photograph of a Ku Klux Klan rally in which a cross is burning in a field. The advertisement asks whether this is occurring in Mississippi, Alabama, or Ontario. Similarly, advertisements for news programs often show real violence (see, e.g., Appendix 16.1, Figures 1–10). Because these images are realistic, they may result in stronger and more emotional reactions than fictional representations since the viewer can identify with the victim.

Theme 6: Power Balance

We define "power balance" as the viewer's perception of the differences in power possessed by the characters in a violent advertisement. Characters who gain from violence are empowered, while those who are harmed are victimized. While most violent acts involve an imbalance of power, the extent to which the viewer identifies with the empowered versus the victimized is the salient issue. This theme can be explained by theories of perspective taking and empathy. "Perspective taking" refers to the imaginative ability that allows people to imagine themselves in the place of another. "Empathy" is the capability to share feelings and understand another's emotion and feelings. To the extent that a viewer identifies with the empowered character, he or she would find the violence acceptable; to the extent that the viewer identifies with the victim, he or she would find the violence less acceptable. In media research, this idea of power balance has been examined using the idea of rewards and punishments—that is, the extent to which one benefits from the violence versus being punished for violent acts (Wilson et al. 2002).

In some advertisements in our samples, the featured product empowers an individual to combat a violent force. For example, a breath freshener advertisement uses phrases such as "to fight the evil Gingivitis" and "to destroy bad breath." One such advertisement (see Appendix 16.4) shows a woman able to fight the "bad breath monster" using the product as a weapon. Similarly, we find a woman empowered by her running shoes in the chain saw commercial (see Appendix

16.3). In horror-movie style, this commercial shows a woman being pursued by a villain wearing a hockey mask. She is able to outrun him, presumably because of the performance of her brand of running shoes.

Violence in some advertisements in our samples does not have a positive consequence for the protagonist. These advertisements depict victimization, including dominance over women and what Kilbourne (1979, 1987, 2000) calls the "dehumanizing" of the character featured in the ad. In a perfume advertisement (see Appendix 16.4 and Appendix 16.1, Figures 1–11), a naked woman is shown with her hands bound behind her back. The central figure in this advertisement is clearly a victim and the product in no way saves her from the circumstances.

In sum, the results of this latent content analysis reveal six important themes inherent in the literature on media violence as well as in the content of a sample of violent advertisements. These themes help to describe the nature of the violent content in advertising. Many of these themes are also found in analyses of violent content in media. Violent advertising differs, however, when its violent content has a positive intention (i.e., the advertisement opposes violence) and in the extent to which the violence has any connection to the main message of the advertisement. All six themes are evident in both the sample of magazine advertisements (Appendices 16.1 and 16.4) and the confirmatory sample of television commercials (Appendix 16.3). They raise a number of interesting ethical issues, which we explore in a normative analysis presented next.

Layer 3: Normative Content Analysis

Our third layer of analysis examined violent advertising from an ethical perspective. Our goal in this layer of analysis was to integrate the latent content analysis of violent advertising with a normative ethical framework.

Advertising has been attacked on moral grounds since at least the 1930s (M. Phillips 1997). Murphy and Laczniak (1981), in one of the first comprehensive reviews of marketing ethics literature, noted that the extant literature was predominantly prescriptive in its normative advice to marketers, and dominated by ethical issues in advertising and marketing research. However, they made no specific mention of violence in advertising and they did not provide guidelines that could be implemented by practitioners.

Nill and Schibrowsky (2007) point out that marketers who have to make real ethical decisions every day are not looking for idealism but for strategies and decision-making systems that work. We propose that rather than specifying a theory and then working to apply it universally to different marketing practices (such as violent content in advertising), it may be valuable to specify a comprehensive set of principles derived from the literature that may be regarded by all stakeholders (i.e., advertisers, consumers, regulators) as having moral value. Practitioners and regulators alike can then undertake a moral calculus that works to balance these principles.

The principles to choose from are myriad, but following social contract theory, the key is finding a small set that can be easily applied. Ross (2002) described one approach for defining such principles. He suggested that a moral dilemma could be viewed as a conflict between certain duties. These duties could be represented as a set of general principles rather than being expressed as absolute rules. In a similar vein, Field (1999) suggests a set of "moral presumptions" to be followed by all unless there is a justifiable reason not to. Using such a contingency approach may be useful in the context of advertising. Field points out that when and if a principle is not observed, then this exception must be justified by a prevailing requirement to satisfy a different principle.

We propose that setting out a small set of principles that captures both duties and consequences may be useful for both practitioners and regulators. There are a few examples of this approach from the marketing ethics literature. Martin and Smith (2008), for example, used the presence of deception, intrusion (violation of privacy), and exploitativeness, combined with a consideration of potential consequences when they studied the ethics of stealth marketing practices. Laczniak and Murphy (2006) developed a normative framework grounded in the centrality of exchange. They begin by stating seven integrated basic perspectives that reflect the ethics literature: people first; standards in excess of the law; responsibility for intentions, means, and consequences; moral imagination of managers and employees; a core set of ethical principles (nonmaleficence, nondeception, protection of vulnerable markets, distributive justice, and stewardship); stakeholder orientation; and delineation of an ethical decision-making protocol. Resnik (1988) provides eight moral principles as standards or guides to ethical decision making and the foundation for a moral community: autonomy, beneficence, trustworthiness and honesty, justice, nonmaleficence, privacy, fidelity, and utility. Each of these approaches captures both duties and consequences.

Based on these various frameworks and our own analysis, we propose a parsimonious set of principles that can be used by both advertisers and regulators to determine whether violent executions in advertising are ethical. We integrate these principles with the six themes developed in the previous section and present these in Table 16.3.

Principles Relating to Consequentialism: Nonmaleficence and Utility

"Nonmaleficence" is the principle of "do not harm yourself or other people." This principle captures President John F. Kennedy's principle of the right to safety (1962). Although Kennedy was referring to the right to safe products and services, we extend the meaning here to include psychological safety because violent ads may induce fear, loathing, or other strong negative emotional reactions. In our use of this term, we not only want to capture consequences but also to apply Gilligan's (1982) "Ethics of Care." This normative theory is especially relevant to marketing, since it is founded on the importance of relationships—the notion of being interconnected with others—in contrast to justice-based ethics, which is founded on autonomy and individuality. In a network of relationships, we have to be conscious of others' needs. We also have to deal with people the way they want to relate to us and be conscious that we do not impose our standards on them. Using this duty-of-care perspective also privileges vulnerable markets such as children.

In applying this principle, advertisers must consider not only the characters depicted in the ad (the manifest level) but also how the action may be perceived by both intended and unintended audiences and the meanings they may construe from the action depicted (the latent level). Questions about the type of media vehicles for the advertisement are pivotal here since control of exposure to the material is media dependent. Our theme of intensity should be considered when making this assessment; therefore, advertisers have to consider not only the degree of harm portrayed but the level of psychological arousal and subsequent emotional harm that may result.

"Utility" refers to maximizing the ratio of benefits to harms for all people. Again, all stakeholders must be considered, and marketers must be conscious not to put their own interests and those of the firms they represent ahead of those of target audiences, minority groups, or vulnerable groups.

The theme of perceived intention has particular relevance when considering this principle. If the violent content is used to build awareness of a social cause, and it works to avoid harm to any group resulting from the ad execution, then the principle of utility would be met. An example of such a campaign is one recently run by Benetton. It is a series of three print advertisements showing women and girls of mixed racial backgrounds with bruised lips and blackened eyes. In each advertisement they stare quietly into the camera. There is no violence in the ad even though their faces bear the results of violence. The ads used the tagline "Colors of Domestic Violence." The use of violence in these advertisements may be deemed in keeping with the principle of utility since the benefits (i.e., awareness of the issue of violence toward women) exceed the harm (i.e., the graphical display of violence and potential emotional harm).

Table 16.3

Six Themes of Violent Advertisements and Ethical Principles

Ethical Principles	Definition	Theme	Description
Principles related to consequentialism			
Nonmaleficence	Do not harm yourself or other people	Intensity	Increased levels of intensity are presumed to be more emotionally harmful to the viewer violating the principle of nonmaleficence.
Utility	To maximize the ratio of benefits to harms for all people	Intention	Some levels of violence may be necessary in advertisements that provide a social commentary (e.g., messages against violence) in keeping with the principle of utility.
		Legitimacy	Violent content in advertisements that show legitimate violence (e.g., police using legitimate force, or one employing self-defense) may help reinforce positive social norms and social contracts in keeping with the principle of utility.
Principles related to intention and duty			
Respect	The duty one has to regard all stakeholders, especially human stakeholders, to be valuable or worthy	Power balance	Advertisements that show individuals being exploited or victimized violate the principle of respect.
Autonomy	The rights to choose and to be informed	Congruence	Violent content in advertisements that is not related to (i.e., congruent to) the product category violates the principle of autonomy.
		Intensity	Violent advertisements that are high in intensity may impair viewers' rational decision-making abilities due to severe emotional reactions, thereby violating the principle of autonomy.
Honesty	The duty not to lie, defraud, deceive, or mislead	Congruence	Advertisements that use violence to accurately convey the violent nature of a product/service are in keeping with the principle of honesty.
		Identification	Advertisements that use nonhuman characters as victims of violence may mislead viewers into the true outcomes of such violence in violation of the principle of honesty.

The theme of legitimacy is also relevant when considering the utility principle. For example, a violent advertisement that shows good triumphing over evil (e.g., a police officer apprehending a criminal) helps to reinforce social norms or social contracts. Such a violent execution would reinforce the role of the police force in maintaining peace and public order (a benefit) and educate the general public about social norms (a benefit). These benefits would outweigh the possible emotional harm associated with the exposure to the depicted violence.

Principles Relating to Intentions and Duty: Respect, Autonomy, and Honesty

"Respect" refers to the duty one has to regard all stakeholders, especially human stakeholders, to be valuable or worthy (Bourassa and Cunningham 2008), and to be treated with dignity. This is the manifestation of the principle embedded in much of deontology, and was expressed by Immanuel Kant's idea that individuals exist as ends-in-themselves. If the principle of respect is followed, issues such as exploitation, noted by Martin and Smith (2008), are avoided. The idea of the inherent value of life is also apparent in various human rights declarations such as the principles that guide the Global Compact (www.unglobalcompact.org).

The theme of victimization is relevant to this principle. When an advertisement uses an individual who is portrayed as a victim, it would be in violation of the principle of respect since victimization reduces dignity. This would be especially true when the victim is depicted as being subservient or dominated by a specific other (e.g., a woman being abused by a male, an animal being beaten by its master).

"Autonomy" refers to the right to choose and to be informed. The principle assumes a rational individual. It has considerable application to advertising with violent content. If the violence depicted is intense or there is excessive victimization, audience members' rational decision-making abilities may be impaired due to the strength of their emotional response to the violence in the advertisement, in violation of the principle of autonomy. The application of the principle of autonomy is also relevant to our theme of congruence. If the violence is incongruent with the product category, and if it is used only to attract attention (i.e., it involves using people portrayed in the ad as a means to an end), it would violate the principle of autonomy by "forcing" the viewer to pay attention to the advertisement, because the choice to pay attention is based not on the relevance of the message to the viewer, but on the violence used to create involuntary attention. The principle of autonomy also applies to audience member selection. In some cases, audience members may be unable to discern between acceptable and unacceptable forms of violence. For example, many forms of violence should not be viewed by minors, as this would violate the principle of autonomy.

"Honesty" refers to the duty not to lie, defraud, deceive, or mislead and is manifest in numerous advertising codes. Advertisers have a duty to adhere to this principle in all types of advertising, but it is especially important to violent advertising, with its heavy reliance on emotion-laden images that may cause distress among some audience members.

Our themes of congruence and identification are relevant in addressing this principle. In terms of congruence, depictions of violence adhere to principles of honesty in advertisements for contact sports and violent games when the violent aspects of these products are communicated to audience members. With respect to identification, when nonhuman characters are used in advertisements, audience members may not identify with the focal character as much as when a human subject is shown. Therefore, such portrayals may mislead viewers into believing that the outcomes of violence are trivial, inconsequential, or short term, in violation of the principle of honesty.

In summary, the results of this normative analysis reveal five important principles that advertisers and regulators can use to determine whether a violent advertising execution is ethical. In the next section, we further integrate the six principles from our normative analysis with the six themes from the latent content analysis to provide a set of practical guidelines for advertisers and regulators.

RECOMMENDATIONS: APPLYING THE FRAMEWORK

We recommend that consideration of the ethicality of violent content in advertising should be conducted using the ethical principles in our normative analysis. In order for our framework to be useful, each advertisement needs to be assessed holistically, using all of the principles. We present below a set of guidelines for advertisers, policymakers and regulators, advocates for better advertising practice, and researchers to follow when evaluating the ethicality of an advertisement with violent content. These guidelines should be applied only under the foundational assumption that the content complies with existing regulations. "Compliance with regulations" is a minimum standard for ethical advertising. Most countries have developed laws or specific codes of conduct for advertising content (although not always for violent content).

Guidelines

1. It is ethical to have scenes of intense violence in advertising only when
   a. the intention is positive (principle = utility), or
   b. the violence is legitimate (principle = utility).
2. It is ethical to use violent content without a positive intention only when
   a. the violence is congruent (principle = honesty), or
   b. the violence has a positive depicted outcome (principles = respect, nonmaleficence).
3. It is ethical to use illegitimate violence only when
   a. the intention is positive (principle = utility), or
   b. it is congruent (principle = honesty).
4. It is ethical to have a negative power balance outcome (e.g., victimization) only when
   a. the intention is positive (principle = utility).
5. It is ethical to use incongruent violence only when
   a. the intensity is low (principle = nonmaleficence/autonomy).
6. It is ethical to use characters with whom audience members will not identify only when
   a. the violence is congruent (principle = respect), or
   b. the violence is legitimate (principle = compliance), or
   c. the intention is positive (principle = utility).

These guidelines provide a general framework, but are incomplete in two ways. First, the guidelines focus on the content of the advertisements only; they do not take into account the nature of the audience member. For example, legitimate and intense violence (as described in 1b) should likely never be shown to minors since this would violate the principle of autonomy (i.e., the right/ability to make an informed choice) for these audience members. This is largely a media placement issue at the discretion of the practitioner. In addition, the low levels of agreement among our coders in Layer 1 suggest that there may be considerable variability among audience members in the assessment of violent categories such as intensity. This highlights the importance of focusing on audience members' perceptions rather than those of the advertisers.

Second, the guidelines do not suggest what to do with very intense violence or potentially emotionally disturbing advertisements. We suggest that these may be ethical under the conditions of positive intention (1a) and legitimacy (1b). Similarly, we suggest that an advertisement displaying victimization may be ethical should the intention be positive (5a). In each of these cases, however, the advertisements would violate the principle of autonomy (i.e., the right to be informed). Based on these two concerns, we add a seventh guideline:

7. It is ethical to use advertisements with intense violence, a negative power balance outcome, or illegitimate violence only when
   a. viewers are provided with a suitable warning and given the right to choose to view the content (principle = autonomy).

For advertisers, we suggest that these guidelines be integrated into the process of creative strategy development. For policymakers and regulators, and advocates for better advertising practice, we recommend that the guidelines be used to direct the decisions of an adjudication panel. For example, television advertising aimed at children in Canada must be screened and given an approval number by the Children's Clearance Committee before such ads can be aired. The panel is made up of representatives from both the industry and the public. Presented with the seven guidelines detailed above, such a panel should be able to determine the ethicality of an advertisement that contains violent content.

CONCLUSIONS, LIMITATIONS, AND FUTURE RESEARCH

Advertising is an important social force, and violence in advertising may have either positive or negative effects on society. Our multilayered content analysis increases understanding of this phenomenon.

Our analysis suggests that there are several important facets to violent advertising executions: intensity, congruence, intention, legitimacy, identification, and depicted outcomes. Empirical research is needed to determine the effects of these themes alone or in combination in advertisements with violent imagery.

Our analysis casts doubt on the generally accepted view that violent advertisements are always unethical, as there may be potentially positive outcomes arising from these advertisements. While our latent content analysis helped us better understand when violent advertisements might be ethical, our normative ethical analysis permits a better appreciation of how to judge whether a particular violent execution is ethical. However, such analysis does little to reveal the actual effects on consumers, and this work needs to be undertaken. Our analysis brings some structure to the ambiguities in violent advertising and the difficulties that policymakers face when attempting to regulate such content.

Inherent in our themes are six latent constructs of interest for future research in violent advertising. As a first step, the six may be used to conduct a more detailed content analysis of violent advertising. The first variable, intensity, would seem to have a direct effect on viewer information processing (e.g., brand awareness, ad recall). Previous research has shown that increasing levels of intensity result in decreasing amounts of memory for ads (i.e., the intended effects) (Bushman and Bonacci 2002). These effects are likely influenced by the other five constructs of interest. At the very least, this suggests that any experimental examinations of violent ads must explicitly control for these potential effects.

Within our analysis of the advertisements, we found a number of other interesting areas for future inquiry. First, it appears that some product categories have adopted a "culture of violence." For example, we found many examples of violent ads for products such as snowboards and skis. These two sports, which have been called "extreme sports," may have aligned themselves with an ethos of aggressive achievement. Second, the issue of personal framing is one that needs further exploration. Life experiences, cultural ideals, personality traits, and other psychological or sociological factors may dictate what is perceived to be legitimate, but also what is perceived to be low versus high intensity.

Violence in advertising is an important social force affecting consumers' perceptions of violence in subtle and unexpected ways. Our analysis suggests that violence in advertising is more complex than previously realized, and that this is an area in need of attention by researchers. Our contribution is to provide a framework for advertisers and policymakers to use in the assessment of such advertisements.

REFERENCES

Abela, Andrew V., and Patrick E. Murphy (2008), "Marketing with Integrity: Ethics and the Service-Dominant Logic," *Journal of the Academy of Marketing Science*, 36 (1), 39–53.

Advertising Standards Canada (2006), "Ad Complaints Report," Ad Complaints Report Archive, Toronto, Ontario, available at www.adstandards.com/en/ConsumerComplaints/2006AdComplaintsReport.pdf (accessed October 2, 2010).

Ahuvia, Aaron (1998), "Social Criticism of Advertising: On the Role of Literary Theory and the Use of Data," *Journal of Advertising*, 27 (1), 143–163.

Anderson, Charles R. (1997), "Violence in Television Commercials During Nonviolent Programming: The 1996 Major League Baseball Playoffs," *Journal of the American Medical Association*, 278 (13), 1045–1046.

——— (2000), "Television Commercial Violence During Nonviolent Programming: The 1998 Major League Baseball Playoffs," *Pediatrics*, 106 (4), e46.

Anderson, Craig A., and Brad J. Bushman (2002), "The Effects of Media Violence on Society," *Science*, 295 (March 29), 2377–2378.

———, Leonard Berkowitz, Edward Donnerstein, L. Rowell Huesmann, James D. Johnson, Daniel Linz, Neil M. Malamuth, and Ellen Wartella (2003), "The Influence of Media Violence on Youth," *Psychological Science in the Public Interest*, 4 (3), 81–110.

Andersson, Svante, Anna Hedelin, Anna Nilson, and Charlotte Welander (2004), "Violent Advertising in Fashion Marketing," *Journal of Fashion Marketing and Management*, 8 (1), 96–112.

Barnes, James H., and Michael J. Dotson (1990), "An Exploratory Investigation into the Nature of Offensive Television Advertising," *Journal of Advertising*, 19 (3), 61–69.

Baron, Larry, Murray A. Straus, and David Jaffee (1988), "Legitimate Violence, Violent Attitudes, and Rape: A Test of the Cultural Spillover Theory," *Annals of the New York Academy of Sciences*, 528 (August), 79–110.

Bourassa, Maureen, and Peggy Cunningham (2008), "Respect in Business-to-Business Marketing Relationships," in *Proceedings of the 2008 American Marketing Association Summer Educators' Conference*, James R. Brown and Rajiv P. Dant, eds., San Diego: American Marketing Association, 86–87.

Boyatzis, Richard E. (1998), *Transforming Qualitative Information: Thematic Analysis and Code Development*, Thousand Oaks, CA: Sage.

Bradley, Margaret M., and Peter J. Lang (2000), "Measuring Emotion: Behavior, Feeling, and Physiology," in *Cognitive Neuroscience of Emotion*, Richard D. Lane and Lynn Nadel, eds., Oxford: Oxford University Press, 242–276.

Bushman, Brad J. (2007), "That Was a Great Commercial, but What Were They Selling? Effects of Violence and Sex on Memory for Products in Television Commercials," *Journal of Applied Social Psychology*, 37 (8), 1784–1796.

———, and Craig A. Anderson (2001), "Media Violence and the American Public," *American Psychologist*, 56 (6/7), 477–489.

———, and Angelica M. Bonacci (2002), "Violence and Sex Impair Memory for Television Ads," *Journal of Applied Psychology*, 87 (3), 557–564.

Cacioppo, John T., and Gary G. Berntson (1994), "Relationship Between Attitudes and Evaluative Space: A Critical Review, with Emphasis on the Separability of Positive and Negative Substrates," *Psychological Bulletin*, 115 (3), 401–423.

Christy, Timothy P., and Eric Haley (2007), "The Influence of Context on College Students' Perceptions of Advertising Offensiveness," in *American Academy of Advertising 2007 Annual Conference*, Kim Sheehan, ed., Burlington, VT: American Academy of Advertising, 69.

Cooper, Tom (2008), "Between the Summits: What Americans Think About Mass Media Ethics," *Journal of Mass Media Ethics*, 23 (1), 15–27.
Croft, Martin (2002), "Must Ads Disgust to Get Discussed?" *Marketing Week*, 25 (June 13), 22.
Dahl, Darren W., Kristina D. Frankenberger, and Rajesh V. Manchanda (2003), "Does It Pay to Shock? Reactions to Shocking and Nonshocking Advertising Content Among University Students," *Journal of Advertising Research*, 43 (3), 268–280.
Debling, Fiona (1998), "Mail Myopia: Or Examining Financial Services Marketing from a Brand Commitment Perspective," *Marketing Intelligence and Planning*, 16 (1), 38–46.
deChenecey, Sean Pillot (2000), "When Is It Right to Use Shock Ad Strategies?" *Marketing* (March 30), 19.
Draucker, Claire B., Donna S. Martsoff, Ratchneewan Ross, and Thomas B. Rusk (2007), "Theoretical Sampling and Category Development in Grounded Theory," *Qualitative Health Research*, 17 (8), 1137–1148.
Field, Richard (1999), "A Practical Guide to Ethical Theory," available at http://catpages.nwmissouri.edu/m/rfield/274guide/title.htm (accessed July 28, 2008).
Freedman, Jonathan L. (2002), *Media Violence and Its Effect on Aggression: Assessing the Scientific Evidence*, Toronto: University of Toronto Press.
FrenchConnection (2008), "A History of FCUK Advertising," available at www.frenchconnection.com/content/marketing/history-of-advertising.htm (accessed May 19, 2008).
Friestad, Marian, and Peter Wright (1994), "The Persuasion Knowledge Model: How People Cope with Persuasion Attempts," *Journal of Consumer Research*, 21 (1), 1–31.
Frijda, Nico H. (1986), *The Emotions*, Cambridge: Cambridge University Press.
Garrett, Jade (1999), "Charities Snub Shock Tactics for Subtle Approach," Campaign, available at www.campaignlive.co.uk/news/28250/LIVE-ISSUE-CHARITY-ADVERTISING-Charities-snub-shock-tactics-subtle-approach—no-longer-enough-agencies-just-upset-public-Jade-Garrett-writes/?DCMP=ILC-SEARCH/ (accessed October 2, 2010).
Gerbner, G., and L. Gross (1976), "Living with Television: The Violence Profile," *Journal of Communication*, 26 (2), 173–199.
Gilligan, Carol (1982), *In a Different Voice: Psychological Theory and Women's Development*, Cambridge: Harvard University Press.
Gosselin, Andre, Jacques DeGuise, Guy Paquette, and Laplante Benoit (1997), "Violence on Canadian Television and Some of Its Cognitive Effects," *Canadian Journal of Communication*, 22 (2), 143–160.
Gunter, Barrie, Adrian Furnham, and Eleni Pappa (2005), "Effects of Television Violence on Memory for Violent and Nonviolent Advertising," *Journal of Applied Social Psychology*, 35 (8), 1680–1697.
Guria, Jagadish, and Joanne Leung (2004), "An Evaluation of a Supplementary Road Safety Package," *Accident Analysis and Prevention*, 36 (5), 893–904.
Henthorne, Tony L., Michael S. LaTour, and Rajan Nataraajan (1993), "Fear Appeals in Print Advertising: An Analysis of Arousal and Ad Response," *Journal of Advertising*, 22 (2), 59–68.
Huesmann, L. Rowell, Jessica Moise-Titus, Cheryl-Lynn Podolski, and Leonard D. Eron (2003), "Longitudinal Relations Between Children's Exposure to TV Violence and Their Aggressive and Violent Behavior in Young Adulthood: 1977–1992," *Development Psychology*, 39 (2), 201–221.
Ji, Mindy F., and Russell N. Laczniak (2007), "Advertisers' Implementation of CARU Guidelines for Advertising Targeted at Children," *Journal of Current Issues and Research in Advertising*, 29 (2), 27–38.
Jones, Morag Cudderford (2002), "Shaken by Ad Aftershock," *Brand Strategy* (July 1).
Jones, Tim, and Peggy H. Cunningham (2008), "Violent Advertising on Canadian Primetime Television: A Frequency Analysis and Potential Impact," *Canadian Journal of Media Studies*, 4 (1), 41–70.
Kennedy, John F. (1962), "Special Message on Protecting the Consumer Interest," in *The Politics of Consumer Protection*, Mark V. Nadel, ed., Indianapolis: Bobbs-Merrill, xvii.
Kilbourne, Jean (1979), *Killing Us Softly*, Boston: Media Education Foundation.
——— (1987), *Still Killing Us Softly*, Boston: Media Education Foundation.
——— (2000), *Killing Us Softly 3*, Boston: Media Education Foundation.
Laczniak, Gene, and Partick E. Murphy (2006), "Normative Perspectives for Ethical and Socially Responsible Marketing," *Journal of Macromarketing*, 26 (2), 154–177.
Lang, Peter J., Michael Davis, and Arne Ohman (2000), "Fear and Anxiety: Animal Models and Human Cognitive Psychophysiology," *Journal of Affective Disorders*, 61 (3), 137–159.
Larson, Mary Strom (2001), "Interactions, Activities and Gender in Children's Television Commercials: A Content Analysis," *Journal of Broadcasting and Electronic Media*, 45 (1), 41.

——— (2003), "Gender, Race, and Aggression in Television Commercials That Feature Children," *Sex Roles*, 48 (1/2), 67–75.

LaTour, Michael S. (2006), "Retrospective and Prospective Views of 'Fear Arousal' in 'Fear Appeals,'" *International Journal of Advertising*, 25 (3), 409–413.

———, and Shaker A. Zahra (1989), "Fear Appeals as Advertising Strategy: Should They Be Used?" *Journal of Consumer Marketing*, 6 (2), 61–70.

———, Robin L. Snipes, and Sara J. Bliss (1996), "Don't Be Afraid to Use Fear Appeals: An Experimental Study," *Journal of Advertising Research*, 36 (2), 59–67.

Lawson, Rob W. (1985), "An Analysis of Complaints About Advertising," *International Journal of Advertising*, 4 (4), 279–295.

Lewis, Ioni, Barry Watson, and Richard Tay (2007), "Examining the Effectiveness of Physical Threats in Road Safety Advertising: The Role of Third-Person Effect, Gender, and Age," *Transportation Research: Part F*, 10 (1), 48–60.

Locke, Karen (2001), *Grounded Theory in Management Research*, Thousand Oaks, CA: Sage.

Macklin, M. Carole, and Richard H. Kolbe (1984), "Sex Role Stereotyping in Children's Advertising: Current and Past Trends," *Journal of Advertising*, 13 (2), 34–42.

Maguire, Brendan, Diane Sandage, and Georgie Ann Weatherby (2000), "Violence, Morality, and Television Commercials," *Sociological Spectrum*, 20 (1), 121–143.

Martin, Kelly D., and N. Craig Smith (2008), "The Ethical Pitfalls of Unconventional Marketing," INSEAD Business School Working Paper Series, Fontainebleau, France.

Murphy, Patrick, and Gene Laczniak (1981), "Marketing Ethics: A Review with Implications for Managers, Educators, and Researchers," in *Review of Marketing*, Ban M. Enis and Kenneth J. Roering, eds., Chicago: American Marketing Association, 251–266.

Mustonen, Anu, and Lea Pulkkinen (1997), "Television Violence: A Development of a Coding Scheme," *Journal of Broadcasting and Electronic Media*, 41 (2), 168–189.

Nill, Alexander, and John A. Schibrowsky (2007), "Research on Marketing Ethics: A Systematic Review of the Literature," *Journal of Macromarketing*, 27 (3), 256–273.

Oliver, Mary Beth, and Sriram Kalyanaraman (2002), "Appropriate for All Viewing Audiences? An Examination of Violent and Sexual Portrayals in Movie Previews Featured on Video Rentals," *Journal of Broadcasting and Electronic Media*, 46 (2), 283–299.

Paik, Haejung, and George Comstock (1994), "The Effects of Television Violence on Anti-Social Behavior: A Meta-Analysis," *Communication Research*, 21 (4), 516–546.

Perreault, William D., Jr., and Laurence E. Leigh (1989), "Reliability of Nominal Data Based on Qualitative Judgments," *Journal of Marketing Research*, 26 (May), 135–148.

Phillips, Barbara (1997), "Thinking into It: Consumer Interpretation of Complex Advertising Images," *Journal of Advertising*, 26 (2), 77–88.

Phillips, Michael J. (1997), *Ethics and Manipulation in Advertising: Answering a Flawed Indictment*, Westport, CT: Greenwood.

Rajecki, D.W., Donald G. McTavish, Jeffrey Lee Rasmussen, Madelon Schreuders, Diane C. Byers, and K. Sean Jessup (1994), "Violence, Conflict, Trickery, and Other Story Themes in TV Food Ads for Children," *Journal of Applied Social Psychology*, 24 (19), 1685–1699.

Resnik, David B. (1988), *The Ethics of Science: An Introduction*, New York: Routledge.

Ross, William D. (2002), "The Right and the Good," in *Moral Writings and the Right and the Good*, Philip Stratton-Lake, ed., Oxford: Oxford University Press, 1–15.

Ruiter, Robert A. C., Charles Abraham, and Gerjo Kok (2001), "Scary Warnings and Rational Precautions: A Review of the Psychology of Fear Appeals," *Psychology and Health*, 16 (6), 613–630.

Scharrer, Erica (2004), "Virtual Violence: Gender and Aggression in Video Game Advertisements," *Mass Communications and Society*, 7 (4), 393–412.

———, Andrea Bergstrom, Angela Paradise, and Qianqing Ren (2006), "Laughing to Keep from Crying: Humor and Aggression in Television Commercial Content," *Journal of Broadcasting and Electronic Media*, 50 (4), 615–634.

Schoenbachler, Denise D., and Tommy E. Whittler (1996), "Adolescent Processing of Social and Physical Threat Communications," *Journal of Advertising*, 25 (4), 37–54.

Shanahan, Kevin J., Charles M. Hermans, and Michael R. Hyman (2003), "Violent Commercials in Television Programs for Children," *Journal of Current Issues and Research in Advertising*, 25 (1), 61–69.

Shimp, Terence A. (2003), *Advertising, Promotion, and Supplemental Aspects of Integrated Marketing Communications*, 6th ed., Mason, OH: Thomson.

Smith, Valerie (2002), "The Free Radical: A Website Outlining Research on Media Violence and Civil Action Against Media Violence," available at www.thefreeradical.ca (accessed November 1, 2009).

Tajfel, H. J., and J. C. Turner (1986), "The Social Identity Theory of Inter-Group Behavior," in *Psychology of Intergroup Relations*, S. Worchel and L. W. Austin, eds., Chicago: Nelson-Hall, 7–24.

Tamburro, Robert F., Patricia L. Gordon, James P. D'Apolito, and Scott C. Howard (2004), "Unsafe and Violent Behavior in Commercials Aired During Televised Major Sporting Events," *Pediatrics*, 114 (6), 694–698.

Tomblin, Mark (2002), "Shock Advertising: Is the Rise in Advertising Complaints Due to Offensive Material or Is the Public Feeling Jaded by the Lack of Relevance?" *Brand Strategy* (November 1), 9.

Trochim, William M. (2006), "The Research Methods Knowledge Base, 2d ed.," available at www.social-researchmethods.net/kb/ (accessed October 20, 2006).

Wilson, Barbara J., Stacy L. Smith, W. James Potter, Dale Kunkel, Daniel Linz, Carolyn M. Colvin, and Edward Donnerstein (2002), "Violence in Children's Television Programming: Assessing the Risks," *Journal of Communication*, 52 (1), 5–35.

———, Dale Kunkel, Daniel Linz, W. James Potter, Edward Donnerstein, Stacey L. Smith, Eva Blumenthal, and Timothy Gray (1997), "Television Violence and Its Context," in *National Television Violence Study*, vol. 1, M. Seawall, ed., Thousand Oaks, CA: Sage, 7–10.

Woodward, David (2005), "When Incorrectness Is a Political Ploy," *Director*, 58 (9), 38.

Zhang, Yong, and George M. Zinkhan (1991), "Humor in Television Advertising: The Effects of Repetition and Social Setting," in *Advances in Consumer Research*, vol. 18, Rebecca H. Holman and Michael R. Solomon, eds., Provo, UT: Association for Consumer Research, 813–818.

APPENDIX 16.1

Samples of Advertisements Used in Thematic Analysis

Figure 16.1 **High Intensity**

Figure 16.2 **Low Intensity**

Figure 16.3 **Congruence**

Figure 16.4 **Incongruent**

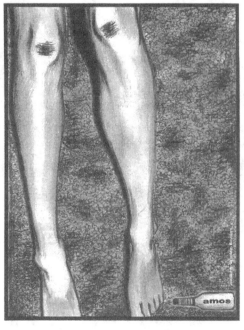

Figure 16.5 **Positive Intention**[a]

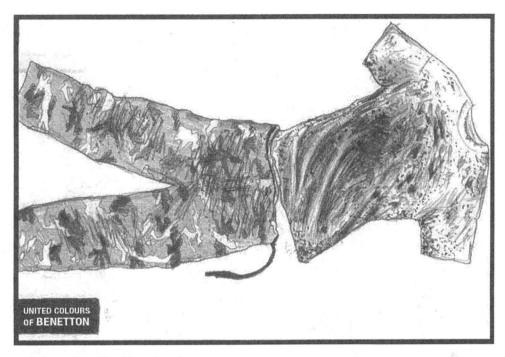

Figure 16.6 **Negative Intention**[b]

[a]The advertisement depicts a soldier's uniform with blood splatters.
[b]The advertisement is for fashion apparel (women's).

Figure 16.7 **Legitimate**

Figure 16.8 **Illegitimate**

Handbag Life

Figure 16.9 **Fictional**

Figure 16.10 **Reality**

Figure 16.11 **Victimization**

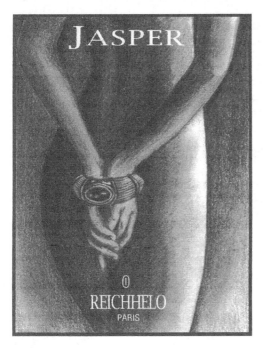

Figure 16.12 **Victimization**

Notes: The advertisements depicted here are hand-drawn re-creations of the actual advertisements. The brand names or tag lines have been changed to conceal the identity of the sponsor (with the exception of the Benetton advertisement, Figure 16.5). The advertisements were redone in this way to avoid copyright issues. Permission to use these advertisements as exemplars of violent advertisements was deemed unlikely.

Appendix 16.2

Coding Scheme Used in Manifest Content Analysis (Level 1)

Content variables	IRR[a]	Categories	Frequency
Intensity (66%)[a]			
Mode of violence	67%	Physical (including sexual)	83%
		Psychological (including verbal)	8%
		Both: physical and psychological	9%
Primary mode of physical violence	69%	No physical violence	14%
		Shooting (with a gun)	44%
		Threatening/forcing with guns	6%
		Fist fighting, pushing, striking	15%
		Hitting with weapons or tools	7%
		Strangling	2%
		Sexual violence	8%
		Kidnapping/tying up/arresting	3%
Primary mode of nonverbal (psychological aggression)	70%	No nonverbal aggression	83%
		Forcing, subjection, pressuring	5%
		Threatening, intimidation	10%
		Irony, scorning gestures	1%
		Other	1%
Seriousness: aggressor's intent	62%	Cannot code	8%
		To have fun	18%
		To threaten	11%
		To insult	1%
		To injure	28%
		To kill	33%
Seriousness: likely consequences of violence to victim (whether depicted or not)	62%	No harm	9%
		Harm to property/objects only	6%
		Mild harm or injuries to people or living things	23%
		Moderate injuries to people/living things (medical care needed)	11%
		Severe injuries (hospital care needed)	10%
		Death	36%
Dramatization: timing of the violent act	78%	About to happen	32%
		Happening	39%
		Has already happened	30%
Dramatization: tone of the violence	64%	Unclear	4%
		Humorous/comedic	15%
		Conflict, fighting	21%
		Exciting, adventurous, sporting, fantasy (games)	28%
		Frightening, threatening, horrific	27%
Dramatization: clarity and vividness of the depicted violence	57%	There is only the potential for violence	19%
		Unclear depiction of violence	17%
		Clear depiction of violence	57%
		Detailed and graphic depiction of violence	6%

Content variables	IRR[a]	Categories	Frequency
Intensity of violence	62%	Mild	53%
		Moderate	42%
		Brutal	5%
Congruence (75%)			
Product category congruence	77%	Inclusion of violence is not consistent with the product category at all	56%
		Inclusion of violence is consistent with the product category	44%
Product category clarity	81%	Product category is clear from ad	13%
		Product category is not clear from ad	87%
Congruence with positioning of brand (e.g., brand/issue)	65%	Inclusion of violence is not consistent with the positioning of the brand	46%
		Inclusion of violence is consistent with the positioning of the brand	54%
Intention (79%)			
Purpose of the advertisement (e.g., brand/issue)	91%	To promote a product/service	80%
		To raise awareness of a social issue	5%
		To promote an upcoming program/movie	11%
		To promote an upcoming event	2%
		Other	0%
Why do you think the creator put violence in the ad?	75%	To enhance viewer interest/attention to the ad	74%
		To make a social commentary about violence	7%
		Because it is a realistic depiction of a particular product category or context	16%
		Other/unsure	2%
Legitimacy (69%)			
Justification: aggressor's intention	79%	Cannot code/unclear	9%
		Intentional violence	73%
		Unintentional violence (including accidental)	17%
Justification: primary motivation for aggressor's use of violence	61%	Cannot code	23%
		To defend another being	0%
		To defend oneself	6%
		Violence as a means to an end	54%
		Violence as a reaction or expression of emotion	4%
		Violence for the sake of violence	8%
Justification: If this violence happened in real life, would it be legal or not?	75%	Cannot code	4%
		Legal	55%
		Illegal	41%
Justification: role of aggressor	65%	Cannot code	16%
		Violence is part of the aggressor's role (e.g., police officer, soldier, hockey player)	41%
		Violence is not part of the aggressor's role	42%
Justification: congruence with context/genre (e.g., war genre/sporting events)	65%	Violence is not consistent with the context/genre	37%
		Violence is consistent with the context/genre	63%

Content variables	IRR[a]	Categories	Frequency
Identification (79%)			
Realism: cultural distance	86%	Fantasy (e.g., sci-fi, cartoons)	12%
		North American culture and English language	82%
		North American culture and foreign language	3%
		Foreign culture and English language	2%
		Foreign culture and language	1%
Realism: temporal distance (setting of the ad)	86%	Current/contemporary (the 1990s and beyond)	1%
		Retro (from the 1950s to the 1990s)	91%
		Historical (before the 1950s)	4%
		The future	3%
Realism: fictionality	66%	A cartoon/animated program	4%
		Unrealistic fiction (caricatured and fantasy characters involved)	16%
		Realistic fiction	62%
		Authentic	17%
Power balance (80%)			
Power: likely sex of aggressor	81%	Cannot code	50%
		Male	30%
		Female	10%
		A group of males	1%
		A group of females	1%
		A mixed group	7%
Power: likely age of aggressor	83%	Cannot code	44%
		Child	1%
		Adult	55%
		People of several age groups	0%
Victimization: likely sex of victim	77%	Cannot code	26%
		A male	31%
		A female	20%
		A group of males	2%
		A mixed group	5%
		Animal(s)	3%
		Inanimate object(s)	11%
Victimization: likely age of victim	80%	Cannot code	36%
		Child	7%
		Adult	51%
		People of several age groups	6%
Glamorization: nature of the aggressor	60%	Cannot code	24%
		A villain or "bad guy"	21%
		Regular person, neither good nor evil	38%
		A hero or "good guy"	16%
Glamorization: nature of the victim	66%	Cannot code	15%
		A villain or "bad guy"	16%
		Regular person, neither good nor evil	64%
		A hero or "good guy"	3%

Content variables	IRR[a]	Categories	Frequency
Efficacy: ignoring the consequences of violence	62%	The victim/aggressor will not /does not suffer any consequences	6%
		The victim will suffer, but it is not explicitly depicted	48%
		The victim suffers and it is depicted	39%
		Both the victim and the aggressor will suffer, but it is not depicted	5%
		Both the victim and the aggressor suffer and it is depicted	2%
Efficacy: extent that aggressor profits by violence	53%	Cannot code	17%
		Not at all	27%
		A little bit	12%
		A lot	42%

[a]IRR = interrater reliability. Perreault and Leigh's (1989) reliability index is calculated as an assessment of interrater reliability.

Appendix 16.3

Television Advertisements Confirmatory Sample: Themes and Exemplars

Theme	Level	Brand	Description of advertisement
Intensity	High	Advertising agency	This television advertisement begins with soft-focus shots of a kitten playing. Then, the barrel of a gun is pointed at the kitten and cocked. This is a metaphor for the effectiveness of the agency's advertising.
	Low	Copier repair service	This television advertisement shows a woman sitting on a photocopier attempting to make a copy of that portion of her body. When an error message requiring a larger paper size appears, she begins to kick and hit the photocopier. At the end of the commercial, the text reads, "We don't care how it gets broken, we'll be there to fix it."
Congruence	High	Sportswear	This television advertisement shows the New Zealand All Blacks rugby team warming up. Interspersed with these images are shots of Maori warriors and rugby scenes. The chants and the actions of the players are aggressive, as is the game itself.
	Low	Auto group car dealership	This television advertisement begins with a scene of road rage in which one driver is verbally abusing another. The angry driver has left his vehicle and is pounding on the window of the other car. The victim presses a button on his dash labeled "Trunk Monkey." This releases a chimpanzee carrying a tire iron from the trunk of the victim's car. The chimpanzee strikes the angry driver with the tire iron.
Perceived intention	Positive	Charitable organization	This television advertisement opens with two teenage boys who are about to try "crystal meth." Suddenly, a wild man appears, jumps onto their car, grabs one of the boys and shouts at him the consequences of taking "crystal meth," including: "screw your brain up with paranoia . . . punch your girlfriend . . . die of a stroke." The text at the end of the commercial reads, "Only you can stop you."
	Negative	Video game	This television advertisement begins with a scene in a lingerie store in which a man tells his girlfriend, "I don't care what she says, you're not too fat to wear a thong." This instigates a wrestling match between two women. The commercial then cuts to scenes from the video game in which two women characters are wrestling. The tag line is, "Get hot girls to wrestle on command."

Legitimacy	High (legal)	Soft drink	This television advertisement shows a BMX extreme sport rider. He does several stunts perfectly and then on his last jump he is hit by a low-flying bird. This accident knocks him off the bicycle.
	Low (illegal)	Sports Web site	This television advertisement begins with shots from a hockey game. It then focuses on two players who battle for the puck. This battle moves from the rink into the surrounding streets, where the players interfere with others and damage property. Eventually they fight their way back to the rink.
Identification	High (realistic)	Fast-food restaurant	This television advertisement shows an office lunchroom scene in which one man attempts to take another's spicy chicken sandwich. The aggressor's shirt is ripped in the process.
	Low (fictional)	Luxury vehicle manufacturer	This television advertisement shows a class for villains in the context of the James Bond franchise. The instructor provides a series of things not to do when attempting to kill James Bond, including "not assuming James Bond is dead before actually seeing him die . . . never, ever ride in anything chasing Bond's XXX."
Victimization	Positive (empowerment)	Running shoes	This television advertisement is a takeoff of a horror movie. A woman has returned from a run and is shocked to see a hockey-masked, chain saw-carrying villain in the mirror. She runs, he follows, and eventually he gives up. The commercial concludes with the tag line, "Why sport? You'll live longer."
	Negative (victimization)	Sportswear	This television advertisement is one of a series featuring Terry Tate, a large lineman in the NFL. In this commercial, Tate is shown tackling someone in an office. The tag line is, "The pain train is coming."

Appendix 16.4

Print Sample: Themes and Exemplars

Theme	Level	Brand/category	Description of advertisement
Intensity	High	Yellé sunglasses (see Appendix 16.1, Figure 1–1)	This print advertisement shows a surf board that has been bitten in half. The surrounding water is full of blood. Floating in the water are several objects that may be clothing and body parts. A shark's fin is in the background. The sunglasses are intact and positioned on one of the surfboard pieces. The tag line reads, "tougher than you."
	Low	Garbage bags	This print advertisement depicts a bull charging a rodeo clown. The rodeo clown is using a garbage bag instead of the traditional red blanket to attract the bull's attention. The tag line reads, "Tear resistant enough for any job."
Congruence	High	Television drama	This print advertisement for a television drama that appears on A&E shows police crime tape and what appears to be a dead body covered by a white sheet. Several people appear to be investigating the scene. The crime-scene tape reads, "They found a body. They have 2 days to find a lead."
	Low	Dymo label printer	This print advertisement shows two men in an office environment. One man is smiling while he sits at a desk that has a Dymo label printer on it. The other man, who is grimacing, is about to strike a printer with a baseball bat. That printer appears to be jammed with labels. The headline reads, "Fast vs. Furious of label printing."
Perceived intention	Positive	Charitable organization	This print advertisement shows a woman and her young child outside a house. They appear to be bruised and despondent. There is an enlarged set of palms drawn into the picture tented over the woman and child. The copy refers to providing abused women and their children safe shelter and counseling.
	Negative	Fashion apparel (see Appendix 16.1, Figure 1–6)	This print advertisement shows a woman being restrained by a man on what appears to be a restaurant bench. She is lying on her stomach and looking back over her shoulder at the man who seems to be either kissing her buttocks or binding her hands. She is wearing a revealing dress and looks disheveled. There is no text in the advertisement apart from the brand name.

Legitimacy	High (legal)	National television news program (see Appendix 16.1, Figure 1–10)	This print advertisement shows several police officers in riot gear carrying batons. In their midst is an unarmed man sitting cross-legged on the ground. The tag line says, "The most comprehensive news from start to finish."
	Low (illegal)	Snowboards	This print advertisement depicts a torture scene. One man is tied to a chair. Blood covers much of his clothing and face. A standing man, dressed in black, appears to be questioning the first man. The scene is very dark. Light is shining through gritty windows in the background.
Identification	High (realistic)	Newspaper	This print advertisement shows the Ku Klux Klan burning a cross with the headline, "Mississippi? Alabama? Ontario?" The copy in the advertisement encourages subscription to the newspaper based on the benefit that the newspaper provides "a range of ideological insights."
	Low (fictional)	Chocolate bar (see Appendix 16.1, Figure 1–9)	This print advertisement shows two characters from the Simpsons television show. Nelson (the bully) is holding a sweating and anxious Bart up by the shirt with one hand while the other holds a chocolate bar. The headline reads, "Nothing feels better in your fist."
Power balance	Positive (empowerment)	Breath freshener	This print advertisement shows a woman dressed in a skin-tight body suit resembling Lara Croft, Tomb Raider. She has a determined face, a powerful body, and is armed with what appears to be an ammunition belt. She is firing a pocket breath freshener at a monster. The headline reads, "The war against evil breath bacteria just got a new hero."
	Negative (victimization)	Perfume (see Appendix 16.1, Figure 1–11)	This print advertisement depicts a naked woman bound at the wrists by a bracelet-shaped perfume bottle. The woman is visible from the shoulders to the knees, and is photographed from the back.

About the Editors and Contributors

Christy Ashley (PhD, University of Rhode Island) is an assistant professor of marketing at East Carolina University. Her primary research focuses on the development, management, and dissolution of consumer-brand relationships. Her research has been published in the *Journal of Advertising, Journal of Business Research, Journal of Public Policy & Marketing,* and *Journal of Marketing Theory and Practice,* among others. Dr. Ashley serves on the editorial review board of *Service Industries Journal* and serves as webmaster for the American Academy of Advertising.

Laurence Ashworth is an associate professor of marketing at Queen's Business School in Canada and has a PhD from the University of British Columbia. His research examines various ways in which social and emotional factors influence consumer judgment and decision making and has appeared in journals such as the *Journal of Consumer Research, Journal of Marketing,* and *Journal of Consumer Psychology.* His recent work on the appeal of violent media with Ethan Pancer and Martin Pyle looks at how viewers can enjoy violence because it satisfies justice and dominance motives, even when they react negatively to the violence itself.

Karen L. Becker-Olsen completed her PhD at Lehigh University and is currently an associate professor at the College of New Jersey where she teaches consumer behavior, marketing and public policy, and services marketing. She also serves as a Bonner Foundation Fellow. Previously she taught at New York University and Lehigh University. Her research interests lie at the intersection of marketing, psychology, and public policy. As such she has published papers in the fields of violence perception, corporate social responsibility, and public health communications. Her work has appeared in the *Journal of Marketing, Journal of Research for Consumers, Journal of Advertising, Journal of Business Research, Journal of International Marketing,* and *Harvard Business Review Latin America.*

Benjamin J. Blackford (PhD), is an assistant professor of management in the Department of Business at Northwest Missouri State University. Ben is a graduate of the University of Nebraska-Lincoln and specializes in marketing, strategic management, entrepreneurship, and human resources. He has published journal articles and made conference presentations in the areas of marketing, strategic management, and entrepreneurship. Dr. Blackford also regularly serves as a reviewer for a variety of journals. He advises several student organizations, consults with businesses and community groups, and has been a member of a variety of professional organizations.

E. Deanne Brocato is an assistant professor of marketing at the Jon M. Huntsman School of Business. Her research focuses on explaining and managing the dynamics of social exchange and social influence (attitude change and behavioral change) in service industries. Current projects in this area address consumer emotional attachment to service environments and the role that other customers play in customer service evaluations. Another area of focus is on the effects of violent media content on children. Her research has appeared in the *Journal of Retailing, Journal of Advertising, Journal of Services Research,* and *Corporate Reputation Review*.

Brad J. Bushman is a professor of communication and psychology at The Ohio State University and a professor of communication science at the VU University Amsterdam, the Netherlands. He studies human aggression and violence. His research has challenged several myths (e.g., violent media effects are trivial, venting anger reduces aggression, violent people have low self-esteem, violence and sex sell products, warning labels reduce audience size). One colleague calls him the "myth buster." His research has been published in top scientific journals such as *Science* and has been featured in the media (BBC, *New York Times,* to name a few).

Michael L. Cappella is the associate dean of Graduate & Executive Programs, and associate professor of marketing at the Villanova School of Business. Dr. Capella's research interests focus on the area of marketing and public policy issues, including topics related to advertising effects, consumer consumption of harmful products, and pharmaceutical sales practices. Prior to receiving his PhD in marketing, Dr. Capella spent nearly a decade in professional sales management with a manufacturer. Dr. Capella serves on the editorial review board at the *Journal of Public Policy & Marketing, Journal of Advertising, Journal of Consumer Affairs,* and *International Journal of Advertising*.

Les Carlson holds the Nathan Gold Distinguished Professorship at the University of Nebraska-Lincoln. He is a past president of the American Academy of Advertising (AAA) and is a former editor of the *Journal of Advertising* and associate editor of the *Journal of Public Policy & Marketing*. He has received the AAA Outstanding Contribution to Research Award and the AAA Kim Rotzoll Award for Advertising Ethics and Social Responsibility.

Magdalena Cismaru is a professor of marketing in the Faculty of Business Administration at the University of Regina. Her research focusing on social marketing and health decision making has been published in the *Journal of Advertising, Trauma, Violence and Abuse, International Marketing Review, Journal of Health Psychology, Marketing Theory, International Journal of Public Health, Social Marketing Quarterly, Canadian Public Policy, Young Consumers, International Review on Public and Nonprofit Marketing, Health Marketing Quarterly,* and elsewhere.

Carlos Cruz is a fourth year PhD student in the communication program at The Ohio State University. His interests lie primarily in advertising and social media research. His ongoing advertising research is examining the effectiveness of advertisements placed in violent video games. He is a member of the International Communication Association (ICA).

Peggy H. Cunningham (PhD, Texas A&M University) is the dean of the Faculty of Management at Dalhousie University in Halifax, NS, and the R.A. Jodrey Chair. In addition to her administrative responsibilities, she researches and teaches in the areas of corporate social responsibility, stakeholder engagement, and marketing. She has received major awards for both her teaching and research. Before joining Dalhousie, she was a professor at Queen's School of Business. She has considerable international and board experience, and she was in industry before becoming an academic.

Leleah Fernandez is a doctoral candidate in Media and Information Studies at Michigan State University, where she earned earlier degrees in journalism (BA) and advertising (MA). She has published on the topics of new media, mobilization, and science communication. Ms. Fernandez has worked as assistant to the editor for *Communication Yearbook* and as a research assistant for a multiyear project on communication and public will. Prior to commencing her doctoral studies, Ms. Fernandez worked in legislative news writing, public opinion polling, and political public relations for various public- and private-sector agencies in Michigan.

Alexa K. Fox is a marketing PhD candidate at the Fogelman College of Business & Economics, University of Memphis. She also serves as Chair of DocSIG, the American Marketing Association Special Interest Group for marketing doctoral students. Ms. Fox's research interests include digital marketing, neuromarketing, online complaint management, and online privacy. Her work has appeared in various journals including the *Journal of Advertising* and *Journal of Transportation Security*, as well as at various national conferences, including the American Marketing Association Winter Marketing Educators Conference, Summer Marketing Educators Conference, and Marketing & Public Policy Conference.

Katherine Gallagher earned her PhD at the University of British Columbia. She is associate professor of marketing in the Faculty of Business Administration at Memorial University of Newfoundland in St. John's, Newfoundland, and Labrador, Canada.

Douglas A. Gentile (PhD) is associate professor of developmental psychology at Iowa State University, and is one of the top experts on the psychological effects of media on children and adolescents. He is editor of the book *Media Violence and Children: A Complete Guide for Parents and Professionals*, which will enter its second edition in 2014. He was honored with the Distinguished Scientific Contributions to Media Psychology Award from the American Psychological Association and was named one of the Top 300 Professors in the United States by the *Princeton Review*.

James Gentry is the Maurice J. and Alice Hollman Professor of International Business and Marketing at the University of Nebraska-Lincoln. He earned his DBA degree from Indiana University. He is the former North American editor of the *Journal of Consumer Behaviour* as well as the former editor of the *AMS Review*. He has authored (or more frequently, coauthored) over 80 articles, 14 chapters in edited books, and over 200 conference papers. His current research interests are the future quality of life of elderly globally, changes in consumption due to life-event transitions, family decision making, and gender roles.

Charles S. Gulas is a professor of marketing in the Raj Soin College of Business at Wright State University. His primary research interest is humor in advertising. He has coauthored numerous journal articles, several book chapters, and a book on the topic. He has previous work experience as a regional sales representative, founder and owner of a small business, and cofounder and former president of a not-for-profit corporation. He has worked as a consultant for government agencies, small businesses, advertising agencies, and Fortune 1000 firms. He is currently on the advisory boards of two small businesses.

Dr. Robert L. Harrison is an assistant professor of marketing at Western Michigan University's Haworth College of Business. His research interests include consumer culture theory, gender and family consumer behavior, qualitative and mixed methodologies, and public policy and ethical marketing issues. He has made numerous presentations at national academic conferences and his work is published in the *Journal of Business Research, Journal of Advertising, Journal of Macromarketing, Marketing Theory, Journal of Historical Research in Marketing, Qualitative Market Research, Academy of Marketing Science Review*, and *Preventive Medicine*.

Ronald Paul Hill (PhD, University of Maryland College Park) is the Richard J. and Barbara Naclerio Endowed Chair, Villanova School of Business and former Senior Associate Dean, Intellectual Strategy. He has authored nearly 200 journal articles, book chapters, and conference papers on a variety of topics. Areas include restricted consumer behavior, marketing ethics, corporate social responsibility, and public policy. Outlets for this research include *Journal of Marketing Research, Journal of Consumer Research, Business and Society, International Journal of Research in Marketing, Human Rights Quarterly, Journal of the Academy of Marketing Science, Harvard Business Review,* and *Journal of Public Policy & Marketing.* His term as editor of the *Journal of Public Policy and Marketing* extends from July 1, 2006 until June 30, 2012.

Mindy Ji-Song (PhD, Texas A&M University) previously served on the faculty in the marketing department at Iowa State University. She currently resides in Ames, Iowa.

Tim Jones is an associate professor of marketing at Memorial University of Newfoundland. He conducts research that examines the content and value of customer relationships and the role of violence in marketing. His research has been published in the *Journal of the Academy of Marketing Science, Journal of Service Research, Journal of Advertising, Journal of Services Marketing, Qualitative Marketing Research, Canadian Journal of Media Studies, Journal of Family Violence,* and in conference proceedings of the American Marketing Association, the Academy of Marketing Science, and the Administrative Sciences Association of Canada.

Dr. Jeremy Kees is an associate professor of marketing and the Richard Naclario Emerging Scholar in Public Policy at Villanova University. His research interests include advertising/promotions effectiveness, intertemporal choice, and consumer risk. His recent public policy related research examines consumer processing of nutrition information, food supplement claims, cigarette warning labels, and direct-to-consumer prescription drug advertising. His research has been published in various journals including *Journal of Marketing Research, Journal of Public Policy & Marketing, American Journal of Public Health, Journal of Advertising, Journal of Interactive Marketing, Psychology and Marketing,* and *Journal of Consumer Affairs.*

Dr. Sarah N. Keller has developed a service learning curriculum that allows her to apply professional experiences from overseas entertainment education and health communication campaigns with Population Communication International, U.S. AID, and Family Health International. Her students have collectively produced annual social marketing campaigns over the past 10 years, including: "Get Tested!" to prevent HIV; "Open Your Eyes" to prevent domestic violence; and, most recently, "Let's Talk" to prevent suicide and depression. Each campaign has been supported by external grants and in-kind services from area broadcast and media professionals, solicited by the professor.

Sookyong Kim (MS, Kansas State University) is a doctoral student in the Department of Advertising and Public Relations at Michigan State University. She has worked as a research assistant at Michigan State University for the Advergame project funded by the National Institutes of Health. Ms. Kim's work focuses mainly on green marketing, ecologically conscious consumer behavior, social marketing, and implications for public policy. She is currently teaching sponsorships and promotions to undergraduate students at Michigan State University.

Russell N. Laczniak (PhD, University of Nebraska-Lincoln) is currently professor and chair of the Departments of Management and Marketing and John and Connie Stafford Faculty Fellow at Iowa State University. Dr. Laczniak served as editor of the *Journal of Advertising* and was president and treasurer of the American Academy of Advertising. His publications have appeared in the *Journal of Consumer Psychology, Journal of the Academy of Marketing Science, Journal of Advertising, Journal of Current Issues and Research in Advertising, Journal of Advertising Research, Journal of Public Policy & Marketing,* and *Journal of Consumer Affairs,* among others.

Dr. Anne M. Lavack is professor of marketing in the School of Business and Economics at Thompson Rivers University in Kamloops, British Columbia, Canada. She has previously taught at University of Regina, University of Winnipeg, and Concordia University in Montreal. Her research interests focus on social marketing. She has published articles in a variety of journals including *Journal of Public Policy & Marketing, Health Communication, American Journal of Public Health, Social Marketing Quarterly,* and *International Journal of Advertising.* She has served as a member of the board of directors for the Canadian Centre on Substance Abuse and for Ishtar Women's Transition Housing.

Hillary A. Leonard (PhD, University of Utah) is an associate professor of marketing at the University of Rhode Island. Her primary research interest focuses on consumer culture theory and understanding how people make meaning in a consumer society. Her research has been published in the *Journal of Advertising, Journal of Business Research,* and *Journal of Public Policy & Marketing.*

Julia A. Maier received her PhD in psychology from Iowa State University. She is an assistant professor of psychology at Waldorf College in Forest City, Iowa, where she teaches courses in social psychology, personality, and research methods. Her research interests are directed toward the study of media and the self, with interests in how experiences with the media are modified by the self and how these experiences can affect the future of the self. She has also incorporated both terror management theory and self-determination theory to explore these relationships on an existential level.

Kim K. McKeage is associate professor of quantitative methods and a contributing faculty in marketing in the School of Business at Hamline University. Her research interests include gendered market spaces and gender identity among consumers, consumer vulnerability and stigma, and economic justice. She also explores historical marketing and consumer behavior themes in food and cooking with a focus on women's domestic roles. Her current research includes macromarketing issues in food systems, higher-education services for first-generation college students, and consumption experiences of transgender individuals.

Patricia A. Norberg is an associate professor at Quinnipiac University in Hamden, Connecticut. She completed her PhD degree in marketing at the University of Rhode Island, where she also completed her MBA and BS in finance. Her main areas of expertise are privacy, information disclosure, incentives, advertising, and behavioral pricing. Her research appears in academic journals including *Journal of Consumer Psychology, Journal of the Academy of Marketing Science, Journal of Advertising, Psychology & Marketing,* and *Journal of Consumer Affairs.*

Dr. A.J. Otjen has developed experiential learning curriculum that has been well attended by students and enthusiastically received by the community at Montana State University-Billings. The curriculum allows her to apply professional experiences from a corporate marketing career of over 25 years including as vice president of marketing operations for Sprint Corporation. Her students produced (along with Dr. Keller's students) the "Open Your Eyes" campaign, which has won 6 ADDY awards as well as the Montana Broadcaster's Association Community Service Award. She is the advisor for the American Advertising Federation club on campus.

Ethan Pancer is an assistant professor of marketing at the Sobey School of Business at Saint Mary's University. Dr. Pancer holds a PhD in management, concentrating in marketing, from Queen's School of Business, where he also completed his B.Com. and M.Sc. in Management degrees. His research interests include consumer judgment formation and decision making, social and interpersonal influences on consumption, violent media, video games, and consumer well-being. His research has appeared in the *Journal of Advertising* and *Journal of Historical Research in Marketing*, as well as several international conferences.

Martin Pyle is an assistant professor at the Ted Rogers School of Management (Ryerson University). His research interests primarily lie in the dual domains of self-presentation and social comparison, and how these theories apply to consumers' choices regarding the appeal of media depictions of violence. In addition, he is also pursuing a research stream in the area of word-of-mouth (WOM), focusing on how consumers use their WOM to present certain images. His work has been published in the *Journal of Advertising*, as well as several top-tier conferences.

Justine M. Rapp (PhD, University of Nebraska-Lincoln) is an assistant professor of marketing at the University of San Diego's School of Business Administration. Justine's research interests focus on the domain of consumer welfare, and more specifically the development and impact of compulsive consumption within the consumer context. Justine's research has implications for a variety of domains (e.g., consumer behavior, public policy, and underrepresented groups), and she has published several peer-reviewed articles in journals such as the *Journal of Business Ethics, Journal of Advertising*, and *Journal of Business Research*.

Tom Reichert (PhD, University of Arizona) is Athletic Association Professor of Advertising and head of the department of advertising and public relations in the Grady College of Journalism and Mass Communication at the University of Georgia. He has been teaching, researching, and writing about advertising since 1993, and his research interests include advertising and mass communication content and effects. He has written or edited seven books about major issues and concerns regarding the uses and effects of advertising on professional practice and culture.

Gitte Kongsbjerg Richards (Jensen) is a PhD student in experimental and applied psychology at the University of Regina, Saskatchewan. Her dissertation and research interests are focused on improving the effectiveness of social marketing campaigns targeting bystanders to domestic violence.

Jef I. Richards (JD, Indiana University, 1981; PhD, University of Wisconsin, 1988), is professor and chair of the Department of Advertising & Public Relations at Michigan State University. He was professor of advertising at the University of Texas at Austin, 1988–2010, serving as department chairman from 1998 to 2002. His research includes advertising regulatory issues, and he has published more than 80 articles, books, and book chapters. He also serves on review boards for 8 scholarly journals, is a former president of the American Academy of Advertising, and is a member of the Advertising Educational Foundation's Board of Directors.

Nora J. Rifon (PhD, Business, MA, BA Psychology) is a professor in the Department of Advertising and Public Relations at Michigan State University. She cofounded and directed the Children's Central Research Collaborative at Michigan State University, and served as Privacy Executive on Loan to the Michigan Department of Information Technology. Her research has been funded by the National Science Foundation, the National Institutes of Health, Microsoft Research, the Michigan Children's Trust, and other agencies, and has been published in marketing, advertising, communication, computer science, public health, and policy journals. She lives in Okemos, Michigan, with her daughter and two rescue beagles.

Marla B. Royne (Stafford) (PhD, University of Georgia) is Great Oaks Foundation Professor of Marketing and chair of the Department of Marketing and Supply Chain Management at the University of Memphis. She is the 2014 president of the American Academy of Advertising and past editor of the *Journal of Advertising*. Her research has appeared in a wide range of academic journals including the *Journal of Retailing, Journal of Advertising, Journal of Advertising Research, Decision Sciences, Journal of Public Policy & Marketing*, and several other publications. She is coeditor of the book, *Advertising and New Media* (M.E. Sharpe, 2005).

Karen C. Smreker (MA, Michigan State University) is a public relations PhD student in the Media and Information Studies program at Michigan State University. She is a teaching assistant at MSU and has taught several advertising classes to Seniors and Masters students. Her research interests include promoting positive health behavior with topics ranging from advergames' influence on childhood obesity to the prevention of cyberbullying. She is also interested in the effects of celebrity endorsers, specifically looking at when a celebrity gets in trouble.

Marc G. Weinberger is Professor Emeritus at the Isenberg School of Management, University of Massachusetts, Amherst, where his advertising work has explored the use of humor and other message devices in magazines, television, and radio advertising. He has coauthored two books, *Humor in Advertising: A Comprehensive Analysis and Effective Radio Advertising* as well as articles that have appeared in the *Journal of Marketing, Journal of Advertising Research, Journal of Advertising, European Journal of Marketing,* and *Journal of Current Research in Advertising*, among others. He serves on the editorial review boards for the *Journal of Advertising* and the *Journal of Marketing Education*.

Timothy J. Wilkinson is Charles Professor and Charles L. Boppell Dean School of Business at Whitworth University. He formerly served as dean of the College of Business at Montana State University Billings. A noted expert in the area of exports and export promotion, he has served as associate director of the University of Akron Institute for Global Business. Dr. Wilkinson has written for publications such as the *Journal of Business Research, Journal of International Business Studies, International Business Review*, and *Journal of Small Business Research*. His articles have also been published in *Business Horizons, MIT Sloan Management Review*, and the *Wall Street Journal*.

Index

AAAA, 250
Aaker, David S., 78
Abuse perpetrators, 217
Acceptance of Interpersonal Violence Against Women (AIV) Scale, 101
Ads. *See also* Advertising, violent content in; Humor combined with violence in advertising; Men portrayed in ads; Sex combined with violence in advertising; *specific product*; Women portrayed in ads
   body image in young girls and, 56
   Cartoon Network, 155
   celebrities in, 134–136, 142–143
   expenditures on, global, 238
   humor in, 62
   Major League Baseball Playoffs, 61
   minority portrayals in, 45, 57
   objectification of women in, 47
   as persuasive communication, unsought, 26
   secondary effects of, 54
   sexist, 218
   sexual content in
      defining sexual words and phrases, 79–80
      effects of, 80–82
      in magazines, 80
      prevalence of, 80, 95–96, 106
   social effects of, 54
   in video games, real-world, 19–20
Adult entertainment, marketing to children, 247
Advertiser Accountability campaign, 154
Advertising, violent content in. *See also* Humor combined with violence in advertising; Multilayered content analysis of violence in advertising; Regulation; *specific ad*; Violent media
   aggression as outcome of, 3–4, 7
   appeal of violence and, 117–118, 238–239, 241, 259
   consumers' perceptions of, research on
      cluster analysis, 31, *33*, 34–36, *35*, 37–38
      design of study, 26
      dimensions, 32–34, *33*, 37
      discussion of, 36–39
      future, 36, 39
      limitations of, 38
      methodology of, 26, *27–29*, 30
      multidimensional scaling analysis, 31–32

Advertising, violent content in
   consumers' perceptions of, research on *(continued)*
      overview of, 4, 23–24, 39
      participant sampling, 30
      procedure, 30
      results of, 31–36, *33*
      stimuli, 26, *27–29*
   defining *violence* and, 82–83
   deserving victims and, 32–36, *33*
   effectiveness of, 19–20
   effects of, 54, 83
   future research on, 36, 38–39, 57
   historical perspective of, 237
   Journal of Advertising special issue on, 3
   Major League Baseball Playoffs ads, 61
   Misattribution Theory and, 57
   overview of, 4–7
   past research on, typical, 24
   from perpetrator's perspective, 32–37, *33*
   policymakers and, 82
   prevalence of, 82–83, 259–260
   protection of, 246–247
   purpose of, 24
   research on, lack of, 255
   researchers and, 82
   response to, 245–246
   scientific research and, 3–4, 7
   secondary effects of, 54
   two-dimensional framework in reacting to, 4, 23–24, *27–29*, 32–34, *33*, 37
   types of
      comedic appeals, 245
      fear appeals, 243–244, 259
      "happy" violence, 244
      informational appeals, 259
      overview of, 241
      print ads, 241–243, *242*, *243*
      shock appeals, 259
   from victim's perspective, 32–37, *33*
Affective aggression, 117
Age and rating systems, 183, 187–191, *190*
Aggression. *See also* General Aggression Model (GAM)
   affective, 117
   arousal and, 117
   children's learning of, 152, 161–162
   culture of, potential for, 106–107

INDEX

Aggression *(continued)*
  defining, 11
  electronic, 142
  hostile, 117
  humor and, 244
  instrumental, 117
  mechanisms that exposure to violent media causes, 117
  memory-based knowledge structures for, 163, 175
  music lyrics and, 17
  online, 142
  in pornography, 87–88
  social media and, 142
  violent content in advertising and outcome of, 3–4, 7
  violent media and effect of, 17–18, 245–246
All in the Family (TV program), 217
Allen, Mike, 229
American Academy of Pediatrics report (2001), 181
American Association of Advertising Agencies (AAAA), 250
ANA, 156
Analysis of covariance (ANCOVA), 222–224
Analysis of variance (ANOVA), 122–124, 126–127
ANCOVA, 222–224
Anderson, Charles R., 61
Anderson, Craig A., 3–4, 62, 82, 96, 137, 163, 168, 191, 256
Anderson, Rachel L., 88
Andersson, Svante, 259
Andy Griffith Show (TV program), 5, 47–48
ANOVA, 122–124, 126–127
Anthes, Emily, 140
Arbesman, Samuel, 3
Armstrong, Gary M., 152
Armstrong, Russell, 140
Armstrong, Taylor, 140
Arousal and aggression, 117
Arousal-transfer, 62
Association of National Advertisers (ANA), 156
AT&T ad, 54
Australian Standards Bureau, 87
Autonomy principle, *270*, 271

Baldwin, Alec, 142
Bandura, Albert, 60, 97
Bartos, Rena, 77–78, 83
Batman character, 13
Baumeister, Roy F., 25, 117–118
BBFC, 248
Behavior change models, 217
Bell Bajao domestic violence campaign (India), 201–203, 207, *211*
Benetton ad, 237, *238*, 241, 269
Benevolent humor, 62–63, *63*

Bernbach, William, 45
Bhadury, Roop K., 57, 245
Bias
  perceptual, 186–187
  self-selection, 223
Bigelow, Kathryn, 11–12
Biocca, Frank A., 83
Bitch Skateboards ad, 243
Blackberry ad, 49, 54–55
"Blame the victim" mentality, 50
"Blonde jokes," 46–47
Bohil, Corey J., 83
Bonacci, Angelica M., 97
Boomerang effects, 217
Bork, Robert, 181
Boyatzis, Richard E., 260, 264
Brady Bunch, The (TV program), 47
Brand effects of sex combined with violence in advertising, 84–86, *85*
Breast cancer prevention campaigns, 217
British Board of Film Classification (BBFC), 248
Bronstein, Carolyn, 94–95
Brown, Chris, 137, 139
Brown, Mark R., 57, 83, 245, 249
Brucks, Merrie, 152
Bruzzone, Donald E., 78
Bud Light beer ad, 48–50, *50*, 55
Bureau of Justice Statistics, 229
Burger King ad, 49
Burt, Martha R., 94
Bushman, Brad J., 3–4, 82, 86, 95, 97, 136–137, 141, 163, 168, 191, 256, 259
Buzz marketing, 249
Bystander intervention in domestic violence. *See also* Domestic violence campaigns
  bystander characteristics and, 203–204
  collective efficacy and, 204
  Latané and Darley model of, 197–200, 208–209
  recommendations for, key, 208–209
  relationship between bystander and victim and, 204
  situational factors and, 204–206
  social disorganization theory and, 204–205
  steps for
    determining appropriate intervention, 206–207
    feeling responsibility to intervene, 203–206
    interpreting the situation as emergency, 202–203
    intervening, 207
    noticing the incident, 200–202
    overview of, 6, 200, 208–209
    role of bystander and, 197–200
  victim characteristics and, 204

CAA, 13
Call of Duty (video game), 12
Calvin Klein jeans ad, 87

"Camouflage" reaction, 60
Campbell, W. Keith, 25, 117–118
Carlson, Bonnie E., 202
Carlson, Les, 175
Carnagey, Nicholas L., 191
Carolina Population Center recommendations for statistical controls, 221
Cartoon Network ads, 155
CARU, 154, 161–162, 175, 247
Categorization, 186–187
Celebrity violence
  backlash from, 134
  case studies of recent, 137, *138*, 139
  celebrities as product endorsers in ads, 134–136, 142–143
  consumers' responses to, 143–144
  domestic violence and, 137, 139–140
  media coverage of, 134
  modeling, 145
  new generation of, 140–141
  overview of, 5–6, 134–135
  reality TV programs and, 140–141
  reports of, 136–137, *138*
  social media and, 145
  strategies for managing, potential, 143–144, *143*, *144*
  teens and, influence on, 141–142, 145
Censorship, 87, 248. *See also* Regulation of violence in advertising
Central Hudson Test, 247
Child Safe Viewing Act (2007), 152, 156
Children
  adult entertainment and, marketing to, 247
  aggression and, learning of, 152, 161–162
  body image of young girls and ads, 56
  desensitization of, 181
  experimental study of effect of violence in TV ads and
    discussion of, 173–174, *174*
    hypotheses of, 170–171
    limitations of, 176
    methodology of, 171–172
    overview of, 170–171
    procedures and measures, 172
    results of, 172–173, *173*
  fantasy versus reality, distinguishing between, 152
  focus groups in study of violence in TV ads and
    children's focus groups, 165–167
    parents' focus groups, 167–169
    results of focus groups, 169–170
  longitudinal studies of violence in TV ads and, 162
  meta-analytic study of violence in TV ads and, 161
  rating systems and
    exposure to violent media and, 151–152
    perceptions of, 181–184, 191–192

Children *(continued)*
  sensitivity to violence and, 181
  violent content and
    exposure to, 151–152, 170–174, *173*, *174*
    fear as effect of, 19
  violent media and
    defining *violence* and, 162–163
    exposure to, 151–152, 170–174, *173*, *174*, 175–176, 245–246
    future research on, 176
    gender differences, 170–175
    heroic characters and, 13, 245
    overview of, 6, 161–162
    perceptions of, 165–167, 169–170
    theory and research on, 163, *164*
Children's Advertising Review Unit (CARU), 154, 161–162, 175, 247
Choi, Sejung Marina, 136
Cline, Victor B., 88, 157, 181, 184
Clinton, Bill, 79
Cluster analysis, 31, *33*, 34–36, *35*, 37–38
CMAA, 13
Cognitive structures, 117. *See also* Consumers' perceptions of violent advertisements
Collective efficacy, 204
Comedic appeals of violence, 245
"Comedic cloak," 244
Comic books, violent content in, 13
Comic Code Authority (CAA), 13
Comics Magazine Association of America (CMAA), 13
Commercials. *See* Ads; *specific product*
Congruence theme, 265–266, 271, *278*, *286*, *288*
Consumers' perceptions of violent advertisements, research on
  cluster analysis, 31, *33*, 34–36, *35*, 37–38
  design of study, 26
  dimensions of, 32–34, *33*, 37
  discussion of, 36–39
  future, 39
  limitations of, 38
  methodology of, 26, *27–29*, 30
  multidimensional scaling analysis, 31–32
  overview of, 4, 23–24, 39
  participant sampling, 30
  procedure, 30
  results of, 31–36, *33*
  stimuli, 26, *27–29*
Consumers' responses to celebrity violence, 143–144
Content analysis, 45, 56–57, 80
Content rating systems. *See* Rating systems
Convergent views of scientific research, 3
Cooper, Anderson, 140
Cosby Show, The (TV program), 47
Courrier, Steven, 157, 181, 184
Courtney, Alice E., 79
Covell, Katherine, 88

INDEX

Crimestoppers Domestic Violence campaign (United Kingdom), 206–207, *212*
Criminal behavior and violent media, unclear link to, 116
Croft, Roger G., 157, 181, 184
Cross, Gary, 48, 54, 56
Cross-sectional research, 18, 221–223
Crowley, John H., 78
Cruz, Carlos, 136–137, 141
Culpability of advertising, 95–96, 152–153, 217
Cultivation theory, 19
Cultural spillage, 53
Culture of aggression, potential for, 106–107
CUT IT OUT domestic violence campaign, 201, 205–206, *213*
Cyberbulling, 142

Dahl, Darren W., 78, 83, 87, 259
Darley, John M., 197. *See also* Latané and Darley model of bystander intervention in domestic violence
Decency Enforcement Center for Television (Decent TV), 154
Deen, Paula, 134
Denigration, 48, 50, *51–52*, 53–54
Descriptive statistics, 182–183, *183*, 222–223
Desensitization
  of children, 181
  defining, 18
  dominance appeal of violent video games and, 127–129
  emotional, 18–19
  humor combined with violence in Super Bowl ads, 70–71
  occurrence of, 62
  physiological, 18–19
  video game violence and, 127–129
  to violence against women, 107
Deserving victims of violence, perceived, 32–36, *33*
Detrimental humor, 62–63, *63*
Discriminatory behavior and racist or sexist jokes, 55
Disney Channel, 156
Disparagement and humor, 46–47
Dodge Nitro car ad, 249
Dodge Ram pickup truck ad, 48
Dolce and Gabbana clothier ad, 87, 242, *243*
Domestic violence. *See also* Domestic violence campaigns
  abuse perpetrators and, types of, 217
  awareness of services and, 219, 224, *226*, 228–229
  beliefs about efficacy of services for, 220, 224, 228–229, *228*
  "blame the victim" mentality and, 50
  celebrity, 137, 139–140
  collective efficacy and, 204

Domestic violence *(continued)*
  defining, 197
  female-initiated, 55–56
  interventions, typical forms of, 215–216
  against men, 55–56
  perceptions about severity of, 219, 224, 226, *226*, 228–229, *228*
  prevention strategies, new, 216
  social disorganization theory and, 204–205
  types of, 197
Domestic violence campaigns
  bystander intervention and
    determining appropriate intervention, 206–207
    feeling responsibility to intervene, 203–206
    interpreting the situation as emergency, 202–203
    intervening, 207
    Latané and Darley model of, 197–200, 208–209
    noticing the incident, 200–202
    overview of, 6, 197, 208–209, *211–214*
    recommendations for, key, 208–209
    role of bystander and, 197–200
  effects of, unintended
    audiences, unintended or excluded, 216–217
    awareness of domestic violence services and, 219, 224, *226*, 228–229
    beliefs about efficacy of domestic violence services and, 220, 228–229, *228*
    boomerang, 217
    culpability, 217
    discussion of study of, 228–229
    future research on, 230–231
    gender differences and, 218, 220, 224, *225*, 226, *226*, 227, 228–229, *228*
    Health Belief Model and, 215, 218–220
    health communication, 216–218
    Heuristic-Systematic Model and, 219
    hypotheses of, 218–220
    interventions and, typical, 215–216
    limitations of study of, 230–231
    methodology of study of, 220–222
    overview of, 6–7, 215
    perception of severity of domestic violence and, 219, 224, 226, *226*, 228–229, *228*
    response efficacy and, 224, *228*
    results of study of, 222–224, *225*, 226, *226*, *227*, *228*
    self-selection bias and, 223
    social norming, 218
    social reproduction, 217
    theory of study of, 218–220
    third-person effect hypothesis and, 216–217
  objectives of, 198
  print ads for study of, 220, *233*, *234*
  self-reported effects and, 223

Dominance appeal of violent video games
  consequences of exposure to, 116
  direct experience of domination and, 130
  mechanisms that exposure to violent media cause aggression and, 117
  overview of, 5, 115, 128–132
  physical dominance and, 118–119, 129–130
  popularity of, 116
  reactions to, 119
    moderation of, 119–120
  reason for, 128
  regulation of, 116
  research on
    analysis of variance and, 122–124, 126–127
    desensitization and, 127–129
    discussion of, 128–132
    Experiment 1, 121–125, 128–129
    Experiment 2, 125–128
    gender differences, 124, 128–129
    hypotheses of, 121, 124–125, 127–128, 128
    implications of, 131–132
    limitations of, 130–131
    mediation analyses and, 124, 127
    moderation of reactions to domination in, 119–120
    motivation for, 117–121
    reactions to domination in, 119
    reasons for appeal, 117–118
    role of dominance in appeal of, 118–119
    vicarious versus real domination and, 125, 131
  role of dominance in human evolutionary history and, 118–119
  "witness perspective" and, 119
Donnerstein, Edward, 96
Don't Ignore It domestic violence campaign (United Kingdom), 201, 206, *212*
Doritos ad, 57
Duncan Quinn clothier ad, 84
Dutton, Don, 220

Eagleton, Terry, 48
Electronic aggression, 142
Elevator Action (video game), 14
Emotional desensitization, 18–19
Emotional response effects of sex combined with violence in advertising, 86–87
Empathy, 267
Entertainment Software Review Board (ESRB), 12, 179, 191, 250
"Erotic communications appeals," 96
ESRB, 12, 179, 191, 250
Ethical content analysis, 260, *261*, 268–269, *270*, 271–272
Everybody Loves Raymond (TV program), 47
Experimental studies, 17. *See also* Children

F-test, 226
Family Guy (TV program), 47, 79
Family Violence: It's Not OK. Are You OK? (New Zealand), 201–202, 206–207, *212*
Family Violence Prevention Fund (FVPF), 216
Father Knows Best (TV program), 47
FCC, 152, 247
Fear appeals of violence, 243–244, 259
Fear as effect of violent media, 19
Federal Communications Commission (FCC), 152, 247
Federal Trade Commission (FTC), 180, 247
Felson, Richard B., 202
Female-initiated intimate partner violence, 55–56
Field experiments, 17
Field, Richard, 268
Fifty Shades trilogy, 77–79, 83–84, 88–90
Films, violent content in, 14, 131, 156, 239, 248. *See also specific film*
First Amendment, 237, 246, 248, 251
Fischoff, Baruch, 192
Focus groups. *See* Children
Ford, John B., 87, 218
Ford SportKa ad, 245, 249
Frankenberger, Kristina D., 78, 83, 87, 259
Freedman, Jonathan L., 82
French Connection UK ad, 79
Frye, Victoria, 205
FTC, 180, 247
Furnham, Adrian, 259
FVPF, 216

Galvin skin response (GSR), 18
GAM. *See* General Aggression Model
Game Boy ad, 242, *242*
Garcia, Enrique, 205
Gatorade ad, 136
Gears of War (video game), 174, 179
Gender differences
  children and violent media and, 170–175
  domestic violence campaigns and, unintended effects of, 218, 220, 224, *225*, 226, *226*, *227*, 228–229, *228*
  dominance appeal of violent video games research and, 124, 128–129
  sex combined with violence in advertising and, 105–106
Gender portrayals in TV programs, 47–48
General Aggression Model (GAM)
  describing, 16–17, *16*, 163, 165
  exposure to violent media and, 117, 175
  function of, 11
Gentile, Douglas A., 187
Gentry, James W., 61
Gerbner, G., 248
Gibson, Mel, 137, 139
Gilligan, Carol, 269
Giudice, Teresa, 140–141

Gladiatorial fights, 12
Glascock, Jack, 61
Globalization
  ad expenditures and, 238
  regulation of violence in advertising and, 248–249
Goffman, Erving, 47–48, 56
Grand Theft Auto (video game), 12, 79, 115
Greenwald, Anthony G., 219
Grigorieva, Oksana, 139
Grossbart, Sanford, 175
GSR, 18
Gulas, Charles S., 83
Gunter, Barrie, 61, 259

Handschuh, Felipe Bances, 249
Hansen, Christine Hall, 118
Hansen, Ranald D., 118
"Happy" violence, 244
Harrison, Robert L., 61
Health Belief Model (HBM), 215, 218–220
Health communications and unintended effects of domestic violence campaigns, 216–218
Heckler, Susan E., 97
Henthorne, Tony L., 95
Hermans, Charlies M., 161, 170
Hernandez, Aaron, 139
Herrero, Juan, 205
Heuristic-Systematic Model (HSM), 219
Hoefnagels, Cees, 198, 201, 204
Hoffman, Adonis, 250
Holland, Dawn, 137
Holsti's reliability, 53
Home Improvement (TV program), 47–48
Honesty principle, *270*, 271
Hoskin, Anthony, 202
Hostile aggression, 117
Hostile attribution bias, 13
Hoyer, Wayne D., 187
HSM, 219
Huesmann, L. Rowell, 62, 97, 184, 245
Humor. *See also* Humor combined with violence in advertising
  in ads, 62
  agent of, 46
  aggressive, 244
  audience for, 46
  benevolent, 62–63, *63*
  "blonde jokes," 46–47
  complexity of, 45
  detrimental, 62–63, *63*
  dimensions of, 65, *65*
  disparagement and, 46–47
  elements of, 46
  object of, 46–47
  power of, to demean, 54
  racist, 46, 55
  sexist, 46–47, 55

Humor *(continued)*
  theories of, 45–46
  third-party, 46
  typologies, 62–63, *63*
  violence and, interfacing of, 62–63
Humor combined with violence in advertising
  "camouflage" reaction and, 60
  male depictions, research on
    backlash to criticism of, 55
    content analysis and, 56–57
    deconstruction of advertising imagery and, 48, *51–52*, 53–54, *53*, 56–57
    denigration of, 48, 50, *51–52*, 53–54
    discussion of, 54–57
    future, 57
    literature review, 45–48
    methodology of, 48
    overview of, 4, 45
    physical violence and, explicit, 48–50, *50*
    power of humor to demean and, 54
    questions raised by, 56–57
    results of, 48, 53–54
    in Super Bowl ads (1989, 1999, and 2009), 48, 53–54, *54*, 64
    violence against men and, 55–56
  overview of, 4–5
  past studies on, 60
  in Super Bowl ads, research on
    background information, 61–63
    change in ads and, 66, *66*
    conceptual definitions, 64–65
    correlation among variables, 69, *69*
    desensitization and, 70–71
    discussion of, 70–71
    frequency of ads, 65–66, *65*
    goals of, 63
    humor in advertising, 62
    implications of, 70–71
    interface of violence and humor and, 62–63
    likability of ads and, 66, *67–68*, 69–71, *69*
    limitations, 71
    male depictions in (1989, 1999, 2009), 48, 53–54, *54*, 64
    methodology of, 63–65
    overview of, 5, 60–61, 72
    parental gatekeeping and, 71
    popularity of, 66, *67–68*, 69–70, *69*
    prevalence of violence in media and, 61
    processes of media effects and, 62
    results of, 65–66, 69–70
    sample, 64
Hurt Locker, The (film), 12
Hyman, Michael R., 161, 170

Identification in vicarious reactions, 119
Identification theme, 267, 271, *280*, *287*, *289*
Informational appeals of violence, 259
Instrumental aggression, 117

Intensity theme, 264–265, *278*, *286*, *288*
Interactive Digital Software Association, 250
Internet, violent content on, 15
Interrater reliabilities (IRR), 263, *282–285*
Intimate partner violence (IPV), 55, 197–198. *See also* Domestic violence; Domestic violence campaigns
Intimate Terrorism abuser, 217
IPV, 55, 197–198. *See also* Domestic violence; Domestic violence campaigns
IRR, 263, *282–285*
It's Not OK. Are You OK? domestic violence campaign (New Zealand), 201–202, 206–207, *212*

Jackson, Sally, 97
Jacoby, Jacob, 187
Jansz, Jeroen, 118
Jeong, Eui Jun, 83
Jhally, Sut, 48, 56
Johnson, Michael P., 217
Jordan, Michael, 136

Kardashian, Khloe, 134
Katz, Jackson, 229, 243
Keeping Up with the Kardashians (TV program), 140
Kennedy, John F., 269
Kenneth Cole fragrance ad, 79
Keystone Light beer ad, 85
Kilbourne, Jean, 45, 48, 56, 77, 268
Kim, Jooyoung, 64
King, Cynthia M., 60
Kirsh, Steven J., 61
Kitty Genovese murder (1964), 198
Kriegal Report, 249

Laczniak, Gene, 268–269
Larson, David B., 88
Latané and Darley model of bystander intervention in domestic violence, 197–200, 208–209
Latané, Bibb, 197. *See also* Latané and Darley model of bystander intervention in domestic violence
Latent content analysis, 260, *261*, 264–268
LaTour, Michael S., 86–87, 95–96, 106, 218
Leave It to Beaver (TV program), 47
Leavitt, Clark, 78, 219
Legitimacy theme, 266–267, 271, *280*, *287*, *289*
Legitimate violence, 266
Leone, Janel M., 217
Lever Bros., 78
Lewinsky, Monica, 79
Lewis, Ioni, 259
Lichtenstein, Sarah, 192
Linz, Daniel, 96
Liz Claiborne Inc. survey (2006), 198
Lohan, Lindsay, 137, 139

Longitudinal studies, 18, 63–65, 162
Loula footwear ad, 84
Loveline (radio show), 140
Lubsen, Graig, 118
Lyons, John S., 88

McAllister, Matthew P., 53
McConville, Maureen, 78
McCracken, Grant, 135
McGraw, A. Peter, 89
MacKay, Natalie J., 88
MacLean, Malcolm, 216
Madden sports franchise, 20
Magazines, sexual content in, 80
Major League Baseball Playoffs ads, 61
Manchanda, Rajesh V., 78, 83, 87, 259
MANCOVA, 102–103, *103*
Manifest content analysis, 260, *261*, 262–264
MANOVA, 34–35, *35*
Mars, Inc., 23
Martell, Dennis, 215, 217, 219, 222, 229
Martial arts, mixed, 15
Martin, Kelly D., 268–269, 271
Martin, Rod A., 62, 65, 69
"Mature content" label, 12–13
MDS, 31–32
Mean world syndrome, 19
Means and standard deviations of aggressive cognitions, 172–173, *173*
MEASURE Evaluation Project, 230
Media. *See specific type*
Mediation analyses, 124, 127
Memory effects of sex combined with violence in advertising, 86, 97
Men portrayed in ads, research on violence against
 backlash to criticism of, 55
 content analysis, 56–57
 deconstruction of advertising imagery and, 48, *51–52*, 53–54, *53*, 56–57
 denigration of, 48, 50, *51–52*, 53–54
 discussion of, 54–57
 future, 57
 literature review, 45–48
 methodology of, 48
 overview of, 4, 45
 physical violence and, explicit, 48–50, *50*
 power of humor to demean and, 54
 questions raised by, 56–57
 results of, 48, 53–54
 in Super Bowl ads (1989, 1999, and 2009), 48, 53–54, *54*, 64
 violence against men and, 55–56
Mentos ad, 239, *240*
Messner, Steven F., 202
Meta-analysis, 18–19, 88, 161
Meyer, Gary, 215, 217, 219, 222, 229
Middleton, Courtney, 87
Mike's Hard Lemonade ad, 49

Miller Lite beer ad, 85–87
Milner, Judith, 229
Minority portrayals in ads, 45, 57
Misattribution Theory, 57
Mixed martial arts (MMA), 15
Modeling behaviors, 62, 145
Moise, Jessica F., 184
Moral dilemmas and presumptions, 268–269
Morreall, John, 46
Morris, Jon D., 64
Mortal Kombat (video game), 179, 249
Motion Picture Advertising Association (MPAA), 247
Motion Picture Production Code (1930), 156
Movies, violent content in, 14, 131, 156, 239, 248. *See also specific movie*
MPAA, 247
Multidimensional scaling analysis (MDS), 31–32
Multilayered content analysis of violence in advertising
  applying, recommendations for, 272–273
  coding scheme used in, 262–263, *282–285*
  data collection, 260, 262
  future research on, 273–274
  interrater reliabilities and, 263, *282–285*
  latent (layer 2), 260, *261*, 264–268
  limitations of, 273–274
  literature review, 256, *257–258*, 259–260
  manifest (layer 1), 260, *261*, 262–264
  normative or ethical (layer 3), 260, *261*, 268–269, *270*, 271–272
  overview of, 7, 255–256, 260, *261*
  principles
    autonomy, *270*, 271
    honesty, *270*, 271
    nonmaleficence, 269, *270*
    respect, *270*, 271
    utility, 269, *270*
  purpose of, 260
  sample ads used in, 262, *278–281*
  themes
    congruence, 265–266, 271, *278*, *286*, *288*
    identification, 267, 271, *280*, *287*, *289*
    intensity, 264–265, *278*, *286*, *288*
    legitimacy, 266–267, 271, *280*, *287*, *289*
    perceived intention, 266, *279*, *286*, *288*
    power balance, 267–268, 271, *281*, *287*, *289*
Multivariate analysis of covariance (MANCOVA), 102–103, *103*
Multivariate analysis of variance (MANOVA), 34–35, *35*
Munoz, Mark, 15
Murphy, Patrick, 268–269
Music and music videos, violent content in, 13–14, 17
Mustonen, Anu, 262–263

Nathanson, Amy I., 61
Nathanson, Paul, 56
National Television Violence Study (NTVS), 61, 151–152, 241, 256
Nelson, Margaret C., 187
New York City Metro card, 237, *239*
Nill, Alexander, 268
Nonmaleficence principle, 269, *270*
Norfolk Constabulary Domestic Violence Campaign, 201, *212*
Normative content analysis, 260, *261*, 268–269, *270*, 271–272
NTVS, 61, 151–152, 241, 256
Nudity, 81. *See also* Sexual content in ads

Obama, Barack, 20
Observational learning, 62
Ocean, Frank, 139
Ogilvy, David, 80
O'Gorman, Rick, 83
Online aggression, 142
Online violence, 249–250
Open Your Eyes domestic violence campaign, 217, 220, 222, 228–231, *233*, *234*. *See also* Domestic violence campaigns, effects of

Paar, Jack, 78
Pagan, Jeffrey, 141–142
Pappa, Eleni, 259
Paquin, Gary W., 207
Parent-Teacher Association (PTA), 191–192
Parental perceptions of violent media, 167–170, 180–184, 187–192
Parents Television Council (PTC), 153–154, 156
Pasadeos, Yorgo, 83
PCS, 230
People magazine, 136–137, *138*
Pepsi Max soda ads, 49, 85, 238, *240*
Perceived intention theme, 266, *279*, *286*, *288*
Perceptual bias, 186–187
Perpetrator's perspective of violence, 32–37, *33*
Personal Safety Survey in Australia (2005), 198
Persuasion Knowledge Model, 266
Pew Research Center, 13
Phillips, Colleen M., 97
Physical dominance, 118–119, 129–130
Physical violence, 48–50, *50*
Physiological desensitization, 18–19
Pile sort, 26, 31
Piliavin, Irving M., 203, 207
Piliavin, Jane Allyn, 203, 207
Pinsky, Drew, 140
Pitts, Robert E., 96
Podolski, Cheryl-Lynn, 184
Pokrywczynski, James, 78
Pollay, Richard W., 45
Pope, Nigel K. Ll, 57, 245

Population Communication Services Project (PCS), 230
Pornography, 87–88. *See also* Sex combined with violence in advertising
Pornstar clothing ad, 88
Poshtakova, Dora, 249
Positive reinforcement, 62
Potter, W. James, 60, 62, 64–65
Power balance theme, 267–268, 271, *281*, *287*, *289*
Presser, Stanley, 221
Principles
  relating to consequentialism, 269, *270*, 271
  relating to intention and duty, *270*, 271–272
Print ads, visual violence in, 220, *233*, *234*, 241–243. *See also* Advertising, violent content in; *specific ad*
Processes of media effects, 62
Progressive Insurance ad, 49
Przybylski, Andrew, 119
Psychological violence. *See* Denigration
PTA, 191–192
PTC, 153–154, 156
Pulkkinen, Lea, 262–263
Pussy energy drink ad, 78, 89

Quaker Oats Gatorade ad, 136

Racist humor, 46, 55
Rape myth, 94
Rapp, Albert, 46
Rating systems
  age and, 183, 187–191, *190*
  children and
    exposure to violent media and, 151–152
    perceptions of, 181–184, 191–192
  current, 153
  exploratory study on
    discussion of, 155–157
    implications of, 156–157
    overview of, 154–155
    results of, 155–156
  for films, 156
  future research on, 157–158
  "mature content" label and, 12-13
  organizational efforts and, 153–154
  overview of, 6, 151
  responsibility for, 152–153
  for TV programs, 6, 153–155, *155*
  V-chip and, 151, 153
  for video games, violent
    age and content, 187–191
    age appropriateness and, 189, *190*
    categorization and, 186–187
    children's perceptions of, 181–184, 191–192
    discrepancy between children and parents and, 191
    efficacy of, 183

Rating systems
  for video games, violent *(continued)*
    exploring rating system and, 181–184, *183*, *185*, 186
    future research on, 192–193
    overview of, 6, 179–180, 191–192
    parental perceptions of, 180–184, 186–192
    parents as gatekeepers and, 191–192
    perceptual bias and, 186–187
    ratings by groups, 184, *185*, 186
    sensitivity to violence and, 181
    understanding age and content ratings, 187–191
    violence perceptions by game, 187–188, *190*
Real Housewives franchise (TV programs), 140
Reality TV, 140–141
Redbook survey (2006), 198
Reducing the Risk domestic violence campaign (United Kingdom), 206, *213*
Regression analysis, 69, *70*, 173–174, *174*
Regulation. *See also specific agency or law*
  of advertising violence
    Central Hudson Test and, 246–247
    children and, 247
    First Amendment and, 237, 246, 248, 251
    in future, 248–249
    globalization and, 248–249
    online, 250
    product and, 247
    school setting and, 247
    state-level, 246
  of dominance appeal of violent video games, 116
  of violent media, 116
Reichert, Tom, 97
Reid, Leonard, 80, 84
Reinforcement, positive, 62
Resident Evil (video game), 179
Resnik, David B., 269
Respect principle, *270*, 271
Revelstoke whiskey ad, 88
Rifon, Nora J., 136
Rigby, C. Scott, 119
Rihanna, 139
Rocco, Sal Jr., 243
Rodin, Judith, 203
Rosenthal, Abraham M., 198
Ross, Dorothea, 60
Ross, Sheila A., 60
Ross, William D., 268
Ryan, Richard M., 119

Sadism, 118
Sandy Hook Elementary School shooting, 151, 247
Scharrer, Erica, 46–48, 60, 63, 65, 71
Schibrowsky, John A., 268
Schlinger, Mary J., 78
School shootings, 151, 247

Scientific research, 3–4, 7. *See also specific type*
SCT, 136, 186
See It and Stop It domestic violence campaign, 205–206, *213*
Self-selection bias, 223
Sensation seeking, 118
Sex and the City (HBO cable TV series), 78
Sex combined with violence in advertising
  age and influence of, 105–106
  brand effects of, 84–86, *85*
  culture and, evolving, 78–79
  emotional response effects of, 86–87
  "erotic communications appeals" and, 96
  Fifty Shades trilogy and, 77–79, 83–84, 88–90
  gender differences and, 105–106
  hypotheses of, 98–99
  implications of, 106–107
  irritation and anger in making women buy products and, 77–78
  memory effects of, 86, 97
  occurrence of, 83–84
  overview of, 5, 77, 88–90
  social effects of, 87–88
Sexist ads, 218
Sexist humor, 46–47, 55. *See also* Humor combined with violent advertising, male depictions
Sexual content in ads. *See also* Sex combined with violence in advertising
  defining sexual words and phrases and, 79–80
  effects of, 80–82
  in magazines, 80
  prevalence of, 80, 95–96, 106
Shanahan, Kevin J., 161, 170
Sheen, Charlie, 134, 137, 139, 141
Shepard, Thomas, 81
Sherry, John, 118
Shock appeal of violence, 259
Shotland, R. Lance, 202, 204
Shuster, Joe, 13
Siegel, Joe, 13
Simpsons, The (TV program), 47
Situational Couple abuser, 217
Situational violence, 24
Slovic, Paul, 192
SLT, 96–98, 106
Smith, N. Craig, 268–269, 271
Smith, Stacy L., 61
Smreker, Karen, 136–137
Snickers ad, 23
Snook-Luther, David C., 96
Social cognitive theory (SCT), 136, 186
Social disorganization theory, 204–205
Social Identity Theory, 267
Social learning theory (SLT), 96–98, 106
Social media, 142, 145, 149
Social norming effects, 218

Social norms, enjoyment of violence and violated, 37
Social reproduction effects, 217
Soley, Lawrence, 80, 84
Sonkin, Daniel, 220
Sparks, Glenn G., 118
Speck, Paul Surgi, 46, 62
Spelling, Tori, 134
Sprint Blackberry ad, 49, 54–55
Stark, George, 142
Statistics Canada Family Violence report (2005), 201
Stereotypes of women, 94–95
Stern, Barbara B., 48, 56
Stiff, James, 37
Straw, Margaret K., 202, 204
Street Fighter (video game), 179, 184
Structural knowledge elicitation technique, 26, 31
Super Bowl ads. *See also* Humor combined with violence in advertising
  audience for, 53
  budgets for, largest, 54
  cultural spillage and, 53
Superheroes and violence, 13, 245
Superman character, 13
Swani, Kunal, 83

t-tests, 222, 229
Tamborini, Ron, 37
Tamburro, Robert F., 61
Tamhanes test, 224, 226
Tay, Richard, 259
Teens and exposure to violence, 141–142, 145, 244
Telecommunications Act (1996), 153
Tell a Gal P.A.L., Violence Against Women campaign, 201, 205–206, *214*
There's No Excuse for Domestic Violence campaign, 201–202, 205–207, *214*
Third-party humor, 46
Third-person effect hypothesis, 216–217
Thomas, Margaret Hanratty, 181
Tonight Show (TV program), 78
Tori and Dean (TV program), 140
Triangulation, 18
Trivialization of violence, 60
Trunk Monkey ad, 265–266
Trusted people, survey of most, 136
Truth as goal of scientific research, 3–4, 7
TV Parental Guidelines, 153
TV programs. *See also specific program*; Violent media
  celebrity violence and, 140–141
  exploratory study, 154–157
    future research on, 157–158
  father roles in, 47–48
  gender portrayals in, 47–48

TV programs *(continued)*
  rating systems for ads and
    current, 153
    organizational efforts, 153–154
    overview of, 6, 151
    violent content and children and, 151–152
  reality, 140–141
  violent content in, 14, 61–63
Twitchell, James B., 54
Twitter, 142, 149
Two-dimensional framework in reacting to violent content in advertising, 4, 23–24, *27–29*, 32–34, *33*, 37
Tyson, Mike, 134

Utility principle, 269, *270*

V-chip, 151, 153
Video games. *See also* Dominance appeal of violent video games; *specific game*
  ads incorporated in, real-world, 19–20
  desensitization and violent, 127–129
  exposure to violent, 12–13
  perceptual bias and, 186–187
  rating system for violent
    age and content, 187–191
    age appropriateness and, 189, *190*
    categorization and, 186–187
    children's perceptions of, 181–184, 191–192
    discrepancy between children and parents and, 191
    efficacy of, 183
    exploring rating system and, 181–184, *183, 185*, 186
    future research on, 192–193
    overview of, 6, 179–180, 191–192
    parental perceptions of, 180–184, 186–192
    parents as gatekeepers and, 191–192
    perceptual bias and, 186–187
    ratings by groups, 184, *185*, 186
    sensitivity to violence and, 181
    understanding age and content ratings, 187–191
    violence perceptions by game and, 189–190, *190*
  violent content in, 14–15, 116, 244
Violence. *See also* Celebrity violence; Men in advertisements; Sex combined with violence in advertising; Violent content; Violent media; Women in advertisements
  actors and, 25
  appeal of, 117–118, 238–239, 241, 259
  as choice, individual, 250
  comedic appeals of, 245
  defining, 11, 64–65, 82–83, 162–163, 237
  denigration and, 48, 50, *51–52*, 53–54
  deserving victims of, perceived, 32–36, *33*
  dimensions of causes of, 24

Violence *(continued)*
  domestic, 55
  enjoyment of and violation of social norms, 37
  fear appeals and, 243–244, 259
  happy, 244
  harm and, level of, 24–25
  of heroic characters, 245
  humor and, interfacing of, 62–63
  legitimate, 266
  against men, 55–56
  online, 249–250
  perpetrator's perspective of, 32–37, *33*
  person-related, 24
  physical, 48–50, *50*
  physical effects of exposure to, 245
  sensitivity to, 181
  situational, 24
  superheroes and, 13, 245
  teens and exposure to, 141–142, 145, 244
  trivialization of, 60
  types of, 24–25
  viral, 245
  visual, in print ads, 241–243
  against women, 106–107
Violence Against Women—Australia Says No campaign, 201–202, 205–206, *211*
Violence Approval Index, 266
Violent content. *See also* Advertising, violent content in; Rating systems; Regulation of violence in advertising
  children and
    exposure to, 151–152, 170–174, *173, 174*
    fear as effect of, 19
  in comic books, 13
  in films, 14, 131, 156
  on Internet, 15
  in music and music videos, 13–14, 17
  processes of effects of, 62
  public health criticisms of, 246
  in TV programs, 14, 61–63
  in video games, 14–15, 116, 244
Violent media. *See also* Advertising, violent content in; *specific medium*
  aggression caused by, mechanisms that exposure to causes, 117, 245–246
  appeal of, 131–132
  children and
    defining *violence* and, 162–163
    exposure to, 151–152, 170–174, *173, 174*, 175–176, 245–246
    future research on, 176
    gender differences, 170–175
    heroic characters and, 13, 245
    overview of, 6, 161–162
    perceptions of, 165–167, 169–170
    theory and research on, 163, *164*
  consequences of exposure to, 116
  criminal behavior and, unclear link to, 116

Violent media *(continued)*
    defining, 162
    defining *aggression* and, 11
    defining *violence* and, 11
    effects of
        aggression, 17–18, 245–246
        desensitization, 18–19
        fear, 19
        research on, wealth of, 255
    exposure to, routine, 255
    General Aggression Model and exposure to, 117, 175
    gladiatorial fights, 12
    historical perspective of, 11–12, 239
    increases in, 239
    "mature content" label and, 12–13
    overview of, 4, 11, 20
    parental perceptions of, 167–170, 180–184, 187–192
    popularity of, 116
    prevalence of, 61
    regulation of, 116
    rise of, 15
    variety of, 250–251
Viral violence, 245
Visa credit card ad, 49
Volz, Gerhard W., 249

Wagner Group, 136
Walsh, David A., 187
WAM!, 249
Warren, Caleb, 89
Warren, Ron, 60, 62, 64–65
Watson, Barry, 259
Weidman, Chris, 15
Weinberger, Marc G., 83
Wells, William D., 78
Westley, Bruce H., 216
Westoff, Charles, 223
Wexlerf, Sandra, 141–142
Whipple, Thomas W., 79
White Ribbon Day ad (Australia), 206–207, *211*
WHO, 24, 162, 197
Wilde, Oscar, 142

Wilson, Barbara J., 61
Wilson, David, 83
Wisk detergent ad, 77
Witness perspective, 119
Witte, Kim, 215, 217, 219, 222, 229
Wolf, Naomi, 96
Women, Action, and the Media (WAM!), 249
Women portrayed in ads, impact of violence against
    culpability of advertising and, 95–96
    culture of aggression and, potential for, 106–107
    in high-violence ad, *112*
    implications of, 106–107
    in low-violence ad, *111*
    memory effects and, 97
    moderate-violence ad, *111*
    objectification of women and, 47
    overview of, 5, 94–95, 105–108
    prevalence of, 95–96
    rape myth and, 94
    research on
        age moderates and, 103, *104*, 105
        discussion of, 105–108
        gender moderates and, 102–103, *103*
        main study, 100–102, *102*
        methodology of, 99–102, *101*, *102*
        multivariate tests, 102–103, *103*
        overview of, 5, 97–99
        pilot studies, 100, *101*
        results of, 98, 102–103, *103*, *104*, 105
        univariate tests, *103*, 105
    social learning theory and, 96–97
    stereotypes and, 94–95
Worden, Alissa P., 202
World Health Organization (WHO), 24, 162, 197
Wrigley's Doublemint gum endorsement, 139

Young, Katherine K., 56
YouTube, 15

Zero Dark Thirty (film), 12
Zillmann, Dolf, 37, 117–119
Zwikker, Machteld, 198, 201, 204